For Pamela Hodas,
who made Patience Worth
visible early on.

Dan Shea

11-25-12

The Patience of PEARL

Patience and still patience,

Patience beneath the blue!

Each atom of the silence

Knows what it ripens to.

—Paul Valéry, *Palme*
James Merrill, trans.

The Patience of PEARL

SPIRITUALISM AND AUTHORSHIP IN THE WRITINGS OF *Pearl Curran*

DANIEL B. SHEA

UNIVERSITY OF MISSOURI PRESS
COLUMBIA AND LONDON

University of Missouri Press, Columbia, Missouri 65201
Printed and bound in the United States of America

5 4 3 2 1 16 15 14 13 12

Cataloging-in-Publication data available from the Library of Congress.
ISBN 978-0-8262-1989-3

∞™ This paper meets the requirements of the
American National Standard for Permanence of Paper
for Printed Library Materials, Z39.48, 1984.

Design and composition: Jennifer Cropp
Printing and binding: Integrated Book Technology, Inc.
Typefaces: Indy Italic, Perpetua, Minion

Contents

Acknowledgments

After the long course of this book's preparation, it is at last a pleasure to thank the groups and individuals whose efforts and advice have helped bring it to completion. I am most of all indebted to the staffs of the Missouri Historical Society's Library, to Dennis Northcott in particular, and of the American Society for Psychical Research and its Director, Patrice Keane, for guiding me to archives crucial to this study. The ASPR's extensive library and archives in New York contain research data, manuscripts from as early as the seventeenth century, and original correspondence from William James, an ASPR founder, Henry James, W. B. Yeats, Upton Sinclair, Arthur Conan Doyle, and Houdini. Founded in 1885 to support "scientific research investigating extraordinary or as yet unexplained phenomena," the society has fostered historical research in its collections of "spirit" photographs and drawings and in manuscripts describing Shaker visionary experiences.

At Washington University in St. Louis, the knowledgeable staff of Olin Library's Special Collections have been helpful guides to the James Merrill collection, and I continue to be grateful to former Dean of the Faculty of Arts and Sciences Edward Macias for timely research support during a semester's leave. Research work by graduate students now beginning their own careers has been invaluable, and I wish to thank Erika Dyson, Jon Naito, Meredith Neuman, Michael Goode, and Franklin Zaromb for their careful and conscientious work. At Washington University, I have profited greatly from conversations with colleagues Miriam Bailin, Steven Meyer, Robert Milder, Henry Roediger III, and Victoria Thomas, and I am grateful for the encouragement of Langdon

Hammer at an important time. Katherine Fama and Rebecca van Kniest contributed their skills to a project much in need of them. Editors John Brenner and Sara Davis at the University of Missouri Press have been wise, encouraging advisors, and I have many reasons to regard copy editor Gloria Thomas as the text's best friend. At the beginning and now at the end of this project, no one has understood better the meaning of patience or exemplified it more lovingly than my wife, Kathleen.

For permission to quote from their poetry I wish to thank Pamela White Hadas and Carl Phillips. The Patience Worth collections of the Missouri Historical Society and the American Society for Psychical Research have been the foundation for much of this study, and I am grateful for permission to quote from their libraries' collections and to reproduce photos from the Photographs and Prints Collection of the Missouri Historical Society. The Special Collections Department of the Washington University Libraries and the Libraries' University Archives office have given permission to reproduce a Pearl Curran inscription and a photo of John Livingston Lowes from their holdings.

Abbreviations

ASPR—American Society for Psychical Research, New York

CPJM—Collected Prose: James Merrill, edited by J. D. McClatchy and Stephen Yenser (New York: Alfred A. Knopf, 2004)

CPW—The Case of Patience Worth, by Walter Franklin Prince (1927; reprint, New Hyde Park, NY: University Books, 1964)

HT—Hope Trueblood, by Patience Worth, edited by Casper Yost (New York: Henry Holt, 1918)

MHM—Missouri History Museum Archives, Missouri Historical Society, St. Louis

PWC—Patience Worth Collection, American Society for Psychical Research, New York

PWM—Patience Worth's Magazine

PWPM—Patience Worth: A Psychic Mystery, by Casper Yost (New York: Henry Holt, 1916)

PWR—Patience Worth Record, Missouri History Museum Archives, Missouri Historical Society, St. Louis

RA—"Rosa Alvaro, Entrante," by Pearl Curran (*Saturday Evening Post,* November 22, 1919, 18ff)

SS—Singer in the Shadows, by Irving Litvag (New York: Macmillan, 1972)

ST—The Sorry Tale: A Story of the Time of Christ, by Patience Worth, edited by Casper S. Yost (New York: Henry Holt, 1917)

T—Telka: An Idyll of Medieval England, by Patience Worth, edited with a preface by Herman Behr (New York: Patience Worth Publishing Co., 1928)

The Patience of PEARL

Introduction

FROM SPIRITUALISM TO VIVISECTION

It does seem odd that a woman who wrote with brief but notorious success less than one hundred years ago could still be, as Lucky Jim once put it, so strangely neglected. The kindly hand of recuperative criticism, reaching out to more movingly dispossessed and marginalized writers, has passed over the quaint enigma she seems to represent. Yet one of her more eligible works, *The Sorry Tale,* earned its writer a place on a list of outstanding authors for 1918, named by the Joint Committee of Literary Arts of New York, chaired by writer Hamlin Garland. Two of her poems in 1916 and five more in 1918 were reprinted in William Stanley Braithwaite's *Anthology of Magazine Verse and Year Book of American Poetry.* All but one of the 1918 poems were rated at some level of distinction in the anthology editor's starring system. More recently, a selection of her poems was reprinted in a New Directions volume, along with poetry by Jean Cocteau, Lawrence Ferlinghetti, and James Purdy, and she has been the subject of a poem-portrait, partly composed of her own language, in Pamela White Hadas's volume *Beside Herself.*[1]

That these works appeared under a pseudonym would be the least of the difficulties confronting a recuperator. The great difficulty, as Pearl Lenore Curran became increasingly aware, was that she had produced the texts associated with her name at a Ouija board, at first calling out one letter at a time to her stenographer-husband, John Curran, who wrote furiously to keep up with dictations that could amount to five thousand words in a single evening. Until her death in 1937, Pearl Curran would insist that the name of the author of her first major publication, *The Sorry Tale* (1917), was no pseudonym but the given name of a "discarnate entity," Patience Worth, who had lived in seventeenth-century England, then emigrated to New England, where she had died in an Indian raid near the end of the century. Resuming speech in 1913, in the Currans' St. Louis flat near the site of the 1904 World's Fair, Patience Worth had come, she announced, to preach a doctrine of love and to write through the medium of her "harp," Pearl. In the beginning it could not have been predicted that the Patience Worth name would appear as author of two collections of poetry, several shorter and three long fictions in dialogue form, and two widely reviewed novels, along with a twenty-nine-volume record of conversations, the Patience Worth Record, by turns witty, contentious, and determinedly inspirational, or that hundreds of visitors would come to witness these acts of invisible authorship. Curran eventually set aside the Ouija board, but Patience Worth's dictations continued through a typewriter and at last through the medium's voice alone. Her novel "The Merry Tale," always in progress, never came to publication. An additional novel in manuscript, "Samuel Wheaton," in which a young Englishwoman disguises herself as an oceangoing seaman, has never surfaced entire, and a final, more seriously edited dramatic fiction, "Elizabethan Mask (Three Days in the Life of William Shakespeare)," which made a young Will Shakespeare its central figure, is also unrecovered.

Whatever the value and interest of the Patience Worth writings, their mode of production under the hand of Pearl Curran has tended to discredit them from the start, tainted as they were by the previous century's history of table-rapping and mediumistic fraud as "spiritistic" revelation and by the power of performative illusion in fleshly entities such as Madame Blavatsky.[2] Studies of the hoaxes arising from nineteenth- and early twentieth-century mediums' claims to communication with the dead, telepathy, and revelation from spheres beyond continue to appear. David Abbott, himself a magician, has systematically demonstrated the deceptions involved in flower materialization, slate writing, and the reading of "sealed billets." A recent treatment by Deborah Blum illustrates the ways in which proof of immortality came to rest on the talents of mediums rather than on articles of faith. Curiosities of alleged visual demonstration captured by the camera were available to viewers of the 2005 Metropolitan Museum of Art exhibit on nineteenth-century photography's attempt to capture ectoplasmic materializations of departed souls.[3]

In the only essay she wrote on her own case for a national audience, the punningly titled "A Nut for Psychologists," Pearl Curran is fully aware of the distastefulness of what she has given empiricists to chew on. "When I let my modest name be coupled with that of a Puritan spinster of some hundreds of years ago," she protests, "I never for one instant realized that Patience Worth and I would be cast out upon the stormy sea of distrust."[4] Beginning her double-voiced project when female suffragism was nearing victory in the form of the Nineteenth Amendment, Curran testifies to hearing a voice that historically had been displaced as too admirably spiritual for the masculinized world of aggressive material competition. As putative "nut," she lodges a contemporary complaint against scientific realism's categorical voiding of her experience and trustworthiness. Slipping behind a male pronoun, Curran disguises only slightly the gendered melodrama that takes place when a writer-as-medium finds "himself a suspected character" in the view of scientists who "humor the subject and listen tolerantly to his effort to prove himself sane, while they cast wise eyes and smile" (*CPW,* 392). In her search for authentication beyond the faithful, it did not help that her dictated art flourished in a period when the Ouija board, evolving from its nineteenth-century origins, was on its way to becoming a name-branded parlor game while the domestic iconoclasm of fiction writers like her St. Louis predecessor Kate Chopin would implicitly have defined her work as retrograde and inauthentic. That, in her public statements, Curran made no claim to agency in producing the Patience Worth text and, until her final years, could not bring herself to alter or improvise on the stream of language she first heard, then spoke, has also tended to depress her candidacy for an attentive rereading.

No one is likely to argue that Patience Worth novels like *The Sorry Tale* or *Hope Trueblood* ought to become a staple of undergraduate surveys, but to express interest in them is more than a perverse test of the hospitableness of American literary histories. *Patience Worth* was and is the name of a problem in judgment. To call attention to curiosities and unexpected merits in Curran's Ouija-board writing can be a losing game. Impressions of linguistic interest or dramatic power contend with annoyance at an artificially antiquarian manner and its limited repertoire of stylistic devices. Amy Tan, glancing recently at the "garrulous ghost" and her "stolid" prose, found equal reasons to admire and to loathe Patience and her medium.[5] Narrative immediacy in the fiction can be compromised by a scrim of trance behind which the action seems to progress; or imagery may come obsessively into focus, like a dream (the Ancient Mariner will enter this story obliquely) that must be told. As a result, the unspoken and yet to come of convoluted plotting can seem more willfully hidden than suspenseful, a covertness reflected in the response Patience once gave to a visitor who inquired whether she planned her stories in advance. "Doth the spider think o' web?" she replied, not quite truthfully.[6]

Historically the voice Pearl Curran called Patience can be located somewhere in the distance between the Puritan and Quaker speakers-out of early American women's history, jailed or hanged for what they spoke or might speak, and the profit-minded mediums of American popular culture who mimicked the dead for a living. Without quite matching the profile of either population, Patience Worth needs to be mapped among them in order to distinguish the lines of culture that limned her contemporarily. Chapter 1 also places Curran in a line of descent from writer-predecessors like Elizabeth Stuart Phelps and Kate Field, who in their first-person inquiries had approached the Ouija board's mechanical parent, the planchette, with a mixture of attraction and suspicion, discovery and disdain. The experience of Phelps and Field needs to be set against representations of female mediums in male-authored fictions of the later nineteenth century. William Dean Howells's *Undiscovered Country* and Henry James's *Bostonians* have been the best known of a short-lived genre in which the medium is represented as inexplicably, even dangerously empowered, but also as spotlessly innocent and therefore a candidate for rescue by marriage.

Chapter 9, the last, focuses on questions raised by experimental psychology and neuropsychology in particular and could be taken as a final step in demystifying the case of Patience Worth, although that is not my purpose. Few readers now need help in assembling arguments against Curran's "control" as a spirit in search of a finely tuned, consummate Ouija board. Increasingly, however, psychology's writing about writing opens new perspectives on the richly complicated neural networks that constitute memory and its creative metamorphoses in art, the Ouija board perhaps a shortcut to activation of those often-hidden processes. To signify a problematic phenomenon rather than an independent personality, I refer to Patience Worth as "PW," but if at one time the PW writings seemed extraordinary because the housewife-medium seemed so ordinary, cognitive experiment and research on the brain's neural processes have made it increasingly clear that the term *ordinary* is an inadequate sign for the potencies of human consciousness.

Between the first and last chapters of this study, I aim to read more fully and closely what Curran's Patience produced and to identify as far as possible the biographical urgencies and textual environments that informed the medium's dictations. As custodian of a newer sort of writing spirit, Curran consciously distanced herself from what she knew of séance behavior and attempts to communicate with the dead—her "control" excepted. Also departing from cumulative stereotype was her husband, John Curran. In contrast to the mesmerizing Svengalis or dominating fathers of fictional mediums, John Curran moved quickly through a brief stage of baffled spectatorship at the crystallization in his home of a seventeenth-century poet and storyteller, to confirmation in his role as stenographer and record-keeper, to business partner in the Patience Worth enterprise, a venture that in the long run struggled to break even.

One might without apology read the PW text and inquire into the private and performative career of Pearl Curran, because no one has yet explored both life and text in any extended way. Narrative approaches to PW have traditionally begun with the discarnate visitor's Ouija-board introduction of herself on July 8, 1913, with the greeting, "Many moons ago I lived. Again I come—Patience Worth my name." That speech came at the end of a year's conversations with a host of spectral visitors involving Curran's mother, Curran's friend Emily Grant Hutchings, and Curran, who was often the least interested among the three. In Chapter 2, I draw on unpublished letters from Hutchings to make clear that Curran's ambition to write, objectified in PW, emerged only by gradual stages and despite Hutchings's letter-writing campaign to undermine her friend as exclusive and indispensable medium. PW's literary debts—to prior biblical novels, or Dickens, or the *Rubaiyat of Omar Khayyam*—were rarely noted by contemporaries and have gone largely unremarked since then. Biographical narratives have displayed little interest in the literary culture of St. Louis in the early twentieth century, ignoring Curran's acquaintance with such writers as Sara Teasdale and Fannie Hurst, a context more immediate than Spiritualism for her literary ambitions.

One might read the PW text because the voice of it very much wanted to be heard. From whatever depth the entity labored in Curran's consciousness, an intention to produce work for the ages can be heard staking identity on output—or "put" or "loaf" or "weave," as PW described her goodwife transmutations of the Ouija-board alphabet. Frequently dodgy and artificial, the persona is often impressive in her skill at turning interrogation by the curious into an occasion for wit. Alternately caustic and compassionate with audiences, both word-proud and a humble "handmaiden" of divine influence, PW regularly suspended conversations with visitors to make the most of her time in the twentieth century as a writer whose behavior suggested an ascendancy of literary faith over doctrinal Spiritualism.

That faith is reflected immediately in the very first words of the narrator-heroine of PW's second novel, *Hope Trueblood* (1918). Speaking in a version of the Victorian novel's first-person narrator, Hope looks back on her childhood and the secrets surrounding her mother's death, her own birth, and the mystery of her paternity. In its confident specificity and sense of the affective picturesque, the text's first paragraph is a cognitive type of other PW productions, confessing drowsy memory's possible fictions but stipulating a story the senses now insist on:

> The glass had slipped thrice and the sands stood midway through, and still the bird hopped within its wicker. I think the glass had slipped through a score of years, rightfully set at each turning, and the bird had sung through some of these and mourned through others. The hearth's arch yawned sleepily upon the black woolen table cover, where yellow fruits cut of some cloth were sewn. It may have been that I fancied this, but nevertheless it yawned.[7]

Because it engages the reader's sense of time in order to assert its own, the PW voice inevitably creates a dialogic text as strategy, a writerly practice that seems most in its element as a voice that does voices. Dissociated from Pearl Curran, PW proliferates into other selves anxious to talk themselves into text. The eponymous heroine of *Telka* (1928), represented as rude and earthy, drawing an arm across her mouth as she finishes a joint of meat, returns often to the difference between her yen for folk realism and the daintiness of her painterly lover, Franco:

> . . . and here be Telka,
> Who aneath doth sorry that ye be an ass!
> Thou shouldst bury 'neath the soil thy pots o' daub,
> And perchance they then shall spring a grain
> More worth to thee. I be no weaver o' rainbows,
> But I stew full well. Thy sup hath sorried sore![8]

Telka is as double-voiced as the one who dictates her. From the mud, her language enacts a barnyard singer, even as she displaces femininity onto, in her idiom, a pettiskirted piddler.

Any study of Pearl and Patience must begin with Walter Franklin Prince's 509-page *Case of Patience Worth,* published in Curran's lifetime (1927) and an invaluable resource for later studies. At this distance, Prince's study amounts to a generous, promotional anthologizing of PW text and talk, with reprintings of supportive critical responses and systematic rebuttals of more negative published views. Among defenders of PW, Prince would have been second only to Casper Yost, editorial director of the *St. Louis Globe-Democrat,* editor of much of the PW writing, and a decorous devotee of the flirtatious spirit who encouraged him to perform a subliminal persona of his own. With scholar John Livingston Lowes and critic-editor William Reedy, Prince and Yost are among the champions and interrogators of PW whose interest in a discarnate female I describe in Chapter 6.

Irving Litvag's biography *Singer in the Shadows* (1972) became immediately useful for its careful reconstruction of Curran's public life with PW, its identification of many of the personalities drawn into the Pearl and Patience circle, which the Patience Worth Record refers to as "the Family," and its recapitulating of the history of controversy over the case. About Curran's transporting of PW to Los Angeles, along with her two maturing daughters, little information was available to Litvag, but it is now possible to document, as I do in Chapter 8, her brief period of celebrity there, followed by obscurity and, near the end, a last quickening of the PW Ouija board. Beyond Litvag's conscientious reporting, it is now possible to enlarge on important dimensions of Pearl Curran's offstage identity and relationships through archival testimonies of which he was unaware. Litvag's reporting of both contemporary newspaper coverage of the PW phenomenon and later retrospectives (*SS*, 264–68) yields commentators mostly satisfied to describe Pearl's Patience as an obvious case of secondary personality along with others who confess failure to resolve the case's puzzles under any single category.[9]

More recently, a dissertation by Mia Grandolfi Wall has made clear that early spiritualist characterizations of the apparently learned and gorgeously elevated PW writings drew on a dichotomy that encouraged characterization of Curran as a quite ordinary if somewhat flighty member of the housewife class. Curran would therefore have been incapable of producing a "Fifth Gospel," as *The Sorry Tale* was described, and could hardly have been the source of poetry that seemed to issue from eternity. By directing attention to "Rosa Alvaro, Entrante," a story Curran published under her own name in the *Saturday Evening Post*, Wall suggests more self-awareness and less dissociation between medium and control than an earlier psychology had found. Though previously identified by Litvag, the story had not been used, as Wall does, to shed light on Curran's literary ambition. The dissertation supplies a useful guide to Pearl Curran's life and career in the form of a biographical time line to which new items of biography can now be added from this study. Wall gives little attention, however, to the published PW texts, including their wealth of historical English usages, and her references to volumes of the Patience Worth Record are drawn largely from Litvag's work rather than from the Record itself.[10] A recent *Smithsonian* magazine treatment by Gioia Diliberto, illustrated with photos of principals in the PW case, reflects continuing interest in questions surrounding an alleged "ghost writer" and provides an incisive, engaging summary of Pearl Curran's development of the PW story while noting its potential for experimental psychological approaches.[11]

The very existence of a twenty-first-century dissertation on a "discarnate entity" and her medium points to the growth in the past two decades of new forms of interest in the interweavings of American Spiritualism and histories of the emergence of women's literary, religious, and political voices from the mid-nineteenth century to World War I.[12] The catalog of women writers drawn to and writing from or about Spiritualism is a long one, of quite extraordinary length if one were to consider American and English writers together. The familiar observation that the growth of nineteenth-century suffragism and the proliferation of Spiritualist orators and audiences were closely connected has readily been expanded to include core elements of American women's literary history as well. To take seriously the argument of Ann Braude's essay that "women's history *is* American religious history" would encourage a linkage of women's literary history with the pattern Braude cites: while women were seen as the "mainstays" of nineteenth-century religion, they were also identifying themselves with movements like Spiritualism that made them leaders of dissent. In the most commonly remarked literary version of that pattern, novelists adhered broadly to orthodoxies affecting representations of female character and to cultural demands that defined satisfactory closure while exploring issues of identity and social role in a counterdynamic that strained against the net of cultural artifice.[13] Similarly, to explore the PW phenomenon is to observe the social definition of a figure who repeatedly turns from parlor audiences to the dictations that will bear her name. At times, that activity can appear as social dissent in unexpected refractions of stock characters, while eruptions of intense anger suggest the limits of patience. The published PW text can regularly be heard speaking over the PW Record's talky, didactic persona even as Pearl Curran, source of both, appears to remain above the fray.

As Elaine Showalter dates the phases of progress in American women's writing following its "Feminine" phase (1840 to 1880), Patience Worth's appearance in 1913 would fall into a transitional period when the later "Feminist" phase (1880–1920), which employed Social Realism to illuminate women's wrongs, was ebbing and before the "Female" phase, with its unapologetic turn "to female experience as the source of an autonomous art," began to gather momentum after World War I.[14] Reduced to an exhibit of automatic writing, Curran could be made irrelevant to such categories or seem regressively Feminine if not for the public career she sought with her revisionist performance of a frequently combative Puritan goodwife. By the time the Nineteenth Amendment was ratified in 1920, celebrity had begun to dim for the medium whose claim to spirit-dictated novels in 1917 and 1918 had diverted some readers' attention from news of the Great War. Latecomer rather than prophetess in the twentieth century, Curran found herself an object of sharp-edged irony in responses from, as we shall see in Chapter 6, working writers like Mary Austin and Dorothy Parker as well as Agnes Repplier, the latter quoted at length by Litvag (*SS*, 192–97). Most psychologists in the generation immediately after William James needed only a glance to decide that Patience Worth was not the "white crow" James had been open to discovering, the anomalous para-perceiver who would force a rewriting of all previous certitudes about the limits of human consciousness.[15]

As a psychological "case," however, Curran was increasingly confronted with studies of dissociation, which she countered with caricatures of the discourse. The confident diagnosis that her automatic writing was the product of a secondary personality derived from researchers' decades of psychological investigation into cases of double or multiple personality, with automatic writing understood as both a symptom and a clue capable of revealing the relation between dissociated personalities and a presumed normal self. Ten years after the Scottish physician James Braid renamed mesmerism "hypnotism" in 1842, the planchette began to appear in France and soon after in America, eventually yielding spirit communication to the Ouija board, first produced in Baltimore in 1890.[16]

However culturally parochial, the conventional dating of the Spiritualist movement from the Fox sisters' Rochester table rappings in 1848 marks a starting point for the later intersection of American Spiritualism with migrating French experimental psychological theories regarding "*désagrégations psychologiques,*" as Pierre Janet described his cases in the 1880s. Between Janet and the most influential of American early investigators into abnormal psychology, Morton Prince, there was a continuity of attention to unconsciously dissociated states—Prince eventually preferring the term *co-conscious*—and to diagnostic and therapeutic applications of hypnosis to multiple personalities. Prince's *co-consciousness* opened up the possibility that extraordinary traits, comparable to those evident in dreams, suggested capacities of which subjects were not consciously aware. One subject, writing automatically as she recalled a dream, produced verse she had not consciously composed but that Prince was willing to characterize as exhibiting "constructive imagination" on the part of a "subconscious intelligence." That Prince noted the poetry was "fairly well written" for one who was "not a poetical writer" suggests the interest Pearl Curran would have had for him when he interviewed her shortly after the emergence of PW.[17]

In 1915, Curran met in Boston with the skeptical Prince, whose empiricism quickly became evident in his aggressive questioning. Curran's abrupt departure prevented her from being added to the gallery of pairings between male mesmerist-hypnotist-psychologists and female subjects who were frequently though not necessarily mediums and automatic writers. In the psychologist-subject pairings to which virtually every historical study calls attention—for Prince it was the case of "Christine Beauchamp" (Clara Norton Fowler)[18]—each figure seems created for the other so conformably that priority between the histories of precocious mediumship and the psychological study of subconsciously dissociated personalities can be difficult to settle. What Franz Anton Mesmer had described in the 1780s as "animal magnetism" in his demonstrations of the induction of "artificial somnambulism" had been as much a technique of mysterious empowerment for a mesmerist-experimenter as an approach to diagnosis and cure by a physician.

As Deborah Coon has observed, claims of paranormal perception constituted a challenge to naturalistic science that psychologists, seeking credibility for empirical assumptions and experimental approaches, could not fail to respond to. Spiritualists like Epes Sargent had sought to borrow the authority of science to bolster their own claims, either by alleging scientists' positive support for psychic phenomena or by pointing across a dualist divide to psychology's silence before spiritual communications. Morton Prince was briefly a member of the American Society for Psychical Research, while William James continued to converse across the widening gap between psychic and psychological research as an early member, then president (1894–1895), of the English Society for Psychical Research, a founder of its American branch, and also founder of the psychology laboratory in which Gertrude Stein and Leon Solomons undertook early studies of automatic writing. After James's death in 1910, empiricists looked to projected work by Joseph Jastrow to undo what they saw as the damage done to the new science of psychology by James's openness to psychic investigation, exemplified in his protracted attention to the trance-medium Leonora Piper. Alluding to "'medium-mad' Bostonians," G. Stanley Hall urged Jastrow to make clear that James had "laid the foundations of all this credulity."[19] Hall was probably unaware that James's final abandonment of Piper could have been heard in his observation that for philosophy and psychology, "[s]ouls have worn out both themselves and their welcome, that is the plain truth."[20]

When Pearl Curran arrived in Boston for a meeting, or "confrontation," as Litvag describes it, with Morton Prince in November 1915, she presented herself in the company of her business-minded husband, John. From the interview in which Prince, addressing PW at the Ouija board, questioned Curran's co-conscious, it is clear that the accumulated experience and maturing strategies he brought to the examination were largely frustrated.[21] In Curran—now a minor celebrity rather than a petitioner for relief—he found a less docile witness than he or any of his predecessors had so far encountered, and in Patience Worth—"'Tis apry ye be"—an evasive antagonist. "Answer my question! You said you would cooperate," was Prince's angry response to a series of archaically phrased evasions and a calculated mention by PW of their mutual friend, Washington University professor of English John Livingston Lowes, who had arranged the meeting and would soon be joining the Harvard faculty.

Prince did not announce failure after the Currans had left Boston but simply told the press that the results of his examination of Curran were "inconsequential and of no scientific interest whatever" (*SS*, 102). His calculation of zero scientific interest might also be characterized as the discovery that he had found himself dealing, however indirectly, with a writer, not a housewife. PW's evasions sound remarkably like those of dodgy writers examined on the meaning and deep sources of their work. What Prince had not yet encountered was an unconscious automatism with the intention of art, one that characterized him as a surgeon who would attempt to end the writer's relationship with her voice. As PW, the processes working themselves out in Pearl Curran at the time of her visit to Prince granted the medium a paradoxical power of control, expressed in Curran's unwillingness, at the cost of "cure," to have their knot definitively untied, and by an external agent at that.

Curran's refusal to let Prince hypnotize her, which she had not signaled in advance, may well have betrayed her reluctance to confront evidence of PW as a dimension of herself, but her wariness had another source as well. By 1919, she would characterize the "thousands of offers" she had received from "doctors, psychologists and the like" as "vivisection, I would call it," with that term's implication of cruelty to animals in the name of science. Her charge against an inquiring neurologist, Dr. Victor Haberman, after a series of PW sessions in New York, suggests a writer reacting to an attempt to net her voice discursively. "Scientists cannot understand me," she countered. "That is why they are trying to call me names. But I don't care. I have the goods—one million and a half words of literature." Vivisection had been a controversial subject in America at least since the 1890s, when Elizabeth Stuart Phelps and her husband argued for a Massachusetts law to control the practice. When *Reedy's Mirror* published in St. Louis a pro-vivisection letter from "Young Barbarian," it called forth a heated reply from Sue M. Farrell, president of the Vivisection Investigation League.[22] Phelps, in late career, translated the code bluntly: "A man may vivisect a woman nerve by nerve, anguish by anguish; nobody knows it. She never cries out." Whatever the range of her reading, Curran used the term knowingly. The angry pitch of her response to those who found her "abnormal" takes its place among the discursive "passions of the voice" that Claire Kahane describes in tracing the development among psychologists of "a virtual psychopoetics of hysteria" in late-Victorian and early twentieth-century studies, beginning with Freud's narrative of Dora.[23]

Curran's awareness of the controversy over vivisectionism takes on period costume in PW's sharply accusatory "Yea, thou wouldst to shed o' the blood o' me and then hand unto the wraith o' me the blood blade to wipe." Whatever forms an unconscious division of labor had achieved, the dynamic underlying these two voices evokes a single body that, when subject to violation, forbids removal of its life-principle—psyche's midwife turning on a would-be surgeon. Maddened by the pointer's wily evasions, "Dr. Prince," according to the Record, replied, "Oh, go away" (*SS*, 100).

While the formulas of Spiritualism failed to contain Curran's experience of PW, her gift did not incline her to translate inexplicable subjectivities into the language of science. Among early twentieth-century writers, such questions had begun to resonate threateningly, as in a recent description of Frank Norris evoking a "fatal surrender to automatistic forces" or Gertrude Stein's experiment-based rejection of automatic writing as inconsistent with conscious art, while others like Yeats and Rilke sought sources of creativity that by definition obviated instructions from craft and culture or diagnosis masquerading as criticism. Helen Sword, who also considers H.D., Sylvia Plath, and Ted Hughes among this group, catalogs a long list of nineteenth-century English and American writers who "dabbled" or "wallowed" in variants of supernormal experience as she frames her consideration of "literary modernism's vexed and often embarrassed fascination with popular spiritualism."[24] In the medium's doubled or multiple identities lay a possible clue to the core enigma of literary creation: who/what if not exactly "I" (and no longer the muse) is the one/many that writes?

Examining the literal doubleness of women's collaborative writing in the late nineteenth and early twentieth centuries, Bette London moves from study of the Somerville and Ross collaboration, to an uncovering of George Yeats's role as a wily medium-nurturer whose responses to her husband William Butler Yeats's leadingly mystical questions engendered his poem *A Vision,* to more obscure English mediums who provided apocryphal narratives of early Christianity and conversations with Oscar Wilde.[25] The most prominent of this group, Geraldine Cummins, declared herself in touch with a spiritual messenger from the period represented in the Acts of the Apostles, receiving extra-scriptural dictations that London compares to *The Sorry Tale,* the PW novel that follows "the bad thief" from Bethlehem to Calvary. (*The Sorry Tale* appeared eleven years earlier than Cummins's *Scripts of Cleophas* [1928].) Approaching the significance of mediumship from distinct perspectives, the London and Sword studies potentiate each other by relating historical constructions of female agency to the culturally and theoretically complicated definitions of authorship called for when physical agency appears diffused among multiple processes for which the sturdily single author can claim little more than complicity or mediation.

That question was posed legally in 1926, London points out, when Cummins sought an injunction against Frederick Bligh Bond to prevent his publishing the Cleophas scripts. Sword mentions that Bond had "typed, punctuated and paragraphed"[26] what Cummins had received, and his collaboration suggests an initial mentoring role since he was already famous for claiming to have received psychic information that led to his successful excavation of lost chapels at Glastonbury. When his role at early Cleophas sessions with Cummins ended, he maintained that copyright for the scripts taken down could not be claimed by a this-world author. In an American commentary, a reviewer of the Cummins-Bond case in the *Virginia Law Review* cited the similarity between the Cummins texts and the work "purporting to be written by 'Patience Worth'" in their use of "archaic English." Having given evidence of her physical authorship, Cummins won her case, the High Court justice regarding the matter as "of the earth earthy" and observing that he "had no jurisdiction beyond the country in which he lived."[27] For her part, Curran took no action against others, such as her friend Emily Hutchings, who claimed communication with Patience Worth.

The surrender, by definition, of a claim to personal authorship even as a text is judged the property of the visible civil self is only one of the paradoxes that mediumship abounds in for Sword and London, including as well its circumvention of traditional learnedness as a demonstration of higher authority and the sacrifice of agency on an altar of service as a means to empowered achievement. Those paradoxes are fully played out in the case of Patience Worth, but cognitive science and neuropsychology must also be called on for an empirical representation of the postmodern anxiety of authorship that tends to make all writing ghostwriting, as Sword observes in citing Foucault and Derrida, with London connecting automatic writing to Foucault's "What Is an Author?"[28] The phenomenon of mediumship, which posits an author removed from a growing script and divides apparent agency at the Ouija board between a pair of visible operators, colors the spectrum of permutations on author theory in ways that have outlived the interest of the communicated messages themselves.

From the perspective of mediumship's gathering history, it is no surprise that a likely classic of modernist long poems, as magisterial in a broken way as it is iconoclastic and centrifugal—James Merrill's Ouija-derived *Changing Light at Sandover*—should exhibit an increasingly familiar pattern of anxieties of identity within the poem while occasioning questions of agency for the poet himself.[29] Described as an epic of late twentieth-century consciousness, its three books published successively, with "The Higher Keys" added as coda, the poem never entirely abandons the Ouija transcriptions made by Merrill and his partner, David Jackson, but never simply concedes the poem to conversations with the multiple voices that spoke through a homemade cloth "board" that displayed the alphabet in capital letters, with a teacup serving as pointer. Unlike Pearl Curran, Merrill reserved to himself the final word, as a comparison of the initial transcriptions ("Drunken lines of capitals lurching across the page") and their remainder in the final poem makes clear. In an interview with J. D. McClatchy, Merrill noted that many transcriptions for "The Book of Ephraim" were unsaved or simply lost, while the second published poem, *Mirabell: Books of Number,* represented "half or two-fifths" of the original, "enormous" transcript, and the "Lessons" in the third book, *Scripts for the Pageant,* appear "just as we took them down."[30]

With many of the transcripts of *Sandover* available to researchers, the work of establishing patterns of revision and fresh discovery, the textual moments when the poet's authority asserts itself over voices that claim priority to conscious craft, remains for future editors. In 1979 Helen Vendler had already isolated in *Mirabell* the result of its expanding universe of ambition on the poet's well-kept island of accomplishment. "Setting aside the effortless jeweled effects for which he has been known"—a polished art that in an etymological sense had tended to define Merrill circumferentially—the poet raises voices whose authority threatens to diminish and diffuse his own. The result for the poet, Vendler suggests, can be "maddening," as when his voice complains to Auden's,

> . . . it's all by someone else!
> In your voice, Wystan, or in Mirabell's.
> I want it mine. . . .
> Here I go again, a vehicle
> In this cosmic carpool.[31]

On his way to becoming the poet not previously visible to even his most entranced readers, Merrill accessed an alphabet beyond the one he had been using by seeking another hand, David Jackson's, giving up individual control in exchange for dialectical revelation, with no assurance what degree of efficacy he could claim in the result. Whatever kind of control is retained in the poem's crafts of expansion and economy or in decisions to silence some of its emergent voices, those acts would lack occasion were it not for the dartings of an automatic teacup. For admiring readers of Merrill's poem, elaborately abstract attempts to reconcile automaticity and agency beyond the text may be beside the point, but as we shall see, psychologists have for some time been enlarging the realm of automaticity without yet fixing its precise borders, and previous studies of dissociation through subjects' automatic writing had already begun contributing to an elegy for the unitary, voluntarist self. Frederic W. H. Myers, researching telepathy through automatic writing for the British Society for Psychical Research in 1885, first put the case for our multiplicity in constitutional terms—we can no longer think of ourselves as "a sovereign state but a federal union," then found science describing an "'animal colony,'—a myriad rudimentary consciousnesses," then fetched incipient modernism out of classical myth by describing "a micro-chaos held in some semblance of order by a lax and swaying hand, the wild team which a Phaeton is driving and which must soon plunge into the sea."[32]

A sample of responses to Merrill's *Sandover* can suggest how ghost writing, already a test of commonsense assumptions about the single self's cognition and volition, also subjects its readers to scrutiny of their ghost reading. For a proclaimed admirer of Gnostic tradition like the critic Harold Bloom, the first book of Merrill's trilogy was "an occult splendor. . . . I don't know that *The Book of Ephraim,* at least after some dozen readings, can be over-praised, as nothing since the greatest writers of our century equals it in daemonic force." The artful vigilance of Merrill's previous polished poetry had until 1976 kept Bloom a confessed "stubborn holdout" against praising a major achievement. He then described himself converted and astonished by *Ephraim*'s "preternatural voices" and their attaining for him an uncomfortable and overwhelming "social plausibility." An iconoclastic rejection of ordinary cognition leaves the invisible icon of Gnostic awe alone on the altar. For Denis Donoghue, the "absence of conviction" in the third book, *Scripts for the Pageant,* leaves it "nowhere to go," so that it runs finally into "camp silliness and giggling." Even if it were calculable, the degree of automaticity involved in the dictation of *Sandover* would be unlikely to affect these critical judgments. For admirers, it is the poetry's scope, ambition, and continuing resourcefulness, intellectual and linguistic, that finally distance it from its predecessors in Ouija-board writing, just as Stephen Yenser, with those qualities in mind, rescues the poet from his expressed "Horror of Popthink."[33]

If Merrill's achievement has power to neutralize the confessional "Nut" tradition, there remains a darker historical version of the bargain the poet as medium strikes with his sources of revelation. Alison Lurie's memoir of her relation to Merrill and Jackson during the *Sandover* period has them at the beginning of their relationship in the mid-1950s turning to the Ouija board for amusement in the domestic setting that provided a table and perhaps a rationale for its operations in a process of celebration, negotiation, compensation, and escape from boredom. In their exploratory early days, Lurie notes, the poet and the fiction writer, both promising, both talented, could approach their alphabet as approximate equals, engaging the creativity of the partners equally and as dividend making more of Jackson's contribution than it might have earned individually. Though initially fearful, Jackson as "Hand" was "more attuned to the spirits' existence," Lurie suggests, her observation confirmed by Merrill's characterization of his partner as "the subconscious shaper of the message" while in his own role as "Scribe" he articulated that message in words and images.[34] Any language that attempted to discriminate an unconscious division of labor at the teacup was potentially misleading. The Hand became more than mere instrumentality. The Scribe furnished more than verbal costume. As Merrill's career grew and Jackson's stalled, the balance that promoted contributions from the two mediums was upset, Lurie believes. Whatever its sources, the board's spellings did not prevent Merrill as poet-editor from exercising a high degree of selectivity among dictations that, assimilated further and translated upward by his sense of a larger mise-en-scène, would bear his name.

That achievement is separable, however, from Lurie's characterization of how a dangerous parlor game might affect the mind of a great poet. More darkly, she remembers arriving at "the feeling that my friend's mind was intermittently being taken over by a stupid and possibly even evil alien intelligence." In figurative language mindful of nineteenth-century warnings, Lurie suggests that "the spirits of the Ouija board had destroyed" the young men who came to it for amusement and enlightenment, while the psychologized metaphysic of her memoir suggests that the "spirits" and "demons" she speaks of had inhabited a little lower layer of the lovers' long conversation with each other.[35]

Like Bloom and Vendler, Lurie sees Merrill attempting to move beyond praise of his poetry as erudite, fluent, and witty to the force and expansiveness of "a major work that could stand next to those of Yeats, Auden, and Eliot." The implicit charge of a Faustian bargain is raised by a series of rhetorical questions asking what risks a poet is justified in taking to make new his poetry and his reputation. Of these, the most ominously phrased asks, "Should one investigate risky ideas—from intense relationships with charismatic but possibly unreliable gurus, or with voices that may be those of demons?" Lurie's expressed admiration and affection for her friend do not exclude terms like *evil* and *alien* as responses to darkly inaccessible dimensions of Merrill's, Jackson's—anyone's—consciousness. The term *demonic* is not, as in Bloom's *daemonic*, a nod to Goethian or Yeatsian genius, nor a literal warning against devilish conjurings. If Spiritualism reveled in paradox, as Helen Sword claims, that paradox, unbound, can revert to Manichean dualism. At the end, Lurie suggests that Merrill's death—from a heart attack brought on by AIDS—could be thought of as a catastrophe in which "all three," the poet and his successive partners, David Jackson and Peter Hooten, had been destroyed by "the spirits of the Ouija board."[36]

The anachronistic trope of Lurie's diagnosis had its precedent in a formidable study of automatic writing by psychiatrist Anita Mühl, who in 1930 at first found the subject "old and somewhat threadbare." Still, Mühl felt it possible to summarize a general understanding that, as a "means of inquiry into the submerged portions of the psyche," automatic writing had its uses in "working off phantasy"—then warned of a danger that the automatic writer might "stir up much that is morbid and unwholesome," even "quite destructive." Mühl's warnings point ahead to Stoker Hunt's horrific recounting of self-destructive obsessions associated with the Ouija board, that continuity in turn lending a clinical rationale to Lurie's figuring of psychic demons. But in a letter to Hunt, who also wrote on Pearl Curran, Merrill happily disclaimed any morbid dependency on the board's revelations, attributing his buoyancy to his "two mindedness, my mixture of joyous belief and amused skepticism."[37] The Hand may have had greater and more vulnerable exposure to the source of the dictations, but the Scribe, who retained the right to revise what he wondered at, was now in, now out, of the game.

A pairing of the names of Pearl Curran and James Merrill may finally depend on no more than the housing of their records and manuscripts in St.

Louis approximately one half mile from each other. The Merrill Collection at Washington University's Olin Library makes available the unpunctuated autograph transcriptions, notebooks, and copyedited typescripts of the Ouija dictations that are given final form in *The Changing Light at Sandover.* A short walk away, the Missouri History Museum Archives hold the twenty-nine volumes of the Patience Worth Record, its typed transcripts beginning in June 1913, a month before the arrival of PW dictations, and ending December 3, 1937, the day Pearl Curran died. (A volume 30, "Odds and Ends of Records and Short Stories by Patience Worth," a collection of miscellaneous PW writings perhaps gathered after Curran's death, follows the Record but is not continuously paginated.) While the typed volumes of the Record are indispensable for tracing changes in the voice and preoccupations of PW dictations and as a record of conversations with habitual and occasional visitors, they do not provide the stenographic originals of PW dictations for comparison with poems appearing in the Record or fictions published later. Merrill's transcripts show unbroken lines of letters needing to be divided into words, but the absence of any stenographic records for PW makes it impossible to determine how much those dictations may have been edited or improved for publication beyond spelling corrections by John Curran or the lining of poems by Casper Yost (see Chapter 1). The absence of original drafts understandably raises a question whether novels like *The Sorry Tale* and *Hope Trueblood* were in fact wholly written at the Ouija board, though two decades of visitors, not all of them friendly, bore witness repeatedly to the spontaneity with which the texts were produced as they watched. In a few cases short passages of typescripted fiction make their way into the Record, but more interesting are entries that contain commentary from the board about its own productions—the reflective PW mulling over choices for a character's name, pleased or displeased with a finished dictation. At a minimum, the proximity of the Merrill and Curran collections supplies materials for an oblique study of two otherwise incomparable writers who asserted that their text had been given them in ways consciousness could not easily explain to itself.

Two further and less significant accidents bring these names together. Merrill would probably not have known anything of the Patience Worth phenomenon, already in decline when he was born in 1926. But much earlier he could have read the name, which came to Curran's attention after she began to receive Ouija dictations. As Litvag notes in his biography *Singer in the Shadows,* a letter to the editor of *Reedy's Mirror* reported (as did Emily Grant Hutchings) that the name *Patience Worth* had already appeared in a best-selling 1900 novel, *To Have and to Hold,* by Mary Johnston. (The novel's heroine adopts the name of her servant, Patience Worth, to disguise herself in escaping to colonial Virginia, but the servant never appears as a character in the novel.) When questioned,

Curran replied that she had not read Johnston's novel until the duplication of the name was called to her attention, a year after PW transmissions began, and that after noting the coincidence she had written Johnston to inquire into her choice of the name and its possible historical sources but had received no reply (*SS*, 111). Walter Franklin Prince dismissed the repetition as coincidence and believed or was told that Curran had never read the novel (*CPW*, 471).

For whatever reason, Johnston's novel attracted the attention of James Merrill's father, Charles, as he presented it to his son on his graduation from primary school, the inscription reading, "To James Ingram Merrill with love from his Daddy, Graduation May 1939."[38] Whether the thirteen-year-old Merrill read the novel is not a matter of record. Nor are we likely to discover Charles Merrill's intention in the year of his divorce from Hellen Ingram Merrill when he gave his son a turn-of-the-century historical romance narrated by a Jamestown soldier who by marriage rescues the polite heroine from a shipment of prospective brides intended for his rough-hewn fellows and who must persuade her to honor the marriage debt by the end of the novel.

Coincidence always aspires to mean something but implores in vain. When Merrill first visited Washington University as a writer-in-residence in 1969, he had been consulting the Ouija board for more than ten years,[39] but he would not have known that the housing provided for him by his hosts was located on the same street and just a block away from the apartment occupied by the Currans in 1913, when Patience Worth first announced herself. Nor could I have known during that sabbatical year when the Department of English rented my house for a series of visiting writers, Merrill among them, that one day, past reason and brain science, I would yield to the temptation to muse on any connection, however faint, between those two dots.

Chapter 1

THE DOMESTIC ORACLE AND HER GENEALOGY

As an emissary from what she called "everspace," Patience Worth preferred that audiences think of her as ahistorical, with time-bound intertextualities no more her concern than the mélange of dialects she seemed to have assembled since her life in the seventeenth century. In the early twentieth century, her supporters were more committed to isolating the PW phenomenon from the history of Spiritualism. To distinguish their project from that of the Spiritualist séance and its history of fraudulent practitioners, the editors of the short-lived (August 1917 through May 1918) *Patience Worth's Magazine,* Pearl Curran and her husband, John Curran, together with Casper S. Yost, editorial director of the *St. Louis Globe-Democrat,* published in every issue the following disclaimer:

> The sole purpose of this publication is to spread and interpret the words of Patience Worth. It is not a medium of occultism nor of psychical research. It will not concern itself with kindred phenomena of any character. It is not related to nor associated with any cult or society, nor has it any theories to present other than those based upon the words and the personality of Patience Worth. . . . She does not "read the future." She does not find lost lovers, lost relatives or lost property. She does not give advice upon business. She does not pretend to be a physical healer. It is, therefore, utterly useless to ask her service in such matters, and it is worse than useless to send money to this publication, or to anyone associated with her, for such purposes.[1]

Establishing a network of communication with the dead—a precious commodity after America entered World War I—made no part of what Pearl Curran's Ouija board offered her public. Yet the very existence of a magazine that published selections from the PW poetry and shorter fiction and featured spirit commentary on public issues, celebrities, and timeless mysteries aligned Curran with predecessors who were either literary mediums or this-world ventriloquizers of other-world wisdom figures. Curran described herself as the richly rewarded temporal site of PW's gift of literature and made no pretense that she communicated with a galaxy of dead writers, instead challenging onlookers with, "We'el what hast *thou* to prove *thee*?"[2] The project's internal contradiction, its attempt to dissociate Curran from a lineage of predecessor mediums while advertising the writer-spirit's claim to historical existence in Old and New England, was evident from the beginning.

As the PW persona underwent gradual construction by its first pairs of hands, those of Pearl Curran and Emily Hutchings, and with Curran's mother, Mary Pollard, as stenographer, the women's deference to icons of American religious history lent allure to a voice that had antique charms lacking in the previous year's sessions at the Ouija board. "It sounds like a Quaker name," Pollard offered plausibly (*SS*, 32). But having shrouded herself in history, PW at first shrugged off questions about where and how she had occupied it. In the Currans' Boston interview with Morton Prince two years after PW appeared, the psychologist asked to no avail for the name of the ship that brought Patience to New England and the names of the colony's governor and the town she had lived in (*SS*, 100–101). In St. Louis, the Ouija-board answers had been no less dodgy, but in a process familiar to psychologists as inadvertent priming, the attempts of questioners to connect PW to the past of their history books gradually supplied a foundation on which the medium could unconsciously build, questions supplying ingredients for answers that acquired an increasing solidity of reference for additional questioners and newspaper writers.

In a sense different from that promoted by her champions, PW was indeed a daughter of the New England Puritanism in which lay roots of what Eugene Taylor has called the "shadow culture" of American religion,[3] just as Pearl Curran, her denials notwithstanding, represented a late-stage evolution of the Spiritualist medium. Disarmingly present as performance, PW as construction arrives in the early twentieth century at the end of a process that began in seventeenth-century New England antinomianism. The figure's double identity as spiritual messenger and unsuspected agent of the medium's literary ambition represented a post-Puritan renewal of the antinomian trope in a way that summarized, at the end of the long nineteenth century, the conflicts of women who had written exploratory fiction at the same time that others, sometimes entranced, sometimes with conscious calculation, lent their voices to powers of revelation. The latent threat to orthodoxy of an antinomian voice, taken as the spelling out of a woman's unnatural familiarity with the unspoken dark, can still be appreciated in the dance of fascinated approach and wary avoidance taken up by Curran's predecessors, Elizabeth Stuart Phelps and Kate Field, whom we shall see contemplating a possible link between the unpredictable freedoms of a planchette and a writing self that verged on spelling their own names. Even more warily, contemporary male novelists like William Dean Howells and Richard Harding Davis unsuccessfully attempted to reduce to fiction the profoundly creative processes set in motion by the female medium, then confessed failure by recourse to an already doddering marriage plot. In fictional mediums, social role prevails over an unchartable, ambitious consciousness. A reading of Patience Worth in the fullest sense begins with mapping the "wee whit gray damie" onto a history she never lived but that constructed her profile and import long before texts bearing the PW name were published.

When Morton Prince, exasperated, abandoned his questioning in 1915 of Pearl Curran's evasive under-voice, he may not have had leisure in his Beacon Street home to reflect on the similarity between his own trial of a woman's errant voice and the civil trial of the antinomian Anne Hutchinson, conducted in 1637 by the Massachusetts General Court under Governor John Winthrop. For all the differences three hundred years would make in versions of orthodoxy, the gradual escalation of temper revealed in the two examiners suggests their common difficulty in pursuing an unstated question. Morton Prince was determined narrowly to demonstrate that his subject's claim to be in touch with a woman who had lived and died in seventeenth-century Massachusetts was a fiction. Winthrop, with his fellow examiners, was increasingly frustrated by Hutchinson's intrepid and minute knowledge of scripture as his Court attempted to demonstrate her stubborn heterodoxy. Historical treatments of the Court's examination regularly point out its climactic moment, when the judges, questioning Hutchinson on her authority for rejecting doctrine preached by leading ministers, heard the witness proclaim that she was given to know what she knew "by an immediate revelation." "How!" responded Deputy Governor Thomas Dudley, "an immediate revelation," which the accused then expanded on no more agreeably: "By the voice of his own spirit to my soul." Hutchinson's domestic gatherings of doctrinally sympathetic church members into extra-ecclesial "prophesyings" need not be seen as an ancestor of the medium's séance in order to observe, as the Court was aware, that the effect of those meetings would be to put Hutchinson, rather than an ordained minister, at a site of revelation. Hutchinson's experience of what Spiritualists would call a gift of precognition was cited at her trial by William Bartholomew of Ipswich, who recalled finding her "very inquisitive after revelations" as they walked in St.

Paul's churchyard in London, where she confided to him that no "great thing" had ever happened to her "but it was revealed to her beforehand."[4]

When a PW autobiography began to take shape, it did so in broad conformity with the migratory patterns and illuminist tendencies of historical predecessors. In the story not fully dictated until August 1916 (*SS*, 142), Patience Worth was born in the south of England in 1649, then, having settled in New England, died in 1694, the victim of an Indian arrow. That final fate relates PW to Ouina, the otherworld guide of preeminent Spiritualist Cora Hatch Richmond,[5] as well as to Hutchinson, who in 1643 was killed in an Indian raid in Westchester County, Long Island, where she had joined her Quaker sister after being expelled from the Massachusetts Bay Colony. As Jane Kamensky has pointed out, the seventeenth-century New England witch was only the most egregious and identifiable example of woman's "unruly tongue." The witch was sister to the Quaker woman preacher, who for Puritan authorities was virtually indistinguishable from the antinomian, the three sometimes spoken of in a single breath. In the year before the Plymouth settlement, Kamensky relates, an Anglican preacher offered the metaphor, though not explicitly linked to woman, that "the *tongue* is a *witch*," but in 1638 the witch's gender is clearly identified in a pamphlet proclaiming that "a Woman's Tongue . . . is the Devil's Seat."[6] PW's preference for the Anglo-Saxon spelling of *tongue* was suspiciously ahistorical; she described herself arriving from the seventeenth century with "buskins, kirtle and much tung." But Curran's Ouija board was ready to concede PW's eligibility for hanging with the accused Salem witches of 1691–1692 when it conceded, "Alor, I be aswing yet," then singled out an outspoken woman from the audience: "did she live her at my day, [they] would set [her] to stock as a witch" (PWR 2:295; 116).

More evidently now than in Winthrop's time, it is clear that the question asked of the female prophet was one of gendered epistemology: how do you know what you claim to know when you do not know *what* and *as* we know? The shock of judges and ministers at the notion of the Holy Spirit whispering in the same female ear that Satan had hissed in stands as a type of conservative clerical recoil extending from colonial Massachusetts to a barely post-Victorian St. Louis. Seventeenth-century students of witchcraft, Kamensky has shown, were not only familiar with such unnatural attainments but quite clear on their source. Witches were known to speak mystifyingly in learned languages while citing biblical texts with a speed that "'no man living ever' could have matched," such that Cotton Mather was moved to describe the discourses of Mercy Short as "incredibly beyond what might have been expected from one of her small education."[7] Curran's audiences expressed equal surprise at superior knowledge speedily delivered throughout her career.

By assuming "supernormal" unchurched authority while serving as handmaiden, PW demonstrated the ease with which the broad faith of the American religious tradition could redeem the witch. Clergy soon joined the audience that heard PW elaborate on her doctrine of love, and a summary titled "What Patience Worth Teaches" in *Patience Worth's Magazine* described immortality as a gift that "all can win and shall win" (*SS*, 173). Emerging from the Spiritualist movement, the medium enacted individualism's assumption of a right to unmediated contact with divinity—whether in the revival tent, the séance room, or the cathedral of nature. As St. Louis editor-critic William Reedy aptly noted after a PW session, "I find nothing but a sort of gloss in root English of Emerson's 'Oversoul.'"[8] With the Ouija board in place beside the Bible and parlor piano, PW carried forward the eclectic spirit of popular religion into the twentieth century, her kindly doctrines constituting an open church while her earthy idiom stitched soul-hankerings onto a cloth of demotic realism. Nondenominational, she was free to say that "[t]he devil hath oft a-tethered him unto a monk's cord" while reminding audiences that a wise man "knoweth the truth athout the parson's drone" (PWR 2:322).

Noting PW's keenness to "clean up on the occult," John Curran was charmed by the downrightness of a leveling theology as he transcribed language that bridged while scrambling the seventeenth and twentieth centuries: "Lawk, dame," PW responded to a Theosophist visitor, "strip the mouthing o' men from the stuff they utter as truth, and find the atom" (PWR 16:2992). Official occultism would not be needed for discovery of that atom because PW's sermonic utterances could blend blandly with the Spiritualist creed as it had developed over the decades since medium and editor Emma Hardinge Britten channeled it.[9] The benevolence of spirit was enacted when PW spontaneously composed "sweets" of poetry for visitors, assuring the poems' recipients that the universe was fashioned in and suffused with love. Eschewing a new cult of personality, PW regularly reminded her auditors that theirs was a shared divinity when she included them in a Whitmanian embrace, "I be Him—alike to thee. Ye be o' Him" (PWR 1:111).

When it came to what Britten called the "Proven Facts of Communion between departed Human Spirits and mortals," the premise of conversations with the Ouija board, it spelled dissent. "I be nay dealer in wraiths," PW had said early on (PWR 4:766), reserving the board for her writer's alphabet. The PW Record names no Spiritualist competitors, but Pearl Curran's unhappy experience with her uncle's Spiritualist church in Chicago (see Chapter 2) probably colors the board's response to a Theosophist visitor who suggested she might have difficulty understanding the idea of reincarnation. Setting aside mysticism as a "pettiskirt" for the "naked soul," PW spelled a sharp reply: "Dame, thee art mouthin' o'er a word. I be a trodder o' this path." Not karmic evolution but a this-worldly sense of barnyard determinism informs PW's craft of theology. "Should God create an ass who stopped at a stile and its master felled it, would He then recreate the ass?" was the board's rhetorical question. "Egad, should He, *'twould stop at the stile.* Nay, rather turn him upon a green pasture" (*CPW,* 222). Odd couplings, characteristic of American traditions of populist religion, valorize one ancient text, the Bible, while its expounding is left to colloquial rather than learned discourse.

Through a fog of truisms, PW's board transmissions can also arrive at a striking mixture of popular and elitist idioms—folk usages, colloquial archaisms, and homely metaphors contending for one kind of attention while self-consciously literary language encourages comparisons with past masters and scripture itself. A middle-class parlor could continue to participate in the democratization of prophecy that had spread like wildfire on the nineteenth-century frontier. Circuit riders made much of their identity with the ordinary, embattled lives of their hearers, as in Nathan Hatch's example of Bible-thumping vulgate: "What I insist upon my brothers and sisters is this: larnin isn't religion, and eddication don't give a man the power of the Spirit. It is grace and gifts that furnish the real live coals from off the altar."[10]

As folk religion, nineteenth-century Spiritualism could be more conspicuous for its vulgarisms than its metaphysics, as when Emerson expressed disdain for the new "pseudo-spiritualists," "dunces seeking dunces in the dark" who preferred "snores and gastric noise to the voice of any muse" and descended into the séance as "the rathole of revelation."[11] One group in 1874 brightened the history of New England witchcraft by celebrating a two-day meeting near Salem "featuring trance speaker Laura Cuppy Smith, a merry-go-round, and a full band."[12] William Dean Howells, the Ohioan, perhaps recalling the Salem fete, devoted several pages of *The Undiscovered Country* to the "profaner flavor" lent the Thoreauvian woods near Walden by a Spiritualist camp meeting with its blown-about food wrappings, a hammock's shirt-sleeved occupant, and complaints of sylvan dullness from one of the visitors: "What you want is a band. You want a dance-hall in the middle of the pond, here; and you want a band."[13]

Charles Beecher, addressing himself ecumenically to "all sincere Spiritualists of every name," summed up the movement as "a household religion, which is rapidly extending throughout Christendom," and in that house, "in one out of four families it is said, a medium will be found."[14] Available statistics, admittedly scant, suggest that the popular image of the medium as female benefited in part from a cultural stereotype and did not reflect actual numbers. In 1859, one survey showed 121 women and 110 men practicing as mediums, not an overwhelming majority. The almost equal number of men could be swept into sexually double-entendre characterizations with the charge, perhaps reflected in characterizations of Curran's Spiritualist uncle, George Cordingley, that "addle-headed feminine men" could be expected to populate the Spiritualist camp.[15] But if more nineteenth-century mediums were women than men, more of the spirit "controls" for whom those women spoke were male. The predominance, 63 percent, of "spirit agents" or "controls" were male, communicating their wisdom through women whose sympathies rendered them ideal receptors.[16]

The virtually unlimited supply of male spirits from history and the literary canon lent collateral authority to the woman who could command their presence and their message. An acerbic and commonsensical historian of nineteenth-century Spiritualism, Frank Podmore, noted that among communications received from "the mighty dead," no name appeared more frequently as "sponsor for more outrageous nonsense than that of Franklin."[17] Male or female, a famous spirit control might further enhance the medium's status by entrusting her or him with new, previously unpublished work. PW made no such claim to fame, but Pearl Curran was writing in the aftermath of American women writers whose homage to predecessors like Charlotte Brontë energized their own writing, as in Louisa May Alcott's story of the triumphantly duplicitous governess Jean Muir in *Behind a Mask* or Elizabeth Stuart Phelps's novel *The Story of Avis,* about the liqueur-induced trance that enables a heroine's communication with a feminist pantheon, which follows Lucy Snowe's dream of Vashti in Brontë's *Villette.*

PW was apparently unaware of these contemporary women's voices, and she was skilled in concealing the medium's literary ambitions. In 1916, when the Currans' Ouija board had been in use by PW for three years, delegates to the Democratic National Convention in St. Louis were greeted by seven thousand suffragists who wore yellow sashes over white dresses and formed a Golden Lane of Silence on the street leading to the Convention Coliseum. Political talk may have been generated among the Currans' visitors, but the PW Record is silent on the demonstration. On issues of interest to women, PW tended initially to communicate stereotypes fatigued by the centuries. Called upon to defend the willfulness of any changes in tactics or subject, the board's strategy ("I be dame") was to accept a reduced charge of fickleness. When a female guest asked PW in 1925 whether in her own time she had wanted to write, the humor of stereotype did service: "List thee, dame, what wench wi' a tung and a mind to wag it, itched for a quill?" More gravely, and speaking entirely at odds with a decade of publication, PW claimed, "Look ye, damie, I hae nae thirst nor yet an ettlin' for to quill. The urge athin thy damie be for to sing a free sweet singin' for the balmin' o' the breaked ones" (PWR 20:3449). By 1920, the accumulated PW writings had registered an undeniable "ettlin' for to quill," evoking the secondary personality of women who wrote in the shadow of their lives as publicly obliging helpmates.

By the 1860s the technology of inspiration, as Ann Braude has described it, made available a more accessible coach to Olympus in the form of a small, heart-shaped planchette, on wheels, with a pencil inserted at its leading point. The "Boston Planchette," advertised as having been made "from the Original Pattern," could be had for as little as one dollar in black walnut, any model predicted to be "full of fun, puzzle and mystery and a pleasant companion in the house." "Planchette," ominously personified, was, however, "full of vagaries," and vendors told families desiring "a novel amusement" that the instrument could possibly divulge "a note of warning for the future."[18]

Nearly two hundred years after the Salem witch trials, a suggestion of invisible agency anywhere in New England was still likely to encounter unstilled tremors. When Elizabeth Stuart Phelps addressed a commentary on the planchette to high-minded readers of Boston's *Watchman & Reflector,* the country's "leading Baptist newspaper,"[19] her levity was balanced by unmistakable caution. In the same year (1868) in which she described a hospitable heaven in *The Gates Ajar,*[20] she put herself forward as "E. Stuart Phelps" when writing about an instrument that occasionally spelled out "Lucifer" when it responded to questions about its identity. At twenty-four, Phelps adopted an unexpectedly jaunty tone as she surveyed the ubiquity of New England's newest antinomian: "Planchette confronts you at the dancing-parties and in the minister's study, in the drawing room and the 'settin room'—is a substitute for the weather and Charles Dickens in the social circle—and the end thereof who can foretell?" Asked about the next president, the instrument responds by drawing a man with a cigar; asked when one will die, one is told yes. Then, on the next attempt, the little plank produces phrases from a foreign language or creates astonishment by writing "the signatures of absent men in their own hand." If only Planchette, as Phelps continues to personify the wily writer, could dependably engage truth rather than darting errantly, the hand that had pointed to *The Gates Ajar* could have rested on it more serenely.

The writer's casual humor disguises the seriousness of the issues for the *Watchman & Reflector* audience. Sober contemporary discussions foregrounded the conflict between science and religion, yet a preference for science over superstition could still be trumped by a darker spirituality, prompting Phelps to observe that "the devil has to do with most things in this world." In that suspicion Phelps only followed her father, a minister and professor of rhetoric at Andover Theological Seminary, who had argued that true religionists could scarcely ignore "an extensive and growing delusion." The most effective response, the Reverend Austin Phelps had argued, would be to preach again to a "demoniac world" the "biblical demonology" that New England generations, wary of repeating Salem, had shied away from. A gathering of Austin Phelps's essays, which includes "Ought the Pulpit to Ignore Spiritualism?" and "How Shall the Pulpit Treat Spiritualism?" suggests the depth of the daughter's conflict as she attempted to move beyond her father's views. "I would say, Vivify the people's faith in the personality of Satan," he wrote.[21] The daughter of the Reverend Austin Phelps kept open a gate of reasonable explanation while also spying in it the movement of a cloven hoof.

Writing ten years before her most important novel, *The Story of Avis* (1878), Phelps was already aware that for the part of her that read as her audience did, the enigma of Avis's Sphinx—what would woman say were her lips loosed?—was a devilishly dangerous one. In the year following Phelps's article in the *Watchman & Reflector,* Epes Sargent made an explicit identification between the gifts of witches and of mediums from his Boston vantage point: "The marvels of witchcraft as they were developed in Salem . . . were of the same class with those phenomena which the present writer and thousands of other persons have witnessed, during the last thirty years . . . and, in the more recent manifestations, through persons called mediums." While she broke from the exclusionary Calvinist past of her father and grandfather, comforting the generation of the Civil War from a standpoint of meliorist universalism that extended beyond the grave, Phelps was never, as John Kucich has pointed out, "an avowed spiritualist."[22]

Any ambivalence in Phelps derives from a readiness to look for benevolent spiritual agency beyond the margins of orthodoxy, paired with great cautiousness about entertaining strange, mediumistic gods. Should the veil drop, what face emerges? If the Sphinx speaks in some incalculable way, who will dare to claim the voice? Even for published writers like Phelps, a psychic approach via the planchette to an unnamed internal authority, from which female voices had been described speaking out of malevolent shadows, could seem a compound of relish for the incalculable and hesitancy before the ungovernable.

Writing the diary of a mobile writing instrument that is and is not herself, Kate Field expanded the subjects on which the "little plank" could instruct its owner. "There be literature and there be writing," she announced in characteristically breezy fashion at the outset of her *Planchette's Diary,* initiating the record of her dealings with "a board that runs about on wheels, and thinks, writes, and swears like a trooper."[23] In a ruse meant to be seen through, Planchette is author, Field editor, in this account of an instrument that cannot do literature but that can taunt, discover, and mirror the woman who would.

By 1868, when *Planchette's Diary* was published, Field had already been to Rome and Florence, where as a member of the Anglo-American community she had grieved at the death in 1861 of Elizabeth Barrett Browning: "[S]he was a guiding light, and will ever remain so, wherever I may be."[24] Presumably she knew something of Barrett Browning's attraction to, then disenchantment with, Spiritualism and would have read Robert Browning's debunking "Mr. Sludge the Medium" (1864). Field's midwestern upbringing and New England education at the Lasell Female Seminary of Auburndale, Massachusetts, would seem to have been left far behind if her letters from Florence are any evidence. Shaping her experience of artists abroad into vendible journalism, Field paid tribute to Elizabeth Barrett Browning in the September 1861 *Atlantic Monthly*, an effort that inaugurated her career as a travel writer, biographer, lecturer, and occasionally produced playwright.[25]

In the end, Field would have to describe her experience with the seemingly autonomous pencil as a "contradictory inconceivable." If not diabolic, the instrument could seem as mercurial as its operator. "P is a creature of magnificent promises, but alas! She breaks at least one half of them," Field complained, as if to an unruly sister. More confusingly, Planchette revealed that the planets are inhabited; that on the other side, Swedenborg, an early favorite of the diarist and her father, is regarded as "only partially illuminated"; and that "once is enough" settled the question whether there are marriages in heaven for the woman who would never marry. For the editor-medium, Planchette existed to provoke, not to lay down truth but to make it the pea in a shell-game of gender and a contest of willings. Like her inquisitor, Planchette was female, but she was an antagonist when she performed an age less than or greater than Field's—sometimes a juvenile "little monster," but often, and more grandly, "Madame," "her boardship," and an "irate lady . . . bent upon administering snubs." When Field complains at the slowness of Planchette's script, claiming, "I can write faster than this," the instrument must remind the writer of the slowness of consciously deliberative processes: "Because, my good gracious! You are not required to express yourself through another's brain."[26]

Agency and identity begin to debate each other at a margin, and audibly. Field feels the prose under her hands as her own only at the last minute, the individual word entering her mind, she says, just before it is written. The "female" board is represented moving past gendered flurries of bad temper and the occasional deception to produce a substantial day's work as text is counted, leaving the newer consciousness it has inaugurated completed and at rest. "Far from being excited, I am soothed by Planchette," Field claims, anticipating Pearl Curran's report of the same experience. But, stresses the instrument, call that accomplishment writing, not the work of a medium: "I am not in harmony with their illiterate minds." Like Phelps, Field can imagine that "agents of hell" are at work, but satanic intervention reduces to domestic impropriety if the plank can be consigned to "a special fire of pitch and brimstone. It is a bad ornament on the sideboard and a bad amusement in the drawing room."[27]

Explaining herself as she attempted to explain Planchette, Field encountered her dead father at the board, as would Pearl Curran. When Joseph Field, actor and European correspondent, died of pneumonia on January 28, 1856, school authorities withheld the news until Kate, eighteen, had finished participating in the evening's musical tableaux. She noted later in *Planchette's Diary* that in February 1856, still grieving, but also suggesting sales of theater properties to her mother as a way to liquidate her father's debts, she had expected to "hear from Father from the Spirit world" and had found the Fox sisters "honest and truthful." Joseph Field's example, like that of Curran's journalist father, was an influential one for his daughter. In 1890, beginning weekly publication of *Kate Field's Washington,* she wrote occasionally "under pen names her father had used, such as 'Straws' and 'Everpoint.'" For Field, the pen names uncovered a voice behind the female voice of Planchette when, at the beginning of her public success, it began talking to her "like a father," filling pages with "words of wisdom . . . the writing being a facsimile of my own."[28]

The growing dialectic of the *Diary* becomes species of both long-winded paternal wisdom and tart-tongued, angry, female repartee. Abstractly, Field never quite makes logical the dramatic preeminence over the father achieved by Madame Board as intrusive "control." Instead, the hands at Planchette obey a more necessary logic, working out a strategy of individuation that obeys the father by moving beyond him. "Why don't you let aids alone?" her "J. F." (Joseph Field) asks. "Ruins confidence in yourself." Despite its multiplicity of voices, the little board had played its part in spelling out the pursuit of a lifelong desire "to act out one's whole nature." Only the voices most allied with a vocational identity remained, an insistent pattern that finally spelled Kate Field, writer, as her own control. In 1868, the voice emanating from Planchette was already assuming the tone of an incipient journalist: "I am not in the mood to discuss so vast a question as spiritual existence. Ask shorter questions."[29]

For the confident male writers of fiction about mediums from the mid-nineteenth century to the beginning of World War I, mystery could be readily dissipated by the exchange of one veil for another, matrimony as saving grace. Henry James's *Bostonians* (1886), with its intertwining of nineteenth-century American Spiritualism, feminism, and reformist energies, has stood for many readers as a summary representation of a pattern already established by Hawthorne's *Blithedale Romance* (1852), in which the mesmerizing manager of a peculiarly gifted and ethereal young woman is defeated so that the young woman's powers may be domesticated by her marriage to an unconvincingly worthy suitor.

An economical derivation of *The Bostonians* out of Hawthorne's *Blithedale Romance,* however, overleaps the considerable body of writing in America on spiritualist experience in general and fiction concerned with female mediumship in particular, a context that constitutes "a relatively coherent tradition," in the view of Howard Kerr, who cites such works as Fred Folio's *Lucy Boston; or, Women's Rights and Spiritualism, Illustrating the Follies and Delusions of the Nineteenth Century* (1855) and Bayard Taylor's *Hannah Thurston* (1863). James evidently knew of Taylor, whom Olive Chancellor mentions in *The Bostonians* as Goethe's translator on the subject of renunciation, but for David S. Reynolds, *Lucy Boston* is an antifeminist dystopia, memorable for its epigraph "This is the age of oddities let loose" and for its image of a "Spiritual University" staffed by the spirits of famous writers and thinkers.[30]

Like the culturally conceived and fictionally enforced marriage plot of which it is a variant, the medium-become-Mrs. plot laid several anxieties to rest. Silence returns once Pandora's box has become part of a household. Predictable order replaces the potential for devilish misrule. And speculative vagaries on what woman wants, intensely importunate in the planchette's wanderings, become a question of domestic management. Even as he wrote empirical psychology, Morton Prince felt the need to represent closure novelistically following his influential study of Christine Beauchamp's dissociation into three personalities. Reviewing his initial studies of 1908 and 1914 in 1929, Prince wrote an epilogue responding to all those who wondered whether Beauchamp's reintegration would be stable and lasting. She had not only "remained well," Prince assured them, "but, like the traditional princess in the fairy story, soon married and 'lived happily ever afterward.'"[31]

As subject matter for fiction, mediumship, with its unpredictable dictations and wayward gifts of vision, presented novelists with convenient occasions for self-reflexive quizzing on the sources of their own art even as they discovered rich possibilities for parody in the social phenomenon. By the time William Dean Howells published *The Undiscovered Country* in 1880, he had earned congratulations from Mark Twain for his skill at reproducing "the nauseating spiritual slang of spiritualism."[32] The convention of contempt could give way to curiosity, however–or grief. Samuel and Livy Clemens attempted to reach their daughter Susy, dead at age twenty-four, through several spiritualists in 1900 and 1901, and Clemens belonged to the English Society for Psychical Research from 1884 to 1902. Howells, following the death of his daughter Winifred, arranged with the American Society for Psychical Research in 1891 to attend a séance.[33]

The difficulty was that the represented medium—the seer and sayer at the center of what was to be exposed—might disturbingly mirror the shape of the writer, an emergence the more troubling for those who made claims to some variety of literary realism. Later nineteenth-century fictional treatments of mediumship, as distinguished from the writing of the mediums themselves, mix realism-minded reportage of the fraudulent with brief astonishment at the inexplicable in their own and others' dictations from the unconscious. Earlier in the century, Hawthorne's representation of "the haunted mind" as a tomb into which the artist descends on sleepless nights also figured the writer, prior to form and at a place of psychic transactions, as a kind of medium: "In an hour like this, when the mind has a passive sensibility, but no active strength; when the imagination is a mirror, imparting vividness to all ideas without the power of selecting or controlling them; . . . things of the mind become dim spectres to the eye."[34]

Closure by matrimony is both triumph and surrender for the novelist who has made the public figure of the medium his textual property. The reader's equal investment rewards the writer for his power to deliver the medium from a threatening psychic wilderness and restore her to the security of hearth and hero. But for the novelist even dimly aware that he and the medium have sought the secret of what they do in the same psychic wilderness, a quality of guilty sacrifice hovers about her deliverance. Howells will represent an interlude of uncanny symbiosis between the consciousness of his medium, Egeria Boynton, and inexplicable stirrings in her immediate material environment. While the medium undergoes socialization, the novelist who represents her can only continue art's communication with the supernormal in the form of ghost stories that vie with complacent realisms for the favor of the duplicitous reader.[35]

Type-naming his medium after a classical prophetess and counselor, Howells, and the novelists who follow him, awards her a potency that, lurking beneath a surface of innocence, enhances the desire of her genuinely innocent suitor, Morris Phillips, who finds Egeria "deliciously abnormal," unburdened by any sense of guilt when she talks with imaginary visitors. As for Basil Ransom in his fascination with Verena Tarrant in *The Bostonians,* the prize greater than the unmasking of a vulgar medium is the acquisition of a pretty young seer who knows nothing, including the possibility that she knows everything. Egeria is therefore "the Pythoness" as well, a pagan serpentine identity understood to be initially the adversary of Apollo, then in defeat his oracular priestess at Delphi. According to Epes Sargent, the encyclopedist of Spiritualism, "pythonism" was also the "bad name" attached polemically to early Spiritualists by the Swedenborgian ministers of Massachusetts. As apologist for Spiritualism, Sargent records but does not share the deep suspicions of the ministers' recoil from the Python as they ask, "'Who cannot in this mythological tradition see the serpent, engendered by the very lowest things of humanity[?]'—Spiritualism, of course," Sargent adds, "being the chief of these 'lowest things.'"[36]

Approaching the medium through a murder mystery, Julian Hawthorne drew on his father's *Blithedale Romance* when he related the drowning of one female prophet and the veiling of another in *A Messenger from the Unknown* (1892). Hamlin Garland, before he wrote *The Tyranny of the Dark* (1905) and the fictionalized conversations of *The Shadow World* (1908), located himself among contemporary psychologists to uncover the "facts" of psychic experience, though his observation of celebrated mediums and attendance at a variety of darkened rooms resulted in no more than a wealth of anecdotal detail. Fiction's freedom notwithstanding, both Hawthorne and Garland overestimate the distance between themselves and the psychic antagonist they construct, as Elizabeth Stuart Phelps and Kate Field did not.

The retrospect of Garland's *Forty Years of Psychic Research* permitted him to reflect on his development from student of his mother's experience "as a young girl acting the part of a medium"[37] to investigator of supernormal claims for the American Psychical Society—not to be confused with the American Society for Psychical Research—which he was obligated to pursue "without fear or favor."[38] Retrospect also dimmed his memory of Pearl Curran, whom he interviewed after she had given up the Ouija board. History becomes fiction when he recalls Curran as "a Kansas woman" and her controlling spirit as "an English girl of the sixteenth century" whose language "belonged to Kansas and not to the England of 1600." The "quaint," sometimes "impudent," persona of PW he found more interesting than the poetry he had awarded with a prize in 1919.[39]

In Garland's *Tyranny of the Dark,* confident control is the virtue of Dr. Serviss, the medical school chemist and biologist whose science will redeem the "slim young witch" of a medium, Viola Lambert, who does battle with the inner serpent bedeviling the half of her that is not "pure and sweet and girlish." Because the submerged power of a female seeress can rise to the surface of her mind with a power that "withers patriarchs," as Nina Auerbach put it,[40] the authority of Serviss must be absolute. Remember, he tells Viola salvifically, "I am now your chief 'control' and there are to be no other 'guides' but me."[41] The tyranny of the dark will be replaced by the known, the governable, and the stoppered subconscious.

Arrived in the twentieth century, the medium acquires titled billing in Richard Harding Davis's *Vera the Medium* (1908) along with the complication of a double life. Vera succeeds Viola and Verena—all three formidable in their virginity, but here a conscious fraud who learned "every trick in the trade" from a mother who had "worked with the Fox sisters before they were exposed." She has also, since childhood, been visited with voices and visions in the tradition of Spiritualist precocity that Cora Richmond had famously exemplified. Her suitor, as if resurrected from New England history, is District Attorney Winthrop, who speaks to Vera as a sensible father, advising her, "You shouldn't be in this business." If Davis cannot emplot voice, he can echo the sound of it, however melodramatically, from within an antinomian-Quaker-Shaker-suffragist tradition:

> "Do you know *who* I am?" she asked. She spoke like one in a trance. "Do you know *who* you are threatening with your police and your laws? I am a priestess! I am a medium between the souls of this world and the next. I am Vera—the Truth! And, I mean—" the girl cried suddenly, harshly, flinging out her arm, "that you shall hear the truth!"[42]

In the Cassandra moment Davis gives her—drained of color, eyes flashing—the medium is both herself and ecstatically not herself, a figure of alienated creativity provoked by nonbelievers to whom a series of fiction writers have given at most a surreptitious allegiance.

Enter, four years after *Vera the Medium,* Pearl Lenore Pollard Curran, who considered herself "not a medium in the ordinary sense." Departing from the pattern of fictions on mediums, she first sat at a Ouija board in 1912, five years after her marriage, with no interest in acquiring Spiritualist credentials adequate to revise the history of American religion at the beginning of the twentieth century. Instead, Curran had occasions to verify the PW claim "I be trickster," as if the persona had its own homuncular subconscious to contend with, one that might enter dramatic process mindless of doctrine. The dialogic association between a dissociated Pearl and Patience, their yin and yangship, or antagonism, or mutual potentiation, is in a way the whole, complicated story. Pearl Curran did not seek to enact a more compelling sister to Egeria or Verena or Vera, but in performance, as the writer who needed to be named twice, she revised their lineage and implicitly served as a rejoinder to their male creators. Her husband, John Curran, from 1915 until his health failed him, was a scrupulous transcriber and guardian of the words he welcomed from her.

Chapter 2

FROM PEARL TO PATIENCE

When Walter Franklin Prince questioned Pearl Curran about her life before Patience Worth, she wrote an "autobiographical sketch" and sat in "the witness box" for him, eager to convince the more sympathetic of the two psychologists surnamed Prince that she was not a fraud. Her aim, sometimes achieved embarrassingly, was to demonstrate her unreadiness to have produced the PW writings. The "discarnate entity" had come to her suddenly, she said, almost without prelude, and in time made impressively clear her status as chosen medium (*CPW,* 11–21). Curran's plea of innocence from calculated deceit required her to describe her education as brief and limited, an argument Prince did not hesitate to accept after questioning her. Later commentators, calculating an achievement gap between PW and her medium, developed a habit of describing Pearl along an intellectual continuum from plain-minded to ignorant.[1] To do so, they emphasized the howlers in her answers to commonplace questions, pointing to her guess that Henry VIII was the king who had his head cut off, that Dickens had written *The House of the Seven Gables,* and that Don Quixote was a Spanish poet, as well as a long list of "don't knows" to questions about book titles and historical figures from *The Canterbury Tales* to Andrew Jackson.

The story of Curran's election as what PW called her "harp" is complicated in ways not previously described. Popular press accounts of a fully formed PW appearing suddenly for Pearl on a spiritualist road to Damascus have admittedly made a better story.[2] For Curran to provide an authoritative inside narrative in Prince's interview (*CPW,* 15–21) would have required her consciously to recall thirty years of formal and accidental learning while delivering an introspective view of its neural networking into available affinities, which with appropriate cues would have emerged in unexpected shapes through automatic speech and writing. It is some help that Curran's miscellaneous replies to Prince sketch the relationships of a musically talented only child, a resourceful, journalist father with a talent for dialect humor, and a mother who prodded her daughter toward performance in compensation for her own disappointments. Linkage of PW's sudden advent in the summer following the death of Pearl's father, George Pollard, often incorrectly given as the single cause for her Ouija-board experiments, ignores the part of mentor played by Pearl's friend and eventual rival, journalist Emily Grant Hutchings. The depth of that rivalry, which climaxed early in PW's Ouija career, appears in separate records left by Hutchings and the Currans, most surprisingly in unpublished letters Hutchings confidentially dispatched to the president of the American Society for Psychical Research, James H. Hyslop, describing Curran as vain, untrustworthy, and profit-minded.

The suspicions, settled beliefs, and ambitions of the original trio of Ouija players—Curran, Hutchings, and Curran's mother, Mary Pollard—argue against finding a fully formed Patience Worth in the board's first spelling of the name. The entity's persona, social and authorial, emerged gradually from the subjectivities of those who evoked it in differing ways until a voice fashioned out of Pearl Curran's early environment and impelled by her ambition was heard above the others. For Curran, pointing to her single year of secondary schooling only made the board's eruption of writings more wonderfully inexplicable, though Hutchings once suggested that, contrary to her public assertions, Curran privately harbored a notion of her own agency.

Socially, Curran qualified as the "bright, jolly, good-natured" fan of moving-picture shows that friends described to Walter Prince, but she had read more, especially from the nineteenth century's canon, than commentators on her limited education chose to notice. In her testimony to Prince, Curran represented herself choosing little but welcoming what was given her—Tennyson a gift from her father, Whitman from her husband, and traditional readings assigned her in the rural schools she attended in Texas and Missouri. Under questioning, Curran was able to identify works by Pope and Gray, knew that Samuel Johnson had written a dictionary, recounted her enjoyment of school-book selections from "Hiawatha," remembered reading *Black Beauty,* part of R. D. Blackmore's *Lorna Doone,* "the Louisa Alcott books" and "Ichabod Crane," and, at about fifteen, *Uncle Tom's Cabin,* "the first real novel I remember reading myself." Close questioning in 1915 by John Livingston Lowes, then a professor of English at Washington University in St. Louis, also drew mentions of George Eliot, Whittier, and Byron.[3] If the 1879 revised version of the widely adopted *McGuffey's Reader*[4] had come into Pearl's hands as a schoolgirl, she would have found selections from Milton, Goldsmith, Hester Thrale, Elizabeth Barrett Browning, and a poem by Felicia Hemans on the Pilgrim Fathers, though she claimed to have learned Plymouth's history only because an audience member had asked PW to speak on "the landing of the pilgrim fathers" (*CPW,* 17). Shakespeare and Dickens, staples of the *McGuffey's Reader,* were also occasions for an intersection of textual and parental memories. Curran's mother, who "read more of Dickens than I ever did" and whose favorite poet was Longfellow, was probably the parent who took her to the two Shakespeare productions she remembered fidgeting through, at last falling asleep after she had "suffered during 'Comedy of Errors,'" but her mother also "taught me a few bits," moving the child from drowsy audience to vocal registering of the iambic rhythms she would later call up.

Of the two parents, Curran recalled her father, a "quiet and gentle man," as the giver of literary presents, while her mother, having written only "some school girl compositions," was associated with music and church and community performance. In a day's few minutes of reading, Curran recalled, she "might look at a fairy tale or a new book daddy had given me," telling Prince that her father read "some of Dickens" to her from the two novels they owned. At some point her father's local celebrity as a humorist writing behind pseudonyms like *Sissy Jupe* and *Tommy Pants* would have caught her attention in the skits he wrote for small-town Ozarks newspapers. Pollard had first attempted life as an artist but sold his studio shortly after leaving school, then became a country newspaper editor and finally a railroad employee and mining engineer in Texas and Missouri. Following his death at sixty-eight in 1912, George Pollard was described in local obituaries as "a writer of pungent paragraphs and rural humor" and "one of the best known Newspaper men in Missouri a generation ago," a "fighting editor" and "versatile writer of verse and prose." In newspapers in Missouri towns south of St. Louis, like the *Potosi Independent* and *Irondale Gazette,* and earlier as owner of the *Charleston Courier,* he "wrote his famous 'Pete Odle of Pucky Huddle' sketches," and at the *Kansas City Times* became a friend of Eugene Field, then the paper's city editor, later famous for children's poems like "Winken, Blinken and Nod."[5]

While early investigations of the PW language noted George Pollard's identification with Ozarks dialect and humor, the frontier humorist's life had begun in New York. Curran did not pass on any reminiscences of Pollard's Bleecker St. childhood or English-Welsh descendancy, but she made a point of saying that he was sent for private education to a military school in Ithaca, New York.[6]

Father and daughter were evidently close. Pollard helped Pearl with arithmetic, but she remembered their mutual interest in art more fondly: "father and I would copy little pictures for hours, just as a game" (*CPW,* 19). The only photo of Pearl Lenore Pollard as a young woman shows her in Sunday white, coaxing a dog that has the attention of her father, who leans against a fence, hands in his pockets, his face partly shielded from the sun by a bowler hat.[7] If George Pollard's modeling of a writer-editor who lived by wit and mimicry was influential for his only child, PW's earthy responses to urban visitors may also have something in them of the frontier editor's relation to his readers. The official cause of Pollard's death in 1912 was recorded as Bright's disease, or chronic nephritis, with cirrhosis of the liver a contributing cause.[8]

Mary Cordingley Pollard made her contribution to the cumulative PW when she modeled both the "desire to be successful as a singer" and the casualty of unfulfillment. In her autobiographical sketch, Curran recalls that at three she had seen her mother cry and describes her as "nervous, keen, ambitious, talented as a singer, aspired to write before marriage at eighteen, no attempt after that and never published." While she remembered her mother reading a popular English periodical, she recalled no writing except for letters and a composition titled "A True Friend," which young Pearl had judged unremarkable except for its "funny curled letters."[9] Nor was love demonstrative in a mother who was "pretty but also . . . too thin to afford me a comfortable pillow, although I wanted to be cuddled" (*CPW,* 11).

Even before she began school, Pearl was taking music lessons because her mother "wanted me to be attractive." Socializing with the wrong group, though, uncovered fearfulness in the parent. Having earned the nickname of wise old "ram's head" from "the darkeys" who worked for the family, Pearl was spanked when she disobeyed her mother by playing with yet another "crowd of little darkeys." Any tears from Pearl go unmentioned, but she has a distinct memory of "'paddlings' by my mother over which my father would almost weep." Having learned that the path to reward lay in performance, she instead embarrassed her mother by voicing an obscure inner impulse that conflicted with ordered ritual. "Once mother took me to St. Andrew's [Episcopal] Church; but had to remove me because I insisted on singing the offertory, which was unfortunately a solo" (*CPW,* 12).

With Prince as audience, the theme of a forbidden but emergent voice spelled itself again. A virtually genetic PW appears when Curran describes herself as a second-grade schoolgirl rising to recite without the forethought of preparation. Rather than be left out of a series of recitations, "I raised my hand and was told to say mine. I knew none, and began babbling, and floundered and swallowed and rambled—perhaps this was a Patience Worth urge! [Prince proves an obtuse sleuth when he footnotes this remark: "The reader will of course understand that this is not meant seriously."]—until the teacher told me that it was so long I had better finish on *next* Friday. I sat down sure she was 'on to me,' and it was my last attempt at bluffing" (*CPW*, 12–13). PW, by implication, is not a bluff.

At her mother's urging, Pearl was introduced to elocution and Delsarte movement instruction[10] and became "quite a 'show off,'" hating what she had become though "mother desired it." At the end of grade school, the shared weight of her mother's disappointments became too much for her: "I broke down the last year (at thirteen) of too much piano, elocution, Delsarte, school and entertainments, and was sent to the Catholic St. Ignatius' Academy for 'rest.'" How much Mary Pollard had at stake in her daughter's life as a performer can be inferred from a memory Curran passed on to her daughter Eileen. Playing Little Eva in a dramatization of *Uncle Tom's Cabin,* young Pearl could not remember her lines, said Eileen, but was "terrified" into giving her "most convincing performance" when her mother "beat the devil out of her, grabbed her by the hair and shook her."[11] The price of heightened consciousness is exorbitant, but the resulting voice takes impressive flight into a fictional character.

Curran's relationship with her mother serves as context for PW's sharp-tongued behavior with Mary Pollard at the Ouija board. Twenty years after Curran's death, in a rambling interview with PW researcher Ruth Potter Duell,[12] a family friend would describe "Mother and Pearl at doggerheads [*sic*],"[13] though Curran had settled for "complex" to describe her mother's being "too timid to assert her talents" while her mother was secretly convinced that "she could excel in any of them and boasted very much." Curran's letter to Prince after her mother's death describes forms of self-punishing discipline from which the only release was a daughter's independent energy. Her mother's household duties were "*virtuous obligations*—she *would* not or *could* not warp the truth for tact—or a good story! She was dainty—loved beauty in all things and created beauty wherever she was—though the beauty was not *comfortable* because she could not be comfortable or relax from the *vice* [*sic*] of her convictions—she was *tense* in all things and her love for me was really an agony—because she wanted to keep me *hers.*"[14]

After a move to St. Louis, only another "year or so" of education—in which she was "put back"—remained for Pearl Pollard, but a pattern of desire and denial at the spotlight's perimeter continued to hold for her. Then there was a descent to Palmer, Missouri, southwest of St. Louis, where her father took a job as secretary to a lead-mining company after he had "lost everything financially and mother was ill and nervous." Threatened with oblivion ("I wanted life and here was desolation"), the artist in her revived. Pearl could only take music lessons by mail, but the local mine owners, "some fine men," taught her poise as they conversed with "Dad" and she was able to forget "how big my feet were etc." She gave adoring attention to a courteous visitor, Mr. Chauvenette, who taught her the accompaniment to "A Warrior Bold," and in St. Louis a year earlier, like her fictional counterpart, Kate Chopin's Edna Pontellier, she had developed a crush on "a handsome actor, J——S——, whom I never met, and perhaps it was he who inspired the ambition to be a prima donna and loveress!" (*CPW,* 14).

In her early teens, no longer in school, Pearl applied herself to voice and piano lessons, first with a teacher in Kankakee, Illinois, then in Chicago, where her lessons were paid for by her father before he suffered a vaguely described financial crash. Shuttling back and forth between Chicago and the small southern Missouri towns where her father found work, Pearl briefly became Willa Cather's prairie lark, Thea Kronberg, responding to a possible destiny of art in the big city. Eventually, Chicago became a metropolitan education for her between the ages of eighteen and her marriage to John Curran at twenty-four (*CPW,* 13–14). Her work as a six-dollar-a-week shopgirl at Marshall Fields and other stores provided the setting for her 1919 *Saturday Evening Post* story "Rosa Alvaro, Entrante," published under her own name after the Patience Worth trademark was well established (as I discuss in Chapter 6). But first came an influential exposure to turn-of-the-century Spiritualism.

Since neither parent "was of a religious turn," whatever Pearl Lenore Pollard knew of Spiritualism came first from the apparently distasteful but clearly formative experience of playing piano for "about a month and a half" at her uncle's Spiritualist church in Chicago. According to his business card, the Reverend George V. Cordingley, "Psychic, Lecturer and Teacher of the Science of Spiritualism," officiated weekly at 8:30 p.m. Sunday services and led a "Psychometric Circle" every Tuesday.[15] Though she found her uncle and his congregation "repulsive," Pearl was attracted by the opportunity at eighteen to exercise her musical talent while earning enough to pay for further instruction. Her early memories of her mother's brother register him as simply odd, but in time she would speak of him with contempt. Having lived with her grandmother Cordingley briefly in St. Louis at the age of four, Pearl remembered her uncle "arrayed in a queer costume for a masked ball (I think as a ballet girl), which puzzled me. He was a medium, though no others of the family were spiritualists" (*CPW,* 11).

So George Cordingley, who comes closest to a family predecessor in the role Pearl would eventually play, disqualified himself as a model by his memorably "queer" theatricality, then by the band of believers he attracted. "I didn't like the crowd that came," she recalled, alluding more vaguely to "things I found [t]here," together with unspecified "home surroundings," which she described as "most unpleasant" (*CPW,* 14–21). A family friend interviewed by Prince confirmed her reaction to Cordingley: "I have always looked upon him as an arch 'faker,'" said "Mr. C.," a businessman. "As I recall, Mrs. Curran never got along with him" (*CPW*, 23).

While Prince made available the evidence of Curran's accidental apprenticeship to her uncle's Spiritualism, he did not include a last-minute contribution that speculated on an association of Curran with her uncle's fraudulence. Fred Stayton Williams, describing himself as an early investigator of Spiritualism in St. Louis, claimed to have known Cordingley there through visits to his $100 séances, whose manipulations convinced him that both he and Curran's grandmother Cordingley were "arrant frauds." When he relocated to Chicago after Cordingley's move there, Williams found the medium-pastor still in business, his character unchanged—"the same old braggart and liar as of old." Williams suggested to Prince that Curran could have been heiress to her uncle's bag of magic tricks, but he believed her opportunities came from living in his house "for some time" and that she "could have" had access to "medeival [*sic*] dialect books."[16]

While Pearl's family had spent a year with the Cordingley grandmother when she was four, there is no evidence that she knew her uncle beyond meeting him again at thirteen, and detailed instruction in a technology of deception under her parents' surveillance seems unlikely to have been part of her education. As a young adult, however, she was a witness to George Cordingley's example of spontaneously spoken poetry as Spiritualist prophecy. Prince's study records nothing of the *"impromptu poetry"* described by Williams as one of Cordingley's "stunts" or of the other poetry he wrote in a trance state and described as messages of wisdom from ancient sages of Egypt. Beyond her uncle's performances, Pearl was very likely also aware of the volume Cordingley published titled *Impromptu Poems*. None of it in historical language, the verse is stubbornly couplet rhymed and clings cloyingly to the domestic scene, its titles eulogizing family members, including "Mother and Her Loved Spirit Ones," "Mother, Music, and Home," and finally "Grandma." The infants he images are more often dead than alive, the better to offer a grieving mother the consolation that "there is no death." The slim, privately printed volume displays its market awareness when the first three poems take Christmas as their subject, while the worldliest of the twenty-eight reports as timeless truth that with the "almighty dollar a lawyer you can tease, / And by its lubrication he will say just what you please."[17]

In one poem, Cordingley spells out a formula, a diluted Romantic statement of faith in a universal soul as muse, which could at this point have begun to shape Pearl Pollard's conception of herself. Far from suggesting that Cordingley has begun to doubt his talent, the title, "He Had No Subject," rejoices in the mind-absentness of the art exhibited by a painter who ". . . has no subject, nay, no idea; no copy, nay, no thought—/ Although he paints his picture perfect in every spot." The poem's language, ambiguous on the source of its control, conforms to descriptions characteristic of early twentieth-century inquiry into automatic writing by William James and others and elaborated in Frank Podmore's turn-of-the-century, psychology-inflected history of Spiritualism: "Entranced his brain had drafted, controlled his wrist became, / Until he had painted thoughts complete as nature itself had done."[18] For the young woman recently arrived from rural Missouri, her uncle's unashamed fluency would have pointed to a resource buried in consciousness but as close as Pearl's piano, the arc from brain to wrist regularly charged by a musician's automaticity.

Exposure to Spiritualism was also an inclusion in its theatricality, a wedding of performance and vision in which Pearl could imagine a future role for herself. Steinway Hall, where Cordingley's congregation assembled, was one of several musical venues she knew in Chicago and would have been by far the most impressive performance space a would-be prima donna had yet seen. Entering that building in 1901 to play piano for the alternative theater of her uncle's church, she would have seen billing for plays, "both Comedy and Tragedy," produced by the Hinshaw School of Opera and Drama, which "guarantee[d] positions for graduates."[19] Shuttling back and forth between the Missouri Ozarks and Chicago, where she continued music lessons and sold sheet music at the Thompson Music Co., Pearl assimilated vocalized text that included "English folk or peasant songs" and the Irish songs of Thomas Moore, while she also practiced solos from a repertoire that included "Faust, a little of Lucia [di Lammermoor], some German songs and . . . one Italian one" (*CPW,* 19).

During the period of PW's engendering, Cora Richmond's Church of the Soul was Chicago's preeminent seeker congregation. There is no evidence that Richmond and Cordingley, he a founding member of the Illinois State Spiritualists Association when it was incorporated in 1896,[20] preached for each other's congregations, but it would be surprising if they were unknown to each other during the time Pearl spent in Chicago.[21] Richmond's national celebrity made her a distinguished guest on the Spiritualist circuit, and her modes of mediumship and prophecy, like Cordingley's, included impromptu poetry from subjects suggested by her audience, a prominent feature of PW's later performances.

Faithful to the custom of nineteenth-century mediums, Richmond called on the spirit of a spectral American Indian, *Ouina,* whose name echoes Ouija and whose dialect continues into the speech that in 1913 constituted Patience Worth's entrance line "Many moons ago I lived . . . " (PWR 1:3).[22] Richmond's "Story of Ouina's Earth Life" begins: "More than three hundred 'harvest moons' ago, my people lived where the head waters of the Shenandoah river rise . . . " Both Ouina and Patience are of English descent, Ouina as the daughter of a beautiful Christian maiden discovered by Indians following the shipwreck of a "huge canoe" with white sails. Both die at the hands of Indians, Ouina at the hands of the Chief, her father, when she prophesies the coming of the white man and the demise of the tribe she has been born into. Patience dies by a single arrow; Ouina says that "nineteen arrows pierced my form," describing how a loving twentieth brave had aimed into the air then joined her at the flaming stake.[23] As Erika Dyson has suggested, while Richmond was able to project herself as "a benign ferryman, paddling her 'spiritual canoe' . . . between the physical and spiritual realms," Ouina's violent death following her "unappreciated prophecy . . . may have been a projection of Richmond's own anxiety over her role as 'seer.'"[24] If Pearl Curran was impressed by a lesson in "Embodied Angels," Richmond's anatomy of souls, it would have been because she valued "personal presence—the oral utterance," delivered in a "lifelike manner as the artist-actor alone is capable," the "glorious" Whitman standing for her as poetry's exemplar.[25]

Whatever lingered of heaven's matriarchal imagery from Pearl's Sunday school experience at St. Andrew's Episcopal Church, where she sang, and the Catholic St. Ignatius Academy, where she went at age thirteen to recover from the stress of elocution, piano, and movement exercises, would have made her fully hospitable to Richmond's call to follow the Spiritualist "Divine Mother, through her Handmaidens throughout the world."[26] The gender paradox of power and submission is particularly evident in Richmond's icon of transcendent female divinity made accessible through the world's teeming population of handmaidens, a term PW used regularly to identify and aggrandize herself, even as her first novel presumed to write its own version of New Testament narrative.

Well aware that fraud often worked its magic behind a veil of consumer-oriented religiosity, Curran claimed little for her spiritual life beyond minimal observance: "I had no inward experience. Was taught at home to say: 'Now I lay me'—that was all. . . . No, I never wanted to be a missionary or do good in any particular way. I wanted to go on the stage and sing" (*CPW,* 20). Curran's stepdaughter, Julia Curran Maupin, testified to conventional piety ("the love of God that we all have") in her stepmother but found it incredible that someone who had been "more a sister" should be capable of what PW dictated (*CPW,* 27, 29). Instead, mother and daughter converged on a language of psychological change. As Maupin recalled it, her stepmother's routine had been indistinguishable from that of any of her middle-class St. Louis neighbors: "housework . . . a nap . . . some fancy work . . . make calls; in the evening she would sing to entertain the family, or very often, the whole family went to a picture show." Curran's domestic complacency made her "a good sport. She lived in her own day"—until, in their overlapping expressions for the culmination of the Ouija-board experiment, "*the bolt fell,*" as Curran put it (her italics), and PW emerged into voice, as Maupin described it, "like a bolt out of the clear sky" (*CPW,* 15, 29). The public language Curran later used to account for her "wonderful privilege" described something like a Puritan's gracious awakening, one that culminated in "a feeling of uplift, a sort of ecstasy." For the once-born Episcopalian medium, PW took on the profile of what William James described in *The Varieties of Religious Experience* as the discovery of the twice-born individual who arrives at "another sense vouchsafed only in small measure to the rest of us," comparable to "traveling in new and unknown regions." In his farewell to Egeria, Howells had in effect anticipated Curran as a doctrinally domesticated serpent: "[I]magine a Pythoness with a prayer-book, who goes to the Episcopal church, and hopes to get her husband to go, too."[27] Aware of Walter Prince's clerical past, if not of Howells's Egeria, Curran appealed to orthodoxy when she called attention to their high church bond in a conscious claim to respectability: "[W]on't you remove for good from the minds of the public that I am a medium with a gold shingle and trances? Pretty, pretty please. Remember, I'm an Episcopalian! It's your duty" (*CPW,* 15).

In John Curran, Pearl Pollard in 1907 married a man twelve years her senior who had been married once before, as her father had before marrying her mother. When he became chief commissioner of the Missouri State Board of Immigration, he welcomed his new father-in-law into his office. The two men were associated for a last time when John Curran died in 1922 and his body was taken to the same cemetery in which George Pollard had been buried in 1912, in Mound City, Illinois. Mound City was also the town in which Pollard and Mary Cordingley had been married in 1871 (the year of John Curran's birth) and in which Pearl was born in 1883. John Curran had not been Pearl's first choice for a husband. At nineteen she was engaged to a young suitor, "had her wedding dress laid out to marry Bob Wyman," according to a family friend interviewed in 1957, but was "forced" by her mother to marry John Curran "because [Wyman] had no means of support."[28]

Though John Curran's published writing had been confined to promoting his duties as Missouri immigration head (*The Business Man Back to Land*), as Pearl's fiancé he made her a present of William Cullen Bryant's "Thanatopsis." She confessed that Bryant's scarcely nuptial meditation on death "was away over my head and he laughed at me and I was ashamed" (*CPW,* 16). His gift to her of Whitman's poetry may have brought husband and father into conflict over the suitability of the spermatic poet's work as Pearl made her transition into marriage. But neither authority could govern what the mind of a musician took in. After four years of marriage Pearl found that she "adored" an unnamed Whitman poem when she heard it recited to musical accompaniment.

The death of George Pollard five years after her marriage may have cued buried knowing for Pearl, but it also made it possible for her to meld her loyalties, with John Curran as amanuensis assuming literature's daylight role.

The only immediate public effect of Pearl's 1907 marriage to John Curran, divorced and a single father, was the possibility that her new name might be confused with that of the pianist-composer Pearl Gildersleeve Curran.[29] If his wife hoped for a comparable musical career, John (Jack) Curran apparently had no objections, encouraging her to continue with her music lessons. As she later told Prince, "I never felt that I had sacrificed anything by marrying." A 1914 St. Louis directory confirms that the Currans had rented a studio near their Kingsbury Avenue apartment, either for Pearl to continue her own training or perhaps as a space where she could take on students for voice or piano lessons.[30] According to his daughter, Julia, speaking after his death, John Curran had "read quite a bit," but from an uncertain sort of work, and "was not literary, though capable of appreciation." For Prince, John Curran's early "exclamations of wonder and delight" at the coming of PW reflected genuine surprise since "he never knew his wife to be capable of anything of the sort" (*CPW,* 30). A lifelong investor in land development, John Curran took a practical view as business manager of a discarnate writer who in the end paid largely spiritual profits. It "wouldn't be so bad," he was heard to say, if psychologists demonstrated that PW was a name for the workings of his wife's subconscious mind. "I'd just as soon have it demonstrated that my wife was the greatest literary genius the world has ever seen."[31]

John Curran was a "man of no mean native gifts," including "quickness of wit (however crude sometimes)," wrote John Livingston Lowes as he began his boardside questioning of PW, noting "unconscious teamwork" but not collusion in the husband's ability to understand dictations that Pearl did not, "and vice-versa."[32] The extent to which John became a faithful, even jealous, custodian of the PW utterances appeared early when he took over stenographic duties from Mary Pollard, then replaced Emily Grant Hutchings as editor of the Record, marking out the transcriptions he and Pearl regarded as genuinely PW's. In the early years, it was sometimes necessary to set down PW dictations and conversations involving five or six—and once eighteen—visitors while recording literary productions in "plain school copy books" numbered consecutively. From his penned records, John then punctuated and paragraphed any prose and poetry to be published, eventually with the help of St. Louis newspaper editor Casper Yost, marking PW dictations separately from conversations, to be typed in five copies by a secretary hired for Pearl. By the time he described his transcription of over a million words in September 1917, John had also prepared an index, which is not extant, to hundreds of PW epigrams, discourses, and parables and a card index naming all visitors. His identification with his task gives the Patience Worth Record its quality of dramatic script, evoking the atmosphere and circumstances of the more remarkable sessions and occasionally translating PW at her most confounding.[33]

Until now, all accounts of Patience Worth's arrival in St. Louis have derived from the work of psychologist Walter Prince and biographer Irving Litvag, who in turn drew on the entries of the Patience Worth Record, beginning on June 22, 1913, with record-keeping taken over from Emily Hutchings by John Curran on January 5, 1915 (*SS*, 28–29). Both the Prince and Litvag accounts make clear that the Currans took over the Record after they became aware of interpolations reflecting the personal spiritualism of Hutchings, who had already contributed to the literature of the soul when she published *Chriskios—the Divine Healer,* in the *Sunday Associated Magazine* of Chicago (*SS*, 21). In Hutchings's letters to the American Society for Psychical Research, however, PW is preceded by a spirit-company of other candidates pursued at the board and promoted by Hutchings in sessions extending back to the summer of 1912 and preceding the death of George Pollard that September. From Hutchings's record of the earliest sessions, it is evident that the name and profile of PW developed incrementally and may initially have derived as much or more from Hutchings's hands as from Pearl Curran's. John Curran's aim, after a year and a half of reviewing carbon copies from the Hutchings record, was to rid the history of what he and Pearl regarded as interpolations, to advance Pearl as the indispensable hand for board communications, and, by deleting Hutchings's idiosyncratic searches, to bring PW on stage quickly after the board's language began to suggest the voice that would name itself on July 8, 1913.[34]

The record kept by Emily Hutchings, which she later sent to President James Hyslop of the ASPR for his organization's use, spells out a larger cast of spectral visitors and, while suggesting that some early messages had come from PW, identifies all speakers as "Board."[35] According to John Curran, Pearl was annoyed and bored by the Ouija sittings and had joined her friend Emily's experiments only for the sake of entertainment. In the end, the admission built a case for his wife's chosenness by constructing a teleology that drew her, willing or not, into the center of the PW phenomenon. By contrast, what remains of the early board sessions recorded by Emily Hutchings has the look of a mediumistic fishing expedition in which a quest for evidence of immortality was the guiding principle. If Pearl's father proved reachable, so might Hutchings's late brother and mother, the board a potentially inexhaustible conduit of spiritual reassurance. Far from Old World Purgatorios, the dead who wafted into American parlors rarely uttered a discouraging word.

Hutchings's accomplishments in an unlikely combination of journalism and attempts at Spiritualist literature had been notable well before the advent of

PW. As a freelance writer, she had filed a story a day for twenty-four weeks of the 1904 St. Louis World's Fair, had written on art and municipal improvement in William Reedy's *Mirror,* and had contributed poetry and fiction to *Cosmopolitan* and the *Atlantic Monthly.* Aiming high in her communication with the dead, she counted William James and John Jacob Astor among her interlocutors, Astor seizing the occasion to apologize to his wife for going down on the *Titanic.* While celebrating gifts of "beautiful poems" communicated through the board by improbable poets—George Pollard and her brother Dolph among them—she also received verse from some well-known ones: "one, I am sure" had been sent from Walt Whitman and in another "my husband said he could trace the style and metrical arrangement of Kit Marlowe."[36]

When John Curran took on record-keeping duties, as Pearl later wrote Walter Prince, he sought "the elimination of the spooks [Hutchings] wished on us."[37] Divergences between the two records suggest how the mixture of conscious and unconscious goals within and between the paired players could give emergent life to complementary phantoms. While Hutchings's communicants had a shorter board life than PW, her spiritualist assumptions created a conjured world for Curran's rivalrous ambition to grow in. Pearl's recoil from spooky spiritualism was on record ("I was raised to think spiritualistic séances taboo" [*CPW,* 15]), but at the scene of Ouija-board performances, networks of unconscious memory provoked to activity by the death of her father were emerging into a new coherence and would push her conventionally trained voice onto a stage that desire had foreseen but not yet occupied.

Emily Hutchings first met Pearl Curran when Casper Yost, as editorial director of the *St. Louis Globe-Democrat* and therefore her "chief," suggested to her that readers might be interested in Curran's experience of life in the "Lead Belt" district of the Missouri Ozarks.[38] And, contradicting John Curran, it was Pearl, Hutchings said, who induced *her* in the summer of 1912 to buy a Ouija board, promising that "we could have a barrel of fun with it." Shortly, recalled Hutchings, with Pearl's mother also at the table, the group was in touch with the spirit of Pearl's grandfather, who, to validate his authority, predicted that "Barney" (the Pollards' nickname for Mary) would be a widow "before the snow flies." (With George "Tolly" Pollard under a doctor's care, the family would already have been aware of the seriousness of his nephritis.) When Pollard fulfilled that prediction by dying in September, neither mother nor daughter would at first go near the Ouija board, according to Hutchings. Shortly, the mourners' resolution faded. If they had incurred guilt with a prophecy of the husband and father's death, they now became his audience when the board-as-George, fulfilling Hutchings's hopes, spoke to their shared experience: "Little did we think, that Sunday afternoon, that so soon I would be talking to you from this side."[39]

At times amused by the board's caprices, Curran nonetheless regularly appears less interested in ghosts than her table-mates, and even less interested in speaking to her father's spirit than they. In the Hutchings but not the Curran record, Mary Pollard believes the board is spelling messages from her late husband. "It's Dad," she says, "come to help me bear my trouble and sorrow." Curran disagrees, with perhaps a glance at her experience of Chicago Spiritualism: "No it isn't Dad. We don't get personal messages." When personal messages follow nonetheless, the mother-daughter conflict is at first resolved in the mother's favor, Emily Hutchings's hand predominating as the board informs the skeptical Curran that her dad has "killed the hindrance of your faith with suffering there." As first scribe, Mary Pollard observes that messages do not come through when Curran is "nervous or impatient. . . . That's always the trouble when it comes badly." Dad declares: "My wife says so!" leaving the daughter both speechless and an apparent obstruction.[40]

Curran may already have become aware that demanding less of the Ouija board would deliver more. Having rejected any "superstitious belief" that the board moved with a "mystic power," she came to think of it, she said later, as a "thought dispeller, enabling me to put my own thoughts away for the moment." In what psychologist Daniel Wegner calls the "mystery dance" of Ouija-board agency, unconscious direction can shift quickly from one "co-actor" to the other or be initiated by or give way to conscious intention. Automatisms, paradoxically, can result from "the attempt *not* to produce the target behavior." The premise that conscious will is an illusion gives way to a push-me pull-you of willing and won'ting; the "desire to resist" an action "creates a tendency to perform" it, particularly when a normal attempt at resistance is distracted by another task. Curran's skepticism prevented her from urging the board to tell her what she could not believe while not silencing unconscious spellings from a deeper counter-intentionality. As coauthor of experiments on "counter-intentional automatism," Wegner provides a plausible explanation for Curran's helping to produce a spiritualist effect despite her announced distaste for her uncle's and Emily Hutchings's dabblings in other-world communication.[41]

By February of 1914, PW's attitude toward Mary Pollard, reflecting Curran's competition for her dead father's indulgent attention, has been made clear. Shortly after announcing herself, PW tells Curran's mother, "Wilt thou but stay thy tung!" And lest the eldest of the three players should demand respect for age, the board boasts, "Why speak for me? My tung was loosed when thine was yet to be" (PWR 1:4). As the mother continues knowingly to pronounce on their visitor's character, PW proves severe and vengeful: "This overwise goodwife knows much that thrashing would improve." To Pollard's expressed wish for less sarcasm two months later, PW instead adds more: PW refers to her "constant wishing the moon may tip for thee," speaks of her "clanging on" like a bell without a clapper, and suggests, "The men should stock her" (PWR 1:11; *CPW,* 37).

Especially for a spirit, these are ungentle words to put before a recent widow, though not implausible ones if their source is a daughter attempting to raise her voice above her mother's. As Hutchings could not fail to notice, "Mrs. Curran's mother, in the early days, always antagonized [Patience]."[42] By September of the year in which PW first spoke, Mary Pollard, after noting "a rebuke," muses, "I wonder if she is particularly fond of Mrs. C., and if that is the reason for her coming always to her." To which the PW reply is: "To brew a potion, needs must have a pot" (PWR 1:10). With a new distribution of authority established by their visitor, Pollard settles into the subordinate role of taking down her daughter's words. She is exasperated—"The idea of her calling me an old goose!"—but reconciled: "Whew! She is rather hard on me, but I am getting used to it" (PWR 1:14).

As spiritualist mentor senior to Curran, Emily Hutchings held her student to the discipline of the board's alphabet much as Mary Pollard had kept her daughter at piano and elocution lessons. The biological mother and spiritualist mother superior formed a natural alliance when they asserted authority over the "fun-loving" Curran, and at times PW could appear to be in league with them when launching testy, impudent remarks against the youngest player. Having found PW "so cranky last time," Curran is ready to be done with yet another version of maternal bad temper one day in March 1914 and expresses a hope that "she won't come at all. . . . I'm tired of her everlasting sarcasm and scolding."[43] In retrospect, one hears PW's minor-key scorn for Pearl adeptly disguising favoritism behind the appearance of ill treatment. When Hutchings complains that PW has chosen to "vent all [her] spleen" on her and Pollard, neglecting Curran, PW disguises her preference by making Curran irrelevant: "Weak yarn is not worth the knitting" (PWR 1:16). Curran's quite conscious vigilance against sermonics comes alive when she responds acidly to another transmission: "Somebody jumped in there with a little platitude." Sweetly scented passages came to be labeled "doubtful," John Curran later assured James Hyslop, while naming no names. None of the "silly or semi-maudlin stuff that came rambling off the board" was considered literature, he wrote, drifting diplomatically into the language of Patience: "[W]hat comes from the other land . . . must be the music of that land."[44]

One month after Pollard found herself wished into the stocks, she joined the Currans and Hutchings in what the PW voice begins to describe as a niggling conversation about the board's diction. PW responds at one point with "Thou wilt, like the goat, devour thy very bed," the metaphor leaving them in "wonderment." Hutchings's apparently inoffensive questioning suddenly provides PW with an occasion for bladed irony:

Patience. Oh, virtue has sway among ye tonight.
Mrs. H. You think us very stupid, Patience?
Patience. Nay, but hide ye behind a mask.
Mrs. H. What kind of a mask?
Patience. Virtue! (PWR 1:23)

Hutchings's insistence on making PW an irrefutable witness in favor of immortality regularly proves counterproductive. Using the metaphor of the meal grinder, which PW will eventually adopt to characterize the circling of the pointer, she sighs at the fruitlessness of her search for final proof. PW sours at the tiresome question.

Mrs. H. It is probably the same old grinding of the grist of doubt. We are no nearer today to the solution of the riddle than they were in her day.
Patience. Ask the cat. She dieth full oft. (PWR 1:36)

Increasingly, PW seizes opportunities to mock the pretensions of the learned and pious: "Drink ye not the muck and swill brewed by seers and creedists," she says in her accent of rural demotic, recommending instead "a full measure of wordy meat" (PWR 1:38). Echoing Curran's protests against platitude, PW grows annoyed when Hutchings reduces language to the task of providing answers:

Patience. I'll tell thee naught save riddles.
Mrs. H. You always treat me that way.
Patience. Why then in the name of the gray goose canst thou not improve thy guessing? (PWR 1:66)

The incommensurability of the Hutchings and Curran programs for the Ouija board is well illustrated by the extended attention Hutchings gave a profane voice, "Pat,"[45] who in the June preceding PW's July 1913 self-introduction presented himself to the three women—John Curran absent for the evening—as surly and in need of salvation and who demonstrated knowledge of local politics by suggesting that John's friend mayor-to-be Henry Kiel avoid public debate because he "is not long on the gab." Curran remained silent while Hutchings remarked on the visitor's "profound dislike" for Mary Pollard, evident in his charge that "she was a vain old party who hoped to marry again and that hell was too nice a place for her."[46]

When the conversation with Pat was later described to John Curran he volunteered unseriously that perhaps the board was hinting at the name of Pat McQuillan, a man he had met in his teens on a recuperative trip to the Indian Territory who "cussed and made jokes about religion" and was later killed in a saloon fight. Hutchings took Curran's hint with utmost seriousness and hoped to convince James Hyslop of Pat's identity by sharing her evidence with him, Hyslop in turn seeking unsuccessfully to ground the case by researching Pat's family and the circumstances of his life.[47] For the Currans, Pat represented a detour on the route to Patience Worth, the early persistence of the letters "p-a-t, p-a-t, p-a-t" a prelude to her arrival. When John Curran later wrote Hyslop to defend his wife's unique access to PW, he argued that only the first three letters of a name had appeared on the board. Offering the story from his western experience, he wrote that he had not realized that his "willingness to supply a ghost on request would result in the building of such a large edifice."[48]

Hutchings's determination to speak with supernatural agents left her ill-equipped to deal with paradoxes of intention and dismayed at the increasingly visible ambition of the Currans, as when she confided to Hyslop that "the more I see of this affair the more I realize that the Currans are mentally incapable of the truth," noting that John "never tells the same story twice alike." In his own letter to Hyslop, John Curran argued that Hutchings's inventions came from her need for an additional spirit to supply a third personality for the immortals she called the Clover Leaf, the first two being her mother and the late George Pollard. Hutchings had simply "conjured out of the air," Curran exclaimed, as when "'a-i-d-a-d-i-d' was read by her as 'aided by dad,'" his rising temper suggested by the fact that the words "in Sam Hill" are still legible after he crosses them out.[49]

The opposition between what Pearl Curran and Emily Hutchings wanted from the Ouija board proved stronger than their partnership. With the PW writings well begun, Hutchings wrote Hyslop that the difference between her "ethical purpose" and the self-centeredness of the would-be medium could be summed up in her memory of Curran saying, "I don't care a hang for immortality. All I'm doing this for is the literature." That Curran went on to offer her Ouija partner a share in any profits only angered Hutchings further, while Curran's occasionally informing "uneducated individuals" that *Patience Worth* was her pen name constituted final evidence of "what this adulation is doing to her head." When she quoted Curran in a letter to Hyslop, Hutchings may not have been aware that Curran's memory of her uncle's Chicago church gave energy to her contempt for the board's sermonizing: "Oh, that has something to do with Spiritualism, and I detest all that rubbish."[50]

Because Hutchings had taught high school Latin, Greek, and German in her birthplace of Hannibal, Missouri, Curran initially deferred to her friend's superior learning. But when she began to receive poetry without Hutchings's participation, Curran "got it into her head that she was the author," said her mentor, describing the vanity that encouraged Curran to spend half a day consciously attempting her own blank verse. Hutchings was delighted with the result: "It was the most ludicrous thing you ever read. . . . She gave it to me for criticism, and it was atrocious. When I scanned it for her, she could not see the faults in the measure, until I showed her on the piano. Then she was disgusted with herself and has never tried again."[51]

At the two-handed board, Emily Hutchings may have been the likelier source for the first version of PW's Old and New England past, alleged age, and physical appearance. In the Hutchings transcript for the date of PW's first identification, Curran is annoyed by the board's repetition of the dates 1649–1694, though she later allowed observers and journalists to cite them as the dates of PW's life: "I don't see any sense to that," Curran says, shrugging off history. "I'm going to quit if it can't give us something worth while." At the same time, Mary Pollard revises her earlier guess that PW was a Quaker, suggesting Puritan instead and adding in a self-reflexive moment, "I know the type, hard and critical and severe." The board demonstrates its severity by asking "Muz," the one "of too much speech," to "pray silence the witch," that is, Curran, who is now amused and a little puzzled at a dead Puritan's knowingness: "Muz, you talk too much and I'm a witch. I wonder how this old lady got on to us so soon."[52] Over time, Curran's developed PW would grow younger, matching her medium's age, but in August of 1913 she is still "that old Puritan woman who came about a month ago."

With greater promise for future readings, Curran seems aware that her friend's conscious intention can be counterproductive when she remarks that Hutchings "never gives up till she has kneaded all the life out of it," while Hutchings is certain that Pearl's moody skepticism made it more difficult to get solid information from their visitor. Two months after the advent of PW, as the procession of spirits continues, Hutchings finds Curran still unimpressed, noting that Curran said, "I confess I've lost all confidence in these people, whoever they are. They made us think they had something great up their sleeves; but I have my doubts."[53] More hopeful, Hutchings began to seek independent contact with her own PW, assisted elsewhere by another "transmitter" friend. By late January of 1914, Hutchings was keen to continue the suspended plot, as she told James Hyslop. Though she had been prepared to serve as "woof" to Curran's "warp," she now found herself encouraged by an alternative PW—still described as "an old lady"—to form a new relationship for spirit weavings. The Hutchings PW proceeds to speak in melodramatic detail about an earthly life in seventeenth-century Maine, vaguely "near Boston." Derived from the more historically informed of the two mediums, this PW explains that the year 1649 had nothing to do with her birth date but was memorable for her time in England as a subject of Charles I. "The planchette moved with slow solemnity—'B-e-h-e-a-d-e-d.'" Although Hutchings maintains that she needed to look up the date of the king's beheading, her memory of schoolroom history is quickly revealed when she speaks of regicide and the English Commonwealth period, guessing that a New England settler like PW might have been a Roundhead and asking this PW's opinion of Cromwell. PW had spoken harshly of the Lord

Protector to Curran, but the Hutchings board records the full weight of a condemnation: "[H]e that gave cousin and kindred to be slaughtered, never yet was called friend."[54]

In the Hutchings version, PW, after the brutal death of her betrothed, one Nathaniel Johnston, had undergone the fate of heroines in popularized versions of early American Indian captivity narratives. She was carried by savage "dastards" on "swift ponies afar," said the board at which Hutchings was joined by another medium, a Mrs. Clendenen. "I dwelt in the tent of the young chief many moons," adds this PW, counting time lunarly as had Hutchings's original PW and drawing on spiritualist prose and a supply of ponies more mindful of Cora Richmond's Ouina than seventeenth-century New England. As the Curran record indicates, it was Hutchings, on March 4, 1914 (PWR 1:41), not a letter writer to *Reedy's Mirror* in November 1915 (*SS*, 111), who first asked PW how her name happened to be in the book *To Have and to Hold,* by Mary Johnston.[55] Curran's response to *Reedy's Mirror,* that "we" read the book in the year following PW's appearance, does not rule out the possibility that Hutchings herself, still dictating messages from Nathaniel Johnston through her board, would have read Mary Johnston's enormously popular historical romance prior to July 8, 1913, her memory supplying her hands with the doubly virtuous name *Patience Worth.* The PW of the Curran record suggests as much in an immediate reply to Hutchings's question about the source of her name: "A faggot findeth the fire should ye cast it.—Hast peeped into the steel?" Hutchings seems baffled at PW's metaphor, but the PW accusation—*have you looked in the mirror?*—is plain enough while also registering an awareness applicable to Curran herself that apparent accidents of association in unconscious memory can derive from goal-minded momentum.[56] In whatever terms, the very existence of PW depended on the principle that the brain goes about its business of fleeting, unaccountable hook-ups without announcing its every move.

Hutchings, in further correspondence with Hyslop,[57] begins to accept that PW might have a special relationship with Pearl Curran, one a "spirit side" transmitter, the other a "material side" medium. By this time, John Curran had already recorded "The Farewell Song" as the first poem produced by his wife with a board partner other than Hutchings. The Curran PW, attentive to the issue of borrowed poetry, is determined to rest "upon twigs of mine own breaking."

> . . . and I
> Shall show myself, myself, not a fanged
> Or painted thing, nor yet the gently smiling
> Oily thing I would crave the world to believe.

Halt thou, in this maddening rush,
And reckon with thyself. Hast snapped
The cord bound round thy book of song
And stopped to read thy note? Or dost thou
Listen to thy heart, which singeth not
One line of borrowed song? (PWR 1:39–40; partially quoted in *SS*, 42–43)

Continuing to oscillate between anger at unimpressive specters and recognition of the surging voice she had begun to identify with, Curran was unaware that Hutchings had begun her own Ouija communications with "Dad," who readily discussed Curran's shortcomings and, reported Hutchings, dictated assurances "through me, who had been more a daughter to him than she of his flesh ever was." Assuming that Dad's spirit knew of conversations in the Curran home and would be aware "that [Pearl] was planning to eliminate me from the work," Hutchings hoped to enlist her friend's father in an other-side search for the historical PW. That PW came to Massachusetts when "most a baby," as Dad reported to her, conflicts with the biography Curran would later recite, but a newly karmic rendering of PW proves wonderfully satisfying. Building on the story of PW's sufferings "at the hands of Indians," Dad suggests that PW cannot "forget and forgive," which Hutchings enlarges to mean that her spirit has come west to St. Louis to heal an "unforgiving disposition" and to make further spiritual progress. "Will [PW] then leave Pearl and progress to higher planes?" Hutchings asks hopefully. "Yes," answers Curran's abducted father, "but she can come back if she so wills."[58] A faithful daughter of the nineteenth century, Hutchings evidently relished a patriarch's blessing, none more eligible than that of her friend's dead father.

Struggling with the generic "Board" in Hutchings's transcript, Curran is inhospitable. When the language of "a rosary of tears" asks for attention, it earns her scorn: "Oh that's trite and stupid: It has been said before. If they can't give us something original, they'd better not try at all." Mary Pollard finds the comment typical of her daughter and unwittingly predicts a chapter of the medium's late career: "If she isn't getting something equal to Shakespeare she is dissatisfied." But Curran, assuming the figure has come from the PW of Hutchings's circle of spirits, remains unmoved. "That's Patience," she says, "and I don't care if she does ridicule me. I stick to it that the rosary of tears is cheap poetry." Hutchings's hand appears to dominate in a sequence that begins with Dad delivering the personal message she had hoped for: "WE DO LIVE ON,"[59] but the pendulum of agency swings again in an event registered in both records, when Curran, described by Hutchings as restless overnight, feels a message about to arrive and telephones her friend to come over. With John Curran present, the PW voice makes an even stronger appeal. "When I would sing,

Thou hast struck me dumb," reads the Hutchings record. "Wait! A goodly lesson is Patience and Worth a wait," read both records.[60]

Curran's transition into her new role has her wavering between denial and an attenuated claim to agency. PW can tell her, "My kerchief holder would hold thy faith," even as Curran complains that she is receiving no credit as a means of producing PW communications. Against cognitive hubris, the board, now fluent in folk idiom, instructs her in fallacies of causation. "So doth the piggie who scratcheth upon an oak deem his fleas the falling acorns' cause." Curran is quick to deny her agency: "Oh, I don't say I am writing these things. If I were I'd improve on most of them" (PWR 1:45). As if in response, "I fain would weave" is taken by John Curran as PW's first expression of a desire "to do literary composition," and for the same session Hutchings records what John Curran does not, Pearl's last resistance to the ingloriousness of mere mediumship, her conventional use of the male pronoun also suggesting the lineage she will draw on and attempt to outdo: "Oh, that's the idea, is it? I am nothing but the iron mould [*sic*]. Well I don't care about doing all this work, just to gratify somebody who couldn't get his stuff published when he was on earth."[61]

The strain between the Ouija-board partners became public with the Currans' discovery that in preparing the Record, Emily Hutchings would "add to and take from and change ad libitum."[62] As Hutchings confided to James Hyslop, she found herself replaced by a copyist retained "to revise the original record" and was politely ignored when she offered to continue as stenographer. Her dismissal, she wrote, resulted from her "uncompromising honesty" when she and her husband refused to agree with the Currans that it would make a better story if all "supernormal communications" were attributed to Patience Worth. If her record showed otherwise, "[t]hen they said, 'So much the worse for the record.'"[63] The intensity of bad feeling that followed the Curran-Hutchings separation is pronounced in Hutchings's letter to Hyslop of March 11, 1915, where she describes a phone call from Curran shortly after editor William Reedy, reporting the PW story in his *Mirror,* had described Emily Hutchings as an "investigator" of Curran, the "transmitter." Incensed that Reedy's information might have come from Hutchings, Curran phoned her, she wrote Hyslop, and in words "that would not bear repeating" threatened "recourse to law" if she attempted to make her own use of the Ouija-board material. When Hutchings next wrote Hyslop, she referred to Curran as her "former most devoted friend" and said she had turned to mediums who lacked Curran's "egotism and skepticism."

In another month, the friendship was unexpectedly but superficially repaired when Curran telephoned again, addressing Hutchings as "dear heart" and describing herself as unable to live "without your friendship." Still too offended to initiate a visit, Hutchings had the pleasure of seeing Curran driven to her house by her husband "in the big touring car."[64] Her sense of loss remained, however. The Currans' appropriation of PW had distanced her from a source of "staggering evidence" that "we do not degenerate into imbeciles after death." Her own talent and learning, she had to admit, had been as irrelevant to the PW transmissions as Curran's deficiencies. As she told professors of English and psychology who saw evidence of her hand in the work of "unprecedented literary quality" that came from PW, the board's writing could not have been her own. Only a "supernormal" explanation, she insisted, could account for the transmission of "forty obsolete words, used with their proper shade of meaning," or details of court life at a Scottish clan castle that found their way into PW's play *Redwing.* As readers after Hutchings would comment, the PW texts not only seemed to contain information Curran could not have claimed, the knowledge was fluently "woven into the fabric of this intricate and remarkable play."[65]

Curran's ignorance came to be a central subject in Hutchings's extended correspondence with Hyslop in the aftermath of breaking into the Currans' "little game," a triumph she had earlier denied herself when she confessed to him that she had been "a very stupid woman," in the sense that "I never see through the machinations of people who play a double game." Her friend Pearl, though a likely enough apprentice medium, had "given her whole life to the cultivation of her voice" rather than to repair of the serious "deficiencies" in her education. Unaware that she invoked a principle linking dissociative automatism to memory's lurking curriculum, Hutchings observed that Curran "works best when her mind is comparatively blank." Her friend's reading was limited to novels (unnamed) "and the kind of verse that finds its way into the lighter magazines." Of Curran's nontranscendent taste in poetry it was enough to say that "her knowledge of poetry is so meager that she likes Ella Wheeler Wilcox. That to me is the final stigma." Bitterness had its limits. At times like this, she said, her voice failed her from "a foolish habit I have, of being unable to talk when I am deeply wounded."[66]

By repairing her national standing privately, Hutchings unintentionally supplied James Hyslop with arguments against the genuineness of the PW phenomenon. When Hyslop wrote a surprisingly antagonistic review of Casper Yost's first national publication of PW writings, *Patience Worth: A Psychic Mystery,* his opposition came unexpectedly for the Currans, but should not have.[67] Though Hyslop granted that the book's selections might be "all good literature," he had previously been told by Hutchings that Yost too was "obsessed with the 'one mind' idea"—that PW dictated only through Curran. Walter Prince, having worked with Hyslop at the American Society for Psychical Research, defended his commitment to "scientific" scrutiny of psychic communications, but he had also learned that "a lady" with "a personal grievance" had prejudiced Hyslop with "unjust suspicions" (*CPW,* 422–23). Perhaps as cover for her double role, Hutchings joined William Reedy and other respondents writing in his *Mirror*[68] who refused to "lie supine while the skeptic annihilates [PW]" (*SS,* 129)—then was happy to construe a subsequent letter from Hyslop as evidence that Curran was not the indispensable PW medium. "I am convinced that you have reached Patience," she wrote to him. Still, "exciting" as the news seemed, Hutchings suggested that "certain touches" of what Hyslop told her he had received from PW seemed not to ring quite true, then introduced a more bizarre element into their correspondence. Her own PW had informed her that she had not written *Telka,* the first long work from Curran's board. Instead, Hutchings's PW told her that "the man who composed it had chained her and compelled her to send it across," leaving Hyslop to imagine the ghostly chains that made PW amanuensis to a bully both tyrannical and immortal.[69]

From the beginning of her correspondence with Hyslop, Hutchings had stressed her need for privacy, "trusting you not to permit this letter to fall into other hands," since she "would not, for the world, have my dear friend, Mrs. Curran, offended or wounded by my recital of her mental or educational shortcomings." An undaunted reporter, Hutchings then wrote to describe the odd result of her published apparent disagreement with his review in *Reedy's Mirror*—a grateful but unexpected phone call from Curran, styling herself "[your] crazy old friend" and unburdening herself of her troubles as in more friendly times. If only from the arch tone the caller had adopted ("Well, Emelina Paris-greena Hutchings . . . "), it seemed possible to her that Curran was attempting to discover the source of Hyslop's information on PW developments. When Curran wondered aloud why Hyslop had "so bitterly" attacked PW, "I told her I didn't know," Hutchings wrote whisperingly.[70]

Even before Casper Yost gave Patience Worth to the world, Hutchings had moved on to a Ouija relationship with Mark Twain, whom she and her husband had met in 1902. Signing himself S. L. Clemens, the author had written that year to thank Edwin Hutchings for accurately transcribing his speech accepting an honorary degree from the St. Louis Art Students' Association, then in November 1902 had responded with jovial diplomacy to Emily Hutchings's inquiries on how to deal with publishers' rejections. Soon after she stopped participating in sessions with the Currans, Hutchings began to cultivate an audience for *Jap Herron,* a novel she said Twain had transmitted to her after his death.[71] A Twainian short story had already arrived from her Ouija-variant "Oriole board," where she had been addressed familiarly as "the Hannibal girl" with the aid of her new medium, the "gifted" Lola V. Hays. Registered as attending PW sessions in the summer of 1915, Hutchings compensated for her demotion by writing that several PW readings were in fact coded compliment, "too flattering to repeat," on her Mark Twain work. Her formerly agnostic husband now faithfully believed that "little intimate touches" in the board's prose stamped the developing text as "coming from the brain of no one but Mark Twain."[72]

While Hutchings felt the novel's climax was "a masterpiece of pathos," its folksiness and sentiment are untroubled by awareness of any of Twain's writing during his dark final years. The only Twain title mentioned in Hutchings's correspondence with the ASPR is his saint's life, *Joan of Arc.* Responding to the dead writer's strenuous urging ("I am rejuvenated and want to finish my work"), she proposed to convey his completed fiction to the ASPR, along with the heavenly Twain's offer to give 25 percent of profits to the cause of psychic research. "Ask Hyslop what he thinks about that," commanded the board. Obligingly, too, a "tirade" from the dead author suggested that the deviousness of Pearl and Patience had not escaped his notice. Hutchings wraps her own suspicions in a Twainian parody of the often self-parodying PW dialect when the board spells, "Well, Emily, Patience and me don't agree. Methinks that Pearl studied o'ermuch anight. Ask Pearl how many o' ye olden tales (oyeold entales, was the way it came) she read atween."[73]

Published in the fall of 1917, *Jap Herron* was predictably associated with St. Louis's "Patience Worth stories." Despite some able representations of dialect, complained a *New York Times* reviewer, the novel was clearly "a feeble attempt at imitation," lacking in virtues to balance "the 'sob stuff' that oozes through many of the scenes." William Reedy, who gave the novel measured praise in his *Mirror,* told a *Times* reporter that while some parts were typical of Mark Twain, others were "awfully sloppy and sweet and sentimental; usual best seller stuff."[74] Reedy's judgment accompanied his delight at reporting a local literary war between rival "spooks," a contest intensified by Hyslop's supportive review of *Jap Herron,* in which he found "abundant evidence that Mark Twain was behind the work" while continuing to describe the PW writings as a deception. Interviewed by Reedy, Hyslop conceded that the novel lacked inherent evidence of Twain's authorship, but, with no mention of Hutchings's lengthy correspondence with him, he declared that on a visit to Boston she and her new medium had given a psychic examiner "indisputable evidence" of the novel's production by a discarnate Twain.[75]

Emily Hutchings would return to a PW session in 1921 with her husband, Edwin, who spoke on the colors of the new Irish Republic (PWR 16:2982), and in June of 1924 she was the subject of a PW poem that began "Today my hand would seek a lute . . . " (PWR 20:3395). Almost twenty years after the death of Pearl Curran in 1937 she had not been visited again by Patience, but she told a *St. Louis Post-Dispatch* writer in 1956 "that she still believed completely in the reality of Patience and that she never had doubted that Patience was truly the spirit of a woman who had died long before" (*SS,* 266). Curran's experience of their strained relationship ran deeper. When Walter Prince's 1927 *Case of Patience Worth* appeared, she expected Hutchings to counter it with her own version of PW. As Curran told the now sympathetic psychologist, "I see no reason why she should wait for me to die—as she has said she would."[76] But wait Hutchings did, until the cessation of PW texts argued that on the worldly plane of authorship and transient celebrity, the Pearl-Patience relationship was a mortal one.

As the processes of PW's emergence began to coalesce, the bond between medium and control occasionally found warm expression. Having made her point, the critical, accusatory old Puritan might withdraw in favor of antiphonal harmony: "Who then denies that from my first voiced crooning thou hast been the vibrant chord?" (PWR 1:57). In October of 1914, Hutchings put the issue on the table by asking PW directly what she thought of "Mrs. C." To which the two operators, hands together, spelled out, "She doth boil and seethe, and brew and taste, yet have I a loving for the wench" (PWR 1:73). One month later, PW found reason to look past the seething: "Her cackle surely will betimes bear fruit. I vum [I vow me]!" (PWR 1:76). Curran's fluent dictations would not suffer when she went on to welcome the multitude of Ouija-board partners, chosen from her visitors, who succeeded Emily Hutchings. For this medium, writing, even automatically, would be the best revenge.

Chapter 3

PEARL VS. PATIENCE: MEDIUM VS. CONTROL

Patience Worth quickly became the dominant fact of Pearl Curran's life as the words of PW, published or reported, became the medium's medium to celebrity. In the months following Curran's first production of a poem without Emily Hutchings at the board, the Currans moved from their modest flat to a large house on Union Boulevard,[1] where Pearl's Patience began to add to her impromptu poetry with short fictions, set vaguely in a romance writer's version of medieval centuries, and to respond with witty evasion or sharp counterthrust when visitors expressed disappointment or disbelief at her answers to historical questions.

Casper Yost, editorial director of the *St. Louis Globe-Democrat,* apparently alerted by Emily Hutchings, was soon attending PW sessions, beginning a long relationship as textual editor and entranced advocate for his discarnate hostess by stirring curiosity in his newspaper on the "the mystery of Patience Worth" and printing early short works like "The Fool and the Lady" and "The Stranger," both of which he put in the paper in February 1915.[2] From different perspectives as journalists, both Yost and William Reedy watched PW's long dramatic fiction, *Telka,* begin to emerge, its awkward but compellingly earthy language and rapid-fire delivery from the Ouija board drawing immediate attention though it would not be published until 1928. The more discreet of the two inquirers, Yost would at first refer to Curran and Hutchings as "Mrs. Smith" and "Mrs. Jones." A committed disturber of the peace, William Marion

Reedy both followed and promoted controversy. His publication, *Reedy's Mirror,* addressed a national and international audience, its masthead proclaiming distribution in London, Paris, and Venice, but its editorial voice, on both literary and political subjects, remained midwestern and no-nonsense realist. The feud between two communicants of a local writer-ghost made an irresistible story even after Reedy had begun to praise some of the PW fiction, *The Sorry Tale* particularly, for its own merits.

After three years of observing PW dictations and printing readers' diagnoses of the phenomenon, Reedy estimated that "if one were asked what personality in Saint Louis is most widely known throughout the country the answer would be Patience Worth. . . . More people of importance and distinction from the world outside Saint Louis visit the Curran home on Cates avenue [as of 1917] than any other house or any institution in the city." Behind the PW transcendencies, Reedy saw from the beginning "nothing but a sort of gloss in root English of Emerson's 'Oversoul'"[3] and cared little for the board's "squeegeeistic" poetry. But PW's cultural scripture of love, beauty, and glowingly divinized nature with Christian tendencies drew on Curran's memories of an oracular mode—FitzGerald's *Rubaiyat* translation, the poetry of Rabindranath Tagore and Whitman—blended with the larks, mists, and moons remaining in the popular downstream of Romantic and Victorian poetry. In what the record-keeper, presumably John Curran, called a particularly "cosy and homey" gathering in November 1916, PW generalized the first person to include "the All":

> I am of Earth, yet builded how?
> As the atoms dance, danced I.
> As the starbeams streamed, so streamed I.
> I am of Earth and All Things;
> For I am His, and He is All Things.

On such evenings, the PW circle, "the Family," could elevate its members to cosmic status and make a potential poet of a visitor whom the pointer told, "See ye, there be an song aneath the napron, dame" (PWR 4:743–44). For her visitors, PW instantiated what Pierre Bourdieu calls the "oracle effect" from "a veritable splitting of personality." The medium, exemplifying an indeterminate "I," gives rise to a voice that speaks in the name of everything, "even in desert places like St. Louis," as John Curran once said.[4] Unlike Emily Hutchings, eager to connect with the spirits of the dead, Pearl Curran became medium for an audience that sought entry to the spaceless source of the PW voice.

As dictations multiplied, it became evident that PW, tart tongue notwithstanding, proclaimed a deeper spiritual life than her medium. In her own dialect, Curran promoted no doctrine other than Patience. Following their disputatious meeting with Morton Prince in Boston, the Currans traveled to New York to meet publishers Henry Holt and Alfred Harcourt, for whom Pearl demonstrated a PW dictation. And in February 1916, Casper Yost's introduction of PW as literary spirit, *Patience Worth: A Psychic Mystery*, appeared from Holt with samplings of poetry, fiction, and table talk. The volume that would now stir speculation and satire equally had been designed by PW, who began the practice of dictating her books' color and cover designs to her publisher. To Harcourt's question whether Curran's picture might appear in the book, the authorial reply came, "She be but the pot" (*SS*, 102–5).

The relentless productivity of PW earned praise appropriate to a daughter of the Puritans. In its first issue, *Patience Worth's Magazine* described the entity as "a hard worker" who "uses every moment constructively," then ran annual totals on the board's activity as evidence of "the industry of Patience Worth." In the year since July 1, 1916, readers learned, PW had written approximately 425,000 words, averaging more than two poems a week at 150 sittings of two hours each. On many evenings fictions were delivered at the rate of 2,000 words per hour. It was notable, said the reporter—Casper Yost or John Curran—that the volume of output had increased enormously each year over the four years since 1913. For Curran, communicating PW had moved from a laborious groping for individual letters, to pointing at letters when there had been no prior mental impression of them, to an "impress upon the consciousness" so complete that letters and sometimes whole words were dictated fluently while the pointer, having become simply a device for focusing attention, circled the board or, when a loud noise distracted Curran, helped return her to her task (*PWM,* Aug. 1917, 5). By "practice and experience," John Curran had learned to keep up with dictations at two-hour sittings gathered three or four times a week.

Beneath the joint success of Pearl and Patience there is another story to be told. What Emily Hutchings missed when she attempted to free PW from Curran's claim to an exclusive property was the formula for conflict between conscious and unconscious knowing, intentional and automatic willing, carried on according to the terms of an unwritten contract between medium and control. Observers of the medium and her Ouija board often noted the conflict, but rarely pressed their inquiry. What surfaces as contentious dialogue in the PW Record is the complex cognitive doubleness of Pearl Curran.[5]

If mutually repelled, medium and control would have had the power to extinguish each other's roles, a deliverance Curran would not seek from a psychologist. Had she staged a medium's revolt by consistently overruling the commands sent from PW's netherworld of language, the misnamed control would have vanished, along with achievement and celebrity, from the site where text unfolded.

At the same time, the implicit PW and the neural processes of memory and automaticity that constituted her were potentially translatable into a mania of fluency, an open-ended "song of my (dissociated) self."

In the period of first fame, equilibrium prevailed. When the subject of "Mrs. Curran's 'dual personalities'" arises from visitors at a board session of November 18, 1916, PW does the math necessary for their production: "Yeaday. 'Twould take a twain o' ye to build up a whole one!" The medium sounds a note of self-assertion but then must arrive at the same sum: one text as the product of two implicitly coordinated cognitive processes—"It's all right, but she's got to have my hands"—then is topped by the PW retort "'Tis well, for the headin' be full o'follies!" (PWR 4:743). The PW voice is both dramatically shrewd and survival-minded. The board's regular characterizations of Curran as confused and inept minimized rather than applauding her emergence from the original trio of board players. With unconscious logic, PW's devaluing of Curran's folly-filled head amounted to a warning that the medium's announced pursuit of a conscious ambition to write, whatever its rewards, could be the end of the automatic flow that flourished under unconsciously collaborative processes. A closely managed automatism vanishes like a spirit called elsewhere.

A trial of psychically interdependent agencies became audible in 1918 when, as John Curran explained, Pearl and he collaborated on a series of "dialect stories" set in the Ozarks to publicize the sale of Liberty Bonds—and for profit, he granted, though the stories have not been discovered. Of the six stories, Pearl wrote three, with John completing another three she had planned for him. The project was one Pearl had "dreamed of for many years," commented John, furnishing more evidence of PW's prehistory and Pearl's continuity with her father's example. The Currans then took down a critical observation, a "stunner," from PW on their dabbling independently in a lesser art: "[Y]e may not husk thy neighbor's grain when thy bin be full," soon followed by "Ye may not peddle tins and sing carols." She is not speaking as a "scold," PW goes on, "but this be a heavy, heavy pack," to which the Currans agree, saying that "we were playing with something the consequences of which we could not fully see" (PWR 7:1291–92). By the fall of 1919, PW was ready to make humor of the attempt at a medium/control division of labor. The more "pifflin'" with "bumpkins" Curran gave herself to, the more room in that "skull . . . for good wheat." But the issue was serious, as William James had made clear in distinguishing between primary (or short-term) and secondary (or long-term) memory, with "PW" representing modes of access to unconscious long-term resources. As if acknowledging the interdependence of memory processes in a single person, PW was ready to push past rivalry to acknowledge a deep pattern of dissociation from a common root: "I say 'tis well that the wench be she. There be within my words a thing she may not deny and within hers a thing I may not deny.

There be two streams runnin' forth from one fountainhead, I say, the throat with two songs" (PWR 10:1968).[6]

Curran soon appeared to find a way of keeping PW in her place while moving into her own on an evening when, a bit blue, she required "jollying." Against PW's complaint that such a request was calling for "ducats" while "castin' pence," Curran laughingly attempts to confine the wordy entity within the formula of words that has bound her. "My secondary personality doesn't suit me," she blurts, temporarily reducing PW by borrowed diagnosis and making light of the heavy pack that was their relationship. Obviously, PW replies, Pearl as medium is calling for the source of authorship in herself to name itself—as if a homunculus could indeed speak revealingly or specific neural processes speak simultaneously as subject and object—and that, by speaking not only through the medium's person but as the shadow of her soul: "Lor' for to be a man's shadow be nuff, but for to be a man's inman's shadow. Lawk!" (PWR 7:1305). (Often complacent about the male pronoun, PW fetched back to *inman* as her term for soul.) The language of control and medium, primary and secondary personalities, while serving as a practical shorthand, would also divert Curran from awareness that alternative cognitive executives could continue to organize depths of the same pool of resources in different ways.

The archetype of truth spoken from behind a mask was reiterated frequently in exchanges between PW and confidante Casper Yost, who came to be identified as "husbandman" and "brother" by the voice he heard from the board. Emily Hutchings found it an excellent proof that Pearl and Patience were "two individuals" when Pearl described PW's habit, sometimes amusing, sometimes embarrassing, of telling Yost things Pearl did not want him to know, the secret writing itself out before the medium could halt its telling.[7] Curran's secondary status, dependent and derivative, could leave her standing "ateeter," whereas for PW a rush of "wording" was regularly celebrated: "'Tis nay trick to set at catch and cast [pitch and toss] o' words, sirrah!" (PWR 7:1264). In the pages of the Record, with its play-script presentation of dialogue, Curran's demanding role at the pointer earns her few lines as a named speaker, relegating the medium to dramatic invisibility. When "the harp be frail" or "the head o' her be amuck," Curran might find her duties temporarily suspended. To Pearl's complaint of a sore thumb, PW responds, "I kenned a man who wi' one limb shoon a nag most perfect" (PWR 8:1458). Curran could sleep, PW never: "'Tis flesh that wearyeth and she doth this thing" (PWR 2:395). Curran's good student behavior might not have been enough for her exacting instructor, who sought an obliging instrument of art, not a bland competitor. When Curran happily visualizes an image of a child in the rain at night, PW warns, "If ye stir the mix, 'tis thy own brew." And Curran: "But Patience, I do see the little girl!" And PW, impatiently: "Welladay then, shew her" (PWR 8:1399).

As if scripted, flarings of PW temper directed at the medium helped minimize suspicion that Curran consciously directed her masquerade. PW left no doubt that she spoke not just of her harp's limited awareness but, punningly, of limited capacity: "[T]hough she be a dame o' worth, yet I speak me unto thee, she be a measure far less the hold o' me" (PWR 2:229). The conscious Pearl Curran, we hear, was employed precisely at the level of her cognitive ability: "[S]he who weaveth be but the bearer o' the words o' me" (PWR 1:134). As Curran's publisher, Henry Holt had reason to dispute characterizations of her as an empty vessel: "She is by no means as devoid of literary faculty as thought by her and some others who believe Patience Worth to be a separate intelligence," he observed (*SS,* 144). In the view of an extra-legal entity like PW, intellectual property is a manipulable concept. No one owns the language, PW could maintain; yet a poem's mother knows her own. When Curran inadvertently spoke of "the poems she was writing," PW objected immediately: "What meanest thou, wee whit dame, that thou shouldst set thee up and o'er thy dame at the bakin' o' wee loaves!" And when Curran communicated the end of a drought in *The Sorry Tale* as "And the rocks hissed," PW, the "word-wench," halted writing to call out, "What say thee? Rocks? I say me stones" (PWR 5:804). "Isn't she perverse," Curran remarked at one point, looking into the crosscurrents of her deep wishing (PWR 2:366).

Shrouded conversationally in sometimes impenetrable utterance, PW can come off as an Anglo-Saxon riddler rather than a middle-American belletrist, creating a script for covertness that gave Emily Hutchings more reason to suspect Curran's motives when she described the board's verbalizations as a "barb wire entanglement . . . calculated to prevent the most daring from penetrating very far in quest of the thought that is supposed to be ambushed behind the words."[8] Hutchings's metaphor captures well the strategic PW and matches Curran's description of her own sometimes indecipherable handwriting, as when she copied out a PW poem for a friend and added apologetically, "My hand writing is 'strange and wonderful'—at times—*nobody* can read it."[9] Protecting the unconscious craft of an inner inner-ear was at stake when psychologists like Morton Prince would "puff up her ahere atelling o' tis the she o' she" (PWR 2:316). For Curran to credit the unremarkable "she" of herself would be to discount the "me o' me," an unconscious revealed only by performance.

From beneath the medium's deceptively frivolous cover came frequent claims to greatness in terms that now seem vastly disproportionate to the published achievement. PW thought well of her work: "[N]eath these hands shall such an word set upt [*sic*], that Earth shall burn with wonder," was the claim that initiated dictation of *The Sorry Tale* (PWR 1:186). The apparent disadvantages of a "prosy spinster," "field wench," and "wee whit gray damie" are made over into a foundation for larger claims. "Man buildeth o' words temples in which he abideth. Yea, and I do build of nothings, much" (PWR 1:185). When the temple was constructed from the homely metaphors of building, baking, and weaving, PW accepted the risk of domesticating and textually reconfining the "wonder-put" of her imagination, a challenge faced by nineteenth-century writers like Elizabeth Stoddard, Mary Wilkins Freeman, and Kate Chopin, who created opportunities for exploration and stealthy triumph within what Susan K. Harris has called the "formulaic covering or overplot" of nineteenth-century American women's fiction.[10]

Flaunting a rural past, PW dares critical judgment to join her in what she calls mire or muck. At the hearth of the "hut," as the Curran parlor was renamed, she renders earth as a leveling site, the last deconstructor of abstractions. Of a play written some twenty years after the story of Telka, PW's field wench, only the poem "The Mire Song" has survived to represent PW's possibly most ambitious work, "Elizabethan Mask," on three days in the life of a young Shakespeare. In the play, "Will" is challenged to write a poem on the unpromising subject of the title. The idiom remains PW's.

> To sing of Mire?
> The silt mayhap of stars, the ash of aged Mays,
>
> . . . .
>
> Lo, it doth cling the shoon as tho' a boon it wert to
> follow thee;
> As though the aged yesterdays spake from the dust,
> and said;
> Behold thou me. A part of thy today.
> I am the stuff of ages, waiting flame that I be
> turned to life again.[11]

To critics who charged that her poetry did little more than quaintly sample the canon, PW maintained, as Pearl the conventional pianist might have, that she was searching, not simply echoing, the territory of voice for the unrevealed secret of her own: "Yea, look ye unto the stringed lutes o' man. Yea, thou smitest one string and there soundeth one note and thou smitest then the string next and behold, I say me that atween these very notes there be melodies that thou knowest not" (PWR 4:609). For the woman who writes poetry as an encumbered heiress of masters, where is language that can serve as "the out-symbol o' an in-urge" (*SS*, 260)? Unseen, PW can claim herself mistress of the unworded: "There be aneath the every stone a hidden voice. I but loose the stone, and lo, the voice!" (PWR 1:92). Named for a fiction, PW relishes the ways of saying she is her poetry. If "[s]ong be the soul's soul" (PWR 1:143), then "I shall sing that thou shalt know what be within me" (PWR 5:801).

Evidencing their own automaticity, PW's critics admired her through comparisons with the male pantheon but were apprehensive that departures constituted mutilations. To John Livingston Lowes's question for PW about willful contortions of diction and dialect from her England of no particular time or place, she responds that, twist for twist, her sense is plain enough: "Atwist ye put it then! Yea, atruth. Did he who fashioned o' the letters buy the right to tung as I do choose?" (PWR 1:92). Capable of joking with company about the prattle of "gab-wenches," she rejects the caricature and, like Elizabeth Stuart Phelps, adapts the figure of the Sphinx to her own purposes.[12] To the suggestion that she may have borrowed from her betters, PW answers, "I hae set no man's wordins" and seizes on Casper Yost's attempt at good humor ("You are no sphinx, Patience") to set a trope Phelps could have appreciated. "Who knows but e'en she might unloose her tongue? Or be it that the Nile sings her words?" (PWR 7:1325).

What writer, finding her words bent to the shape of a critic's agenda, would not harbor some version of "Yea, they seek and set the word o'me ameasured athin their word-pack . . ." (PWR 2:278)—or when "sages' mouths . . . fall achatter o' naught," could suppress a feeling of rightness in the image of critical jawing as "Dry bones ahinge" (PWR 1:185)? Creating an effect of otherness was in a sense Curran's greatest performative achievement in PW. Once worded, the medium's silently presided-over strategy becomes a surly, taunting apologia that its source will not apologize for. Pamela White Hadas quotes while also renewing and re-creating this quality in "The Riddle Patience Weaves":

Sing ye the song o' why? Why? Why?
Aneath every stone a hidden voice.
Will ye see aneath the pettiskirts o'me?
I am Patience Worth, I strut
To teach ye I be me.[13]

When, after three years of dictating literature, Patience Worth decided to become a godmother, her further intrusion on Pearl Curran's apparent autonomy should have tested the medium's readiness to serve. The intrusion plays against a subtext, however, since the co-desired co-maternity of Pearl and Patience extends their symbiosis to a new, more visible stage. Married to John Curran six years before PW entered their lives, Pearl Curran was a stepmother just as she was midwife to the text entrusted to her. John Curran's daughter, Julia, spoke affectionately of her stepmother and lived on apparently easy terms with the family, which included Mary Pollard. In ordinary circumstances, the Currans' decision to adopt a baby would have followed credibly from the assumption that Pearl was unable or unlikely to conceive. The domestic omnipresence of

PW made the circumstances extraordinary. Proliferating newspaper and magazine coverage at the time, followed by later interviews with the Currans' adopted daughter, who was born October 7, 1916, and whom they named Patience Worth Curran and referred to as "Patience Wee," transformed the adoption into a new chapter in the PW scripture.

When one evening's session began with PW saying she wished to speak on "a sumpthing close, yea close," Curran had no difficulty delivering the sense of the alphabet before her: "She wants us to get a baby" (PWR 4:643). As Litvag summarizes: "The Currans . . . insisted that they had given no thought to adoption until this night [August 16, 1916]. They asked for further information and the ouija board responded: 'Thou shalt deliver o' the goods o' me [meaning the income from publishing her books] unto the hands o' this one, and shall speak its name, 'Patience Worth'" (*SS*, 137). Consistent with what she preached, PW urged the Currans and their larger circle to rescue "one that needeth sore" from those who could not care for a child and to do so on receipt of the first check from her novel-in-progress, *The Sorry Tale.* That check would be "for the tidy sum of $3600," Emily Hutchings had heard; she told James Hyslop the money was being divided between Pearl Curran and Casper Yost.[14]

Specific directions from PW would govern their choice. The child was to be a girl, since any boy grown to man would have enough "cunnin'" to survive, whereas a woman—"ah, I be aknowin'." Brought home, the child would need to be outfitted "spinster-prim," "bonneted o' white" and "gray caped," a history book's illustration of a Puritan maiden save for an unexpectedly iconic cross "bout the wee neckin'," which PW stipulated as an accessory. The child would be in all respects as if she were "the flesh o' me," and in future would be well versed in her godmother's weavings, but her raising would be left to all members of the PW circle, already called "the Family," which the Record took to mean that "each of us, even Mr. Curran's child, Julia, should have full share in doing for the child" (PWR 4:644–45).

Specific mention of Julia Curran lends some credence to the suspicion, voiced by a family friend, Mrs. A. P. Holland, eighty-four when she was interviewed in 1957 by Ruth Duell, that the timing of the "Patience Wee" adoption coincided with "the time Julia was having an affair with a professor. Julia disappeared at the time of Patience Wee's birth and adoption. About the right time for Patience Wee to have been Julia's child."[15] The suggestion has the undeniable attraction of cutting acidly through the sensationalism and pop spiritualism with which newspapers and Sunday supplements, typographical volume turned up, treated the heaven-sent adoption. "Patience Worth Appears in the Flesh / Ouija Board Spirit Orders Adoption / Girl Baby Is Legal Child of Currans," proclaimed the *St. Louis Republic* on October 20, 1916 (*SS*, 140), with the next day's follow-up story adding, "Patience Worth has promised to keep a watchful eye on her namesake and to do all in her spirit power to lead her to become a great and good woman." Language used by the PW circle to describe the child's availability for adoption from a mother about to give birth—"the merest accident," "a mere acquaintance,"—emphasizes the providential and invites suspicion: "The father of the expected child had been killed by a mill accident. The mother, who has since died, was poor" (*PWM,* Aug. 1917, 8).[16]

Again according to Holland, John Curran's continuing deep investment in the welfare of his adopted daughter—"even thine, laddie," PW had said—reverberates strongly when, after a friend suggested the child should be spanked for making noise at the table, he threatened, "I will——[*sic*] anyone who touches her." At the time of the child's fourth birthday, John Curran quotes himself in the Record as he says, "I want Patience to write me something about my baby" (PWR 14:2672). PW's reply, "Trothed twixt thee and me. God grant I keep it," could suggest a shared secret or no more than another expression of fairy godmotherhood. PW apparently honored the request several weeks later with the poem "My Baby" (PWR 14:2715). Heroines bear illegitimate children in *The Sorry Tale* (1917) and the never-published story "The Madrigal" (*CPW,* 396–97). Patty Curran, the adopted daughter, named her own first child Hope, after *Hope Trueblood* (1918), the novel's eponymous "brat." Apart from the Holland interview, however, there is no evidence of Julia Curran's maternity, and after her beginning violin lessons in May 1920 (PWR 13:2453) draws a poem from PW, she disappears from the pages of the Record, reappearing in Walter Prince's interview of her as Mrs. Maupin. The 1957 Holland interview is also alone in suggesting that "[Julia] and Pearl did not get along"; Holland mentioned no date or circumstances for any conflict in that interview.

Against the possibility that the Curran Record invents a PW cover story for a Julia Curran pregnancy, there is the matter of Julia's age in 1916. When Henry Holt reported on "that Patience Worth baby" to his readers in 1917, he quoted at length from a letter Curran had sent him in which she describes Julia as sixteen and raised since age five by Curran and her mother. In 1916 Julia would have been a high school student. Holland's term, a "professor," would imply a college or university faculty member but could have been used broadly. Pearl Curran cited Julia as the reason she and John, if not PW, would have preferred a boy as their new addition, though "now that it is a girl we are satisfied."[17] In the Record, PW's early preference for a girl is clearly registered. In advance, the Currans would not have known the sex of any potential mother's child, and in the period of their search "to look over some babies" (PWR 4:650) they had conveyed to friends PW's instruction that the child must be a girl. Members and guests, often named when newspapers referred to the Patience Worth "cult" or "clan," had been alerted for two months to PW's profile of the desired adoption and would need to have been either unaware of or uniformly silent about a story involving Julia Curran.[18] During the gestation period of a Patience Wee, the Record would also have been at its most disingenuous when its keeper, presumably John, described the Currans as "nervous at the thought that somewhere the child we wanted was waiting for us" and concerned that "about its parents there should be no taint" (PWR 4:645).

Another kind of lineage may be read in the Ouija-board transcripts. By establishing herself first as a writer, then seeking motherhood, PW reversed a pattern that had characterized American woman-as-artist fictions from Elizabeth Stuart Phelps's *Angel Over the Right Shoulder* in 1852 to her namesake daughter's *Story of Avis* in 1877. Both texts represent mothers whose art has been sacrificed to domestic duty, their artistic ambition supported only in vague benignities by indifferent husbands. Readers of *Avis* are aware at the novel's conclusion that the heroine's looking ahead to fulfillment through her own daughter, named Wait, is a bitterly ironic comment on the pattern of deferral that had passed from the first to the second Elizabeth Stuart. For all the textual domesticity of its "bannocks" (unleavened flat bread) and "beaslings" (a cow's first milk after calving), the PW voice had been clear in the year before it ordered an adoption, with the enormously ambitious *Sorry Tale* begun, that writing had so far come first: "'Tis ne'er a dame who weaveth with babes at the skirt o' her" (PWR 1:177).

The writer's production had preceded motherhood rather than vice versa, and despite the overweening involvement of the PW voice in the raising of young Patience, writing continued to flow. The coexistence of the two roles appeared theatrically when newspapers reported that the PW baby had not been injured when "Mrs. John Curran, authoress," carrying the baby, slipped on a rug and fell down nine stairs, turning at the last moment onto her right arm so that the baby, held in her left arm, "escaped without a bruise."[19] In the dialogues of the Record, PW's spoken motherhood becomes as much a dramatic representation as any of the published fictions. A dissociative wanting that did not have the appearance of being willed was Curran's path as both writer and mother. Still, John Curran was right to describe PW's adoption order as "an epoch in our relationship with her," one that brought a fictional maiden more fully into their social lives and suggested how control and medium were moving in the same direction toward the same ends. Referring to transcriptions of *The Sorry Tale* taken from a voice that days before had instructed them to find a foundling, the Record notes, "We realized then that the child was the symbol of the book and of her work also" (PWR 4:649). John Curran, faithful record-keeper, is representing a parthenogenetic writer who reproduces herself in cape, bonnet, and text, while beyond the PW margin he keeps curtained conversations with his wife, authoress, and new mother.

Both Pearl and PW were pregnant with the idea of a child before August of 1916, its profile appearing under Curran's hands well in advance of the birth that took place on October 7 of that year. Two years earlier, the board had dictated several paragraphs titled "Lullaby," which began, "Oh, baby mine, soft upon my breast press thou and let my fluttering throat spell song to thee. . . ." Emily Hutchinson's presence at the board makes the source ambiguous, but Curran's reaction, registering denial, impatience, or both, was clear: "Let's stop this foolishness," she chided (PWR 1:640). In the next year, the Record for February 10, 1915, anticipates the subject of nontraditional maternity when PW observes, "A dame may mother a waif do she choose" (PWR 1:84). With the arrival of the waif, a visitor suggested that in her own lifetime PW had no doubt wished for a child and heard confirmation from the "primmed spinster" that she had indeed "housed such an warrin' heartie that ached and lo'ed and hungered deep" (PWR 4:701).

The maze of indirection that is PW can be traced to linkages as minor as Curran's continued fascination with red hair, a theme that sheds oblique light on the question why she could not simply write, or could not straightforwardly adopt, when she wanted to do these things. That the board gave orders specifically for a red-haired child seems at first an oddity, as if PW were contrarily daring the folk stigma that made a red-headed stepchild a traditional figure for rejection. The subject was not a new one, however, either in the Record or in the Curran household. Curran's second daughter, Eileen, remembered her mother saying that as a child she had "wanted red hair desperately" and had "tried red pepper and water solution," apparently without lasting success. From early attempts to establish PW's physical appearance, hair color was one of the few hints Emily Hutchings recalled from the Ouija board's repetitions: "Three times she has referred to red-haired persons in a way to make us think her own hair was red."[20] A fourth time would have been evident in the board's greeting to Pearl and John Curran on the day they brought home the object of PW's search, swaddled perhaps beside the board, which now spelled triumphantly, "See ye, I did for to say me that thy handmaid was at the merryin'; for look, she hath ta'en a tinder-top!" (PWR 4:698B). Inadvertently, John Livingston Lowes supplied further evidence that PW, control, was a medium for the engendering of a baby already imagined yearningly by Pearl Curran. Mostly interested in the anomalies of PW's historical English, Lowes inquired whether Curran had made any attempt at serious writing as a younger woman. As an example of the "humorous poem or two" she had tried, Curran passed on to him a poem titled "To a Red-haired Girl," which, Lowes told psychologist Morton Prince, bore "no similarity with [the?] ouija-board poetry."[21]

Authorship and motherhood were most clearly related to each other when in the month following Patience Wee's adoption, Curran took up a pencil, not a Ouija pointer, and excusing herself from the family circle for half an hour, wrote in her own hand using the thickly Scots variant of PW language a three-stanza poem called "The Wonder Babe," which began:

Ye wee wonder babe,
Wi' heaven still aclingin' ye!
The angels fashioned ye
And gaed ye o' their gracin's. (PWR 4:742)

In Burnsian dialect or any other, Curran's direct production of a PW-sounding text was potentially damning evidence. Those who said she had knowingly fashioned the PW mask out of herself—conscious duplicity rather than "secondary personality" their theme—would have been right all along. Describing himself as "stumped" and "thoroughly frightened," John Curran wrote that "in view of many antagonistic theories about the work, it looked as though, if Patience Worth was what she claimed to be, that she had placed within Mrs. Curran's hand a blade and bared her breast. And why? Why?" After "a visit to the pictures," for relief and reflection, "the Family" returned to quiz the board and was told that the short poem had after all been "ne'er a deal o' sweets" and was given on this one occasion simply as a reward for Pearl. "See, hath she not ta'en unto her breast the wee flesh o'me? This song be o' this thing and be dealt unto her" (PWR 4:742; *SS,* 143–44). But the appearance of mediumship and authorship merging would continue, Curran moving past the successes of dissociation as the gap between selves narrowed for both mother and writer. In the newly launched magazine bearing her name, PW proposed through her medium that women begin to form adoption clubs, dividing their "attention and expense" for homeless or neglected infants ("The root of evil be within the cradle") who could be placed with "some good woman with time" (*PWM,* Sept. 1917, 11).

Never far from the "wonder babe's" development, her doting spiritual mother poeticized endlessly—"Two dimple hands have given me the key / And Heaven is mine!" (*SS,* 141)—in ways that should have reminded Curran of her uncle Cordingley's wettish word-pack. In other moods, PW was a possessively maternal spirit bent on claiming "the wee fleshie that be mine, mine, mine" (PWR 5:805). Often enough, PW as mother would assert the same kind of superiority and control that she had claimed as author, describing Curran as at most a loving caretaker (*SS,* 141). Conflict followed. Prefiguring her behavior later in life, the four-year-old Patience Wee one evening "had been naughty and rather unmanageable" and was sent to bed before she could greet Casper Yost, due to arrive for a PW session. The board quickly registers discontent, mounting an argument that the mother's decision was "wrongfu'," not as a punishment but as a broken promise. PW pictures the "bairn" sighing in "a sea of tears" and urges Curran to awaken her so that she can join the company. Curran's dialogic inward struggle, spelled out, has a happy ending: "little Patience" tells Yost that she has been dreaming "about fairies dancing about the stars." An appearance of divided authority counts less than the emergence through PW of Curran's remorseful second thoughts, for which she endures a scourging description of herself as "a wench wi' a slit tongue. . . . thee'dst nae sayed the thin' loud athout thy damie had voiced it" (PWR 15:2919–20).

Nearing seven in September 1923, Patience Wee faced the question of having two mothers by flattering her "angel Patience" with a note of imitation and reconciling herself to visible authority. "Dear Patience, I love you and sometimes I have wanted to speak to you but I was outdoors. You are just like a wee whit angel. Dear Patience, I love you millions. I am going to mind my mother." The habit of communication between PWs great and wee continued up to "Patty's" marriage at the age of eighteen, when the bride and namesake, used by this time to addressing a hierarchy of mothers, received a blessing in discarnate Scots signed "Thy Mither" (*SS*, 141).

In taking on a "babe o' the flesh o' me," PW moved toward convergence with her medium by objectifying more of an earthly body, another way of saying that Pearl Curran had begun to possess more of herself. Having claimed something of the earth in her child, PW then remembered the earth claiming her. Ten days after the desire to become a mother was read from the board, Curran was moved to spell details of PW's life and death. This too was close matter, and the board's pointer "circle[s] very slowly" as its "I" begins "aseekin words." The communication carries again the note of "an wistful yearnin' that eat thy damie's heart," quickly imaged as the sea voyage of a young Patience Worth from Old to New England. "Such bleaked walls o' stone! Such rockin' seas! Such empty lands!" Just as quickly, the narration leaps over the historical question of which New England settlement was being recalled.

What happens next objectifies a mortal PW. Curran takes over, with no protest from PW. The death of PW is given as a picture in Curran's mind but is introduced in the language of the board spoken in the third person. The precedence of picture over word was not unusual in Pearl's mediumship, and the narrative itself has the quality of historical romance, of, for example, Mary Johnston's *To Have and to Hold,* which Curran had by then read, or of Gertrude Atherton's *Patience Sparhawk and Her Times.* What is exceptional is the exchange of the familiar PW voice for a narrative idiom that translates what Curran was seeing into the bookish imagery of violent death: "Here the picture showed Patience, a small, wee figure in grey, come out of the copse of pine on the bluff top, speeding, speeding to the bluff, then half running, half falling, down, down to the beach where the waters seethed. Within her breast an arrow stood and the small hands held it as she ran and fell, and half raised to her knees."

Without pause or reprimand at this writerly intervention, the voice of PW returns, interrupting the more formal voice to respond directly to the represented experience. "And then, and then, when the tide had come unto—Look, Look. Ye know! See. See. 'Twere sunk deep." The romance narrator then resumes the story, promoting the pathos of what it tells by inventing, then occupying, the eyes of a dying Patience Worth: "The dear eyes looked across the sea, straining to find the dear home-land afar. But all grew misty and the yearning eyes grew dim, and she sunk on the sand by the sea's waters like a wounded swallow, a mere bit of grey along the vasty shore" (PWR 4:660–61).

On other occasions Curran had demonstrated in comparable prose how she experienced "visual preludes" to the experience of dictating PW (*CPW,* 321–31). What began to happen just as "The Wonder Babe" was about to be dictated was not only the further construction of a persona—PW's representation taking on a life and look she did not have in July of 1913—but a development of the author–medium relationship as a kind of contrapuntal agency rendering Curran increasingly authorial in language and ambition, novelistically aggrandizing the heroine whose voice she presumably served.

By 1921, Curran came to see PW not as an old lady, but "much younger," about thirty, her own age in the inaugural year of 1913 and more appropriate to a heroine of historical romance. The revised portrait had been provoked in the Record by Casper Yost's plan to verify in England the inner circle's assumption that PW had lived in Dorset. Asked on July 4 to preview what Yost would discover, PW unfolds a series of "mental pictures" for "Mrs. Curran" into which the medium can step as actor. Curran finds herself climbing a hill to observe a monastery, first in ruins, then in its original condition—iron-bound doors, hinges, and a square turret described in detail—before she discovers the village PW had described on June 27, making "a couple of manor houses" from PW's one, confirming the smithy, and accepting the Scottishness of a dialectally misplaced "kirk." While PW is given as the scene's source, Curran is subject here, Patience object, as the Record sketches a heroine embarked for the New World on a "three-masted schooner," revealing beneath her hood hair that is "dark red, mahogany" and that falls "in big, glossy soft waves." Impressions of "clammy skin," "desolation," and "heartsickness" arise from a transaction between writer and character, the Record's Curran present enough in the scene to hear the creaking of the ship's spars while she appears to act as medium for the feelings she reads in Patience, "lips trembling and hands nervously moving on the rough rail where she has laid them" (PWR 15:2931–37; *SS,* 226). Entering more consciously into the narrative of PW's voyage, the transported Curran brings with her figures like those she had dictated in previously published texts: a young mother mysteriously alone with her child, perhaps in flight, a boy quickly become an orphan, weeping into the skirt-folds of Patience after his mother has died in her sleep. Curran's visualizing of a Patience Worth at sea had been novelistically persuasive, yet the PW voice, set apart, undercut those attractions in a poem titled "The Real Patience," implying strongly that Yost and the Currans were together creators of a temporally "concrete" PW.

> Not what I wert but what I am.
> I am resurrected from out the cunning
> Of thine imagination.
> Yea, I have poured that which is me
> Unto the cup of thy day, a molten stuff,
> And become anew, manifest,
> Without place or instant.
> I am conceived
> And become concrete.
> What is the answer?[22]

The stumped final line appears to keep open the question of a historical Patience, and Curran continued publicly to insist on their separateness as agents. Henry Holt told readers of his *Unpopular Review* that he doubted the spiritist interpretation of the PW writings, but that Pearl Curran did not, quoting at length from a letter in which Curran contrasted her conscious writing with the speed and quantity of PW's automatic production. The letter had taken her "almost all afternoon" to write, she wanted him to know, "while if it had been *The Sorry Tale* or a big poem, I would have done three thousand words in an hour and three quarters and forgotten about it." Among the 900,000 words dictated to her by 1917, none of them, she said, had been "consciously or voluntarily produced by me." Estimating that she spoke with "as clear a mind as the average," Curran could only conclude that PW was a "discarnate entity" who spoke to her "from a state of actual existence outside, beyond or different from, the ordinary life of mortals."[23] Neither to her publisher nor to herself could Curran speak in her own voice of a dialogic history now narrowing the distance between her dissociated yet cross-referential selves.

All that was lost as an immediate effect of Curran's independent writing efforts was the Ouija prompt. Two days after the *Saturday Evening Post* published a story by Curran in November 1919 (see Chapter 6), PW suggested the board's retirement, saying, the "follied one" had grown tired of "the grister" (*SS*, 212). The board that had seemed indispensable to a flow of production was becoming an encumbrance. Following PW's advice that she "[c]rawl before thou runnest," Curran began dictating word by word rather than letter by letter (*SS*, 212). While John Curran had worried that his wife's movement into magazine authorship under her own name might raise further questions about the legitimacy of PW, he had little difficulty adjusting to her new mode of production, noting that a poem delivered on January 5, 1920, arrived at the rate of 110 words per minute (*CPW,* 344–45). At first, Curran found her idle hands unsettling and held a scarf pin offered by Casper Yost (PWR 12:2239), then she discovered that with practice she could deliver dictations at a typewriter without conscious effort (*CPW,* 345). Launched into automaticity, she continued to hear the words and see the pictures she believed PW was giving her, along with "the pressure on my head" that she had first reported in March of 1914 (PWR 1:45). At the typewriter, without a partner, she was again conveying literature without forethought, although, as she told the March-April 1920 readers of "A Nut for Psychologists," "if I become conscious of the change I have to go back to the spelling" (*CPW,* 403).

However startling to her immediate audience, Curran's transition to the typewriter participated in the relation well under way by the turn of the century between Spiritualism and new technologies. As Pamela Thurschwell, following Friedrich Kittler, has pointed out, what is pre-verbal is taken for spiritual because undetectable and, as yet untextual, then through the typewriter enters a material, mechanized world that does the word's emergent bidding virtually without effort. Mark Seltzer notes that Henry James's late-career secretary, Theodora Bosanquet, already inducted into mediumship and automatic writing, saw herself as a medium for James, preferably "without a mind," between the writer's spoken and her typed word, with James asserting that after five years his dictations were "intellectually absolutely identical with the act of writing."[24] For the musically trained Pearl Curran, the Ouija board was a clumsier kind of piano, the typewriter a mechanically more satisfactory mode of conjuring the word.

What emerged at the turn into the 1920s was the medium's greater awareness of the terms of a Pearl-Patience cohabitation. Struck by the contrast between the difficulty of her conscious composition and the ease with which PW operated beyond or beneath her consciousness—"My own writing fatigues me, while the other (Patience Worth's) exhilarates me"—Curran proposed an experiment in May 1920. She would write a letter to her friend "Dotsie" Smith while simultaneously calling out to her husband the words of a poem as PW gave it to her. The language John Curran recorded is that of the unrepentantly poetic PW ("Oh you marshlight flashing / Across the marshes, beckoning!"). What he did not hear, a silently penciled letter, is pure Pearl, slangy and flustered, as she complains to her friend, "I don't like it, honey. It's like baking bread and stirring soup. I am sick of the job. . . . This is a mess of a letter, honey bug. I'm nuts!" (*CPW,* 285–86; *SS,* 214). It was not incredible, commonplace even, that an unmoored feeling of doubleness should result from Curran's experience of the power of a control who sotto voce spoke her medium as prima donna.

Chapter 4

WHAT PATIENCE WROTE

> I should sing even though the winds arose and blew down my throat my song.
>
> —Patience Worth (PWR 8:1433)

Let PW be a subset of neural processes in Pearl Curran's capacity for unconsciously attending to, recalling, then reconsolidating language and imagery from continuously revised forms of implicit memory; or a demonstration of oscillating flow in the hydraulics of conscious and subconscious intentionality. More fancifully, let her be seen as an antetype of someday's nano-level, dark-matter telepathy in a space-time continuum when neuropsychology finds itself immersed in quantum mechanics. If writing can be an out-of-body experience, by all means let her be a discarnate entity. She will remain "a word wench," PW would say, "and ne'er a ghost for see" (PWR 1:157). Pragmatically, none of these explanatory gestures is more or less useful in reading what PW spelled.

Just as the PW persona coalesced over the period of Pearl Curran's increasing proprietorship, the PW text, including both published works and the unpublished conversations and poetry of the Record, develops through discernible stages, peaks in the latter years of World War I and adoption of the Nineteenth Amendment, then falls off into a long decade of repetition and self-imitation, concluding in the mid-1930s in Los Angeles with a burst of Shakespearean ambition whose textual product remains to be located, much less appraised. While the poetry of Patience Worth attracted early attention, and the habit of delivering it without second thoughts extended throughout Pearl Curran's career as medium, it contains few surprises. A brief survey of the poetry may justify itself most by emphasizing places in which the PW voice, not bound by narrative, created a space for the surfacing of attitudes less reverent than its hymns to love and nature. The two novels most newsworthy at the time of their publication were *The Sorry Tale* (1917) and *Hope Trueblood* (1918). Not only their production at a Ouija board, but PW's agile movement from one popular genre, the biblical novel, to another, the "Victorian" plot of a heroine ultimately found not guilty of illegitimacy, drew praise, some of it mixed, from national reviewers. But PW, clearing her throat, had first served an apprenticeship as fictionist with shorter tales in vaguely Arthurian-medieval settings, published by Casper Yost in the *St. Louis Globe-Democrat* in 1914 and 1915. At the same time, *Telka,* finished by 1915, became the first novel-length, dialogue-based fiction to be completed at the Ouija board. Its publication in 1928 was anticlimactic following the early interest in its idiosyncratic Anglo-Saxonisms, seized on by supporters as evidence that PW wrote from beyond. Of the fictions that followed *The Sorry Tale* and *Hope Trueblood,* only *The Pot Upon the Wheel* (1921) found a publisher, and much of the work produced in the twenties went unpublished as Curran moved PW's energies to public appearances on tours across the country.

No single critic followed PW's literary career from beginning to end, but William Reedy would prove the most open minded and unillusioned of her readers during the Ouija board's early, productive years. By giving serious attention to novels like *The Sorry Tale* and *Hope Trueblood,* Reedy undertook a characteristic act of literary sympathy in his role as editor of *Reedy's Mirror* while minding the gap between the spirit world's "wee whit gray damie" and the madam of a local house of prostitution he had married. Judging only what PW had written, Reedy stationed himself between a circle of true believers and satiric fellow journalists who portrayed Ouija-board writers as, by turns, addled grannies and fraudulent competitors. Reedy may even have seized his own opportunity for satire. In an issue of his *Mirror,* there appeared under the name of William Trowbridge Larned a poem titled "Ballade of the Last Straw," which in a headnote cites PW's enormous productivity and then in verse warns the brothers of the writing fraternity, "Behold in Patience Worth—the super-She—/ *Our bread and butter swiped by lady spooks!* " The poem's satire cuts both ways with its implication that the masculinism of the literary industry's "Princes," the "success de steam" generated by the "sole man-power of a fiction factory," may have to give way to "the perils of this new psychology."[1]

It may now be surprising that the PW text could be taken seriously by a critic like Reedy, whose hard-boiled style was sometimes offset by eruptions of learnedness. But PW had happened to Reedy when, as a guest at the Currans' home, he watched an extraordinary act of textual production, letter by letter, as he had not in the cases of other writers he championed—Kate Chopin or Vachel Lindsay or Theodore Dreiser. Repeatedly, he had seen Curran's pointer resume where it left off and with no recursiveness or consulting of notes plunge unhesitatingly into the Bethlehem and Jerusalem of the time of Christ to tell a long, many-charactered story with its climax on Calvary.

To take PW seriously was to take her at her transcribed word, particularly when the board became its own subject, pointing again and again to the proliferating quantity of its text. If the text was real, so was she. Her version of *scribo ergo sum*, at its most self-important, ran: "He who buildeth with peg and cudgel but buildeth a toy for an age who will but cast aside the bauble as naught; but he who buildeth with word, a quill and fluid, buildeth well" (PWR 1:68). More viscerally, she sounded most like a testy earth-bound writer surrounded by scholarly mediocrities when she told Professor John Livingston Lowes, "I be a trickster and thou a piddle-spiller" (PWR 1:90). To catch sight of self-proclamations from PW may be an additional opportunity to understand what was at stake for a writing woman in the new twentieth century. Precisely because the PW text will not bear comparison with Kate Chopin's or Willa Cather's, its anger and oblique ambition within sight of the looming canonical make it representative of a larger number of singers in the shadows.

I. The Poetry

In its beginnings, the heightened PW language arriving letter by letter would not have looked like poetry. As Casper Yost informed readers in 1916, the lining into verse of the board's stream of words represented a series of editorial decisions. Some lines, it was decided (Yost's passive voice sets aside Pearl Curran as her own copy editor), might have as few as six syllables, some as many as sixteen, the only observable breaks for auditors coming with the medium's pause at the end of a sentence. Line length and punctuation were decided in as close accord with "the principles of blank verse" as possible while leaving the words, sequence, and spelling of PW dictations untouched, Yost explained (*PWPM,* 65–66). In the Ouija board's first days the difference between amusing banter and an emerging intention of poetry became clear: a week before naming itself, the board spoke of "rising Venus in a mountain lake" and a bluet springing "from 'neath the moss," then asked pleadingly, "Oh, why let sorrow steel thy heart?" (PWR 1:2). John Curran began to suspect Emily Hutchings of interpolation when PW was recorded as saying "Can you catch a star? Then, and only then can you alter the Great Plan." Hutchings also seemed likely to have been the polished hand in an early poem, "The Bitter Cup," whose rhyming trimeter lines alternate regularly with lines of unrhymed tetrameter.

Smothered under heaped-up beauties, the PW poetry begins to move its conflicts to other terrains. One is the shadowland of agency between Pearl and Patience; another is the disharmony between a voice instantly ready to condemn fools and fervently pouring forth its nondenominational orthodoxy of love. While audiences grew used to accepting that what they saw in Curran was not what they got in PW, they learned directly from the poet that a signifying mask was at any moment its own trial of identity. In the midst of gorgeousness, the PW text grows angry to the point of self-betrayal at its easy mastery of the masking game, as in "The Deceiver":

> I know you, you shamster!
> I saw you smirking, grinning,
> Nodding through the day,
> And I knew you lied
> . . . .
> And your hands shook
> And your knees were shaking.
> I know you, you shamster.
> I heard you honeying your words,
> Licking your lips and smacking
> O'er them, twiddling your thumbs
> In ecstasy over your latest wit.
> I know you, you shamster!
> You are the me the world knows.[2]

Aware that the tongue, "a cunning implement," cuts both ways, the speaker knows herself. It may decapitate a brother or undo the speaker, awed equally by the mind's straining for wisdom in "cocksure Faith" or by arguments with God that "reorganize his creation / Upon a foundation of words" (PWR 14:2753; *CPW,* 190).

PW was not a literally autobiographical poet, but for Curran the poetry served as a species of self-writing. Her PW spoke of "Lost Children" in a way that identified a limbo of children yet to be with ghosts of unfruited ambition. As a condition of the trope's birth, the medium who delivers a dissociated "I " from a mist in consciousness may be as inaudible as the mist's "half-begottens," both "wan-cheeked babes" and "half-begotten hopes" that, "condemned, pass phantom-like within the mist" (PWR 15:2945; *CPW,* 135). The medium–specter dialogue weaves together art and motherhood, ambition and devotion that neither entity alone could pattern to any satisfying effect. More often, PW's menu of doctrine and decoration varies more according to the needs of imploring visitors than to the dictates of her privately held fund of invention. When Herman Behr, become a wealthy supporter of Curran in the 1920s, selected and compiled poems from the Record to be published as *Light from Beyond* (1923), he gave only brief space to PW's "personal" poems while reflecting the greater quantity of poetry on such subjects as consolation, God, and immortality.

In a 1914 poem, "War," anger at war's false promises breaks through the benign calm of all-shall-be-well to condemn the Great War for providing so many fatal occasions for Ouija-board communicators. As war undergoes a gender change from false god to "masquerading fiend, / The harlot of the universe," her speaker's lips are "becrimsoned in her lover's blood," a lover warned to discover her "raiment o'er-spangled with a leaden rain." Beneath the enemy's martial visor, the warrior-lover will "see the snakey strands" (PWR 1:72). If war is gendered as Medusa, death becomes tombstone sex in a poem that takes its stereotypical givens as far as they can go while characterizing the conventional warrior as unknowing and deluded.

A poet born of doubling is energized by conflict. Heaven's God is the antagonist in a poem that has the PW voice hovering between accusation and acceptance. The rhetorical ploy is transparent: the speaker's righteousness has not been adequate to a Job's trial; anger and winey indulgence are short-term responses to a divine plan for long-term harvesting of souls. Often enough, PW does not earn her name, enacting impatience or repeatedly invoking a patience of unnuanced faith based on eyes-shut speculation that debates the likelihood of either bruising or restoration in a later harvest. Still, the poem's tone and the riskiness of its role-playing could have seemed daring for its earliest audience.

> Ah, God I have drunk unto the dregs,
> And flung the cup at Thee!
> The dust of crumbled righteousness
> Hath dried and soaked unto itself
> E'en the drop I spilled to Bacchus,
> Whilst Thou, all-patient,
> Sendest purple vintage for a later harvest.[3]

Just as Curran had rolled her eyes at some of the board's early offerings, PW, committed to spontaneity by birthright and spurning revision, sometimes confessed disappointment in what was produced under her name. After taking on an audience challenge to use both free and blank verse for a poem on an approaching storm, PW comments, "This may be singing but it's a muckish tune" (PWR 15:2905). By contrast, PW was pleased to have visitors to the Curran parlor call out the names of her presumed neighbors in eternity—Burns, Shakespeare, Sappho—then ask for updatings, a final word passed on. Allegedly deprived of the high school graduate's erudition, Curran could wander in a newly capacious memory when she saw Shakespeare as a beggar knocking at the gate of immortality, then entering when he "oped his soul / As a polished steel reflecting [Eternity]" (PWR 12:2305). A requested poem on Sappho drew PW's prediction that her tongue, loosed, "would be most lustful in its melody" and would "sip seductively at the nectar of expression," a sipping that continued into a poem in which Sappho is seen "dreaming dreams from out the tabernacle of the flesh . . . / E'en to today. . . . " (PWR 17:3100).

Strategically it was important that Curran disclaim any sources other than PW. Signs of popular bookishness or alertness to current literary chat could erase the border between the medium and her control, as did an occasional leakage of her own slang into historical vocabularies. When a friend of Curran's suggested "character is destiny" as a subject, the response spelled a medium rising to claim her own first person, struggling to hold on to a Burnsian "Sae" with one hand and her own slangy "mug" with the other. The PW who asserts her writing as her being gives way to another voice that sounds uncertain who is trickster, who is chump, before trailing off flat and stymied.

> What a hapless mug I be,
> Baffled by incident,
> Flung into chaos by doubt,
> Clothed in a tattered raiment
> Of learning, stitched of wisdom.
> What I BE trends my day!
> Is this a jest 'pon me?
> Or my jest at the day? . . .
> I am wondering . . . (PWR 20:3439)

The company, says the *Record*, "thought this a strange philosophy, unlike Patience." If the PW voice occasionally found its identity failing in the cushioned confines of hopeful poetry, Curran could not help expressing discomfort. Better to reassure the puzzled audience that they heard no more than the debility of aged centuries: "mine ain, when thee art oldin' as thy damie, thee hast unlearned many a true-put sayin'." The dialogic poem lends itself hopelessly to hope:

> What have I to do
> With this labor
> Save the lending of myself unto it
> Unquestioningly?

There was nothing local in this, or of the closely set, red-brick houses the Currans regularly chose as their St. Louis homes. Once, though, on an evening when neighborhood noises interrupted the medium's concentration, described in the Record as "a time of interruptions and confusion," the PW voice, straining to launch immortal lines, clothed the city's distractions in English country manners:

I tune my lute and let my fingers strum
When lo, a gander squawks. I sigh
And sing, and out the belfry chimes
The bell wi' cracked sides and a heavy tongue.
I ply me listlessly and wait, and lo,
A jogging cart goes clattering by.
I dream me of a carol gay when lo, some wail
From out a distant spot breaks in,
Yet I must sing! (*CPW,* 197)

The heedless proliferation of PW poems, even with their occasional flarings of interest, can make the choice of some poems over others seem futile. Or the poems can be seen as a single act, performing PW's insistence on poetry as a soul's soul that marshals a fluent alphabet toward an unspellable "I" with no visible referent. To reach that center, Pamela White Hadas braids the PW idiom with her own in "The Riddle Patience Weaves." Creating a Patience in search of Pearl, Hadas makes the medium's buried voice PW's quarry, a shift of power so marked as to seem a trick were it not a mystery demanding to arc the synapse between wound and tongue:

Aye, when I found my Pearl, *her foot were abruise*
With the rugged road. It was but for me to bite
Her lily-lip o' lonely red and trick her pout
So willow-worn wi' the put o' the me o'me.
Think ye my body's naught, ye can unweave
The flesh o' my puts and spare the world
Its mystery? *Teach me I be ye.*[4]

II. Short Fiction and "Playlets"

I tease from the eons fanciful puppets, which walk,
Aye, stalk majestically, or prance in mimic measure. . . .
—Patience Worth (*CPW,* 81)

No one at first suspected PW of harboring fiction. But in September 1914 the Ouija board tossed off a brief sketch, untitled, that seemed to promise work on a stage larger than poetry could offer. After noting that her medium was not above stealing corn from a neighbor's crib, PW dipped into a private store of picturesque pastness as the pointer began "haltingly" to spell:

> At Sabboth house, at midmorn prayer, one, Faith Todd, did smile ahind her hymnal, and good man Pritchett did look a lesson upon her. Poor Faith had but espied a stinging fly smashed upon the words, "Jesus, I my cross have taken." And believe me, she told me after she read it so, "I my *crush* have taken." (PWR 1:63)

The anachronism of romantic "crush," a word Curran had used for herself,[5] is symptomatic of the contemporary feel of the sketch while the lineage of historical romance appears in Faith's name and looks ahead to the novel *Hope Trueblood.* More noticeable is the hymnal text made to serve punning humor by the same PW whose treatment of the Crucifixion in the long novel *The Sorry Tale* would be praised for its scriptural power. In conversation PW regularly characterized herself as an easily distracted woman of the pews she claimed to occupy in Old and New England. Here, the hymnal is a prop for the writer who brokers Faith's heartfelt text to a new audience.

In the earliest PW fiction, the preferred setting is a stagey, idealized England of agrarian and courtly charm populated by roisterous, good-hearted hut dwellers and a mixed population of knights, ladies, and loutish lords populating and occasionally emerging from the castle above the village. Illustrated, her pages have the look of an operetta, derivative visually from pre-Raphaelite painters like John William Waterhouse, Edward Burne-Jones, or William Holman Hunt and continuous with the American Arthurianism of the enormously popular Howard Pyle and the school of illustrators he founded.[6] The imagery of these first efforts at fiction is summed up in a 1920 PW poem titled "From A Turret Window," its vista suggestive of young Pearl Pollard as a Lady of Shalott in a desolate Missouri small town, "like a lady" shut away with her voice, looking out on a "dusty highway" of passing warriors, a pig-farmer "dolt," and a Tennysonian landscape of "barley / Stream with tangled beard where larks / Flutter, half prisoned in the heavy grain." (Compare in Tennyson: "only reapers, reaping early / In among the bearded barley, / Hear a song that echoes cheerly . . . ") The PW speaker, a Lady of Shalott who has survived, hears it all, "haunting as an old memory," and recalls the "leaden hours" of her dreamy spectatorship from a turret "as I thread[ed] the golden threading / of my soul through the leaden hours" (PWR 12:2240).

The Missouri "lead belt" towns of Ironton, Bismarck, Palmer, and Potosi had been no Camelot for the girl who took in the "desolation" of her surroundings as she listened to a touring Mr. Chauvenette recite what she remembered as "The Lady of Charlotte." Communicating fiction, the adult Pearl had to construct Camelot from her memory of the actor's recitation and the "mire" and "muck" of her small-town upbringing. Even as advocates found evidence of PW's freedom from time, the medium was demonstrating her immersion in the tastes and historicisms of her environing culture.

Heroines in the earliest PW fiction divide into two sorts: aloof ladies of the turret, physically unsighted or wounded in heart, largely silent and living out the terms of their enforced gentility; and peasant-stock wenches who share the rural origins of the persona credited with inventing them—colloquial, voluble, of the earth, but no earthier than a popular taste for the romanticized medieval might allow. When PW adopts the figures of weaving and baking—a "loaf" is the story she is currently working on—she makes a connection between her wenches and the cookery-based writing she turns to as ballast against Arthurian dreaminess.

The proximity of the lady's turret and the wench's kitchen also evokes the kind of rivalry PW once enacted on an evening when the godfather to Patience Wee complained of an overly serious literary diet. "Oh, if she would only give us something plain and simple!" wailed Dr. Woodruff, a family friend. To call for something Quakerish was to play to PW's strength. She obliged by interpreting her guest's lament as a request for "A puddin' bag, and a puddin' within it." In "A Song or a Loaf," which the Record describes as "whimsical," a knightly lover would make a kitchen of his lady's turret, PW supplying the subtext for her project from its beginning:

Oh, I sat upon a silver couch
And strummed a silver lute,
And sang a lay
Which made the day
Seem grey and melancholy.
I sat and sang a wordy tale
Of pettiskirts
And ruffled shirts
And shields and lances feathered.
Oh, I sang a lay that caused the thrush
To hang its head in shaming!
I sang my song
And warbled long
My song in sweetness streaming.
And lo, my lover sat in pain
Aweary growin', gaping,
"Mine ain," he said,

"Come turn the bread."
But I was singin', singin'. (PWR 10:1978)

By the time Casper Yost first presented early PW writings to a national audience in 1916 in *Patience Worth: A Psychic Mystery,* he was able to publish the stories "The Fool and the Lady" and "The Stranger," a snippet from the five-act play in verse *Redwing,* and a sampling from the long fiction *Telka,* as well as several parables Yost described as "cryptic," leaving the reader "to ponder o'er their meaning." Another selection included in the book, in verse for two speakers, titled "The Phantom and the Dreamer," he characterized as a "weird allegory" and "the most mystical of Patience's productions" (*PWPM,* 255–64). In longer works, PW either wrote closet drama in which characters' speeches are linked by occasional narrative, as in *Telka* and the intermittently composed "Merry Tale," or in more conventional novels like *The Sorry Tale,* made dialogue the staple of the story and relegated narrative to the tasks of setting the physical and tonal scene or foreshortened action.

The Record itself might be characterized, until the death of John Curran, as a dramatic text, a series of dialogues between PW and her visitors, just as *Patience Worth* was a name for the medium's conversation with herself. Commentators on Curran's limited education who totaled only her reading missed the large experience of entertainments and performances available to her in the small towns of her childhood, in Chicago, and relatively abundantly in St. Louis, including reviews, vaudeville shows, selections of operatic arias, and, in time, the newest of popular art forms, movies. The environmental mix of music and theater makes clear again how much of her education Curran took in by ear, performing heightened diction as delivered by melodramatic characters and dictating rhythms of lyric expression that were part of her earliest voice and piano lessons.

In a convergence of popular and elite tastes, there was the phenomenon of the American Shakespeare. She had never actually read Shakespeare, Curran told Walter Prince in 1926, but had learned "a few bits" from her mother and had been a young spectator at two plays during her earliest trips to the theater (*CPW,* 16). In 1915, the list of authors read that John Livingston Lowes drew from her placed Shakespeare last ("not much"), just after Byron. Yet Pearl would not have needed to read Shakespeare directly in late nineteenth-century America. Until the end of the century, Lawrence Levine points out, "Shakespeare *was* popular entertainment," gradually separating from popular forms like burlesque into the middle-class appetite: "Nineteenth-century America swallowed Shakespeare, digested him and his plays, and made them part of the cultural body."[7]

In St. Louis, the mass appeal of a Shakespearian pageant drew half a million spectators over five nights in 1914 to a "Community Masque," based on *The*

Tempest, written by Percy MacKaye and later performed in New York.[8] (Curran titled her final dictation "Elizabethan Mask.") The occasion for MacKaye's ambitious project—some thought it hugely overblown—was the tercentenary of Shakespeare's death in 1916, and trial performances took place in St. Louis in May of 1914, several months before PW began to explore a dramatic mode in her fictions. There is no record of the Currans making part of the half million spectators, but the masque, performed in the city's Forest Park a few blocks from their apartment, would have been difficult to ignore. A photograph shows an audience of 150,000 at one performance and describes 7,500 of them as participants.

Reactions by Pearl Curran's contemporaries, astonished at the stylistic and historical range of her Ouija-board fiction, remain instructive as a study in cultural myopia. Her most literary observers were impressed by PW's ability to range from English to European to Middle Eastern settings and characters with, they believed, uncannily appropriate stylistic and dialectal variations. Yet the PW text predictably mirrors literary tastes predominant in early twentieth-century St. Louis, a conservative city of traditional culture in the aftermath of the 1904 World's Fair. Defenders of a spiritually autonomous PW were quick to argue that Curran had not read any of the works alleged as sources, but they would have had difficulty removing themselves from the climate that had delivered Literature to them and that Pearl Curran breathed in as well.

The first PW story, "The Fool and the Lady," suggests the lineage of the early fiction. The story of a hunchbacked fool, his monkey, and the lady for whom he sacrifices himself seems less a specific borrowing than a variation on the *Pagliacci* story, as Irving Litvag suggests (*SS,* 47), or, to cast a wider net, Victor Hugo's *Hunchback of Notre Dame* or Anatole France's story "Our Lady and the Juggler," later an opera, *Le jongleur de Notre-Dame,* by Jules Massenet, which had its American premiere in 1908. Specific details are not lacking. In Rugerro Leoncavallo's *Pagliacci* (1892), Beppe is a member of a troupe of traveling actors. PW names the Fool's monkey Beppo. Tonio is Leoncavallo's hunchback, in love with Canio's wife, Nedda. In PW's story, Tonio is the name of her innkeeper. Pearl Pollard's recuperative year in the Catholic St. Ignatius Academy (*CPW,* 13) may well have acquainted her with the story of a juggler who expresses his devotion to the Virgin by a performance of his humble art. The widely disseminated story needed only to be part of a culture of convent-school Mariolatry to create a bridge in imagination between the Lady who bends to bless Barnabas, her juggler, and PW's Lady Lisa, who kisses the Fool's hand as he dies, her blue and gold raiment, the colors adopted by her victorious champion, mindful of chapel statuary and of France's blue-mantled Mary wiping the sweat from her juggler's forehead.

Charmed by her Puritan-maiden persona, few visitors inquired into PW's acquaintance with Romish material or attempted to match it with Curran's experience at a Catholic academy, which continued to be influential when she chose to have her daughters educated by nuns after her move to Los Angeles. In "The Stranger," a Christmas tale described by Casper Yost as "weird, mystical," it is unsurprisingly the blind, "mad" Lady Marye who sees what others cannot in the shadowy Christ figure tending his sheep and who plays the pipes "most mournfully." Her intuitions of order and disorder are difficult to reject: "I fear me lest I see too much" (*PWPM,* 131), but she is no more mad than her roaring vinous father, Sir John, is peaceful. An unsighted figure—the Lady Ione in *Telka* is another—speaks for Curran in Lady Marye's "I but loosed my fancy from its tether to gambol at its will, and they do credit me amiss" (*PWPM,* 127).

More visible from our distance are PW heroines who repeatedly confront versions of male power, the historical setting obscuring Curran's suffragist present. Provoked by a castle full of "wine-soaked," "feed-drunkened" lords, Lady Marye resolves to confront their lord, her father, and "wage him war at words!" The story only hints that he may be guilty of something more, most eligibly the death of her mother, but elaborates on associations Marye feels, with the fallow deer slung across her father's saddle, and with the "billowed lace" of her mother's bridal gown. Wrapping herself in her mother's gown, Marye first takes in her father's arrogance at her approach—"So, lily lip, thee'lt scratch! Thy silky paw hath claws eh?"—then sees him recoil from the symbolic shroud and its "scent o' graves." Like her *Sorry Tale* successor, Theia, Marye dances first, then forms her accusation, making clear that the "flags[tones]" under her feet "are but my heart and hers, and do I bruise them well for thee?" (*PWPM,* 138).

Once begun in her historical mode, PW would write until she had exhausted its possibilities. The "first of her long compositions" was *Redwing,* said Casper Yost when he introduced it to readers of *Patience Worth's Magazine* in September 1917. Running consecutively in six issues of the short-lived magazine, this "playlet," as Yost called it, was also the most comic of the early dictations, particularly in its characterization of the giggly, doddering rake, Prince Charlie, waving his kerchief, "[w]et with scent and age-water from his eyes" (*PWM,* Sept. 1917, 4). *Redwing* was presumably completed by the early winter of 1914–1915 since dictations of the longer and more serious *Telka* began in February and would run to 60,000 words (*SS,* 84–88). That the Anglo-antique idiom had become automatic for Curran is evident when it continues into "The Merry Tale," begun as a cakes-and-ale antidote to *The Sorry Tale.*[9] Yost, having decided not to publish *Redwing* among his "psychic mysteries," made a point of remarking in its magazine publication that it was "the only one of Patience Worth's productions that has no discernable spiritual significance."[10]

As principal character, the Troubador, dubbed "Redwing," could owe something to Curran's acknowledged familiarity with Giuseppe Verdi's *Il trovatore*. PW's witch figure, Hoody Mack, though no child stealer, makes a comic-benign analogy to Verdi's vengeful gypsy, Azucena, when she is recalled crooning to rest the infant Troubador; and a tanner's hammering song ("Up, up, up, and down, down, down!") in Act I may be the remainder of an anvil chorus. John Livingston Lowes's interest in the character of the father, King Charles of the Iron Fist, was piqued by PW's representation of his stuttering speech—"and I a fool / For p-p-p putting thee amid a p-p-p pack o' fox" (*PWM*, Feb. 1918, 9)—since, as Lowes observed of Charles I, "the Cavalier King really stuttered." Characteristically evasive when questioned on history, PW first suggested a family "blood taint," then argued a writer's freedom to "pettiskirt" her character as she chose (PWR 1:100). Lowes also noted that the play borrows its motley of historical English from a longer span than a medieval romance setting should allow. At one point the text refers to the spinning jenny, invented in 1764.

As heroine, Princess Ermaline will marry her age-appropriate lover, the Troubador, but first finds herself engaged by her mother the queen to Charlie, the tee-heeing "Prince of Dodders," which draws a vow from her to "pass as mute until his going." The sharp-tongued Hoody Mack describes Prince Charlie's voice as "a kettle aboil, and he doth spatter more" as "slime bubbles gather them like clustered grapes / At his mouth corners" (*PWM*, Sept. 1917, 4). The prince is smitten only with himself: "My calf, set off with garter jewel, / Doth set the ladies at unrest" (*PWM*, Oct. 1917, 11).

The Troubador's triumph owes something to his wit but more to his art. No "armoured [*sic*] knight," he calls himself a "Knight o' Song," "for song hath ever been my armor" (*PWM*, Oct. 1917, 13). When he once followed the redwing's song into Spring's "ice-loosed" fields, recalls the Troubador, his sight of Ermaline elicited his song and a pledge to join her kingdoms, for which task he robed himself as "Redwing" (a kind of English thrush, notes Yost). The story, told at last to the queen and Ermaline, is punctuated by the bird's "a-cheer," a motif that had identified Pearl Pollard, musical child, to herself when she discovered a youthful "power of taming birds, which came to her when she whistled."[11] Compared to the more ambitious fictions that followed, no place was found in *Redwing* for the artist as woman, carnal or discarnate. At most, PW's Troubador makes a beginning when he locates the space in which voice and knowing will issue from their opposite. "I but pipe," he tells the queen:

> I but pipe; but pipers know the stars,
> And he who knoweth them knoweth solitude,
> And he who knoweth solitude knoweth silence. (*PWM*, Oct. 1917, 12)

III. The Longer Fictions

Telka: "Atwist o' Tung"

Not published when it was completed in 1915, and studded with linguistic curiosities, *Telka: An Idyll of Medieval England* drew little of the interest earned by the two Holt-published novels, *The Sorry Tale* and *Hope Trueblood,* that brought national attention to PW and her medium in the three years that followed their publication. For its language, *Telka*'s most interested reader was probably Casper Yost, whose essay "The Evidence in *Telka*" appeared in Walter Prince's 1927 study, *The Case of Patience Worth,* and in the following year served as an appendix to *Telka* when devoted supporter Herman Behr subsidized its publication by the suddenly invented Patience Worth Publishing Co.[12] Yost's confident assertion that 90 percent of the work's locutions derive from the Anglo-Saxon while also exhibiting a southern England variation in dialect (*CPW,* 358–59) does less to place the text historically—a pointless task for the philological puzzle—than to shore up his assertion that the work is "a literary miracle."

More significantly, Yost fails to read the story in the poetry. Familiar as its plot devices may be, *Telka* is written in code. Superficially, that code is the strained attempt of its language to sound unapproachably remote in time, with the result that the text is neither convincingly medieval nor readily accessible as historical drama. Yet the reader who shrugs off annoyance at the gnarled, compacted speech of *Telka*'s characters can find PW deploying an array of literary languages bespeaking her art, or artfulness, or tricksterhood. Past dialect lies a reverse image of the woman as artist, rudely unqualified for the "new Beauty and Wisdom" promised by Behr in his brief foreword. In *Telka,* the yen for beauties gets displaced scornfully onto the male artist, Franco, while Telka undergoes a process of grudging, angry arrival, first at motherhood, then at an artist's vision, while preserving her pitiless "tung." "Yea," PW says as the curtain comes up on *Telka,* "I have constructed with Cunning! / And the meat of the word and the treasure in the casket—I have hid!" (*T,* vi).

With one concession only, *Telka* might be associated with nineteenth- and early twentieth-century portraits of the artist as a young woman—but as their precise opposite. Telka is the anti-artist, crudely literal and practical, her jibes at her husband, Franco, styling his painterly ways as girlish and ineffectual. Nor is she maternal simply because she becomes a mother, appearing largely indifferent to the needs and attraction of her babe, the "Telka Wee." Franco, playing his part in the exchanged costumes of role reversal, is the one who rises early from bed to comfort their wailing child. Standing the *kunstlerromane* on its head, PW, as she had warned, has set warp against woof and made cunning one of her threads.

The gender consciousness of *Telka* differs in important ways from pronouncements PW made to her admiring circle. Telka is an unfeminine heroine in her earthiness, physical strength, practicality, and disdain for romantic ritual and religion. "Thee art dull as prayer," she says to the heaven-destined Marion (*T,* 14). Most of the more common masculinisms are assigned to Telka, while the passive Franco is feminized as a dauber of paints and a dreamer. Telka's jealousy and hot tears betray her love for Franco, but she expresses no admiration for him, calling him "Polly-coddle" and "a-prattle / O' a pot o'color and dead man's chant" (Franco was raised by monks) and offering scornfully, "I shall fetch thee a ribbon, Franco, / And a fluffed pettiskirt" (*T,* 5). More earnestly, she announces her intent to save Franco by rooting him "in the earth" and argues speciously that he must marry her to redeem her from public jesting about her wrathful jealousy:

TELKA. Then thou shalt buy thy spoil! Aye, I know thee
For a saint a-clothed in piety, but a maggot
Rot aneath. Thou dost wed to me Franco!
FRANCO. But Telka, I be not a-wish to wed!
TELKA. Aye, but I be! And thou, like to the
Black sheep, jumpeth at my start! Aye and more! (*T,* 15)

Symbolically burying her prospective husband's paints under a dungheap, she suggests that

. . . they then shall spring a grain
More worth to thee. I be no weaver o'rainbows,
But I stew full well. . . .
Do ye then but put a word amiss Franco,
And I do swear to lay ye cold! (*T,* 16)

The text assigns itself a challenge: to represent a woman's awakening to more of herself through archaisms cut off from any enlivening contemporary reference to the increasing economic visibility of women who wrote as journalists, novelists, and dramatists. At risk is the possibility that the narrative of Telka's becoming would reconcile her to medieval domesticity by attenuating the blunt, angry assumption of power that made her interesting in the first place.

Tongue, or "tung," is the leading edge of Telka's characterization. She is the "tinderwench," seconds away from enflamed speech in nearly every early scene. Franco, though no match for her, is roused to anger himself: "Telka, Telka! Drat thy barbed tung! / Cast thou the bolt!" (*T,* 29). In the language of Telka, *tongue* is another name for temperature. Well past clichés of the untamed shrew, an embodied burning drives the heroine and commands the attention of others even as she threatens to explode. Franco identifies the eros in Telka's behavior when he tells her father, Baba, "I do love the lass like I do love / A loaf. She be a-hot, and loaf a-hot be puffed!" (*T,* 18). Marion tells him what he already knows: the gentler Telka he dreams of, "Less the wrath and round, be winter's dreary!" (*T,* 31).

Telka's path toward a wedding of heaven and earth will make its way more through her language than her marriage. Introduced in the first scene as an earthy organism who tracks fellow creatures unpoetically, she "drats" the gnawing of beetles when Franco sees them as "wonders" (*T,* 3). In a kind of Anglo-Saxon *flyting* between two poets, Franco, speaking first, muses on nature's wonders in dainty imagery akin to "the fairy / Who painteth rainbow." The answers, he says, could take their cares away, but against Franco's delicate music, Telka delivers a version of braying nature and its daft designs:

I do wish to find the sprite who put the
Curl within the wee-squeals' tails! Aye, and yet
The one who tuned the asses' song
And strung the earth with fools, and pinned
A pettiskirt 'pon he who piddles in the daub. (*T,* 48)

Telka will not be instructed, much less redeemed, by her fragile husband. Franco reddens when she kisses him and retreats to the friar and his monastery when she taunts him for his painting.

If PW is Curran's veil, Telka is PW's, with puns on the entity's surname betraying a writerly presence behind the character who scorns art. Telka notes that "a maid o' worth" can out-trick the devil (*T,* 2). Ione foresees "a harvest of worth" when the missing-mother note in Telka's song is supplied (*T,* 97). In a remark that might stand as epigraph for much of the PW idiom, Baba tells Franco that he is blind to the secret of Telka's blossoming in Ione's company: "'Twill be a task o' worth for thee to ravel out / The knot that she hath tied" (*T,* 118). In the case of Pearl Curran, an adoptive Patience Wee was sought in the year after a fictional Telka Wee was conceived. Telka delivers her child nine years after her marriage, the span from the Currans' marriage to their adoption of Patience Wee.[13]

As if Curran were retracing the path to her enabling doubleness, Telka travels from a single-minded misreading of the world she knows materially better than others in the company of blind Ione, her opposite. As fostering mother, identified by the touch of the child's outstretched arms, Ione wonders at their bond,

Is't not a joy to see not?
For though her eyes be bright and she doth see
She like to me be blind—I at eye and she by youth! (*T,* 91)

From seeing to telling would be a single step for Telka when Ione wants to teach her to "spell" but must conclude, "Ye see aright but be atwist o' tung" (*T,* 95). When the Wicked Lord dies, faithful retainers are compelled to represent as still in its glory the crumbling, windswept castle in which his blind daughter lives. Others spell him to her empty eyes, just as she matches the Telka she hears with the character spelled to her by others. Her attempt to match images lingering in memory to words that evoke those scenes is much like the creative process Curran described in which pictures arose in her mind before the PW voice gave words to them. Ione says,

'Tis such a joy to search amid the every scene
A-hid athin my heart, and conger days
To fit the spelling o'one who words the scene! (*T,* 95)

Seeing herself through Ione's "congering" undoes Telka's armor of anger and sends her home, eyes reddened, while a warm wind "mother[s] her"; once home, she lifts her sleeping child into her crib. Unsighted Ione has made Telka aware of her own and others' seeing as both creative possibility and limit since she also becomes aware of her eyes as entrapping: "'Tis the wish o' me to see, but spite o' it / The eyes o' *me* look but from the eyes o' *me*!" (*T,* 100). As critic of Franco's painting, his "smear," she sees him also entrapped, "o'ersure o' thine eyes" and unaware that others' eyes "do see afar a-more than but their sight" (*T,* 102).

The growth in Telka's self-recognition crystallizes in a new relation to the patriarchal castle. Enacting the fictionality of the medieval setting in which PW has brought her to life, Telka takes charge, instructing the other characters to sustain for now the Lady Ione's illusion that her father is alive, only "ridden off unto the havoc-fields." With Telka's domestic generalship established, she becomes director of an illusion—the castle's ancient glory. Now a PW in deed, Telka imagines a cast of fictional characters with Ricardo, an aging knight, called on to play all the parts to his audience of one, Ione. The second-sighted Lady's idealized seeing can only be worded by the voice of a country wench, the Patience-Pearl dialogic creative life reflected in their interdependence.

The conventional artist fulfilled in parenthood will be Franco, who keeps his promise of a "wonder work" by holding their child up to Telka, while Telka returns him his paint pots, announcing that these "ghosts did rise." Franco judges the pots empty as against the full "coffers" of his vivid wench and her babe. The "tracker o' the sky" and she "a-rove 'pon fields" have come together at last: "The sky doth ever lead / A-back to earth . . . " (*T,* 242). The conflict between didactic spirituality and ambitious art, healing patience and fruitless anger, is not so much resolved in *Telka* as displaced to two subsequent novels in which a heroine's art and anger would be given a larger stage. Less than two weeks after she finished her first long fiction, PW began to dictate "a story of the time of Christ" and, before its conclusion, the terms of her long-awaited motherhood.

The Sorry Tale and Salome's Sister

PW audiences had already been convinced that extraordinary productions were the usual thing for the Curran Ouija board, but the biblical story begun on July 14, 1915, and concluded on February 17, 1917 (*SS*, 92, 147), made further demands on their fund of superlatives. Whether the new work was regarded as spiritual revelation (Yost) or literary tour de force (Reedy), *The Sorry Tale*[14] raised the stakes on questions that had already divided observers. Even those who identified the PW text with a secondary personality of Pearl Curran granted the moral attractions of a narrative that demonstrated the self-destructive effects of hate and the final triumph of love in this story of Hatte, or often and more baldly, "Hate," the bad thief destined from birth to hang from a cross by Jesus's side on Calvary. For PW's most dedicated allegiants, the novel's authenticity of religious feeling was evidence of the immediate witness they saw in descriptions of the look and feel of the Holy Land at the time of Christ. When Casper Yost, as the novel's editor, contributed an appendix of historical annotations, his unstated intention was to argue the accuracy of PW's history and to reconcile the known travels of the historical figure Tiberius Caesar with a plot that makes a Greek slave and court dancer the mother of his bastard son. The perceived distance between what Curran could have known about the Middle East at the beginning of the Christian era and what PW seemed to know, locating herself in a timeless "here," gave the novel the authority of a latter-day revelation for many readers.

National reviewers found both extraordinary merits and off-putting defects in the 637-page novel. Already made suspicious by Emily Hutchings's portrait of the medium's self-centered ambition, James Hyslop told readers of his American Society for Psychical Research *Journal*, "I could find no interest whatever in it" (*SS*, 154). In *The Nation*, readers were advised to consider the book "not merely as a psychic phenomenon but as a piece of creative fiction," and William Reedy described *The Sorry Tale* to his *Mirror* readers as "the most remarkable piece of literature I have ever read," arguing that it deserved the "highest consideration" of critics, whatever "the psychological mystery" of its origins.[15] Critic H. W. Boynton of the *Bookman* had seen enough to catalog remorselessly PW's literary sins and Yost's apologies for them. Boynton thought PW's obliquity-as-antiquity language bad enough—"a strange farrago of strained and clipped and grammarless utterance"—but he found the writer's manner even more irritating—"a kind of self-consciousness, a deliberate smartness, as of a spook posing." But joining a company of fellow reviewers, he then found "the Oriental detail of the narrative . . . amazingly lavish and vivid" and the five-thousand-word chapter on the Crucifixion "a composition of appalling force and vividness, and an interpretation upon a high and sincere plane" (*SS*, 161–62). Or sincerely deluded, implied Dr. Wilfred Lay, a psychoanalyst. Granting poeticism in the PW language, Lay invoked both the unconscious and the phenomenon of "split-off personalities" in recommending to Curran the "most modern of scientific instruments of precision, psychoanalysis," when he discovered evidence of masochism and the mother imago in the character of Hatte (*SS*, 163).

The Sorry Tale fully earned its mix of reviews. Indictment of self-conscious "and-it-came-to-pass" scripturalisms accompanied praise for the power of the novel's concluding scenes on Calvary and its evocation of the costumes, food, trades, and multiple cultures of a Roman-occupied Holy Land. Characters enlisted from the ancient world—Greeks, Romans, Jews, Indians, and Egyptians—receive individualized attention in their names, in the gods they worship, and in their vividly drawn fixations and animosities. Economies of narrative summary are rare, most often put in the mouths of characters who explain what we could not know otherwise. In mid novel especially, lengthy, labored dialogue alternates with repetitive monologues to tax any reader's patience. The novel gains momentum as it moves toward Calvary as "the end of paths" (*ST,* 631), but scripture's plot often gives way to the narrator's discursiveness or repetitions of obsessively intense mother-son moments from Theia and Hatte.

Useful as it might have been to discover that Curran had consulted Greek mythology or a book on the Holy Land under Roman governance, it should also have been clear that the medium dictated from her own culture's reverent taste for historical novels that culminated in the Passion of Calvary. A genealogy of late nineteenth-century Christian-scriptural romances like *Ben-Hur* (1880), *Barabbas* (1893), and *Quo Vadis* (1896) was well established when *The Sorry Tale* was published in 1917. One reviewer of Curran's addition to the genre made an explicit comparison with *Barabbas,* doubly appropriate given the mystical, Theosophical orientation of Marie Corelli, that novel's author, at whose death *Barabbas* was in its fifty-fourth edition.[16] A broad similarity among the biblical novels, including *The Sorry Tale,* is their strategy of focusing on characters like Barabbas, discovered at the periphery of the Gospel narratives, then drawn into the novel's center. To that scheme—PW's bad thief perhaps a less likely choice than the good one—*The Sorry Tale*'s voice attempts to gain authority by taking on a Gospel writer's idiom as its own.

Several closer resemblances to popular fictions like *Barabbas* are worth noting. Well before PW demonstrated her fondness for "prating" and "bibbing," Corelli had exercised the same habit, as in "Cease thy prating," "a prating infant," and "Rufus hath been wine-bibbing." A Magdalene type appears in *The Sorry Tale* as a reformed Greek woman, Mary, but was preceded by Corelli's prototypical Magdalene, whose "yellow-haired vileness" is scarcely hidden behind her "golden veil,"[17] while PW's unrepentant Indra has her *Barabbas* equivalent in Judith Iscariot, a pun PW was able to resist. Henryk Sienkiewicz's *Quo Vadis* modeled, directly or indirectly, numerous repetitions of "Whither goest thou" in the dialogue of *The Sorry Tale.* PW's explicit directions for the spelling "Jesus Christus" inclined toward the Latin represented in the Christian voices Sienkiewicz has rising from a Roman amphitheater to proclaim "Christus regnat."[18] Sienkiewicz's Ligia and PW's Legia are both Roman, but Ligia more nearly approaches heroine status when she is finally united with her lover, Vinicius, whereas in *The Sorry Tale* Legia is a youthful concubine waited on by the aging Theia and is notable in the Record when Pearl has difficulty retrieving the spelling of the name (PWR 4:748). There is some resemblance too between the idealized dead beauty of Edgar Allan Poe's Ligeia—her "skin rivaling the purest ivory," "the raven-black, the glossy, the luxuriant and naturally curling tresses," and her "jetty lashes of great length"—and PW's Legia: "Dark her locks and glistened o'er of gold dusts and her white flesh gleamed and her eyelids lay their lashes long upon it" (*ST,* 495).

Three years before Pearl Lenore Pollard was born, Lew Wallace established the genre of American biblical romance when he published *Ben-Hur* in 1880. Wallace's hero too has an encounter with an Egyptian Magdalene named Iras, who for irony's sake is the daughter of Balthasar, one of Bethlehem's three kings. "Call me Egypt," she says, greeting Ben-Hur, then later deserts her father for the Roman Messala, Ben-Hur's antagonist, whom she eventually kills, having discovered that "to be a Roman is to be a brute."[19] Less plainly put, the same formulaic charge is hurled at Tiberius by PW's Theia, who will succeed in executing a minor Roman brute.

Rome's carnality is too well established a trope to be identified with any single text, but one feature of Balthasar's odyssey in *Ben-Hur* has significance for *The Sorry Tale.* The white camel he rides on his way to Bethlehem is one of three, the other two ridden by Gaspar (Wallace's spelling) and Melchior, each unaware before their meeting that his camel is "of the whiteness of the others." Though it has no scriptural basis and more likely derives from Islamic tradition, the white camel as a portent of the coming of Christ appears early in *The Sorry Tale* in a prophecy made by Theia and taken up by Hatte that promises his deliverance will coincide with the revelation of his father's identity and the appearance of a white camel.[20] As Curran began *The Sorry Tale* in 1915, she was very likely aware that Wallace's novel had been adapted for the stage and was appearing throughout the United States, with six stops in St. Louis between 1901 and 1918, including an extended run at the 1904 World's Fair.[21]

Silent film versions of the life of Christ had also appeared prior to dictations of *The Sorry Tale.* A 1913 Italian version of *Quo Vadis* included a character named Lygia, in love with a Roman soldier.[22] Curran would likely have gained most from the first film done on location in the Holy Land. *From the Manger to the Cross* was released in October of 1912, a month after the death of George Pollard and several months after experiments with the Ouija board had begun, then was rereleased in 1917. On-site filming of the Sphinx's desert setting, scenes from Bethlehem and Jerusalem, the use of local populations in crowd and market scenes, including sheep and camels, and the general sense of a population little changed in costume or customs over nineteen hundred years would have constituted memorable visual information for a member of the picture-show audience.[23]

With Theia's assaultive/beguiling dance at the center of PW's *Tale,* the story's costuming required richer resources than an alleged Puritan could provide, even for readers who imagined her free of time's constraints. Contemporary films, dramas, and other theatrical productions had increasingly featured exotic versions of Middle Eastern dance and music. Its circumambient imagery, at once alien and hallowed, was sponsored by the greatest story ever told and made compelling as an originary site for temptresses both sordidly fallen and happily redeemed. Whether in high- or low-culture versions, Orientalism offered a distinctly transgressive flavor to turn-of-the-century American tastes. In St. Louis, a thriving theater scene provided venues for touring companies offering such exotica as *An Arabian Night,* performed at The Olympic in 1912, starring Otis Skinner as Hajj the Beggar, and, simultaneously, *The Cherry Blossoms,* which "introduc[ed] the Egyptian Enchantress 'Cleopatra'" to audiences at The Standard.[24] The central figure in any array of veiled women was of course Salome, whom Oscar Wilde gave consummate representation in his 1893 play. By 1909, observes Toni Bentley in her study of "the Salome craze," "there was not a variety or vaudeville show that did not offer a Salome act as part of its entertainment," and "three one-reelers of her dance were filmed within months of each other in America."[25]

As a cultural sister of Salome, PW's dancer, Theia, is in turn a sister of contemporary dancer Loie Fuller and a Greek cousin of Isadora Duncan. Described as "the Electric Salome" by Rhonda Garelick, Fuller made her reputation in the Paris of the 1890s and beyond through "a careful choreography of veils, lights, stagecraft, and machines," her magic a "manipulation of fabric and costumes."[26] With the discovery that her dancing was not being singled out for appreciation, Fuller made her costume as much an instrument of performance as her body. A reviewer for the *New York Spirit of the Times* described her 1892 appearance much as *The Sorry Tale* would present Theia, as entering into "a white light which makes her radiant and a white robe which surrounds her like a cloud."[27] When Theia declares her intention to revenge herself on the Roman "mighty seat," she provides herself with a comparably diaphanous costume that will be identified with her throughout the novel: "And she brought forth the robe of mists, the white wool, thin, that hung soft and like clouds, the curling wool scarce held together" (*ST,* 30).

Theia's creator need not have heard of Loie Fuller or the aesthetically Grecian dancer Isadora Duncan, though it would be surprising if their fame never reached her. As a schoolgirl casualty of "too much Delsarte," Pearl Pollard had been exposed to instruction that codified the zones of the body according to their spiritual significance, emphasized health and strenuousness, and "actually recommended a 'Greek' costume" for its students."[28] Duncan's mother had come from a wealthy St. Louis family and, raising a family in San Francisco, had taught dress reform, Delsarte, and "defiant feminism" to her daughter. Duncan's visionary reach extended from Greece, which she visited as the birthplace of the body's natural forms, to a prophetic imagining of her successor: "Oh, she is coming, the dancer of the future, the free spirit who will inhabit the body of [the] new woman; more glorious than any woman that has yet been."[29] Like-sounding prophecies would be characteristic of PW's visionary Theia, Greek in origin, who wanders from Rome into the Holy Land, where the PW text charges her with the enchanting and verbal scourging of empowered male costumes.

Though populous, the longest PW fiction centers itself on Theia, who is unconfined by any of the book's three divisions (titled "Panda," "Hatte," and "Jesus"). In Greek mythology, Theia the female Titan is a minor goddess, but her name alone suggests female divinity, and as mother of Helios, Eos, and Selene she is progenitor of light, a theme PW regularly insists on. Theia rewrites Salome as part of PW's overwriting of the Gospels. While Herod and John the Baptist make obligatory appearances, Theia's real object is to confront and accuse her former lover, Tiberius. His casually arrogant rejection of her when she became pregnant inspires her vengeful anger, complicated by what remains of her early love for him. The text attempts no portrait of Tiberius, but Yost provides explanations that reconcile references to him with his withdrawal to the Isle of Rhodes before he became emperor as an escape from gossip surrounding his adulterous wife, Julia (*ST,* 642n8).

Hatte, in turn, is the embodiment of what his mother feels: "And Theia suckled the babe at the breast of hate, that it wax stronger of hate" (*ST,* 30). In maturity, Hatte searches for the source of his mother's victimization while demanding his own recognition and ascent to the status of his royal father. The parallel births in Bethlehem of Hatte and Jesus assure the reader that hate will die before love does, but the trajectory from Theia's first wild condemnations as she is about to give birth to an apparent rejection of hate after she meets Mary, Joseph, and their son approaching the temple is accomplished prematurely. Theia expounds a theodicy that describes her own son as darkness and Mary's as light, earth requiring both: "Theia hath born a need if she but bore the dark" (*ST,* 44). As she tells the fatherly Panda, "[T]he gods are but the streaming tongues of priests," and, as a woman formerly accustomed to dancing "her path unto the King's own door," she is revolted by the hut in which a fishy midwife is about to deliver her son: "She hath a face like Dagon, I swear! Panda, I fear lest her sides should show a scale!" (*ST,* 3–5).

As PW spells it, motherhood will be indivisible from Theia's sexuality, aggression, and aesthetic, her dance expressing elements of all these, the medium participating, said an onlooker, by pointing a finger at the Tiberius she was dictating. Temporarily, dance transforms the dancer by creating the prospect of reunion with her son: Theia proclaims herself cleansed of hate, "and the light broke out anew and she sung as a child" (*ST,* 72–73). In its multiple significations, dance becomes both weapon and speech, revenge and celebration, and continues to call upon the resources of an aging Theia's identity even as she finds herself a forgotten competitor for Roman favor among second-rate Salomes. "Dancing," she later tells a young Roman concubine, "maketh the sky seem nearer; maketh the moon many, and the stars many, many, many more" (*ST,* 498). Left to his own wanderings under the care of Panda, whose "saffron skin" types him "a desert's child" (*ST,* 8), Hatte was to be an incarnation of Theia's art: "Thou art the flesh of Theia's dance, for she hath loved and lived but dance" (*ST,* 10).

As if in synchrony with the wise men's setting out, Theia's vengeful journey begins hours after giving birth when she visits Herod on her own business, an assertion of pride and a challenge to his current favorite, Claudia: "And I, Theia, shall rise and unwind the robes of me and cast unto the winds and clothe but with the rose" (*ST,* 9). Dancing to the music of her own laughter before the drunken and diseased Herod, she loosens her hair, which "flew like golden mists behind, or like to wings of gold," then quickly strikes the drooling king on the cheek. Her turn from seduction to aggression is all dark heroine, but PW chooses from a palette that included Corelli's Magdalene as "a yellow-haired wanton" to fashion her golden "white-skin" Salome. Theia escapes from her assault on a "wrathed" Herod by declaring laughingly that she has drunk too much to become his slave, then bounds away as he falls into a locust-wine stupor.

On course to a climactic confrontation with Tiberius, Theia instigates a brawl between Jews and Roman soldiers at a Jerusalem market. She pelts them with fruit, springs at them, and leaps at the throat of her chief tormenter to "claw with nails within his flesh." As the Jews protest that no woman should be harmed and begin their own fight with the soldiers, Theia is recognized by a Roman sensualist, Alexis, who misses the dangerous marks of a trance-murderess-dancer when he proposes to keep her past secret for a sexual price. Instead, Theia calls prophetically on a revelation yet to come from the East, stabs her assailant, bloodies herself, and "swayed and spake as in a dream 'Hate! Hate! I love thee'" (*ST,* 133–34). Arrested, she laughs and spits at her captors, kicks the dead body, and shakes free her golden hair to dance away into captivity, where she is made to confront the corpse and the "stained metal" she has killed with. Theia takes the occasion, hissing, to drive the blade into Alexis once again (*ST,* 151). For a discarnate entity, PW proves a ruthless and indefatigable writer, blading, as she words it, both the tongues and the hands of her heroines.

Theia's trial becomes an opportunity for an even more intense performance. Against her captors, the rage of a "she-wolf" baring her teeth has the overwrought quality of silent film, and Rome's opulent decadence, too, has a look of early Hollywood. The procurator's seat is hewn of black wood spiked with gold, "and there ranked at the sides seven black men, eunuchs, bared, who swayed of tufted grass that scented of the airs." When the faithful Panda and his friend, Joel, attempt to save her by claiming guilt for themselves, Theia earns guilt beyond their capacities while disguising her relation to them: an imprisoned Panda would rob Hatte of his guardian. The bizarre intertwining of mother love, radical rage, and theatricality is on final display when the procurator proposes that the three who claim guilt each be given a chalice of wine, one of which will be poisoned. Fatalistic about her wine, Theia will not be outperformed in claiming guilt and counters the trial of cups with another dance. As her audience watches "cold and frightened," she puts on the late Alexis's bloody mantle, paws the floor "as doth the charger upon the battled field," and slashes her wrists for blood to cover her face and spill on the stones. Joel, more expendable than Panda, succumbs to the poisoned wine, and Theia's voice becomes shrill music cutting the air like yet another "bared blade" as she extols the sacrifice of an innocent to the as-yet-unrealized divinity she addresses as "Thou of the East" (*ST,* 153–54).

With Theia consigned to the pit, the plot belongs to Hatte, whose development from boy to man moves him closer to the secret of his paternity, then into a self-destructive search for acknowledgment by Tiberius. While Hatte and his mother invest their identity in a nobility that will be denied them, the didactic PW accumulates their spiritual compensation. Theia will voyage to Rome, but as superannuated dancer will find herself "handmaid to harlots," attending younger concubines. Hatte will grow into his role as bad thief, slaughtering and stealing, roaming the countryside as a kind of junior Lear who rages at storms and descends into madness, accompanied only by his fool and boyhood companion, the habitually empty-netted Aaron.

As "madwoman" and "madman" in their turns, Theia and Hatte advance toward Calvary interdependently. Hatte, become roving criminal, has slashed sheep and cattle by night, assaulted a beggar, and been identified as killer of the merchant Jacob. His withered leg, matted hair, and a hand crushed in a snare

are the physical marks of the outcast, and his progressive madness carries him from a megalomania of royal descent, to embittered weeping, to complete dissociation. More surprising than the reclamation of either character is the development of the mother's and son's yearning for each other as a version of saving grace, its oedipal intensity driving their language of soul-hunger. Theia's status as female castaway enables her to move from one version of banishment to another. When her fluency in the language of the markets leads her captors to ask if she is a Jew, she replies, "A Jew? Yea and a woman! But dross for Rome!" Taking on the voice of those under the "heel of Rome," she adds a third population, aware now that "Rome despiseth the black-skins she slaves."

The great God's "wonderwork" will be to reverse history's pattern of victory and defeat, with Theia as apparently defeated Greece. Greece is female, Rome is male. Rome's light will fall into shadow, what Rome has made shadowy will come to light. Theia can affirm "I am a Greek," confident in her prophecy of rising again. "Greece waiteth, sire, waiteth; for even out of dusts of ages shall her dead beauties arise." Theia and her dance celebrate a resurrection of art's beauty over power and her defiant speech capitalizes on Tiberius's earlier reference to her as "dead woman": "Fetch forth thy musics and bid 'the dead woman' dance!" she says. "'Tis but play; for she danceth upon thy heart and knoweth it" (*ST,* 505). Tiberius now joins the series of Romans who found her treasonous, "for they had heard not such a tongue as this of Theia" (*ST,* 150).

By the time Theia is delivered from the pit to become senior advisor to women in a Roman harem, she has relocated her faith from Greece and Rome to Jehovah, the God of the Jews, as a more powerful ally in her cause. Among the fallen women is the repentant concubine Mary, who has loved Hatte since they were children; Indra, an orphan who grew up with Mary and Hatte; and young Legia. Weathered and unillusioned, Indra is closest to Theia in the spectrum of Magdalenes, expressing bitter realisms about men, survival, and her own attractions that require the narrator to dismiss her as "follied-drunk." Indra makes finer distinctions. Her revulsion at Mary's attempt to reclaim spiritual chastity spills out: "Snowy white! . . . Ugh! Thou lookest as a man who hath vomited the night through. Pale! Pale! Ugh!" Exasperated by Mary's mourning for her lost soul, she asserts an impeccable identity: "Is not a woman's flesh pure e'en though she doth leave filth to touch it, if she batheth her? For what may cling unto Indra's spirit that she hath done unto her flesh?" (*ST,* 475–78). Inspected for leprosy, Mary must display her nakedness before her arranged marriage with Arminius, who "shall teach thee new tricks of loving" (*ST,* 460), Indra assures her. The scene is managed as if PW were announcing its filmic potential, the actors bathed in the lighting of a morality play. Slaves strip away her mantle as Mary covers her breasts, Indra laughs, and Arminius stands "as one . . . carved out of stone."

Approaching her final dance, Theia is already an aging Isadora or Loie when she recovers her sandals, armlets, golden latchets, and a peacock feather from Indra's treasured relics of her mother and relives the scene of Caesar's bidding her to dance in a hall lined with "peafowl's flaunts. Yea, and Theia was the bird—the sign of vanity!" (*ST,* 301). In three pages of glorious vanities, Theia recalls the triumph of her initial encounter with Tiberius. A cornucopia of imagery is her response to Panda's call, "Enough!" and she tells him smilingly, "Nay, Rome would on with the play!" And indeed Romans sip wine from her hand and greet her when she enters carried on a golden salver: "And this was Theia! This was Theia! This!" For the moment, Tiberius admires Theia with "honeyed words" as the hall shouts her name and she amasses spiced wine to be drunk from a golden bowl with lotus-lily cups, inducing the "dream-god " among banqueters who will sleep "like flies swarmed and stilled o'er filth" (*ST,* 301–3).

For her climactic scene, Theia counsels Legia on the brevity of a courtesan's career. "Ah Venus, lend thou thy spell" is her failed prayer, an admission that her robe of mists has been exchanged for another, woven out of her own silvering hair. The vain hope of rewinning Tiberius gives way to an autopsy on his character. He must be aware, she tells Legia, that those around him would hang him "even with their glances." What she sees of his future will make personal revenge unnecessary: it is written, she says, that Tiberius will die with his eyes open. His tongue "shall lap at the airs as a dog lappeth waters," a prediction Yost matches with Suetonius's story "that Tiberius was strangled by Caligula, his successor" (*ST,* 499n). In her final dialogue with Tiberius, Theia taunts him, aware that he seeks his son only to rid himself of an affront to his dignity. Not only is his flesh visible in his son, Theia charges, Hatte is his fled soul, leaving the father "an empty carcass." The son "is a Caesar," the father merely Tiberius (*ST,* 505).

For a biblical novel, the Ouija pointer must shuttle between melodrama and moderate orthodoxy, seeking tenable common ground that favors undogmatic monotheists—Hindus, Arabs, or Jews—the latter sometimes represented as seers of a revelation that will become a kind of eschatological spiritualism triumphing over materialism and power. PW differentiates monotheistic Arabs and Jews by broadly recognizable markers, sometimes using anachronistic details—like her use of the crescent for a time period before Mohammed's birth—which elicit puzzled explanations from Yost (*ST,* 643). Nada's father, Nadab, prays to Allah for mercy and weaves his faith and prophecies into the designs of his rugs (*ST,* 114). Theia is able to join Panda and her coconspirator against Rome, Ahmud Hassan, in praising Allah as a God who comes out of the east (*ST,* 282), and Panda and Nada imagine their dead son as a swallow flown into a pre-Mohammedan paradise (*ST,* 325).

PW's Jews do not divide neatly into proto-Christians or deniers of the Messiah, but the cultural force of that dichotomy, available to Curran from any of the pulpits she sat under, is apparent even as she modifies it. Theia's earliest prophetic speech, spoken to Simeon, explains that a building up of "atoms of hate" will kill the infant that Mary is bringing to the temple, and more hate will later "build up a stone that shall crush these Jews through ages" (*ST,* 44). Theia must then contend with the irony that she has raised her son to enact her prophecy when he says, "Panda, I Hatte, do hate these Jews!" (*ST,* 123), and she must be silenced by Panda, who evokes the suffering of the Jews under Roman rule while also condemning their priest-collaborators. Up close, PW gives her readers good Jews—Levi—and bad Jews—Jacob—and a mixture of sentiment and, in the marketplace, predictable caricature.

In an apparent digression into the Hebrew scriptures, PW returns late in the novel to the Jerusalem marketplace and a scene between a young Isaac and an aged, suspicious Abraham. The two are not father and son, but their scriptural originals frame Abraham's skeptical testing of the language of divine instruction when Isaac expresses innocent wonder at Jesus's words and devoted following. Abraham responds by raising the question of signification itself and the problematic situation of the medium as artist. Words only shadow the infinite, Abraham says, and serve as signs of faith's referent, which cannot be fully written into existence. Theia adds paradox: "and he who knoweth silence well knoweth the great God's shadow" (*ST,* 501), reaching well beyond the linkage of solitude and silence in *Redwing.* "Writ words make no sound," pronounces Abraham, "yet loud noises. Out of the shadows which are scripts man plucketh him a thing that is his" (*ST,* 490), as if PW, to Pearl, were that thing.

Spelling Calvary in a single session of five thousand words (PWR 5:820), the Ouija board had little time for the good thief, who speaks his sympathetic part and is invited by Jesus to "enter the new land" with him. Hatte earns the blessing of a smile from Jesus at the culmination of agonies whose duration and intensity are represented graphically. As the crowd beats on Jesus's pierced feet, "the flesh quivered like unto a host of maggots beneath the flesh." On his cross, Hatte falls forward, "the hands torn loose and the knees broken," then is lowered, adjusted, and raised into place again (*ST,* 634). Given the novel's charge to adumbrate Christian revelation, the narrative advances Hatte's instinct to identify Jesus (whom he calls the Seeker) as brother, since both have absent fathers, a bond renewed by their mutual experience of desertion on Calvary. Before PW grants Jesus his scriptural cry, "My God! My God! Hast thou forsaken me?" Hatte asks unscripturally, "Is the God sleeping?" and with a glance at Jesus addresses the silent heavens: "Thou too, even as Tiberius, hath betrayed thy son" (*ST,* 632).

Out of his own Calvary, Hatte qualifies as oedipal patricide in his dream of an as-yet-unnamed father whose lips open to reveal a serpent whose scepter ball "shrinketh unto a rotted fig," and whom he would confront with a golden scourge for "the slaying" (*ST,* 238–39). At his hate-filled worst, he spits at, but misses, Jesus. The passage illustrates the self-defeating habit of an automatism that adheres to its enabling dialect no matter the cost. Miracle goes comic when it refuses revision: "And behold, Jesus stepped Him back that the spat fall not upon Him, and lo, where it fell He bended Him down and plucked up a white bloom" (*ST,* 526).

What Hatte cannot have is his mother, and he is unaware that Theia cannot free herself from her residual love for Tiberius: "Down deep beneath Theia's scorn the love lay laughing" (*ST,* 544). His ardent friend, Mary, recognizes Hatte's fixation and speaks to him as Theia; that is, a former sex slave and his would-be lover takes on a voice she expects Hatte will recognize as that of his mother, a convergence that did not surprise the psychoanalytic reviewer. "I would fill thee up of me, of me, of me! Yea and I would fill up of thee, of thee, of thee! . . . Theia loveth thee. Theia's arms have ached as thou hast craved her bosom" (*ST,* 625). When Jesus, calling on Hatte as "Brother," urges him to "[g]ive forth love. This is the mending," Hatte cries out his mother's name—six times. In this newer testament, Jesus, surprisingly encouraged by each "Theia!" describes the mother's name, not his own or Jehovah's, as a protective "regal garment." Strengthened face and form return Hatte to the look of Caanthus, his claim in youth to a Roman name (noted as Greek by Yost), the grace of that regression now rendering him "peace-filled" on the day of his execution (*ST,* 53n, 626–27).

At her most fictional, PW most insists on her authority, punctuating the novel's final pages with sentences that begin "And it was true that . . . " As the crowd cries "Crucify them" to reject the pair who claim themselves Son of God and Son of Tiberius, the text invokes tempest and earthquake and takes final account of the Rome that distributes skins of wine among "the rabble" and presides "fatted, comfort-full and smiling." With Theia's arrival—she leaps from a camel and loosens her locks for a last dance—Hatte translates her desire for his ennoblement into a vision of a white camel ridden by the Christus, "And before it danceth Theia!" Hatte dies before Jesus does, but Theia's script and dance come last of all. She writes "The Son of Tiberius" in blood on her mantle, dances before the dead until dark, "uttering sounds that [chill] the echoes into phantoms," and dies under Hatte's cross (*ST,* 635–37).

Having repeopled Calvary, PW forgoes the challenge of a Resurrection. The task of closure falls to the conventional living—Panda, Nada, and their new infant, Hate, now only a name, says its mother. The last sentence is given to simple Aaron, "seeking, seeking, dragging his nets, and laughing, laughing." The text makes clear that it will leave any further script to others: "And it was true that the dark came, and the dead things hung silent, leaving silence to be filled by the tongues of the coming ages" (*ST,* 639). Patience would have its reward in an abundance of testaments, including one that implied it was the dancer's story that needed telling.

The Great Expectations of *Hope Trueblood*

The sudden arrival of "mid-Victorian" language, plotting, and historically accessible characters in the next PW novel, *Hope Trueblood,* which one publisher subtitled *A Mid-Victorian Novel by a Pre-Victorian Writer,* astonished Casper Yost and others even as they failed to notice that *The Sorry Tale* had been no less "Victorian" in its preference for translating scripture into Holy Land historical romance. PW's readiness to undertake a second novel suggests that she harbored a deep fund of gestating fictions that awaited only time and a stenographer's endurance to be put into print. While rapidly dictating *The Sorry Tale,* PW had apparently also been conceiving the new work, which she began two weeks later, in March 1917 (*SS,* 148). She followed this period of prodigious output with yet another novel, now lost, "Samuel Wheaton," begun five months after *Hope Trueblood* was finished in October 1917. Introducing the second published novel, Yost described Curran as having looked up "round-eyed and wordless" (*HT,* iv) when *Hope Trueblood,* with its sound of "modern" English, began to flow, while PW, a month into Ouija-board dictation, found the new project "nay task. 'Tis nay a trick for to pluck that that groweth" (PWR 5:898).

The novel's increasingly convoluted plot, as mysteries get explained with further contrivances, argues against its being conceived entire. Until the pen falls from her hand at the end of the novel, Hope as narrator constructs the past that she needs to understand, her election to that duty still characteristic of PW's preference for the first-person voice with its immediacy of feeling and speaking. If *Hope Trueblood* is not an impressive imitation of memorable nineteenth-century novels, its narrative voice has impressive moments representing acts of retrieval from buried memory. Narration apart, Hope also enacts a roaming consciousness that, PW-like, floats timelessly above events. On principle, PW would not allow Curran to speak of her as a reincarnation. But that voice was engaging the medium in implicitly remembered idioms of nineteenth-century fiction for the sake of performing another kind of past self.

At an early point, the young Hope is conscious of doubling herself when she enters sympathetically into the mourning of a shrunken, silver-haired woman who in her turret bedroom rocks the empty cradle of a child, also named Hope, alive only in the woman's fantasy. Swaying in sympathy, young Hope feels herself leave the manor-house bedroom to dance in a green field with the mourned-for Hope she is now urged to embody. "Oh, the joyous dancing we had! And always, always, it seemed, we were to be together, the little lady's Hope and little me. Then the beautiful day ended and in the midst of a joyous dance I found myself in the middle of a [four] poster, dancing" (*HT,* 115). The passage is at once another entranced dance, an act of enlarged self-creation, and a metonym for the whole of the PW text presided over by one visible self and one invisible counterpart. The literal plot of *Hope Trueblood* is merely confusing. The symbolic plot spun out of Pearl Curran for her own discovering—the self will be named only when memory has been searched through to its origins—is the novel's subtext and resists unraveling even past the death of its narrator's voice.

In updated costume, the central character of *Hope Trueblood* is again a wronged woman. Beginning as "a nameless waif" whom PW had already identified in a poem previewing the novel (*HT,* iii–iv), Hope grows to pained awareness of the apparent illegitimacy that makes her "a sign of sin" to the pious members of a small, chapel-dominated village (which nevertheless boasts a Church of England vicar) after her mother, Sally, or "Sarah," has died. A true religion of mother-love is again set against its opposite in a father to be named later, but PW devotes greater energy to satirizing hypocrites and directing her heroine's rage against the piety of village moralists. The death of Sally, who takes the secret of Hope's father with her, begins a lifetime of returns to the words of the mother's fevered farewell.

The hourglass sands Hope Trueblood contemplates in the novel's opening paragraph count the minutes of her unhappy visit to the cottage of Patricia and Reuben Passwater, sister and brother, where she first hears herself named "a brat," the dour Patricia's reaction to the child's forwardness—Hope had asked whether Patricia's facial moles do in fact move, as a village boy told her—and to the brand of her presumed bastardy. Home is a shelter under the eaves of the Gray Eagle Inn, where she lives with her mother and will be carried back by the long-legged Reuben, who absents himself from much of the novel in a fruitless search for the man he knows to be Hope's father and his own rival, years past, for the love of Sally Trueblood. Returning in the darkness to her mother, Hope in bed whispers her discovery:

> "Sarah Trueblood, I am your brat."
>
> She did not answer and I made ready for sleep and lay wondering, seeming to see Miss Patricia's moles and I fell asleep listening. I thought it was blowing without, for a sighing sounded. But I know now she wept. (*HT,* 11)

Within days, Sally Trueblood is dead, having exacted from Hope a promise to play the game of waiting for a "Mayin'" celebration yet to come—a projection, we learn, from a happy earlier time with Hope's unnamed father that arises from Sally's unwarranted optimism that he would someday return to claim his daughter. The realization that her mother has died comes slowly to Hope when she hears in the village of a "deader" to be brought to the graveyard, the novel's summary trope as holder of secrets, and she goes eventually to live with Patricia, who has long mourned the childhood death of her brother Willie Pimm Passwater and who gradually becomes a curt but caring parent to Hope. Hope's immediate grieving is relatively brief, but over the novel's span of time she dwells recurrently on her love for her mother and expresses a mixture of pity, ardor, and need toward a succession of women. These include Sally's sister, Felicia, also wooed and abandoned by a man and believed to have preceded Sally to the graveyard; Sephira Gifford, whose lonely pregnancy mirrors Sally's experience; and Geneva Willoughby, the elegant only daughter of the family whose history Hope learns is intertwined with her own. Felicia is the lady of the turret who recognizes her sister, Sally, in Hope and who had inexplicably gone "mad at the May" (*HT,* 331) before bearing a child, who was subsequently taken from her. In the graveyard lies another Felicia, her and Sally's mother.

Hope's visit to the Willoughby manor as a child is an introduction to the family's baffling genealogy and, in the turret scenes, the reader's first sustained experience of PW's ventriloquizing of Dickens. More striking than any physical resemblance between the silver-haired Felicia and the indefatigably bridal Miss Havisham of *Great Expectations* is the shared pathology of their withdrawal into time stopped at the moment of a past sorrow. For Hope, as for Dickens's Pip, a child's innocent bewilderment is enlightened only by a vague sense of serving to console or amuse a mysterious old woman who will not outlive the doom of her original loss. Felicia throws herself from a turret window, just as Miss Havisham dies despite Pip's attempt to rescue her when her "faded bridal dress" catches fire at her lonely hearth.

As in *Great Expectations,* secrets of parentage are disclosed only at the end of *Hope Trueblood.* PW is more prolific of clues than explanations, but both narrators are, in Pip's language, "hot on tracing out and proving" not only their own origins but the larger web of relationships their stories have revealed. Mysterious initials appear on the items left in Sally's box of treasures—a buckle, a locket, a silver ring. Nameless faces smile from a small ivory and a large oil painting at the Willoughby manor. The largest number of males who might be suspected of paternity are Willoughbys, a surname associated with the confessed "cunning fool" and handsome rake of Jane Austen's *Sense and Sensibility,* though Austen (but not George Eliot) went unmentioned in Pearl Curran's inventory of her reading.

For the perplexed reader, the Willoughbys' most successful camouflage is a sharing of names between father and son. Hence there are two Obadiahs just are there are two Stephens, and the difficulty goes beyond the repetition of names. One suspects serial improvisation of characters' pasts, as if PW's plotting were a postdated check to be guaranteed through gradual payments on a debt of promissory revelation. What Hope calls "the stream of mystery" finally yields Obadiah Willoughby the younger as her father and the husband, however briefly, of Sally Trueblood. In an Edenic Maytime, the two brothers, Stephen and Obadiah, wooed and, as we later learn, married the Trueblood sisters, Felicia and Sally. While Obadiah was both in love and in drink, Stephen married Felicia in an attempt to reap the benefit of a Willoughby claim against the Truebloods. When the senior Obadiah learns of Stephen's plot, Stephen murders him, an act witnessed by a horrified Sally. Because the villagers wrongly believe the younger Obadiah to be the murderer, and because Stephen persuades his brother that Sally has been faithless to him with Reuben Passwater, Obadiah flees, leaving Sally behind to bear their child, Hope, and to keep silence until her death. Stephen Willoughby's broad protective shoulders suggest at first that he may be the novel's romantic match for Hope, but in a blackmailing plot he becomes the last murder victim, following the elder Stephen, "a sodden lout" who had fathered young Sephira Griffin's illegitimate baby before being killed by an outraged yeoman, Rudy Strong.

Like many of her fictional sisters, Hope Trueblood Willoughby is of gentle birth, combining the pathos of apparent orphanhood with the redeeming grace of discovered gentility. Her relationship with her found father will be meager and unfulfilling, but she has already sought to legitimate herself by other kinds of naming, countering "the lash" of the pious village that sees her as the "heathen" daughter of the "deader." Discovering that she is a "brat," she understands from the euphemizing Reuben Passwater that "[a] brat is an elf" (*HT*, 11) and thinks of herself as that, a creature familiar from her mother's story-telling. A chance meeting with Geneva Willoughby inspires her to a pompous performance in the dark space under the eaves of "Sir Lilyfinger Dappergay," a game her mother, drifting into death, encourages her to continue to play. As narrator, Hope watches herself play at becoming the speaker we hear until, as her speech trails off, she calls for her manuscript and erases the word "shame" to write "love."

More than the emotional freight of dead or absent parents migrated from Dickens to the Curran Ouija board. Dickens's narrators take their bearings from parental graves, Pip as an orphan first seen among the tombstones of his parents and siblings, David Copperfield evoking his father through "the shadowy remembrance that I have of my first childish associations with his white gravestone in the churchyard." Introductory portions of *Hope Trueblood* ("It may have been that I fancied this . . .") adopt a tone familiar from Pip's retrospect on his youth in *Great Expectations* and from David Copperfield's thinking, "This may be fancy . . . ," when he retrieves a distinct image of lying in his basket while his mother lay in her bed, even as he grants that "Betsey Trotwood Copperfield was forever in the land of dreams and shadows." The pasts Pip and David speak into being lie in some borderland between the invented and the retrieved. "I have an impression on my mind," David says, "which I cannot distinguish from actual remembrance."[30] Hope makes the same confession as she begins ("I may have fancied this . . . " [*HT*, 3]) and regularly invites the reader to watch her seek herself in the past: "I seem to see myself now as I write, one bare foot and the gray stocking . . . " (*HT*, 74), she muses, or, "All of this was so very, very long ago and yet I see myself, wide-eyed upon the tangled path . . . " (*HT*, 105).

Explicit ventriloquizings of Dickens point back to the productive dissociation in Curran from which the PW text was generated in the first place, represented in the novel by the speaker's sequential orphaning of successive selves. Hope's "I" hears "my voice" extrinsically, unaware, she says, that it is "letting forth the things that I had pent up through the years" (*HT*, 178). When Teeny Gifford, one of the vicar's prying children, asks if she is a "sneathen," Hope inquires archly after the disfigurement of her inquisitor's split lip: "What cracked it?" and later, coldly, "Did God do it?" Supping porridge with the perpetually tearful Nebuchadnezzar Gifford, young Hope discovers a gift for caricature, wondering if he "cried upon his in-take or his out-go. There was certainly no mark between" (*HT*, 29–31). When Patricia and Hope are stared at by the congregation as they visit the church graveyard, Hope's narration performs at the level of maturity it describes: "I haughtily arose and spread my scant skirt and curtseyed," she says, noting that Miss Snifly's "nose was lifted up as though she smelled something" (*HT*, 99).

In full flow, Curran's metamorphosed memories of reading Dickens or of hearing her father speak Dickens went unremarked by her contemporaries. Referring to a subplot involving two greedy solicitors, John Curran recorded a conversation on what he called "the *unique* characters of Brumby & Brumby" (my italics) at their first introduction. When PW explained that the characters were typical "o' the tide [time] o' me," types of the "trumphery" (*sic*) of the "uppin' ones" (PWR 6:1021), "the Family" and Casper Yost readily agreed that the type, presumably thieving lawyers, persists, but they could as well have referred to a Dickens typology—vivid cartoons embodying the dominant trait of a humours character, identities summed up in physical tics or verbal tags and suggested by evocative names.

Of Dickens's characters' names, PW's name *Brumby* comes closest to that of the pompous petty tyrant Mr. Bumble, who as parish beadle officiates at the workhouse where Oliver Twist is taken in. Important notes of a more general ventriloquism are evident in brief excerpts. One Brumby brother is tagged "the wreckage," the other "the bulk." At their introduction, Hope observes, "The wreckage was immediately animated and bowed profusely. I imagined I heard his hinges creak. Then there showed a wider crack and the form of the bulk toward the wall where a shadow like some ominous cloud showed. Miss Willoughby waited that the wreckage bid her in. I stood looking upon the scene with the spirit of mirth welling up." The pair's synchronized, slippery officiousness inhabits not only the language but the speech rhythms of disingenuousness familiar from predatory characters in Dickens like Uriah Heep.

> "I dare say," he went on, "I dare say, my dear Miss, you understand our crushed spirits at the loss of so worthy a gentleman as Strong, of Strong & Strong."
>
> "Crushed," moaned the bulk.
>
> "Crushed," piped the wreckage like an evil echo. (*HT,* 297–98)

If conscious plagiarism is ruled out in such passages, what remains is the mimetic skill of a pianist unaware that while seeming to invent she has drawn on memory to play a recognizably Mozartian or Chopinesque composition. The momentum of automaticity, outpacing conscious recognition, makes it difficult to praise that skill unless the pianist, brightening, concedes, owns, and improvises on the phenomenon as part of her repertoire.

Our moral guide throughout the novel, Hope nevertheless becomes capable after her mother's death of flaring into rage of the same temperature as Telka's or Theia's, suddenly ready to return the figurative stones cast at her. When the dissolute Stephen Willoughby offers her a purse of gold coins for a kiss, she empties the purse and throws the coins in his face, leaving him "saying things aloud that I would not listen to." Further on, she passes "a group of village lads" playing quoits, staring at her and remarking her shame. When one of them finally encircles her waist and whispers something, Hope hurls the metal disks at the boys, attracting a larger crowd, which she attacks with disks and stones, facing them "like a beast at bay . . . wild, panting" (*HT,* 177–78). As Theia had learned, the feeling that fills the mature Hope has a name, "and after this I learned to call it hate" (*HT,* 84), her ordination to a counter-pulpit. When she ascends the steps from which Vicar Gifford speaks, she scorches villagers with their hypocrisy and drags the most pious to the graveyard, where she retitles her identity: "I was a thing, not a woman, a wild thing, a beast" (*HT,* 222–23).

At the end of memory's sequence, Hope is conscious of attempting to write her final self into being when she returns to the Gray Eagle Inn for a spectral conversation with her mother. From a dreamless sleep she awakens to a Mayin' celebration, a fulfillment of her pledge to her mother, but something she can no longer participate in. She lifts a mirror to her face and sees herself as Sally Trueblood, with white hair and her father's brown eyes. Trying "to trace the words" to their origin, she eavesdrops on her parents in the time before her narrative began. "Oh, I would bring you the truth, but I know it is yours and his" (*HT,* 362), she says to Sally of her and Obadiah, arrested by the primal event of her conception. Her "sire" is now physically present to her, but weak, declining, and in her care. "I took him, her love, to me," then asked, "Was he mine? He was hers." The only attraction of an indifferent father is as medium to the lost mother (*HT,* 361). Without speaking, Hope places the armchair of the "helpless" man so that he can view the graveyard, his destination in the paragraph to follow.

For *Hope Trueblood* PW wrote two endings in an inadvertent tribute to Dickens, who in *Great Expectations* first put Pip and Estella on separate paths, then whisked away the shadow of their parting in a second ending that had them walking hand in hand into their future. In both the American and British editions of *Hope Trueblood,* the heroine's voice trails off in midsentence and an authorial voice intoning "And" sets a scene of the deserted interior of the village chapel. On high, the "Word" of its Bible is illuminated by the sun while the wind loosens notes on which are written "Sally" and "Obadiah," evidence of their marriage at the time of Felicia's to Stephen Willoughby, whose name also flutters to the floor.[31]

The Patience Worth Record tells the story of a rejected ending. Two were dictated, sharing only a final sentence that takes in "the mounded chapel yard," nodding larkspurs, and a rising white butterfly (*HT,* 363). When PW remarked on the need to conclude the novel as a "pressin task," she was alluding to the deadline of the New York publisher, John Curran observed, but also to the need to make the legitimacy of Hope's birth more explicit. John excerpts from the rejected ending, which notes Hope's passage from youth to age "until she died with the record in her hand." A dialogue follows between Rudy Strong, now a church elder, and a newly arrived vicar, Mr. Brighton, who inquires about the meaning of scraps of paper in the ragged church record that mention Sarah and Obadiah, in effect providing evidence of their marriage by his duly ordained, previously unmentioned father. Holt's impatience notwithstanding, Pearl Curran tells her husband and Casper Yost that PW has had second thoughts and wants "musicin'" for a new dictation—the one that will finally be printed. The rhythmically dispensed imagery of the new paragraph then obviates the explanations of the Strong–Brighton dialogue. In an empty chapel, the wind simply stirs the Bible's pages and loosens the evidential scraps of paper while a "playful" sunbeam dances to illuminate them.[32]

To John Curran, the relation between medium and control seemed to change over the six months prior to his Record entry of March 20, 1918. Reviewing the period of *Hope Trueblood*'s dictation, John stated that Pearl might be "totally oblivious" to a sentence she had dictated or would announce that she heard characters speak differently "from the words that she dictates off the board" (*SS*, 183–84). Conversations in the Record show a writer consciously wondering whether she has got it right. Throughout the day of October 29, 1917, Pearl suggested that PW preferred the name *Sir Gildegraces Foppinjay* to *Sir Gilleyfinger Poppinjay* in the game Hope plays with her mother in chapter 2. "It be cunniner," PW explained, but until the publisher's proofs arrived, PW continued to worry Pearl, asleep and awake, the Record reporting two more revisions of the name until a final "impression" arrived during a nap. The previous candidate, Pearl advised her husband, should now be changed to Sir Lilyfinger Dappergay, "which I think is the final name" (PWR 6:1188–89).

"The Family's" process of choosing a title for the completed *Hope Trueblood* has the sound of a Ouija-board recreation. At first PW teases her company, suggesting a series of dashes as a way of signifying the no-name status of her heroine, or a "quizzing sign" (question mark), which leaves the company looking at each other "in a daze." With a "what 'ud ye think," PW wonders whether to repeat one of Hope's final utterances, "Shame," to be visibly crossed out with "Love." When the board evades the issue by beginning a story about a hunchback boy and a monk, John Curran loses patience, exclaiming, "Well! Of all the—! What the Sam Hill!" The chase ends when it appears that PW had all along preferred the title "The Lash," now coldly calling it "a tickler," but that candidate does not make it out of St. Louis. The term had been used numbingly in both PW novels. It may have been a Holt editor who turned conventionally to an eponymous heroine for help naming the book (PWR 6:1078–79).

IV. "Adieu to the Ouija Board": Patience at Sea

The period from the end of World War I into the early 1920s added dictations and another published volume of poetry,[33] but PW was not prescient enough to advise Curran that *Hope Trueblood* would be the last of her "as given to" publications to win wide readership. The sun rising over an English "Inne" on the novel's cover—an embossed design dictated by PW—had begun to set. By February 12, 1920, Curran had accepted the challenge of dictating her new, but never published, novel, "Samuel Wheaton," without using the board, having made "her adieu to the ouija board, we feel for all time," her husband wrote (PWR 12:2240).

Even greater career and life changes remained for Pearl Curran, but PW had now reached what Irving Litvag would call "the top of the hill" in his biography *Singer in the Shadows.* The next book-length publication after *Hope Trueblood* could not have done much to advance PW's reputation as a vendible writer. *The Pot Upon the Wheel* (1921) had to be published in St. Louis by the Dorset

Press, whose trusteeship papers were discussed by an inner circle that included Yost and a half-dozen other regulars (PWR 14:2759). In the intervening years, PW had produced fiction vigorously but with divided attention, returning to "The Merry Tale," beginning a new "Old Europe" story, apparently never completed, and continuing "Samuel Wheaton," though with difficulty. "I be nay jaded nag," she told a visitor (PWR 14:2763). A brief *Patience Worth's Magazine* synopsis had suggested that the next fiction was again going to focus on an artist figure, a boy "whose body is too frail for the spirit within it," who plays the viola "wonderfully" while living in an abbey with nuns and "a Padre tutor" (*PWM,* Jan. 1918, 13). When the story's setting changed from Spain to France, the *Magazine* saw evidence of PW's acquaintance with French history, manners, and customs in allusions to François Villon "and a certain Basselin whom we had to look up in the old-time Who's Who."[34] Despite what the *Magazine* called publishers' "intense interest" in the manuscript, it was set aside in favor of "Samuel Wheaton," a novel that was not completed until October of 1923 (*SS,* 236–37) and never published. The Spanish-French story has disappeared, for now at least, without a trace. Passages from "Samuel Wheaton" appear in both the Record and *Patience Worth's Magazine* for May 1918, but no manuscript has surfaced.[35]

In "Samuel Wheaton," the setting again is a small English village whose "Dorset Lane" suggests a further attempt to reify a PW birthplace in the south of England. Unsurprisingly, a birthing is the story's first event as a hum of voices is heard coming from a room above a shop whose sign reads "WHEATON," then below, "GENERALS," followed by FASHIONER, CLOCKSMITH / COFFINS. BLADES AND FIREPIECES" (PWR 7:1233–34). Within the shop hangs a "ghastly line" of empty uniforms as if listening to a "death watch" of ticking clocks, while above dark stairs a birth is taking place. References in the Record suggest that the newborn Samuel Wheaton is in fact a girl, a development foreshadowed when a slim, black-clad figure records the name as, alternately, "Samuel" or "Estella" (the latter name again evoking *Great Expectations*), before settling on "Samuel." A reference to a trust stipulating Samuel Wheaton as heir to all Wheaton claims appears to dictate the substitution of a male for a female name. The question of how far the imposture could be carried would have come into play when PW sent Samuel Wheaton to sea, when the shy girl's transformation into an adventurer would have enlarged horizons both literal and figurative beyond those set by Hope Trueblood's claustral village. In a later scene, Samuel eyes a model of the "H.M.S. *Gloucester*" while wearing a red greatcoat, feeling "most grand" under its high shoulders, though "the tiny form within seemed forlorn and the steps seemed uncertain" (PWR 7:1259). In an isolated passage representing the heroine on board, a shipmate, Pommer Pringle, addresses Samuel and is described as catching "her arm as she started aft," then commanding, "Sit down mate." Her identity still unrecognized, the cross-uniformed Samuel salutes Pringle and observes "Aye, aye, sir, . . . We may as well understand, man to man" (PWR 14:2778).

Available passages record an awareness of ship talk that might have been rare among St. Louisans acquainted only with the Missouri and Mississippi rivers, but for others, PW's nautical slang probably had the flavor of leather-bound treasure islands and lending-library mutinies. The story of PW's ocean crossing to New England was compelling enough for Casper and Anna Yost to travel to Dorset in July 1921, hoping to locate landmarks that PW had suggested would identify the birthplace from which she set out on her transatlantic voyage. Their exploration was an attempt to memorialize the earthly Englishness of a Patience they imagined occupying a pew and singing hymns yawningly in the same church that Hope Trueblood would recall.[36] Yost reported that they had found the ruined monastery of Abbottsbury that PW had shown Pearl—and in the village of "Portisham" (*sic*), which "fits exactly" with her description, the small chapel "with a square Norman tower" that would have been there "in Patience's day." Yost could say with certainty that he had stood "where she has stood" and could "see the sea where she has looked." His retrospect had been modeled when PW encouraged her knight's "quest" with a poem that likened his twentieth-century crossing of the Atlantic to her narrative of emigration in the seventeenth century. The poem reflected as well Pearl Curran's venture into Ouija writing: "With little faith in the chart . . . / Seeking the harbor of chance" (PWR 15:2931).

V. Patience as Potter: A *Rubaiyat* of One's Own

In an English village, at sea, or on Calvary, the PW text had enlisted impressively varied cultural idioms and historical settings as material evidence of its claim to spiritual authority. The next published and least noted work, while drawing on widely available Orientalist formulas, spells out how closely Pearl Curran was tied to elements of the St. Louis arts scene, a linkage largely disregarded by local PW followers. The change to an Orphic Middle Eastern voice in *The Pot Upon the Wheel* falls short of the exotic but also dispenses with anger and caustic wit, mostly preferring the kinds of vaporous dialogue that for years had appeared in PW's meaning-of-life conversations with faithful inquirers. Not the least of these was the text's editor, Casper Yost, who continued to appeal regularly to PW for hints about eternity as he prepared to write his own wisdom book, to be titled *The Task.*

When Curran told Walter Prince that her reading of the *Rubaiyat of Omar Khayyam* had made the "deepest" impression on her (*CPW,* 16), she supplied only a portion of what went into the dialogues of PW's Middle Eastern fable. Nearer at hand were the St. Louis Potters, a group of determinedly antibourgeois St. Louis women who had come together first as the Self and Mutual Admiration Society between the World's Fair year of 1904 and 1907, the year of Pearl Pollard's marriage to John Curran, to publish their own art in a handcrafted magazine they called *The Potter's Wheel.* Poet Sara Teasdale would later have the most public career of the group whose leader, Williamina Parrish, and her sister Grace, both students of the new pictorialist photography, found their way into the inner circle of PW watchers. It was Williamina who, though described as "a born tyrant" over her fellow artists, emphasized their need to support one another's talent and who composed a poem, "The Rubaiyat of Friendship," for the fourth issue of *The Potter's Wheel* in 1905. The stitched-together pages on which the artists created their work were bound within a cover that showed two men, "naked save for a loin cloth"—the phrase appears twice in *The Pot Upon the Wheel*—facing each other on opposite sides of a potter's wheel, one turning a new piece of pottery, the other painting a finished one. Over them hovers a vaguely Egyptian, winged female, their Muse. With no mention of the Potters, Yost's introduction to *The Pot Upon the Wheel* has Curran first receiving a picture of an "old man seated at a rude potter's wheel," together with a poem, "The Potter," which speaks of the clay as crafted to "unloose the steed of my soul / Which is pawing for release."[37]

Although Pearl Curran was not part of the original company of Potters, disbanded in 1907, the group's alumnae became an enthusiastic audience for PW gatherings in the years 1924–1928 and "flocked to the Patience Worth séances on a regular basis."[38] From the edge of the post–World's Fair arts community, its network of social relationships tight and white, the names of its members a kind of local aesthetic currency, Curran gained acquaintance with the Potters' work and the group's more prominent members. On April 17, 1912, she sang settings of poetry by Sara Teasdale and future playwright Zoë Akins, appearing with them on a program of the Papyrus Club honoring "St. Louis Poets of Power." In the year before PW arrived, Curran's local reputation as a singer was graciously noted by the evening's program: "To those who know her voice it is unnecessary to say she will do [the songs] justice." Personalities that would be involved in the period of PW's celebrity appear in Papyrus Club programs. On the evening in 1912 when Curran sang, Casper Yost is listed on the program as the club's president, Emily Hutchings as assistant hostess.[39] Post-PW, on May 12, 1914, Curran sang four poems of Rabindranath Tagore while Emily Hutchings delivered "an appreciation." Hutchings's husband, C. Edwin Hutchings, is listed on the program for that evening as president, and John Curran and Casper Yost are listed as members of the Program Committee. In November 1915, an entire program would be devoted to PW, speaking from Curran's

Ouija board, with Yost giving a talk titled "Smiles from the Invisible," Reedy describing PW in "My Friend from There," Dr. E. George Payne balancing things with "Psychology and Patience Worth," and, in celebration of her arrival among local celebrities, Curran giving a speech titled "The Pack a-packed by Him."[40]

Correspondences between the content of PW's imagination and the artistic tastes of the Potters are striking. The group's discovery of art for art's and their own souls' sake had publicized to a large audience the romanticized roles and genres available to educated, aspiring daughters of St. Louis's upper middle class who sought to reinvent or at least recostume themselves.[41] In Carolyn Risque, Curran would come to know the artist who had created the facing pair of potters for the inaugural November 1904 magazine, *The Potter's Wheel,* predecessors to the character Khadjas in *Pot Upon the Wheel.* Grace Parrish hung framed reproductions of Edward Burne-Jones's *Hope* and Rossetti's *Beata Beatrix* in the group's clubhouse. Williamina Parrish wrote a Salome poem, and as photographers, the Parrish sisters practiced Pictorialist photography, creating portraits like the Salome of Strauss's opera that lent themselves to or derived from theatrical poses.[42] Vine Colby submitted to the group's magazine a "medieval parable about love," while Celia Harris contributed "Wind Play," a play whose setting was "a castle on the blasted moors of Scotland," its heroine "the free-spirited Margret, reminiscent of the tragic heroines of Pre-Raphaelite literature." An anthology of love poetry selected by Teasdale in 1917, the year of *The Sorry Tale*'s publication, included a poem by Akins and others by Potters Edna Wahlert, Vine Colby, and Williamina Parrish, as well as Curran's admired Ella Wheeler Wilcox. Years later, when Williamina Parrish reminisced about Sara Teasdale, she evoked a Tennyson-tinged Arthurianism as the setting, which PW had also made use of in creating Lady Marye in "The Stranger": "Sara lived the life of a Princess in her Tower, as far as I could see," Parrish said.[43]

While the *Rubaiyat* was a direct resource for them, the Potters appear to have adopted their identifying trope from the Scottish divine John Watson, who wrote under the pseudonym *Ian Maclaren* and died on a U.S. tour in 1907. Watson adopted the potter metaphor for the title of his turn-of-the-century volume on soul-making, *The Potter's Wheel,* in which he posted as epigraph a poem that began, "Ay, note that Potter's Wheel, / That metaphor . . . "[44] An echoing poem in the second number of the Potters' magazine exhorted again, "Aye, try that Potter's wheel!" and encouraged hesitant artists to leave their "impress on the clay." Whatever Pearl Curran's debt to the Potters and to their models in turn, her own *Rubaiyat* has the look of a belated bid to her sister artists for associate membership. The summer of 1919, when PW first began to dictate *The Pot Upon the Wheel,* also marked the appearance in the Curran living room of Dotsie Smith, Pearl's incorrigibly devoted friend in her final years. In a letter to the director of the Missouri Historical Society in 1957,

Smith wrote that *The Pot Upon the Wheel* had been written for her, to answer her questions about "life."[45]

At the board, Curran's memory of canonical literature made it possible to associate her moving hand with its "moving finger" of fate. While Edward FitzGerald as translator of the *Rubaiyat of Omar Khayyam* had written indelibly that not "all thy Piety nor Wit" could revise its lines, he could not prohibit widespread emulation, even supernormal supersession, of its manner or of references like "a surly Tapster" or colloquial registerings of "daub" and "Pish." The role of speaker for Eternity is given to Khadjas, the potter, whose turning wheel engages a seeker who begins as the question-filled, innocent Child, then as Ancient arrives at a wisdom that marks him as Khadjas's replacement. By dramatizing the stages of a single pilgrimage, PW links a series of illusory victories and the promise of eventual enlightenment but excludes the rueful double vision of FitzGerald's speaker, who admits at one point that he "was never deep in anything but—Wine."[46]

A single theme, the fullness of emptiness, is shared by the *Rubaiyat* and *The Pot Upon the Wheel,* encouraging PW to identify the shaping of the wheel's product with the medium's role. Consulting the Record for March 9, 1926, Prince found PW saying, "Song is born of thirst, and all things are poured into it" (*CPW,* 323). Incurious about the art of worldly women, Casper Yost maintained that Curran would have known nothing about a potter's wheel, insisting that her latest PW communication had been "impressed upon her consciousness by the same power" and included "too much that is utterly unknown to Mrs. Curran, to accept them as products of her imagination"—unknown, that is, unless her sister artists' homage to the *Rubaiyat* had prompted a reimagining of the potter's hands as an analog of her own at the board. Khadjas comes closest to declaring a creed of unconscious intentionality when he tells the youth, "Within the pot there is no desire but to become a pot; and it becometh the thing."[47]

Pearl Lenore Curran at the outset of her career as medium to Patience Worth. Reprinted by permission from the Missouri History Museum, St. Louis, MO, Photographs and Prints Collection.

John Curran, Pearl's first husband, brought entrepreneurial support to the Patience Worth venture and was the faithful keeper of the poems and conversations of the Patience Worth Record. Reproduced from *Picturesque St. Louis* (St. Louis: Finkenbiner-Rich Publishing Co., 1910), by permission from the Missouri History Museum, St. Louis, MO.

Though a committed believer in Patience Worth from the beginning, Emily Grant Hutchings soon found Pearl Curran an unlikely and possibly unworthy medium. Reproduced from *Notable Women of St. Louis,* by Anne Johnson (St. Louis: Woodward, 1914), by permission from the Missouri History Museum, St. Louis, MO.

A Spiritualist minister and Pearl Curran's uncle, George Cordingley led a Chicago congregation that Pearl found repugnant during the period she served as church pianist for him. His practice of delivering impromptu poetry nevertheless reappears in Patience Worth dictations. Reproduced from *Impromptu Poems,* by George Cordingley.

As editorial director of the *St. Louis Globe-Democrat*, Casper Yost printed and publicized the early writings of Patience Worth, edited and annotated later novels, and was a devoted member of the group attending the Ouija-board sessions in the Currans' parlor. Photo originally appeared in *The Bookman* 45:6 (1917).

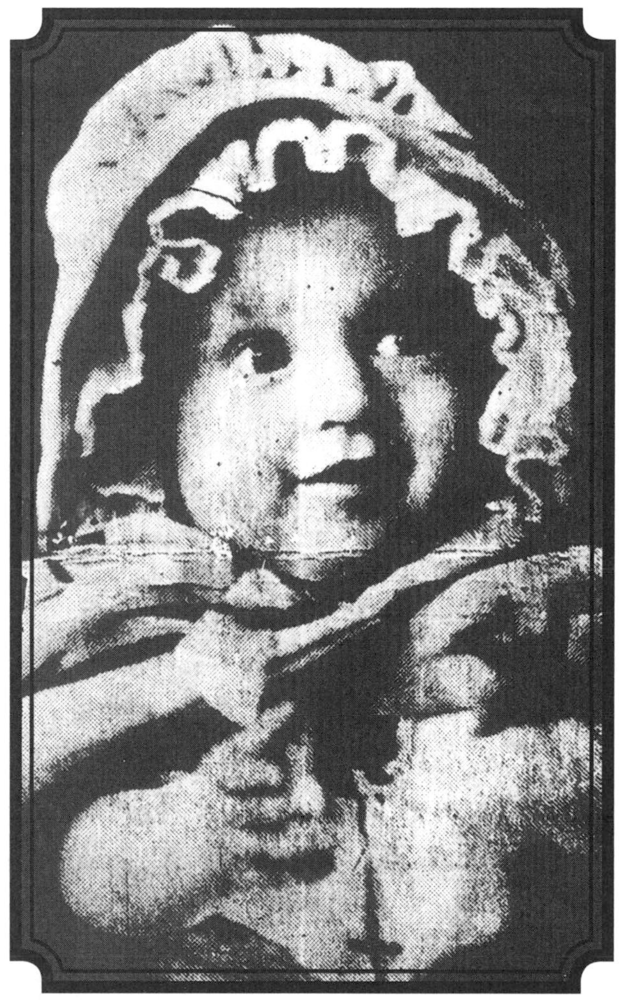

Patience Worth Curran, "Patience Wee," was adopted by Pearl and John Curran in October 1916. They dressed the child in a bonnet to evoke her discarnate Puritan godmother. Reproduced from *Patience Worth's Magazine,* November 1917.

Nov. 3rd 1921

Mrs. John H. Curran
"Patience Worth"

"To the common hunger of the day, a bread set forth with the salt of love upon it."

"Patience Worth"

H. S. Hadley

Inscription by Pearl Curran as Patience Worth in a friend's copy of *The Pot Upon the Wheel.* Courtesy of Department of Special Collections, Washington University Libraries, St. Louis, MO.

Walter Franklin Prince gathered an enormous number of notes, records, and interviews for his book on Patience Worth and tilted toward a "supernormal" view of the case, remaining a lifelong defender of Pearl Curran's honesty.

(Opposite top) William Reedy, journalist, critic, and publisher of *Reedy's Mirror,* took a satiric view of "spook writing" but praised Pearl Curran's talent. Patience Worth styled him "Fat-A-Wide." Reprinted by permission from the Missouri History Museum, St. Louis, MO, Photographs and Prints Collection.

(Opposite bottom) Drawn to the idea of centuries-old English language and literature, John Livingston Lowes quizzed the Ouija board unsuccessfully and soon ended relations with the Currans, accusing them of bad faith. Courtesy of University Archives, Washington University Libraries, St. Louis, MO.

(Above) A surviving photo of Pearl Curran and her daughters shows Patience Wee, *left,* adopted on instructions from Patience Worth, with younger sister Eileen, *right,* born six months after her father's death. Reproduced from *Poems from Patience Worth for Williamina Parrish, 1924–1928* (typescript), Missouri History Museum, St. Louis, MO.

Pearl Curran had fully matured into her role as "authoress" by 1927, following publication of novels *The Sorry Tale* and *Hope Trueblood,* as dictated by Patience Worth. Missouri History Museum, St. Louis, MO, Photographs and Prints Collection.

St. Louis lawyer John Cashman became a regular attendant at a number of Ouija sessions before and after John Curran's death and was questioned on love and faithfulness by Patience Worth. Reproduced from *Prominent St. Louisans* (St. Louis: Henry Brown & Co., 1916), courtesy of Missouri History Museum, St. Louis, MO.

Chapter 5

AN OCCULT VOCABULARY AND THE PROBLEM OF KNOWLEDGE

Casper Yost was the first PW observer to point to the "problem of knowledge." How could Pearl Curran deliver up historical language and dialects, ethnic names and place names and local markers of a foreign culture out of her modest education and limited reading and do so while dictating fiction at a speed and with a fluency that amazed visitors, *unless* some supernormal agency was involved? Examples of facile mimicry give themselves away throughout the PW texts and Record, but even a limited inventory of the vocabulary's uncommon resources suggests that Curran was rightly awed when she pronounced beyond her ken. Awed at what, one still might ask. Rephrased in Chapter 9, the question will become: what does the medium's verbal performance at the Ouija board suggest about the complexity and multiple capacities of human memory? For now, Curran's experience of language summoned unaccountably from its ancient home raises its own questions.

Like historical romancers before and after, the literary PW created a textual claim to citizenship in the centuries she wrote about. That claim can initially be seen as the fictionist's gaining plausibility for apparent historical knowledge through dictations that are no more than a matter of stylistic manner. The Ouija board's customary idiom, in responding to visitors' questions, gave an impression of olde England much like that of the signage on America's familiar beef-and-ale restaurants. When philologically astute visitors questioned PW's use of words from different periods and regions, the board celebrated its freedom to roam the history of the language, a boast that asserted stylistic willfulness more than it explained: "Ye shall find whits o' this and that ta'en from here and there . . . " (*CPW,* 343). Mouthing variously, as a matter of mood or audience or occasion, the writer created an illusion of speech made grandly whimsical by the centuries. No longer "atrack 'pon clay," she was free to weave "o' the spill o' time and 'tis the cloth o' me. Let any man then weave o' such" (PWR 2:278).

When she spoke as unsuspecting medium, Curran was perfectly willing to describe the language of the board as a "manufactured English," but she gave no evidence of curiosity about its origins apart from an occasional trip to the dictionary when an unfamiliar word had been dictated. A deliberate and disingenuous Curran must remain a logical possibility. That medium would have sought out arcane usages and consulted historical grammars and medieval and early modern texts unobserved, though one could argue that ill-informed research by such an uneducated person would have consumed valuable time and created an unconvincing deception. More difficult and interesting questions are raised by considering the PW lexicon as a network of coded verbal memories, cognitively occult in Curran well before ingredients of the "wonder-put" were prompted to issue fluently into an appropriate context. As the medium moved the Ouija board's pointer, the phenomenon repeatedly claimed for itself what Curran did not—the resources and prerogatives of the conscious artist. "I be afull o' word" said PW (PWR 1:116). A reader of the PW Record is likely to take away an impression of affectation and verbal role-playing, but in the domain of what Curran did not know she knew, there remains a core of historical, colloquial English accessed with apparent facility and put to apt use, contributing often if not consistently to the lively concreteness of PW texts.

Not even PW's defenders could avoid characterizing the antiquity of PW's language as performative costume. Walter Prince, noting the repetitive use of the prefix *a-* as rhythmic filler, was exasperated enough to call the dialect "half-artificial" (*CPW,* 343). No one would write in a tongue "so clumsy and so objectionable," never spoken "anywhere at any time," granted a contributor to *Patience Worth's Magazine*—probably Casper Yost—if the purpose were simply to sell books (*PWM,* Mar. 1918, 4). From the beginning, the appearance of *'tis* and *dost* announced a stale convention. Then idiosyncrasies of spelling began to appear with an insistence on older but entirely recognizable forms like *merrie, tung, milch, linon, ribband,* and regular use of expressions like *a-lack a-day.* Some word choices suggested only idiosyncratic variations on what was familiar, to *dud, bedud,* or *pettiskirt* (as a verb) serving as metaphors to suggest pretension, decoration, or concealment. A usage like *knee breaks* is close enough to "breeches" but makes length explicit, as when Hope Trueblood observes a mysterious host "clothed in 'knees' and white leggings" (*HT,* 112) or when PW remarks, "A man loveth his wife, but ah, the buckles on his knee breaks!" (*PWPM,* 20). Emily Hutchings was warned, "Ne'er leap afore ye search," when she questioned how loosened "points" could allow hose to drop, until the dictionary supported PW by putting "lacings" in them (PWR 1:46). For some, the inconsistency of PW's word store was sufficient proof of an ignorant ruse. Insistently English in communicating "a bit of treacle" and "prating" of Martinmas, PW travels to colonial New England for "pine-shillings," is a Washington Irving New Yorker when she refers to "knickerbockers," then is shamelessly anachronistic when she scorns "lollypops" or refers to a "hurdy-gurdy." When Curran placed a short story under her own name, PW said she was reminded of "a lout who fetched four pound tripence [not thruppence] peddlin' wry ["twisted"] fish" (PWR 10:2001).

In an essay printed by Walter Prince, "The Evidence in Telka," Yost granted that there was "no uniformity in [PW's] language" but still believed that he was conversing with someone who had "an uncanny knowledge of the English tongue at all times," having combed authorities on Anglo-Saxon and a dictionary of English dialects while consulting the texts of Chaucer, Layamon, and Wycliffe (*CPW,* 375, 359). Admittedly "eclectic," the PW language, he believed, registered a predominant South of England influence, particularly in the ambitious early work *Telka.* Prince also felt able to support the claim of an alleged PW lifetime in Dorset when he detected several resemblances, including frequent use of the *a-* prefix, between portions of the PW dialect and language in nineteenth-century poems by William Barnes (1801–1886), a Dorset poet.[1]

Earlier, Yost had attempted the greater challenge of quizzing PW, who spoke with no accent other than Curran's, on Dorset pronunciation, such as the *o* in *go* and *boy.* While Yost felt rewarded by phonetic pronunciations spelled out on the board with an air of authority, his questions could be leading, Prince believed, when they suggested possibilities for choice. Yet Prince largely accepted Yost's conclusions, citing spellings in Barnes that indicated pronunciations agreeable to what Yost had recorded, for example, PW's preference for "a longish o-o-o" for *go,* the correction of Yost's pronunciation "zoo" to "tzoo" for *so,* and a suggestion that his "by" for *boy* might have "a bit o' a sound 'pon the o"—the board finally accepting Yost's "bwy" with a "Yea" (*CPW,* 341–42). No natives of Dorset appear in the Record as arbiters.

Tracking the number and variety of PW's historical usages would have been a daunting task for any examiner. In first presenting the "psychic mystery" of PW to the public in his book *Patience Worth: A Psychic Mystery* in 1916, eleven years before Prince published his exhaustive casebook *The Case of Patience Worth,* Yost offers only a few samples. In the Christmas story "The Stranger," he intervenes several times as editor with help from a dictionary. The blind Lady Marye is first seen "fingering the regal," which Yost informs the reader was a "small portable pipe organ used in the sixteenth and seventeenth centuries." His readers learn that the verb *ettle,* which became a staple of PW's conversation, is "to have a strong desire," *aslaunch* is "aslant or obliquely," and *chamming* is an obsolete form of "champing" (*PWPM,* 123–25, 135). Yost was struck by PW's use of *jane o' apes* as a variant of the masculine *jackanapes,* which in Shakespeare had expressed monkey-like tricks and apish behavior. The coinage *jane o' apes,* he believed, appeared only in a play by Philip Massinger (1583–1640), a source also listed by the *Oxford English Dictionary,* which quotes from Massinger's *Bondman:* "But we shall want a woman. . . . no, here's a Jane-of-apes shall serve" (act 3, scene 3).[2] As dictated, *cock-shut* was recorded wrongly as "cock's hut," then was understood to be a figure for twilight, as in Shakespeare's *Richard III,* "much about cockshut time" (*PWPM,* 57–58).

With manuscript accumulating, Yost pursued fewer particulars but eventually allowed Prince to include his essay "The Problem of Knowledge" in the study he published in the same year (1927) as John Livingston Lowes's anatomy of Coleridge's imagination. Yost was less interested in such individual curiosities as PW's use of *napron,* a Middle English form of "apron" derived from French, than he was in arguing the dictations' broad understanding of the Anglo-Saxon roots of common English words, their relation to a variety of British dialects, notably including "the lowland tongue of Scotland" (*CPW,* 376), and in his notes to *The Sorry Tale,* the verifiability of PW's Holy Land settings and personalities.

Yost was himself part of the problem of knowledge. As sympathetic audience, he did not allow for the possibility that his own learning might emerge without notice to accommodate or fill in gaps in what PW offered, or for the possibility that the board's rush of performance, its spelling a dialect, any dialect, might have successfully created in him the illusory perception of a voice speaking from the past. Walter Prince went further than Yost in his research when he inventoried the dusty volumes Curran had stored in a cupboard since the death of her father. He proved an incurious reader of the 290 volumes, almost half of them nineteenth-century fiction, and concluded that most appeared to have belonged to John Curran before his marriage to Pearl, or to George Pollard, though he was aware that as a child Pearl had been read to by her father. Prince was more diligent when he looked at two lives of Jesus but noted that they came into the Curran house after completion of *The Sorry Tale,* and he searched for but found no copies of *Ben-Hur* or *Quo Vadis.* He lists Dickens's *Child's History of England* and two biographical volumes, *Famous Actors* and *Famous Actresses,* without comment.[3] A promising discovery was *The Old Spelling of Shakespeare,* but Prince found its pages partly uncut, the edition a reprinting of *All's Well That Ends Well* from the First Folio, and its spellings unlike those of PW.[4]

A systematic categorizer, Prince devoted three pages of *The Case of Patience Worth* to compiling a PW dictionary of what he describes as rare, obsolete, or "dialectic" words (*CPW,* 338–40). For the most part the vocabulary Prince assembled repeats examples of PW's most characteristic mannerisms—*atwain, atrap, aneath*—but it also reflects, and extends, the practice in early modern English of using one part of speech for another—*holy* and *heavy* as verbs, *grow* and *tarry* as nouns. Many of the usages are standard fare—*hey-day* said in "frolic," *yester* for "yesterday," *tide* for "time," and, predictably, *dame* and *wench*—but Prince is unwilling to distinguish between flavoring—PW's preference for *neckabout* or *egotry* over "necklace" or "egotism"—and genuinely Old English usages, such as *shoon* as the plural for "shoe."

A more biographically grounded challenge to PW's free-range historicity came from commentaries that stressed the influence during Pearl Pollard's youth of time spent in rural Texas and the northern reach of the Missouri Ozarks. American regional speech carryovers from Britain point to both old and new worlds at once. PW uses *grister,* as in "grist mill," to refer figuratively to the Ouija board. The expression *to rid up,* or *ridden up* or *righted up,* used in *Hope Trueblood* (*HT,* 80, 82, 211), has *Oxford English Dictionary* citations for Swift and Hardy but was also common among U.S. dialects to mean clearing the table, washing up. *Oxford English Dictionary* references that would reveal a *slaunch-eyed* character (PWR 3:416) as slanting-eyed are all drawn from American sources, including Texas, beginning in 1913. Two of PW's favorites, *bannock* (a round flat meal-bread) and *I vum* (for "I vow me"), survived from Old to New England in Elizabeth Stoddard's *Morgesons* (1862). If the Puritan poet Edward Taylor (1642–1729) wrote the soul in his Meditation 8 as a bird in a wicker cage, Pearl Pollard's rustic memories could readily have yielded the image of the "wicker" and its tenant with which Hope Trueblood begins her story.

As respondents to James Hyslop pointed out when he adopted the Ozarks explanation for PW's language, regional American survivals do not appear in great enough numbers to characterize the PW vocabulary. A *pudding string* might have secured either an English or rural American pudding, of innards and meal, beef or mince, boiled in bags, but the term realizes its definition not as an egregious item on a list but woven integrally into the PW text: "Were I to tell thee the pudding string were a spinet's string, thou wouldst make ready for the dance" (*PWPM,* 20–21). Words that have a look of forced archaism, like *leggins, ceil* for "ceiling," *ope* for "opening," and *loth* for "loathe," appear to have been common British usages from the seventeenth to the nineteenth centuries. The *Oxford English Dictionary* has both a 1763 British and a Washington Irving entry for *leggings* but cites the 1861 Bentley Ballads for *ceil,* quotes nineteenth-century descriptions of tower and cathedral windows for *ope*, and gives a 1667 Pepys entry and a phrase from *Silas Marner* for *loth*.

And curiosities persist, including the use of *twittle* for "to chatter." As individual items, PW's *I wot* ("I know") or to *up a bumper* ("fill a cup with," e.g., ale) might have been recalled from readings or performances more readily than abstractions, but having village boys play at *quoits*, or adopting *catch and cast* to describe a back-and-forth game, or summoning the name (*bascinet*) of a medieval helmet worn with armor suggests a further reach. The narrator of *Hope Trueblood* uses the archaic *yelk* (89) and *sheething* (252) for "yolk" and "sheathing" (as when "the rain sweep[s] the shutter in sheething sounds"), knows that a *tidy* (4) is an antimacassar, in her mental England can speak of a *liquored* rather than a "candied" apple (292), and can refer to "cold round and black bread" (295) without needing to explain that the meat is beef usually cut from the haunch. In conversation, PW's oath *Bally!* a euphemism for "bloody," goes unremarked, perhaps because she speaks more invitingly of *harebells, larkspur,* and *May-thorn.* (The *Oxford English Dictionary* quotes Elizabeth Barrett Browning: "I receive the maythorn, and its scent outgive!")

PW aphorisms are dotted with historical nuggets. The expression "'Twould *pleg* thee sore should thy shadow wear cap and bells" (*PWPM*, 21) appropriates a genuinely archaic spelling of the word *plague* to set beside the traditional image of a fool, and when PW has it that "Sages' learning is but a shrunken *clout* for naked fools" (PWR 1:28), she diminishes to a patch or "small or worthless piece of cloth" erudition's attempt to undo her. The *Oxford English Dictionary* cites G. Fletcher (1591): "They use to go naked, save a clout about their middle." In "The Fool and the Lady," the Fool's place in the social hierarchy is implied in his sardonic word choice when he says that village crones "wear their necks becricked to see [the King's] *palfrey* pass," his "*sumpter-cloth* . . . trail[ing] like a ladies' robe" (*PWPM*, 116). Part of the passage's ironic effect is its pairing of a small saddle-horse for ladies with the cloth used as a covering for a sumpter or pack animal, as in the *Oxford English Dictionary* citation of *The London Gazette* (1666), which describes "thirty seven mules with their Sumpter Cloaths nobly embroidered with Gold." When a poem's stream is *wappered*, or fatigued, it "threads like a crewel" (PWR 8:1538). Among look-alike words: *wabble* is a readily guessed variant of "wobble" in "age-*wabbled* brother," but a wattle perhaps familiar from Curran's rural experience, is "a fleshy lobe," red and pendant from the necks of turkey and other fowl. Hope Trueblood speaks of "a fat person . . . whose cheeks surprised his shoulders by *wattling* upon them" (*HT*, 108). If *wizened* can describe a shrunken, dried-up face, *weasened*, an alternative spelling, serves Hope to describe a failing, barely lighted candle in a dark room (*HT*, 297).

PW confided that in her time children who asked too many questions were disciplined with "a saplin's *quirk*," the sting of its twisted part (PWR 5:942).

No editor explains as does the *Oxford English Dictionary* that wrathful language like that of the *bumboat's woman* in *Hope Trueblood* (228) would have been the coarse talk of scavengers and provisioners, female or male, who in the seventeenth century removed "filth" from ships lying in the Thames and in the nineteenth century sold fruits and vegetables but earned notoriety by also supplying sex. The usage is casually knowing in Hope's narration but may have a nearer source, the sanitized bumboat's woman Little Buttercup of Gilbert and Sullivan's *H.M.S. Pinafore* (1878), whose song in her own name ("I've treacle and toffee, I've tea and I've coffee") would have been widely popular by the time Pearl Pollard began piano lessons. The *Oxford English Dictionary* describes *smalls* (*HT,* 102) as "formerly breeches," later "underclothes," presumably under a coat, or as William Thackeray describes a footman in *Vanity Fair,* "in large plush smalls and waistcoat." *Tansy,* a bitter herb ingredient in Easter puddings or omelets, was "formerly much used in medicine as a stomachic," and PW proposes it as a treatment for a "sorry belly" (PWR 1:32) or a *quinsied* ("swollen") throat.[5]

Patience Worth celebrates her text not as etymological wraith but as a writer's intent to speak "that thou shalt know what be within me" (PWR 5:801). That intention is explicit, Prince notes, when PW describes herself as "a builder 'pon word," ready to "make o' that that be not that that be. Theeds't merry at the word awaked that knoweth not its self." To a visitor who remarked on her vagaries of language, she spoke with writerly defiance to assert that it was her imagination, not a historical period, she strove to incarnate, promising that she had words of "flesh for to show that be not fish nor fowl nor water nor wine! Nay she shall for to cunger [conjure] until the folly-smirkin' be froze upon the face of fools!"(*CPW*, 336–40). Since Yost seems never to have heard of Gerard Manley Hopkins and could not have read Dylan Thomas, he credits PW with reviving the "almost forgotten art of compounding words," that is, repeating the formula of Anglo-Saxon metaphorical kennings, like the ocean as "whale-road" in *Beowulf,* without precisely duplicating any historic original. Yost has in mind the instances when PW speaks of a bird as a "snow-chirp," prattle as "quack-gabbing," a shepherd's crook as a "chide-rod," and admires a "dandy-flower" and calls a dogged questioner a "blunder-mucker" and turnips "marrow root," informing the confounded, "Ye be at the callin' o' such turnips" (PWR 5:951).

The device serves to set a winter scene as "The Merry Tale" begins: "The hoof-pound 'pon the soft snows set them asqueak, and feather-float fell soft upon the white."[6] In providing a long list of PW's compounds, like *dally-path, sleep-stalked, whine-wind, woe-songster, gab-wenching,* and *sprite-toe* (*CPW,* 367), Prince makes clear that PW's Anglo-Saxonisms are an imitative art rather than linguistic archaeology. Four years before fetching *marrow root,* PW had been willing to say "turnips" (PWR 1:18); growing audiences encouraged her to enhance her dialectal powers by compounding fresh archaisms. To praise of her coinages, PW once stopped to explain the associative quality of metaphor: "Ye see, a word needeth o' its brother's blood atimes that it bring forth fruit" (*CPW,* 337).

Inspecting text alone, Yost found himself impressed with the predominance of Anglo-Saxon derivations in the writing of *Telka,* "about ninety per cent," he estimated freely (*CPW,* 358), but he often simply counted words of one syllable, in effect remarking an absence created by PW's stylistic vow to avoid polysyllabic words. When the board spells it that a cover on steaming herbs "will but modify the stench," Yost rightly points out of *modify* that "a word of this degree of Latinity is very rare with her" (*PWPM,* 20). The shunning of Latinity puts PW to the trouble of using connectives and bridges like the prefixes *a-* or *be-* or infinitives as verbs so that she can produce her characteristically iambic and anapestic rhythms. "A heart a-hungered, aye, or sored" (*CPW,* 357, 367). To admit polysyllables of Norman French and ultimately Latin origin or to modify action adverbially would have been to take tautness from a performance of rural antiquity. In a mode of succor, PW was more likely to liquefy and soften surfaces in the poetry than in the dramatic fictions. Whether or not there is more to it, as Yost and Prince believed, there is this much in plenty.

Patience Worth's naming of fictional characters can be unsurprising, oddly off, or unexpectedly resourceful. The name *Franco,* in *Telka,* simply serves to locate the reader in a region closer to the Mediterranean than the North Sea. Without introduction, a medieval Lady Marye can plausibly make her appearance anywhere in the Christian West. Other names fit less well. Cato, the comic-relief roisterer of the unpublished "Merry Tale," could recall Joseph Addison's soberly patriotic Roman for some readers or remind Americans of a generic name applied to enslaved African males rather than suggesting a lineage of profane court jesters. Inexplicably, given the character's merely custodial role, *Panda* was at one time under consideration by PW as eponym for *The Sorry Tale.* A worshipper of Allah and named as a slave of Caesar for his skin color, according to a Roman character, Aurelius, Panda advises and stabilizes, but only an obscure piece of zoological information provided by Yost informs the reader that Theia's protector was named for "a small, carnivorous animal found in the Himalaya region" whose fur is "reddish brown" (*ST,* 342n).

As events in *The Sorry Tale* move closer to their scriptural base, the Gospels govern characters' naming if not their imagined speeches, as in the cases of Herod and Simeon. The names of other characters point in opposite directions. A shamelessly allegorical and nonbiblical name like *Hatte* only exercises a didact's right to be morally insistent. *Theia,* however, qualifies as either a well-researched borrowing or an appropriate inspiration. Her name shedivinizes her, typifies her visionary gift, and as aureole diminishes the constructions of sexual slave and palace dancer. As Titaness of sight, therefore of knowing, Theia was the daughter of Gaia and Uranus, sister and wife to Hyperion. Her children were Eos, the dawn, Selene, the moon, and Helios, the sun.[7] Indeed, a minor character named Helios appears toward the end of *The Sorry Tale,* and in Hesiod's *Theogony,* Theia has a sister named Rhea. In the PW novel, a Rhea is stepmother to Hatte in Theia's absence.

"That could hardly be coincidence," says Yost, though he is addressing another issue as he alleges historical evidence against a critic of *The Sorry Tale.*[8] But some issues may have been too local for Yost to acknowledge, particularly when they arose from Curran's desire to associate herself with a St. Louis literary aristocracy. In the year of its writing, 1915, *Telka* would not immediately have suggested a novel of pre-Raphaelite medievalism or rural maidenhood, but the name could well have reminded St. Louis readers of the brilliant, well-traveled Thekla Bernays (1856–1931), friend of Kate Chopin and Sara Teasdale, educated in Europe, member of a distinguished family, one-time foreign correspondent for the *St. Louis Globe-Democrat,* translator, reviewer, and contributor to *Reedy's Mirror.*[9] The name *Trueblood* argues itself an irreproachable choice to Yost in the PW novel that excited suspicions of its heroine's legitimacy. However appropriate given the novel's subject matter, though, the name could have surfaced from a stroller's view of a Civil War memorial dedicated to the Confederacy in 1914 in St. Louis's Forest Park. Wilbur Tyson Trueblood was an architect who helped design the memorial for the United Daughters of the Confederacy, of which Anna Parrott Yost, Casper Yost's wife, was a member, and his name appears on the memorial.[10]

In the conversations of the Record and in some of the poetry and published fiction, PW can be heard wandering north to Scotland. Since a Dorset-based Patience Worth was unlikely to have known Scots words and their spellings, their use could add to the problem of knowledge, but as we shall see, their use also links PW to a local environment of Celtophiles in an instance of how Curran's immediate environment could nourish unconscious fluency. PW as stage Scot sometimes avails herself of the most obvious markers, as when a ship's builder has "trigged her bonny and taut" (PWR 5:799) or when John Curran is described as having "braw [brave, handsome] hands" (PWR 4:774). But in the PW text, a word like *weason* (PWR 4:790), a Scots variant of the Middle English "weasand" (gullet or windpipe), is considerably more obscure, as is *besom* for straw or twig broom, a term Telka extends to "besom-head," or misbehaving female, in berating her husband, Franco (*CPW,* 284). Curran's eye would need to have fallen with adequate attention on enough instances of Scots dialect to supply memory with originals for her use of *flaen,* "flae" being the Scots version of "flay," which PW uses in a poem to describe villagers "going to church" as if they were "flaen forth" (PWR 4:686). In poetry, PW's Scottish dialect was publicly illustrated in a December 2, 1917, contribution to the *St. Louis Globe-Democrat,* "To the Boy in France." Apparently unconfused, PW was able to call out, as if speaking from Ayreshire, to the boys across the Channel:

> Be ye lone, laddie, lone?
> Then I'd send to thee a token, laddie dear.
> Just a whit o' earth and blossom
> From thy mither-land's ain breast.
> Lay ye doon then 'pon thy pillow,
> Place it 'neath thy weary head. (PWR 6:1112)

Doughboy readers might have been as perplexed as Curran herself was when she received from PW the poem's inquiry "Be ye greetin'laddie / Greetin' greetin' sore?" but a footnote helpfully translates the Scottish dialect word *greetin',* still current, as "grieving."[11] John Curran believed his wife totally unfamiliar with Scottish dialect, a difficulty more evident in another December 1917 session when PW explained her slowness in getting started on a vignette titled "The Turrible Scut" set "somewhere in France." "I haed for to loose his tongue," the board spelled, referring to a Scottish soldier in the sketch who narrates following a brief introduction. Two soldiers occupy a lookout post and one of them, in a kilt, "has just made a hurried entrance from above, urged by the peevish trilling of machine guns and the din of bursting shrapnel close by." The remainder of the sketch is a monologue by a "Scut" responding to a comrade's concern. "Na. A Scut mind 'e Sandee, a scut cun sup oot a deid mun's cup when the finners be stiff wi' the grippin o' death. A-a-i! . . . I tell 'e, comerd, the diel be fellow wi' the Scuts, und Hells a wee bit fireside to the Scuts" (PWR 6:1140–41).

Robert Burns's poetry is fully eligible as a memory-stored text that could have supplied PW with an alternative dialect. In "The Wee Cot in the Gloamin'," another December 1917 production, there is no disguising the Burnsian voice:

> Ach, the days hae slipped by me apacin'
> Wi' sairies and gladsomeness filled,
> But the tide that be dear
> Is the gloamin' sae drear
> When I mind the sma' cot on the mead. (PWR 6:1123–24)

PW's specific acquaintance with Burns is more clear than any other dialectal debt. Though not a direct quotation, a poem in "The Merry Tale" even borrows

Burns's Jeanie, "I leaved thee, Jeanie, at the spring / And sought afar, afar, awa' O"; and its refrain is mindful of Burns's in "The Lea-Rig," "My ain kind dearie O."[12] In 1920, when a Mr. Hamilton requested a poem on Burns, PW balanced affection and disapproval by sketching a poet who dipped his quill in verbal honey-pots as well as the "swill" of a sheep's track, then concluded,

> Aye, who could jest o' mice and men,
> Who singed wi' a lover's singin'
> Yet jested wi' louts in an inne.
> A brothel, egad, spilled 'pon a harp! (PWR 12:2305).

At the turn of the century, widespread St. Louis interest in the life and poetry of Burns argues that with PW arriving in the next decade, Curran wrote for and from the region in which she found herself. Among its other exhibitions, the 1904 World's Fair had included a replica of the Burns Cottage at Alloway, including a number of its original furnishings. Those treasures became the stock for the founding of a local Burns Club and the inspiration for a statue of the poet as ploughboy near the site of the original exhibition. By 1913, the year of PW's first appearance, a printing of addresses delivered at annual Burns Day suppers included "Burns and English Poetry" by John Livingston Lowes (1911) and "Burns, the World Poet" by William Reedy (1912), though Reedy, like the medium he had yet to meet, had to confess that in college, "the dialect was too much for me."[13] Casper Yost, after the height of PW's production, became a member of the Burns Club in 1925, gave the annual address in 1930, and became club president in 1938, just after Pearl Curran's death.[14] As of 1908, the Burns Club was housed in the St. Louis Artists Guild building at 812 Union Boulevard in a room set aside to resemble the hearth of the Burns Cottage. The Currans' addresses on Union (1363, 1395) in 1915 and 1916 put them within the club's compass, and in 1918 the Yosts moved into nearby 1316 Union Boulevard.[15]

In her Potter apprenticeship period, Sara Teasdale elected a range of voices that would eventually give way to her own, among them a taste for Scots dialect. Vine Colby, keeping the group's *Log* in 1906, observed that "for the maist part" her pen would need to run to "the unworldly Scots tongue, for Sara [Teasdale] would not descend to plain Anglo-Saxon at all. She out-Barried Barrie and out-Ian Maclarened Ian Maclaren."[16] Colby alludes to the James M. Barrie not of *Peter Pan,* but of *The Little Minister* (1891, then a 1913 film) and cites the pseudonym of the Potters' admired John Watson, who used *Ian Maclaren* when he wrote his popular stories of Scottish village life. In a period of regionalist writing and attempts to recover Scotch/Gaelic roots, Barrie's Thrum and Watson's Drumtochty are thick with dialects past mastering, but not sampling, by a midwestern American, and they adopt the same genially comic attitudes toward clerical "auld lichts" and "dominies" as do PW's versions of English village residents.

Sara Teasdale made an exception to the chronological limits of her *Answering Voice* anthology for "Auld Robin Gray," by Lady Anne Lindsay Barnard (1750–1825), suggesting a widely shared taste of which PW's Scots-flavored dictations are only one example. Barnard's words were newly set to the tune of an old Scottish air and included dialect staples that appear in PW's talk and texts: *muckle* and *sair, gi'ed, didna',* and *couldna', wraith* for "ghost," and, as in the poem sent to soldiers at the front, *greet* for "grieve." That Barnard's poem belongs to a Scottish air suggests another avenue to Curran's literary memory unexplored by either Yost or Prince. Whether or not Curran read or was audience for local readings of Scottish poetry, she could well have sung settings of Burns or any number of other dialect songs as a student of piano.

What may have seemed least familiar to PW's observers was the writerly certitude of the ungraspable woman who wrote from an imperative prior to vocabulary, the edict of a queenly single-mindedness that her words be taken as they were given. In PW, Yost heard someone "absolutely sure of herself," though he still found it necessary as editor to document, for example, descriptions of "the religion of the Arabs." When Yost reported that he could not confirm some "mooted points," the board remained unmoved by his appeals, or if PW "condescended to clear a doubt," said Yost, she simply "emphasized the original assertion" (*CPW,* 386–87). The authority of a discarnate writer is likely to melt away with confessions of historical error, a vulnerability PW defended as performative versatility, idiom as mood and mouth position, when scholar John Livingston Lowes questioned her closely: "Do I then tung from mouth awide, I then do put questions at awide. Or do I prate through mouth aslant, 'tis then aslant and crooked tale I spin" (PWR 1:91).

For guests at a PW weaving of "knottins unto the warpins" (PWR 5:816), anachronisms and inconsistencies were passed over in favor of the overpowering past-life-likeness streaming through the medium. In performance, the arrival of obscurities carried more than historical prestige when the awed medium herself announced, "I don't understand this—I see a tall cart piled high with furniture and things of that sort—like a moving day." When the poem that followed described a moon that "ascended like a toppling bride's wane / Cross the sky," and a visitor consulting the dictionary translated *wane*[17] as "cart," in this case one that carries the new bride's furniture, vision and diction seemed inseparably part of the same text (PWR 21:3500). The processes of memory and inventive recombination that were PW will not wholly submit to footnotes. Enough that, for many who heard her, it seemed plausible enough that a Shakespearean Victorian displaced from Scotland to Dorset to New England had made a linguistic appearance in a midwestern river metropolis.

Chapter 6

DISSECTING A SPECTER

Vivisectionist or not, attempts to explain the Patience Worth phenomenon regularly accompanied publications like *Hope Trueblood* and public appearances by Pearl Curran. Curran's attempts to explain her "gift," as in her essay "A Nut for Psychologists," took part in this widespread conversation and should be seen in the context of arguments, sometimes reflexive, sometimes evidential, made by supporters and skeptics. The writing of "Rosa Alvaro, Entrante" was not only Curran's attempt to advance her own talent lest it become invisible in the shadow she cast as medium; the story also seemed an attempt at self-exploration in its characterization of a young Chicago salesclerk and her Spanish-inflected double personality. But the effort was not a totally independent one. Help unmentioned by the Currans came from sources other than PW and emphasized clinical dissection rather than romantic masquerade. As we shall see, studies of Spanish lady dissociation, which Pearl Curran would have heard about even if she did not read them, were undertaken both before and after the publication of "Rosa" by Morton Prince, Walter Franklin Prince, and Charles Cory, an observer at PW sessions and a faculty member at Washington University. And the genre of Curran's *Post* story owed something to Fannie Hurst, whose increasingly successful career as a fiction writer took her from St. Louis to New York and whose early short stories provided a magazine reader with useful examples of urban realism applied to the wage-earning woman.

It would be misleading to characterize PW skeptics as predictably male, the specter's champions as invariably female. Casper Yost never wavered in his conviction that Patience Worth had become a spiritual presence in the city where he labored as an editor, even when he found cause to doubt Pearl Curran's commitment to record-keeping. Walter Prince deployed skepticism strategically while gathering evidence that gave supernormal influence more than equal status with as-yet vague theories of the subconscious (*CPW,* 509). John Livingston Lowes hoped to connect the abundance of what he knew about English literary history with what a genuinely historical spirit could verify, until his disappointment turned to angry rejection. While Curran's quest and PW's accomplishments gained favor with younger women aspirants to art in St. Louis, writers like Agnes Repplier and Mary Austin, who had competed in a male literary domain to gain a national reputation, were quick to see regression in the example of a fetchingly named spirit-control. The dialogue between PW's champions and interrogators faded with Curran's newsworthiness, but its terms are unlikely to disappear from the continuing discussions of "ghost writing."

I. The Case of Multiple Rosas

It may be, as Mia Grandolfi Wall has argued, that by publishing "Rosa Alvaro, Entrante" under her own name, Pearl Curran divulged the secret that had been her relation to Patience Worth.[1] The autobiographical patterns of the story's dual personalities vividly dramatize the internal pairing psychologists had pointed to in Curran from the beginning. In the Record, John Curran suggests that "Rosa," finished on September 1, 1919, was written with the help of PW and "reeks" of her. PW characterizes it as "a babe's mixin'. But nae sae sorry a loaf" (*SS,* 203–4). The Currans briefly kept the story a secret from Casper Yost, perhaps believing he was less interested in Pearl's career as a fiction writer than in his oracle, Patience. To Pearl, it seemed "almost a sacrilege" (PWR 10:1973) to mix her glossy writing and its sales-counter argot with the transcendencies of PW.

As magazine fiction, "Rosa" succeeds well enough. The story of a department-store salesgirl who is suddenly able to relieve her drab existence and find true love by taking on, or being taken over by, the personality, accent, and demeanor of a Spanish dancer was unquestionably well timed. Published on November 22, 1919, in the *Saturday Evening Post,* the story capitalized on trends in parlor spiritualism that would peak in the 1920s. A Norman Rockwell cartoon depicting a young couple seated across from each other, fingertips on a planchette, would appear on a *Post* cover for May 1, 1920.[2] In the tradition of medium novels, she is entranced by the unseen, he is entranced by her. And in the May 22 *Post,* Dorothy Parker's lampoon of the Ouija-board craze would appear, caricaturing practitioners as bluestocking reformers and sentimentalists of the afterlife. From the wisecracking humor of "Rosa" and its avoidance of spiritualist themes emerges the profile of a Pearl Curran who temporarily preferred to ignore what the PW voice had to say while continuing to inquire into her relation to it.

Other short stories Curran appears to have written at the time of "Rosa" reveal her as an interested and amused inquirer at the opposed temples of science and the supernormal. For two of these stories, "Old Scotch" and "The Fourth Dimension," we have only Walter Prince's inspection of them as authority. Although he believed two of the four to have been published in the *Post,* short-fiction bibliographies of the period list only "Rosa Alvaro," of which Prince makes no mention though it is the story that best fits his description of having been "clever" enough to have scrambled "onto the ground floor of the *Saturday Evening Post*" (*CPW,* 413). "Old Scotch," in his description, features an actress who owes her sudden success to an unspecified influence, represented variously as spirit possession, suggestion, or "ancestral memory" as discussed by "two goggle-eyed professors" (*CPW,* 414). "The Fourth Dimension" takes on "spiritualistic fakery," represented in "Rosa Alvaro" by the "flapdoodle" and "mediumistic chatter" of Madam M. Martin. Prince juggles several explanations for the success of Curran's self-credited fiction, estimating that her "exercise of subconscious capacities" as PW might have given her confidence to write "Rosa" as her own agent, for which she earned $350.[3] With a maximum of breezy dialogue and a minimum of authorial commentary, "Rosa" is written to recipe: the dreary life in Chicago of a stocking-counter clerk, Mayme Ladd, made just bearable by her tough-talking, heart-of-gold buddy, Gwen Applebaum; Mayme's escape into the power and exoticism of an alternate personality, Rosa; double-edged satire on fraudulent clairvoyants and omniscient psychologists; and a satisfying denouement in which it is revealed that, having developed a Rosa within, Mayme can do without her Spanish costume and that Mr. Peacock, the department-store supervisor charmed by her accent, has proposed to and married her.

As a nine-dollar-a-week hosiery clerk in Chicago, Mayme Ladd goes numbly through tasks Curran might have remembered from her job at Marshall Fields, where she too would have waited on "little-finger-in-the-air" customers and rattled home nightly on the El or streetcar to her boarding house. The effect of the mechanical round on Mayme is serious, says buddy Gwen Applebaum, even threateningly terminal: "Mayme's handed over the counter about the last of her, and is sellin' off the remnant." The god of the department store owns her soul, Mayme fears; "I ain't nothin' but a stockin' box and when I'm empty y'can find me in the dump" (RA, 91).

Defeated and docile, Mayme makes an excellent subject for the clairvoyant Madam Martin, who does "life readings" for two dollars and whose type and parodic profile Curran knows well. Madam Martin quickly offers the suggestion that her new client is "psychical" and puts her in touch with a spirit named Laughing Water, if not directly a comic version of Cora Richmond's Ouina, certainly an allusion to the tribe of spectral Indians that regularly danced behind spiritualist veils. When "Laffie" withdraws from the entranced medium, her diminishing voice compared to that of a ventriloquist, Mayme has received her diagnosis, but no cure, until the "cracked, childish" voice tells her "she be controllum by big longtime-dead Spanish lady, name Rose, Rose, Al—Al—Alvaro, Rosa Alvaro. . . . You homely. She lovely. She make you Spanish bootiful" (RA, 19). For Curran, Madam Martin is pure hokum, informing Mayme that Rosa "was a child of Napolyun Bonypart." Artifice briefly becomes knowingness when Madam Martin reads Mayme as if predicting Pearl's career with PW, saying, "You should develop, deary. I ain't nothin to what you'd be" (RA, 19).

Rosa, or Mayme as Rosa, is an unquestionable success, impressing the streetcar conductor, changing Mayme's mood from dejection to assertiveness, and as Gwen looks on, "playin' baby vamp to Peacock," her smitten manager. What is worrisome is that Rosa's willfulness will dominate her host's life. Curran evokes Shakespeare and the pythoness in Gwen, who wants no part of it: "I ain't no Cleopatter. You don't catch Gwenny nussin' no snakes." Far from praising a dissociative gift, Mayme admits that she both loves Rosa and is afraid of her. "It ain't me. It's what I used to be before the world buried it" (RA, 88). More worrisome is Mayme's decline as an imperial Rosa takes increased command over her miniscule salary while Mayme "is dyin' more every day" (RA, 91).

From the diagnostic language that flourished around the case of PW, Curran assembles a cigar-smoking psychologist, Dr. Drew, who sounds an alarm. Dissociation can lead to obsession and a submersion of primary identity; it "may even lead to insanity," he confides to Gwen. Differing only in dialect, Rosa conforms closely to the profile of PW generated by her examiners when she argues that her distinctive pattern of seeing and saying is superior to that of the host self: "Mees Ladd ees what you call *nada* een my *lengua.* You sabe senor?" What Rosa knows may come from the previous life she describes for Dr. Drew, living in Madrid "centuries ago," dancing for "Ferdinando" as his "*favorite,*" then ending at the point of a dagger, a death she enacts pathetically, then laughingly, leading Gwen to call her a "little devil" (RA, 93). Submitting to hypnosis, which Curran would not do, she is both "childishly trustful" and a wily confessor when she betrays Mayme to Dr. Drew by revealing that Miss Ladd "has a leetle book" from which she learns Spanish (badly). Rosa's confession could be taken as Curran's as well, but it also reproduces charges tiresomely familiar to her and in a story that satirizes Mayme's investigators.

For Dr. Drew, Mayme's consciousness is a circle within that of Rosa but also overlapping it: "I can lead Miss Ladd up to a certain point and then Rosa slips in. It is only by the use of hypnosis that I can keep the two separated" (RA, 94). As in her published introspections, Curran now appears to suggest an underlying continuum of selves, revising her original fear that a hypnotist's separation of Pearl and Patience would silence the voice that won fame.

Still, Mayme resists. Dr. Drew is a representative of Science, and Science is not the experimental method, but the machinery and instrumentation of the vivisectionist male kingdom. Mayme asks derisively what she will do with the independence from Rosa-life that Dr. Drew would restore her to: "'What can I do with it? That ain't the cure. . . . Science, science,' she said evenly. 'I guess they want to empty the box and tag the goods for stock.'" Dr. Drew's friend, the elegant and calculating Agatha, is enlisted to link popular song to the strategies of reason's kingdom: "Poor butterfly!" she says. "What an enviable death, to die by inches while science takes notes!" (RA, 98). Dr. Drew's proposed cure would return Mayme to a self emptied of the creativity and sensuality of the Rosa-words that "seemed to scorch her lips. For she licked them with her scarlet tongue and swallowed as though thirsty" (RA, 93). The cure, wholeness by subtraction, would be worse for Mayme than the disease.

When it arrives, Curran's resolution appears to borrow from a self-help, human-potential movement yet to come. The decisive moment, she tells Gwen, came when, touching bottom as if in "a dream, a nightmare," she chanced on Madam Martin's card and, out of the living Gwen had said the world owed her, spent two dollars on her future. Yes, she knew the clairvoyant was "a fake," but the better idea of Rosa Alvaro was real enough for Mayme to will herself out of her circumstances: "I just made Rosa out of a shawl and a bunch of rag flowers. . . . I forgot myself in Rosa and commenced kiddin' the world back" (RA, 98).

The idea of Mayme's consciously manipulating identities solves a narrative puzzle as simply as Dr. Drew's sketch renders dimensions of consciousness. Recursively, though, it fails to cover Mayme's apprehensions about what is happening to her, relegates to dialect the influx of power that had felt beyond her capacities, and leaves her with the question whether to continue invoking a secondary personality to maintain her conquest of Mr. Peacock. Dr. Drew claims to have cured a case of dissociation, but Agatha dissents with, "Cure indeed!" Mayme and Mr. Peacock, now married, board a Lake Michigan tour boat, Peacock continuing to address his alter-wife as Rosa, and "Señorita" at that. To his wife's heavily accented question whether she should disappear into yesterday or remain into tomorrow, he pleads, "Forever, *amor mio!*" "*Siempre jamás*" comes the accented answer, suspending the reader between a Mayme unwilling to be confined to a role and a Rosa forgetful that dissociation can make no promises. Continuing to exclude Mayme from the action, Curran has "Rosa's little head [fall] confidingly upon Mr. Peacock's shoulder," rewarding the groom for his illusion. Gwen offers psychology as the real subject, but there is no scientific last word as the lake steamer whistles and vapor rises over the lovers in the "cunningly wrought form of a giant interrogation point upon the sky" (RA, 98).

The image fits Curran's story well, and its decoding of Rosa as a consciously manipulated secondary personality is consistent with Emily Hutchings's claim that Curran cited PW as her pen name. But for all its interest, "Rosa Alvaro" is not the key that finally unlocks the case of Patience Worth. The story's commercial viability and reader-friendly conclusion create too slick a surface for self-exploration or confession, conscious or inadvertent. As "Nut," Curran would continue to ask how it was possible to enact a writer whose sources she could not name and whose productivity and literary triumphs were contingent on an absence of conscious control. It was one thing to concede, in the jaunty realism of Gwen Applebaum's summary, that "Mayme just pulled off a movie reel all to herself, bein' the star and support both," but it would be something else for introspection's limited view of automatic processes to assert agency for the shopgirl as writer (Spanish grammar in hand), director, and producer as well.

Pearl Curran was not original in drawing on a population of Spanish ladies who had become objects of psychological study. The fantasy of an alternative life as a Spanish beauty registers the nineteenth century's popular image of Lola Montez ("Whatever Lola wants . . . "), the Irish-born "Spanish" dancer and mistress of King Ludwig I of Bavaria. Two years after the publication of "Rosa Alvaro," Curran's nemesis, Morton Prince, reported to the American Psychopathological Association on his year-long treatment of a patient, the beginning of their meetings undated, who as "Juliana" experienced visual images, wrote automatic script, and made sketches of herself as a reincarnated thirteenth-century Spanish dancer and singer who "danced barefooted before the King of Spain and his court." Speaking "broken English with a foreign accent," Prince's subject also crafted a "mass of neologisms" into what he referred to as "the lingo," just as Curran's Rosa refers to her own *lengua*. Like PW, the secondary personality spoke grandly of her talent: "Pandora's box is poor compared with all I hold within." Little as he learned from PW, Prince now identified a "glorification" of talents denied expression until subconsciously discovered by the subject.[4]

Nearer at hand, and in the month when "Rosa" was completed, Curran found herself referred to as "very intelligent" and of a "quick intuitive understanding" in a September 1919 article on PW by Charles Cory, chair of Washington University's philosophy department, whom Walter Prince links with the mention of "goggle-eyed professors" in "Old Scotch."[5] Had he discussed "Rosa Alvaro," Prince could readily have connected Curran's apparent invention with a study of dissociation Cory published in October 1919, reporting on the case of a woman, A, whose secondary personality, B, expressed her sexual desire in Spanish-accented English and occasionally in a "tongue" made up of fragments of Spanish and traces of Italian. The article reproduces a swatch of Personality B's "tongue," indecipherable save for proper names like "Maria Rozell Rosa" and "Reyos Ferdinando III" of the "Palais Rayals Madrid Espana." Cory suspected that his subject had overheard fragments of Spanish from three Mexican students at the convent school they attended together, the language appearing later in automatic writing the woman turned to after the suicide of her father. The possibility of sexual abuse by the subject's father is not raised by Cory, but he is alert to a connection between Personality B's bold "sex impulses" and her "delirium of fear and suffering" under hypnosis, a "house of horrors" in which she saw "the body of a lover who had taken his own life" at the same time that her father, "an habitual drinker," had committed suicide.[6] The subject's linkage of sexual desire to things Spanish, Cory reports, derived from Personality B's attraction to a Mr. X, "many years her senior," whose Spanish mother lent him a "strongly Spanish" appearance.

Appearing in the month before "Rosa," Cory's article directly followed another Morton Prince study, "The Psychogenesis of Multiple Personality," in the *Journal of Abnormal Psychology*, which Prince edited. Prince and Cory may already have corresponded on their Spanish-lady cases, but it is also likely that Cory's conversations at PW sessions supplied Curran with key features of "Rosa" before her story and his and Morton Prince's journal articles were published. Studies of dissociation also appear to have contributed to how Cory's subject articulated her own "case." His Spanish-accented "B," Cory notes, had read Morton Prince on Christine Beauchamp as well as several other works in "abnormal psychology."[7]

Though silent on "Rosa Alvaro," Walter Prince too had written on a Spanish-speaking woman, Señora Z, with allegedly supernormal powers two years after the Cory and Morton Prince studies of 1919 and five years before he met Pearl Curran.[8] Not himself the initial investigator, Prince traveled to Mexico to oversee the work of Dr. Gustave Pagenstecher, "a materialist" who had written for the American Society for Psychical Research on the "peculiar powers" of the daughter of a governor of a Mexican state. For Prince, Señora Z's intellect and erudition alone could not satisfactorily explain her capacity for "apparent prevision" or the graphic panorama she provided of a royal Egyptian funeral from the touch of an amulet. His neglect of Curran's "Rosa" allowed him to refrain from any mention of the network of studies connecting PW's medium to Spanish-inflected studies of dissociation.

Pearl Curran, authoress, may have profited from forms of support near at hand. Fannie Hurst's early short stories are a lesson in the shop talk of *Saturday Evening Post* fiction. Admired and encouraged by William Reedy, Hurst had her first story published in his *Mirror* in 1909, the year of her graduation from Washington University. Barely an anecdote, the story earns its title, "The Joy of Living," from a husband's department-store promotion to "ribbons and laces," news that prompts his wife, Mayme, to sigh, "Ain't we lucky, Charley?" against a backdrop of kitchen realism.[9] Another of Hurst's early stories, "The Gropers," was published in the *Mirror* in 1910, before the coming of PW but after the Currans had settled in St. Louis, and assembles a group of dateless young women behind a department-store cosmetics counter to display their slang ("Ain't you lucky, kid?") and to give readers glimpses of their attempts at modishness. In this story, where a minor character is spelled "Mame," the place of Curran's Mayme Ladd is occupied by Mary Kantorwitz, presumably disadvantaged by her ethnicity and impoverished wardrobe. A confident, well-coiffed friend, Ethyl Tracy, comes to Mary's aid with the offer of her own party dress, setting an example for a speech from one of Curran's characters in the brief excerpt from "Old Scotch" reprinted by Prince: "Sister, I'm going to tog you out tomorrow in some of my own gay rags. For once you're going to slip into some nifty cloth."[10]

The two-page Hurst stories are skeletal, but the precedent of their idiom and of the working-woman characters who were a staple in Hurst's early fiction may have helped Curran imagine a route to national publication. In September 1912, as Curran tentatively approached the Ouija board, Hurst published "Summer Resources" in the *Saturday Evening Post,* with flirtations at a summer resort conducted in dialogue lines like "I wish I knew if you was jollyin' me or not." Up to the time of Curran's "Rosa," Hurst had published enough work in the *Post, Metropolitan Magazine* (including "Sob Sister," 1916), and *Cosmopolitan* to be collected in 1919 under the title *Humoresque and Other Stories.* For Curran, Hurst was both a local celebrity and predecessor as one of William Reedy's discoveries. More unexpectedly, she was attracted to a sitting with Patience Worth.

The session recording the Hurst-PW conversation appeared in *Patience Worth's Magazine* along with a letter of permission from Hurst expressing "keen anticipation" of the magazine's arrival, describing herself as "deeply interested in your new enterprise," and observing from New York that *The Sorry Tale* "is receiving the sort of reviews its high literary quality warrants." An unlikely admirer of *The Sorry Tale*'s artificial biblicisms, the tough-minded Hurst had nevertheless "come over to get acquainted with Patience," she said. In the session she found herself the object of some of the board's most strained and incomprehensible dialect: "Ye be at the fetchin' o' a wench that be at the uppin o' her sleevin' and takin' o' grain's meal that be not e'en bolted through the nettin', and maketh fittin' loaves for the eat o' the hungered."[11] Decoded, PW's tribute alludes as much to Hurst's robust ambition as to her social sympathies, which are noted when the board contrasts the "sunnin' smile" of Hurst's self-presentation and the suffering with which she shaped "cups for to hold the sorryin' wine," alluding to the writer's characteristic mix of comic caricature and the struggles of her working-class, urban characters.

Poems adopting a visitor's first person to represent their inner life were a staple of PW sessions. The poem written as if by Hurst goes beyond praise for the writer's desire to sing her success. An unnamed darkness PW alludes to may in particular refer to the genteel anti-Semitism that was a mostly unspoken part of Hurst's experience of St. Louis society. The poem concludes: "I could rejoice in my God / Did I not know the shadows, shadows, shadows" (*PWM,* Oct. 1917, 6). Lacking a proper literary agent, Curran would have benefited from an established writer's introduction to magazine editors, in which case Hurst may deserve credit for the uncharacteristic appearance of a short PW poem, "The Golden Bell," in *The Smart Set: A Magazine of Cleverness.*[12] Emerging from a context of case studies and imitable models, the appearance of "Rosa Alvaro, Entrante" may be anomalous among Curran's productions, but not mysterious.

II. Champions and Interrogators

Casper Yost: Brotherly Love

Of all those who expended energy on the case of Patience Worth, Casper Yost as first champion would have had most to lose, personally and professionally, if the Currans were shown to be conscious frauds. Named editorial director of the *St. Louis Globe-Democrat* in March of 1915, he steered the conservative paper through World War I, at first opposing then advocating American entry and describing passage of the eight-hour workweek as "the most pusillanimous act in the history of the American Congress." His combination of moral stringency and gentility earned him the nickname "Arsenic and Old Lace," and his high-minded editorials earned him four honorary degrees and election as the first president of the American Society of Newspaper Editors.[13] Yost was described as "frail, gentle, and soft-spoken" by the one-time head of St. Louis's Mercantile Library, who had observed him spending hours poring over the library's holdings, "wrestling with the problem of the archaic language of the [PW] stories and poems."[14] The conservative voice of the editorials he wrote would have harmonized more closely with that of a Puritan spinster had the specter singing a doctrine of love flirted less fetchingly with her editor. Yost's mission was to authenticate what was edifying. The warmth of his inquiry wrote another script. For a self-educated journalist who was said to have "the distinguished honor of having collected the dullest editorial page in metropolitan newspaper history,"[15] PW was an exotic source of spiritual truth and he kept her company religiously.

In some quarters Yost's forwardness in the case raised suspicions that the PW writings were his own. A former St. Louisan, Dr. William Porter, wrote from Mississippi to ask his friend, William Clark Breckenridge, about the identity of Patience Worth. "I thought she was C.S. Yost. Now she seems to be Mrs. Curran." Soon Porter was expressing concern, noting that "it is risky to work off a joke on the public. I fear for the expose or the explanation. . . . Is it all up to Yost? Are the Hutchins [*sic*] mob in it?" Breckenridge, replying, doubted that "a Puritan lady" would write a poem to the Virgin Mary and echoed Porter's concern that an explanation would have an "effect on someone's future," while confiding that "Mr. Curran is in high feather" and that "Mrs. Curran is keyed up so high that something soon will snap." More darkly, Breckenridge added that his knowledge of Missouri writers led him to suspect someone he could not yet name: "But mind you, only a suspicion so what I am telling you is to be regarded as confidential."[16] There is no evidence that either correspondent pursued his suspicions.

Since Yost staked his own reputation and the credibility of his newspaper on his five articles describing the coming of PW, at first leaving Pearl Curran and Emily Hutchings unnamed, it is "almost eerie," as Litvag understates the case (*SS*, 178), to observe his relationship grow into exchanges of love poetry with a persona he could only know through the voice of Curran.[17] Yost had not been a part of the original Ouija circle, and according to the Record did not make his first visit to the Currans until October 1914 (*SS*, 53). In December 1916, he described to "the Family" an "uncanny" resemblance between a phrase, "beyond the skyline," impressed on him six months earlier as he dreamed of Kipling's poetry and which he developed into a poem, and a recently dictated PW poem that began with the same words. The repetition was "nay wonderwork," PW offered, since as the source of both poems she might "smite thy lute" and dictate her own art as well. The Record went on to quote Yost's poem, emphasizing the line "Have *patience* yet awhile" (PWR 4:781A, 781B).

At its beginning, Yost's relationship with PW was familial. They were to each other "brother o' the flesh o' me" and "beloved sister," related in their fellowship as writers. When PW spoke of her words as her flesh, the adopting of an incarnational metaphor to herself seems not to have bothered Yost; voicing a buried spirit into publication was their shared carnality. As editor of the PW texts, Yost was titled "husbandman." As indispensable friend to the Currans, he became godfather to Patience Wee, for whom he made a "baby book" following PW's earlier proclamation of herself as godmother to the Yosts' grandchild, Dolly (PWR 4:719–20).

Initially Yost depended on his word-sister to articulate the secret life he lived in his days at the *Globe-Democrat.* That buried experience PW characterized as a "vast pang of kinship and surety," which in Yost was the response "o' lo'e unto lo'e"—as if *v* were the body he had left behind. Encouraged, Yost moved past a request that PW write him a poem on God as love and love as God to ask for another, "on love's constant impulse and urge to creation," an impulse he said he felt was absent from his current writing, which "seems barren without the magic of your words" (PWR 10:1873). While Yost refrained from speculating on PW's relation to Curran's buried life, PW was "ateeter to tell" about the "queerish mix" audible in Yost's attentions. His love as editor "for the put o' me"—the stream of her letters—was obvious to all, but PW also identified a "love that hath been alain away at the go o' her he loved adeep, the dame o' him. Yea, tis smiled I be" (PWR 2:343). While blessing the marriage of Casper and Anna Yost in the past tense, PW remarked a dormancy in what had been "alain away." Anna Parrott Yost, whose voice is rarely heard in the Record, was left to contemplate the import of a smile she could not see.

Casper Yost as loving husband had already, in 1907, written a book of advice on marriage in the form of letters from a fictional husband to a fictional son. John Sneed, Yost's advice-giving stand-in, announces himself a firm believer "by ginger!" in equality for women even if some of its advocates "do run over the line," and so long as the doctrine of "different spheres of action" is observed, "a mannish woman or a sissy" being "equally unnatural and abhorrent." From within his wife's domestic sphere, where "there is no better exercise in the world than housework," Sneed is happy to say that even after thirty years of marriage "I . . . am still in the midst of my honeymoon" and exhorts his engaged son, "You should never cease to be lovers."[18]

In the company of PW, Yost was disregarding John Sneed's chipper advice to his son: "[A]nd of all things on earth deliver me from amateur poetry, particularly when it's maudlin."[19] Over more than a decade, he received more than his share of the poetry dispensed to visitors, an imbalance occasionally righted by a poem to Anna Yost, "a dove, and puffed verily," as she was characterized in the first year of her visits to the Currans (PWR 1:157). Seven years later, PW reassuringly adopted Anna's voice, imploring "make me not afraid" and expressing the hope to remember the "same love which I accepted long agone, grown sweeter" (PWR 17:3111). With reserves of polite dalliance exhausted one evening, Yost erupted: "You're the greatest dame in the world or out of it" (PWR 8:1405), reviving the ardor of a pre-Christmas dialogue of 1917 that had him caught between her heaven and his earth:

Buz [Yost]. I know what I'd like to give you.
Patience. Lor', this be like unto the swain who would but canna and canna but would!
Buz. I'd like to put my arms around you and kiss you!
Patience. I said it were so!
Buz. I'm going to do it some time if I have to chase you all over heaven.

After PW urges her suitor to "tarry," complaining that spinsters are too often "plegged" by men thrice a grandsire's age, the dialogue continues:

Buz. . . . This is only brotherly love, Patience.
Patience. Lor', I hae heard that too! (PWR 6:1143–44)

Eventually, suitor-and-coquette light comedy gave way to the quest of an aging child-inquirer before Wisdom's seer. Without mentioning PW, and finally dedicating the book "to one whose faith needs no argument—My Wife," Yost undertook an ambitious inquiry into major questions of faith, finally publishing *The Quest of God: A Journalist's View of the Bases of Religious Faith* (originally titled "The Task") in 1929. Between PW writing sessions and within the smaller circle of what the Record calls "the Family," he proposed sequences of unanswerable questions ("Now tell us about the Resurrection" [PWR 2:289]) and read out entire chapters of his manuscript for the approval of his Puritan Egeria. After reviewing Yost's writing on immortality, PW spoke resignedly of his dependence on her: "I did to set the toddler 'pon path and yet he holdeth ever to the hand o' me" (PWR 1:151), a view Yost echoed two years later when he told his guide, "[Y]ou know what I want, Patience, better than I can tell it" (PWR 5:918). By 1919 "my book" became "our book." If the chapter on God fell short, Yost said, it was because there was "too much of me" in it and not enough Patience (PWR 10:1873), though eventually that voice could not help remarking, "what I be thou hast created . . . " (PWR 15:2830).

Through the time Yost worked on *The Quest of God,* Pearl Curran was moving PW from Ouija board to typewriter, diminishing mystery and bringing him closer to the medium's own voice. It is difficult to believe that Yost would never seriously have entertained the possibility of PW's being a dimension of Curran, awed though he may have been by language and gravitas he could not associate with her. Curran's awareness that she was medium to a radiance not associated with an editor's office appears in an image given to her by PW, she said, of Yost by his inkstand, weary with writing but looking up occasionally at a "quaint little figure" of PW resting on his desk in "whimsical costume." The poem that followed, "The Playfellow," dwells on the editor's gray days and "grind of labor" before pledging "I would become a bauble in thy hand" (PWR 13:2575). So perfectly sublimated into the great mysteries was the Pearl-Casper relationship that PW had no need to say to Anna Yost what she once told a visiting Theosophist, Mrs. Hotchner, as her husband looked on: "Nay I be not ahungered for thy laddie, dame! Lor, but thy handmaid might set him scorched!" (PWR 4:655).

After the death of John Curran in 1922 and Pearl's subsequent remarriage to Dr. Henry Rogers in 1928 (see Chapter 7), it became evident that the editor and the medium were traveling different paths. Casper Yost did not in print express second thoughts about his work on behalf of PW. A letter to Walter Franklin Prince, however, shows him clear-eyed on the subject of the medium: "If records depended on herself there wouldn't be any, and since her husband's death there has been no systematic preservation and duplication of records. She has always been personally more or less indifferent."[20]

As Pearl Rogers established her new base in California, where she moved with her new husband in 1930, Yost found himself at the periphery of the PW picture, soon leaving it entirely and outliving Pearl by only four years. In early 1930, as a guest at one of Rogers's return visits to St. Louis, he received a poem that seemed intended to bring up to date an old relationship. "Oh, my beloved, I ken! I ken!" PW began familiarly and went on to recall "those mute communions" begun in 1914 that had quenched his "ever-fretful thirst" (PWR 26:4032). Listening now to the voice of Mrs. Rogers, Yost no doubt concluded that he had already heard the last of the real PW.

The Puller and the Deep Well of Imagination

John Livingston Lowes's inquiry into the matter of Patience Worth was brief compared to Casper Yost's, but its lessons informed the major work of his scholarly career. *The Road to Xanadu,* published nine years after his move to Harvard in 1918, is a monumental study of the sources that supplied Coleridge's recombinative imagination in *Kubla Khan* and *The Rime of the Ancient Mariner* and an assiduous researching of what Coleridge read, or must have read, in order to write his poems.[21] In his preface, Lowes explains that the "substance of the book" had informed lectures at Harvard and Radcliffe as early as 1919, but he writes no preface to his preface. The work is dedicated to Mary Cornett Lowes, "who like the wedding guest could not choose but hear" and who also, as the Currans' guest in 1915, had heard PW along with her husband.

Like other university faculty drawn to a local phenomenon that had interest for professors of both literature and psychology, Lowes approached the Currans balancing skepticism against curiosity.[22] In the end he happily left the field to others, angered by what he regarded as the Currans' self-serving and dishonorable behavior. To read Lowes as a reader of PW is to discover a rough-draft prologue and unmistakable rehearsal for the "demystifying tactic" implicit in his study of Coleridge, a narrative, as Christopher Norris describes it, that "extenuates [*Kubla Khan*'s] visionary strangeness" by accounting for the "circumstances which surrounded its writing."[23] Despite his misgivings, however, Lowes's wondering admiration for what he saw of the earliest PW fiction already bore marks of the contradiction Norris sees in his "forked paths to Xanadu." That conflict pitted the remains of a quasireligious literary faith in the

Coleridgean Imagination, with its repetition in the finite mind of the infinite "I am," against the beginnings of materialist cognitive psychology, evident in Lowes's description of associative processes that serve as the "hooks and eyes" of literary creation, a metaphor in debt to Epicurus and contemporary psychologists like Morton Prince.[24] In 1915 Lowes was already struggling to reconcile his impression of a creative imagination with a psychology of "forgotten reading" operative in Pearl Curran's "secondary personality."

As professor of English and dean of Liberal Arts at Washington University, Lowes had no more allegiance to Spiritualism than Pearl Curran. But the PW tongue was Lowes's library speaking to him, its talk mindful of the language and literature that were his passion and profession, drawing him in with its mélange of regional British dialects and whimsical archaeology of periods. His 1911 address to the Burns Club of St. Louis had expressed a powerful nostalgia for an English language lost, portraying Burns as the last poet to speak with the "spontaneity" and "careless audacity" of the Elizabethans, who themselves had spoken "in a diction which was often like the large utterance of the early gods." In Burns he found language from the original stock, "racy with the tang of the soil" and giving promise of a new kind of "authentic speech" for English poetry.[25]

In PW, Lowes found a little of everything. The question was what, and how much, to make of it. Emily Hutchings, quoting Pearl Curran quoting Lowes, wrote that he had said, holding a page of the *Telka* manuscript, "If I could have written this, I would be a made man. My fame would be established."[26] In the end, Lowes felt fortunate to have preserved his reputation from the notoriety he felt was the Currans' element. But from March to November of 1915, a period that embraced the Ouija-board dictations of *Redwing* and *Telka* and the first short pieces of fiction, he took PW seriously enough to question the board on seventeenth-century English and New England history, conduct experiments with Curran on telepathy, travel to Boston to research Worth families in early New England, and, climactically, arrange a meeting between the Currans and Morton Prince in an attempt to apply "the scientific point of view." When Curran refused to submit to hypnotism—Lowes had understood that her willingness to put herself at Prince's service constituted prior approval of the experiment—he felt obligated to apologize to Prince for her "breach of faith," particularly since the Currans had made the abortive interview more sensational by promptly giving the story of it to the press.

Privately, Lowes kept notes on his interviews with Curran and in a series of letters forwarded them to Prince as "starting points for your own investigations should you use them,"[27] aware that the psychologist had already published *The Dissociation of a Personality* in 1906. By seeking a professional opinion, Lowes was attempting to enlarge his understanding of the mental processes that produced the PW text, in contrast to the quick, categorical study of a colleague like Edgar Swift. Emily Hutchings described Swift, a professor of psychology and soon to become chair of that department at Washington University, as an exemplar of "the oldest variety of intellectual snobs" after he gave a lecture comparing the "mental operations" demonstrated by Curran to those of a "trained horse that could apparently spell and do sums in arithmetic."[28]

Lowes would not finally have agreed with philosophy professor Charles Cory's judgment that Curran exhibited a "high degree of rationality" and was not subject to the pathology of dissociated personalities he had known. Cory's willingness to describe PW's "genius of no mean order," though, had been linked to his diagnosis of its workings as a release from "inhibitions that clog and check a normal consciousness." If Cory contributed to Lowes's thinking on Coleridge's experience of the imagination, it was in his description of PW's tranceless dissociation as a freeing from the world of sense into the strength and facility of "a dream without chaos" (*CPW,* 431–34). Applied to the PW writings, the term *genius* also appears in a Lowes letter to Morton Prince, and in *The Road to Xanadu* registers what was beyond investigation in Coleridge's "deep well of unconscious cerebration."[29] In the early going, Lowes already estimated that what was produced at the Ouija board fell "little short of talent of the highest order"—"even genius," by which he meant "artistic coherence, insight into character, and a rich naked vividness in its portrayal, richness of imagery, and the like."[30] Speculating, he associated the coming of PW with Curran's loss, unmentioned elsewhere, of her singing voice, and he passed on the family physician's remark that "'patience' [*sic*] really stood to Mrs. Curran in the place of a child." Both Currans had become wholly identified with the characters of *Telka:* "They really live and move and have their being in the thing." Between them, Lowes felt "unconscious *team work* [*sic*]," one understanding at times what the other did not, "and *vice-versa.*"[31]

In effect, Cory predicted the limit of Lowes's later research (and of mine) when he observed that even an inspection of Curran's reading "from childhood" could not establish all unnamed resources and would still leave open questions of attentional cues and memory triggers and unavailable information taken in without conscious attention. When Christopher Norris speaks of Lowes's "documentary detective work" he refers to an ambition Lowes told Morton Prince he had no time for, the "detective work" of looking into Curran's "past and probably forgotten reading."[32] Yet the persistence of habits and methodological assumptions developed in his investigation of PW appears early in the Coleridge book. Beginning his chapter on the imagination's deep well, Lowes uncovers an increasingly revelatory, or incriminating, series of passages in Joseph Priestley's *Opticks* that qualify as the basis of imagery in *The Rime of the Ancient Mariner.* The unfolding inquiry, connected by a string of clues and "aha!s," begins with Lowes confiding to the reader, "I cherished a stubborn suspicion (why, need not concern us now) that he had read Priestley's *Opticks.*"[33]

In the late fall of 1915, Lowes arrived at a darker view, telling Morton Prince after the Currans' trip to Boston that he had not at first realized the Currans' capacity "for abysmal and incredible folly." Until then he had been a close but sympathetic questioner, drawn to the speech of PW despite its "many glaring solecisms," finding the narratives "saturated with imaginative quality."[34] Beginning in March of that year, Lowes displayed what John Curran described as an "insatiable appetite" for the language of PW, joining Pearl for the dictation of *Telka,* asking whether Patience had known "Will Shakespeare" or George Fox, and requesting permission to smoke in her presence. Drawn into PW's verbal performance of pastoral England, he attempted an echo of it as compliment: "Your speech is racy of the lanes and hedge-rows; of spinsters and of knitters in the green." The board's nonchalant use of *steel* for "mirror" suggested to him that PW was quietly aware that metal mirrors persisted into the seventeenth century, but he grew suspicious when the board spelled *russet* for "rustic," when *bergers* who prattle had to be respelled, and when shepherds rather than Wise Men were said to have brought gifts of frankincense and myrrh to Bethlehem (PWR 1:106–7; 2:225).[35] Even more dubious was PW's maintaining that, except for consulting "His book," the Bible, she had not read the authors of her own time while obviously echoing later poets. As he attempted through questioning to place PW among the New England Worth family he had investigated, Lowes found the medium under "unusual nervous strain" and the board's responses fragmentary or distorted or desperately bad guesses, even when he willed a coherence on them, making "Dorset" out of *Dove coo,* for example.[36]

Often credited with reading the personality and history of visitors, PW characterized Lowes as an academic "puller o' grass" who was "packed past carry. Aye, but 'tis the tickle [o'] the word o' me that fetcheth o' him" (PWR 1:106, 137). Lowes seemed aware that he had found a revealing mirror. "You said to me that I did but pluck the grass, not gather o' the blossoms of the world. 'Tis so," he granted, before moving on to his next question and the remainder of his career (*SS,* 86; PWR 1:107). When, following a summer consultation with Morton Prince in Boston, Lowes told the Currans that he now viewed PW as a secondary personality of Pearl, his judgment "seemed to cast a gloom over Patience," John Curran wrote in the Record, since as historical confidante PW had counted on Lowes's fidelity "to all she had given to him of herself." The gloom quickly gave way to counterattack. When Lowes, no longer enamored of the board's language, observed that PW had become content merely to pass out "sweet things" to her audience and was beginning to repeat herself, the board took careful aim at the scholar's most vulnerable point: "Aye and thou hast pulled asour atimes." If it was literature he wanted, "e'en though thou deemest I be not me," PW urged him to follow the progress of *The Sorry Tale,* "mine reckoning with thee, for thou shalt sorry much o'er the putting o' it" (PWR 2:224). The tool of scholarship could only pull up what a creative imagination had planted.

Mentioning his break with the Currans, Lowes told James Hyslop in April 1916 that the PW archaisms were susceptible "of a comparatively simple explanation," sharing the Ozarks theory with him, and concluded that Yost's assertions about the language were "untenable." He was happy "to be absolutely out of the thing." When he wrote Morton Prince in the previous November that "all the King's horses and all the King's men can never again drag me near this, or anything remotely resembling it," he had only one regret, which he lingered over before writing again four days later. Yes, he granted, the Currans were as innocent of science as "a pair of unborn babes" and unable to distinguish "an archaism from an artichoke," but it was also true that Prince knew nothing of *Redwing* or the much longer *Telka* and would be unable to appreciate Lowes's initial enthusiasm for a "genuine creative imagination," with the result that "I am in the rather embarrassing position of having had the case tried without my only evidence!"[37]

It would be a stretch to suggest that Lowes's attempt to make out the genealogy of *Kubla Khan* from an upstream reading of Coleridge's tributary texts would not have occurred to him without his experience of Patience Worth, but he may well have carried forward to 1927 the warning against approaching literary texts only as a "puller." His familiarity with experiments on automatic writing led him to deprecate for a larger audience the "crassly mechanical" in favor of the mysteriously "involuntary and automatic operations" of the Well of Consciousness and its "forgetful pools." The endless flux in the artist's mind, its mingling of conscious and unconscious, is "only half the story," he argues, the rest belonging to a "shaping spirit." Lowes's alternative to literary archaeology, Christopher Norris points out, is to enact mimesis as criticism. To illuminate the poem to which Coleridge had attached his famous dream as a note of explanation, Lowes reports his own "wild night of fantastic dreams," culminating in familiar images, like that of "a sunny dome." With memory's pictures arriving in unexpected juxtapositions, Lowes finds himself reenacting the poet's experience of the priority of dream images to "the poem as a poem." The same experience had been described by Curran as a typical gift from PW. If PW lingered for Lowes on his road to Xanadu, it was in the phrase he repeated in a newly valorized cause: "All the king's horses and all the king's men" could not have accomplished the unearthly combinations he found wrought in Coleridge by the distinctly female "Imagination Creatrix."[38]

A tone of self-consciously frank admission in the preface to *Road to Xanadu* conceals the momentum that underlies Lowes's will to reunite the seeker with his primal library: "The Story which this book essays to tell was not of the author's choosing. It simply came, with supreme indifference to other plans, and autocratically demanded right of way,"[39] much as, for Pearl Curran, "the bolt fell." At another remove, the reader-critic who reads Lowes reading Coleridge through the lens of the PW phenomenon unavoidably adds to a series of Russian dolls.

Dear Doctor: The Other Prince

Walter Franklin Prince wanted it understood that he was not related to Morton Prince or "to his methods,"[40] though both psychologists had established themselves as early students of the dissociation of personality. Morton Prince's 1906 book on the subject, with its discovery of a succession of selves in "Christine Beauchamp," pronounced cured through his therapeutic hypnotism, earned him description as the "informal leader of a Boston salon of psychopathologists."[41] In the decade after Freud published his 1905 study of "Dora" as an example of hysteria traceable to oedipal-sexual conflicts, and shortly after Freud's 1909 visit to America, Walter Franklin Prince produced a two-part study of "Doris," as if introducing a nominal cousin of Freud's subject.[42] Walter Prince identified what would later be described as classic symptoms of multiple personality disorder, now called dissociative identity disorder (DID), and related the origin of the Doris personalities, or alters, to the childhood trauma of physical abuse by the father, noting the emotional triggers underlying "switching behavior" among personalities he termed Sick Doris, Sleeping Real Doris, Margaret, and Sleeping Margaret. The absence in the early twentieth century of any diagnostic boundary between alleged psychic phenomena and symptoms of DID is suggested by Prince's relation to James Hyslop, president of the American Society for Psychical Research and author of the preface to the ASPR publication of Prince's Doris study. Until 1920 Prince was assistant to Hyslop, then became executive research officer and editor with the Boston Society for Psychic Research, under whose auspices he published studies of "American slate-writing mediumship" and "past events seership."[43]

A further blurring of boundaries, both experimental and therapeutic, is evident in Prince's relation to the subject of his study, Doris Fischer, or "Theodosia," as Prince and his wife, Lelia, called the young woman they adopted in 1912 at the age of twenty-three after she had come for help to the Episcopal church in Pittsburgh at which Prince was rector. In his diary-like book *Psychic in the House,* a briefer continuation of his original Doris studies, Prince records a domestic drama played out in three "psychogenetic" houses as the Princes and their adopted daughter change addresses variously productive of rapping sounds, apparitions, crystal gazing, and automatic writing of messages to Theodosia from dead acquaintances, all these incursions attended to with intense professional interest by the man she called "Papa." By this time, Doris-Theodosia's personalities had disappeared or coalesced into one, Sleeping Margaret, who announced that from the age of three she had been charged to protect her host personality and was capable of discussing subjects in philosophy and psychology "that transcended Doris's ability."[44]

In Prince's treatment, Sleeping Margaret appears never to sleep. Keeping watch by night from a morris chair at his adopted daughter's bedside, Prince conducts conversations with the psychically talented remnant of the dissociative disorder he and his wife had attended to therapeutically. Appearing in the Princes' bedroom ("Mother, the spirits are acting dreadfully tonight"), Theodosia reported bed-shakings and mattress movements, which Prince confirmed by occupying the suspect bed himself and confirming with Theodosia next morning his experience of a "tremendous wriggling motion" sufficient to make his stomach "wamble." Prince's wife found experiences of the "uncanny" not fully respectable, but he made use of her testimony nonetheless to document rappings and other incidents that supported his observations. Confident that "my mind is not easily suggestible," Prince rejected the possibility that his foster daughter's behavior after her "cure" might have been a response to his own expectations as well as a more benign continuation of the original disorder. He rejected that implication even when his wife reported a house free of psychic activity during his absences—"as if my presence in some obscure way actually aided their production or they were produced for my benefit." When Prince began his PW investigations in 1926, his wife had been dead for two years. Theodosia, presumably remaining in Boston when Prince made his trips to St. Louis, would outlive her adoptive father, but her later life has not been documented beyond hearsay reports from a surviving associate of Prince's that she relapsed into insanity.[45]

An amateur magician "acquainted with the tricks of mendicancy," Prince attempted to distinguish between "evidentiary" psychic phenomena and skillful fraud; "the detective instinct is very strong in me," he claimed.[46] Having written an 1899 Yale dissertation titled "Three Studies in the History of Crime and Punishment in the Colonial Period," he believed himself a scientist of the psyche but in his career as a psychologist acted on the hypothesis that science would verify spirit. In practice he presented himself as a devil's advocate keen to expose fraud[47] for the sake of rare but genuine instances of the paranormal, and as an ex-pastor, he practiced therapy as a doctor of the soul. Most important for his relation to PW, he saw automatic writing as therapy rather than symptom and recalled a case in which he had recommended automatic writing to a woman who was evidently depressed. Released into automaticity, she had leapt "at the paper like a wolf at a lamb" and when finished writing, though disclaiming her agency, she rose from her chair "with color in her cheeks, and she has done well ever since."[48]

For Prince, Pearl Curran's ignorance of slates and crystals argued strongly for a true psychism, but not as strongly as the continuously arriving PW text. To that phenomenon he brought an announced enthusiasm for puzzle solving, selective flourishings of stern common sense, and large confidence in his ability to read character. His methodological empty-handedness and endlessly anecdotal approach would mean that for all its 509 pages, *The Case of Patience Worth* tells an experimental psychologist very little. Following a first stage of "Sherlocking on their heels," as he describes his investigation of previous mediums (*CPW,* 278), Prince reports that he became a PW confidante (after Casper Yost's advocacy had run its course).

When he published a preliminary report in 1926 on his investigation, subtitled "Conducted in a Scientific Manner by a Serious-minded Seeker after the Truth," it should have been clear that Walter Prince had decided quietly to oppose Morton Prince's view that Curran was being disingenuous. Describing a fellow investigator as holding "confirmed and inflexible" views, he declines to name the psychologist who had poked Pearl Curran with his finger, asking a putative PW, "Do you feel that?" Since Curran was without "hysterical stigmata," Prince argues, the poking had understandably left "an unpleasant impression." Her decision against hypnotism was well advised, he notes, since the same technique that might elicit certain facts could also privilege suggestions from the hypnotist. Prince's article is a forecast of the book that would follow, exhibiting PW's poetry, folk aphorisms, and Puritan-maiden views of the twenties, when flappers "dare what the past hoped for."[49]

Surprisingly, in view of his Doris study, Prince finds no more evidence in favor of a subconscious phenomenon, one whose "potencies" await further description, than he does for "some cause operating through" Curran, the two options he believes an investigator must choose between (*CPW,* 509). His fulsome displays of PW accomplishments amount to their own argument. In one table the quantitative PW is represented by the total number of words dictated on any given day over a period of three months while writing three works of fiction, numerous poems, and delivering quotable conversation (*CPW,* 346). The writer's "stunts," as Prince calls them, sometimes originate with PW but sometimes are prompted by her examiner, who asks her to write a poem in which each line begins with a letter of the alphabet in sequence, skipping X, and to deliver at an instant's notice passages in the style of four of her works (*CPW,* 282–85). Though fascinated by these performances, Prince comes to no conclusion that would link dissociation, automaticity, and exceptional verbal behavior in his juxtapositions of Pearl and Patience.

That Curran gradually learned to trust Prince and to count on him as a vindicator of her honesty and sanity had much to do with her discovery of the hopeful pastor behind the proclaimed scientist, a patient listener whose zeal was noncommercial. In the aftermath of his book's publication he wrote

Curran to say how much he valued the good opinion of PW, as if asking a friendly servant to take his part before her mistress: “I wish you would ask Patience herself what she thinks of the book. I feel a sort of affection for Patience, that very vivid entity, who is so wonderful in her mental endowment. And you know that I had some flirtations with her, though I have a very powerful rival in Mr. Yost, of whom I am very jealous.” In reply, the newly married Mrs. Rogers wrote that, to be sure, Patience was “bound to have a word,” which followed in the customary dialect of a Puritan coquette: “Sic a flurry as thy damie hath aneath her bibbin! A billet o’ her *ain*—and for a swain—! Lawk Sirrah and I’m sayin wooin a wraith be sorry fillin—eh?” If it did not seem “uppin’” on her part—before a parson at that—PW wanted to agree with her champion. “I ken much,” she asserted, while granting the occasional error that suggested she had not “kenned all.” What if he had found his “ladye” dull, “what then might keen thy quill or urge it pon thy script?” Desire, her parson should know, is the invisible writer’s name: “Ye see, I ken *thee* sirrah—and hae a loein’ for thee.”[50]

What Prince appreciated inadequately in Patience Worth and Sleeping Margaret both was the dissociative syndrome’s potential for drawing a self-appraised Sherlock into its fiction, investigation undermining itself as, in intimate circumstances, it invites construction, layer by layer, of what becomes dialogically real. The investigator too obeys a script, responding to a boldness of speech that denies its fictionality in a persuasively fictional voice, as PW did at the letter’s end when she forbade contradiction as “*P. W. herself.*” Rogers added, “(The lady seemed bound to have a word so I send it as it came original copy. Mrs. R.)”[51]

As beneficiary of Curran’s trust, Prince became the occasion for a final emptying out of her sense of betrayal and injustice, accumulated over the previous fourteen years. Their correspondence goes to the core of her revolt against examination. “You see,” she explained, “I have not been treated fairly *once*—and it still rankles with me.”[52] Still doing battle with Morton Prince “and his ilk,” she granted, “If he wishes to convey the idea that in the ‘Patience Worth’ idea I have unconsciously lied–that is one thing & there is a prettier and safer way to state it.” Her real failure, she argued, was in not providing him with evidence “on which to base his theories—consequently I *had* to be a liar. It is very hard to stand such things Dr. Prince.” To her fairest judge, she submitted accumulated grievances: against Hyslop, who got off “even without hearing my testimony”; against Emily Hutchings, who had “busily spread” her rival account “quite slyly since she first began to lose credit for the phenomenon”; then, in a raised voice mindful of her control, “and now Prince prances forward bravely and we must let him spout—!” Even a psychic “*may* be truthful,” she asserted, and in her own voice.[53]

A latent uneasiness about Walter Prince's book was evident when Curran wrote him in the last days of 1926, concerned that she had heard nothing of progress toward publication. The depth of her concern quickened the mother nerve that was interwoven with so much of the PW text and that Curran gave figurative form in defending herself against "vivisection." Womb and voice were one when she described herself to Prince as "sort of in the [same] position as [a] mother who had delivered her dead child's body for autopsy might be—both as to Patience and whatever part my own personality may play for or against her." When Curran apologized within the week, "I talk too quick, too much & too often," Prince moved to regain her confidence with news that he had deleted Emily Hutchings's version of the genesis of PW and fully accepted hers. As for Morton Prince, "I have hit him quite adroitly several times in the book," he wrote, referring to his systematic refutation of "Dr. Hyslop's criticisms" (*CPW,* 420–28).[54] Though he had known of Hutchings's attempts to discredit Curran, he was evidently unaware of Hutchings's correspondence with Hyslop when he suggested that his former ASPR colleague apparently had a secret informant, which together with "defective scientific handling" resulted in "very doubtful justice" (*CPW,* 423).

For all his efforts, Prince soon had to wonder whether his labors were appreciated when he heard nothing from the new Mrs. Rogers following publication of his book. In addition to his inquiry to Yost, he complained to T. H. McQueary of St. Louis, a high school teacher turned Episcopal minister, and expressed concern that not only had Pearl grown silent, he had received no expressions of interest in his book from the PW circle of friends, which he said "surprises and saddens me." McQueary assured Prince that Pearl was "delighted with the book" and seems to have passed on Prince's concern. Pearl's period of silence overlapped with her marriage to Dr. Rogers, but replying on the same day as McQueary she told Prince, "Surely no one could have treated the subject more fairly. . . . I am deeply indebted to you."[55]

Seven years later, prompted by Prince's inquiry to a mutual friend and with much of her PW identity diminished, Pearl wrote in 1934 to ask Prince: "I wonder, being a woman, what you have found to prompt you to wish to hear from me." With Prince as with Yost, Pearl had felt most sane in the company of paternal authorities who validated her phenomenal self, even when their awe derived from the character of their own seeking and carried with it an implication of her ordinariness as the basis for estimating PW's mind and work. Looking ahead from Santa Monica to a further sharing of "interesting experiences too long and intricate to write you," she urged Prince, "do write me," and, now married a third time, signed herself "Pearl L. Wyman."[56] In the remaining six months of Prince's life, illness may have prevented him from replying. He died on August 7, 1934.

I-Mary (Austin) and Patience

It is not difficult to understand why popular interest in the PW writings took on a look of regression to women like Agnes Repplier and Mary Austin, whose writing lives represented a hard-won victory over entrenched editors and reviewers. Repplier (1855–1950) made Patience Worth the object in 1918 of a notably acidic treatment. A contributor to the *Atlantic Monthly* for thirty years, Repplier counted herself among the anti-modernists who, as Jackson Lears has shown, embraced chivalric medievalism and deplored "the decay of sentiment" among the urban bourgeoisie. Her counterattack on the demythification of the past and her expressed preference in 1886 for the picturesqueness of medieval faith might have disposed her in favor of the author of *Telka* had she spoken after its 1928 publication. Instead, her detection of counterfeit medievalism and huckstering spiritualism in the case of Patience Worth made her an unqualified antagonist. With graveyard humor her only hedge against expressing outright contempt, Repplier singled out PW in an essay titled "Dead Authors" for the absurdity, opacity, and unrelenting didacticism of her writing and for what Repplier found PW's greatest threat to the reader—her undead desire to continue to add to the mounting total of her published words.[57]

The most searching criticism of claims made for discarnate dictation came from Mary Austin, writing in response to Curran's "Nut for Psychologists." Though Austin's mature aesthetic is sometimes described as mystical, her criticism of PW is consistent with her struggle to become the artist she had felt herself to be from childhood. Only recently has Austin been given adequate attention as a writer drawn to the folkloric culture and native inhabitants of the American Southwest in such works as *The Land of Little Rain* (1903) and *Lost Borders* (1909).[58] Austin first charted her development from an alienated midwestern childhood to her discovery of an identity of the imagination in an autobiographical portrait of the artist, *A Woman of Genius* (1912), then in her later autobiography *Earth Horizon* (1932), either of which could be taken as a basis of sympathy with Curran's ambitions. But Curran's readiness to displace her writing life onto a specter, together with what seemed naïve marveling at powers beyond her own, failed Austin's stringent test of artistic sisterhood.

Mary Austin too had made much of a secondary personality, which she called "I-Mary" in *Earth Horizon,* as if taking up a challenge from contemporary investigators of female dissociation, invoking at once a more than first person and her awareness of its role in the dynamic of her identity. The entity is neither a Doris nor a PW but an invulnerable core of self superior to such events as the deaths of a doting father or of the younger sister on whom Mary doted. As if her death were negotiable, I-Mary must prevail over rejection, as when her mother at the sister's grave cries, "Why couldn't it have been Mary?"

From that pit, I-Mary becomes the standpoint of Austin's detachment from, yet ambitious wording of, the world and the stream of "pictures" it will offer its temporary custodian. Austin's PW, unlike Agnes Repplier's, is no laughable cartoon. Austin's dispassionate itemizing of the common experience of writers, set against Curran's claims of extraordinariness, has a deconstructive but not a destructive tendency. Austin lays bare Curran's reports on her experience as being simply uninformed, along with Austin's certainty that what PW has written is "all literature." Having grown up in Carlinville, Illinois, Austin does not attribute naïveté to limitations of region or education. What Curran does not know, Austin implies, is herself. Unnecessarily welcomed as Other, dissociated creativity seals off the writer from herself, Austin warns. When she reached back to an early memory of tall white "Presences," Austin learned to understand them as the working of her "own subliminal self."[59]

As part of his *Case of Patience Worth,* Walter Prince reprinted portions of Austin's naturalization of creativity (*CPW,* 464–70) in order to assemble a dogged rebuttal of it, demanding that explanatory space be left for the "supernormal, whether telepathy, spirits or the Great Cosmic Puddle be called in." Yet Austin's discovery as a writer, during the period that involved her glance at PW, was that the natural was supernormal enough. When she first began to write, Austin had experienced "I-Mary" as a "stream of knowingness . . . creating certainties for which no warrant was to be found in my ordinary experience."[60] In her first experience of the American West, she called on the language but not the traditional faith of mysticism when she discovered "a lurking, evasive Something . . . insistent on being noticed . . . yearning to be made human."[61] The arrival of that "Something" in one's text provokes "a mild form of ecstacy [*sic*]" in the writer, whose most important processes may "take place out of sight"—Austin notes *Kubla Khan*—but the Freudians are wrong to suggest that "deleterious effects" follow from repression if they fail to understand that revision, even "censorship" of instinct, is what writers call craftsmanship.[62]

More than any of Curran's inquisitors and, one might argue, more than PW's champions, Austin made the most serious attempt to value the writer reduced to medium by returning the medium to herself. She had heard enough of Curran's "great natural gifts" to hope that she would throw off the obsession with Patience Worth in order to make "genuine contributions to the elucidation of the Unconscious."[63]

Chapter 7

PEARL AND PATIENCE IN THE TWENTIES

A Circle of Art

By the spring of 1921, when her story "Rosa Alvaro, Entrante" appeared as a film from the Goldwyn Studio, Pearl Curran had reason to believe that whatever the economic returns from PW's continuing dictations, her career was gaining momentum. Instead, the decade's early years would unscroll more difficult transitions than she could have guessed. The sudden death of William Reedy in the previous year had had no obvious effect on PW's productivity, but his passing from their circle of support deprived the Currans of a tough-minded and respected national publicist. Though unsuccessful in promoting *The Sorry Tale* as a film, he had passed along his high valuation of the novel to Anna George de Mille (mother of choreographer Agnes de Mille), who replied with a letter suggesting that he advise Curran that the local "movie staff" had had difficulty reading PW's prose, "although I get it very easily," Reedy wrote back to de Mille.[1]

For Curran, access to *Reedy's Mirror* had also meant connection with a larger circle of St. Louis women writers, a population largely ignored in studies from Walter Prince's study onward. When Reedy wrote his final dispatch from California to *Mirror* readers on July 29, 1920 ("Then it's ho for Catalina island and the port of Avalon"), he could count among them a number of women who had earned his critical imprimatur and whose careers he had, in one way or another, been involved with. Welcoming Reedy, the Currans would need to have been extraordinarily innocent not to have registered something of his past, including his affair, circa 1905, with the young Zoë Akins, later a Pulitzer Prize–winning playwright, but at eighteen the recipient of Reedy's middle-aged tributes to "the dawn spirit of you, the fresh, free spirit of you."[2] The range of Reedy's hospitableness to women who wrote is suggested by his early printing of Emily Dickinson poems, his support of Kate Chopin after her return to St. Louis from Louisiana—Chopin used Reedy as a model for the young wanderer in "A Vocation and a Voice"[3]—and his welcoming of a young Fannie Hurst, who had been excluded from the St. Louis women's art club, the Potters. ("I would rather be a classic failure than a popular success like Fannie Hurst," said an unnamed Potter.)[4] He gave equal encouragement to Akins, an Ozarks native, and to Sara Teasdale, born into wealth, past the time when his affair with Akins had ended and before the two writers found fame in New York.[5]

The subtext of Reedy's encouragement to women writers was another matter, lupine in the case of Fannie Hurst: "Hello, college girl. I am going to print your story 'Episode.' It is as wobbly as a new calf but there is talent in it. Come into my office and let me meet you," and as a frustrated voyeur when he described Teasdale as "a middle-westerner who bathes under a sheet."[6] A strain of his Catholic education may have persisted in his enthusiastic praise of *The Sorry Tale,* but an instinct for his readers' taste led him to reprint Theia's defiant dance before Tiberius, and he flaunted his reputation for philandering in the titles of reports like "My Flirtation with Patience Worth," published in his *Mirror* on October 7, 1915. By the time he earned the nickname "Fat-A-Wide" from PW, he had settled into rural domesticity with the second of two madams he married, his third wife, Margaret (or Margery or Gretchen) Rhodes Reedy, who often accompanied him on their visits to the Curran house for her own "sweets" of poetry, but found PW's treatment of her not to her liking ("That's real mean of you Patience, and I'm mad at you."), as when PW pronounced her a "tinder-wench" who "dost touch off the tinderspark and run ye awhither to flee the fires." Margaret Reedy nevertheless returned in the fall following her husband's death to receive a PW poem on "his Departure" (PWR 2:250; 14:2703). On the day following news of Reedy's death, the Record observes that "it seemed the world was black for some of our dearest friends" (PWR 13:2553).

While daughters of the grande dames of the Mississippi sought an audience with the author of *The Sorry Tale* and *Hope Trueblood* as patron saint of their creative ambitions, Pearl Curran was accepting invitations from their sites of cultural clubship, the Theosophical Society, the Papyrus Club, the Psycho-Success Club, and the Wednesday Club. As a newcomer among St. Louis's traditional elite, she was a petitioner at the city's gates of wealth and respectability and to its guardians of art and religion, while, with PW at her fingertips, she was widely seen as custodian of revelations to which she alone had access. Not all visitors who came to hear PW were named in the Record, but a significant number had gained their own celebrity, including the World's Fair president, later Missouri governor and ambassador to Russia, David Francis (PWR 12:2269). Names firmly established as part of St. Louis history—Chouteau, Blewett, Danforth, Hadley, Schlafly—were often represented by husband and wife on an initial visit to PW, then by the wife alone. Others, like the Countess Kingston—domain unspecified—and a Mme. Ballu, who told Patience "you are like our own Jean d'Arc" (PWR 4:723), suggest that the Curran parlor was among stops of interest for foreign visitors. Hadley Richardson, Ernest Hemingway's first wife, was taken to the nearby Curran house by her theosophically inclined mother, Florence, who had been widowed by the suicide of her husband in 1903, but Hadley "remained skeptical about it all, even though Mrs. Curran prophesied great things for her future."[7]

For every Sara Teasdale or Zoë Akins who expanded their horizons by leaving St. Louis—and the émigrés would eventually include both the founders of the Potters and Pearl herself—there were dozens of others appearing on the Curran guest list who aspired only to identify their psychic talents with their invisible hostess. At a Red Cross fund-raising evening in November 1917, Rosalind Day, a frequent visitor to the Currans, had played a violin solo described in PW's *Magazine* as "a special delight" (*PWM,* Jan. 1918, 13). Several years later, a fully initiated Day, "who had never composed before" (PWR 14:2607), took her place by Curran's side, providing settings at the piano for PW poems and claiming to receive her inspiration, "both words and music," directly and simultaneously from PW. Running a total in the following year, John Curran announced that the collaboration had produced forty-six songs, the result, PW said, of a mutual "throbbin'" (PWR 16:2958, 2968, 2608).

Maizie Fitzroy, an artist and a musician, occupied herself on one of her frequent visits by sketching an intuited portrait of PW that has to be imagined from its subject's comment on a winking eye and twitching smile (PWR 5:996). Adept at automatically delivered sketches of departed spirits, Fitzroy had moved PW to praise her "stir o' wraiths," leading to an agreement that she would illustrate "The Merry Tale" (PWR 2:363). It made little difference that her initial drawings seemed to have nothing to do with the story since that meandering diversion had arrived, after "a muck o' a put," at "a pretty rough place" (PWR 5:838–39). PW made clear that Fitzroy should not think of herself as a maker of literature: "thou art at the weavin' o' a cloth thou knowest not o'" (PWR 5:862).

Similarities between the automatic arts of Fitzroy and Curran drew the attention of philosophy professor Charles Cory when he wrote the last of his PW studies, an inquiry into the subconscious promptings and physical manifestations he observed in sketches made by Fitzroy, whom he identifies only as a fifty-year-old, unmarried St. Louis woman. At about the time of Curran's first trial of the Ouija board, Fitzroy discovered that her hand moved without effort or control as she sketched faces not summoned by conscious forethought, the experience of automaticity inducing "a degree of anesthesia" that could become a general numbness when she drew blindfolded.[8]

Fitzroy's vivid, almost "hallucinatory" visual imagination led Cory to inquire into the connection between what professional judges described as the "considerable" merit of her portrait sketches—though they resembled no one she knew—and her lifelong repression of "strong feeling" behind a "reserved" exterior, emotion turned further inward by her loss of hearing, beginning at age twenty. That none of the attempted sketches, of a man or woman, extended beyond head or bust prompted Cory, with no reference to Freud, to theorize that matters "of a sex character" suggested a pattern of repression, while a vital freedom had appeared in Fitzroy's relations with "the world of art and literature"—"*and only where the mind is free is it receptive.*" Fitzroy's drawings had surfaced from processes of transformed memory, Cory suggested, and he might have added, from the priming effect of PW's example. For students of the subconscious, he reproduced two of her sketches, one a possible trial of her assignment as "Merry Tale" illustrator of a character like Cato, a jowly, peasant-capped PW attempt at a Falstaffian character.[9]

For women whose careers as artists were already established, PW's invisibility qualified her as a widely adaptable and respectable muse. Amy Beach, America's most accomplished female composer when she visited the Currans in January 1918, was appearing with the St. Louis Symphony to play her Piano Concerto in C-sharp Minor. An enthusiastic review by the *St. Louis Post-Dispatch* described Beach as "a composer of brilliant genius irrespective of sex."[10] In return for her visit, she received from PW a prayer, which she said in a letter used as a testimonial in *Patience Worth's Magazine* had "helped me more than I can express in words" (*CPW*, 68). More memorable yet, she added, was the impression of power left by PW's dictation for *The Sorry Tale,* which resonated with Beach's ambition to compose music beyond historically gendered criteria of polished delicacy.

If a path to Hollywood was cleared for Pearl Curran by a St. Louis woman, it would, again, have been Fannie Hurst, who in the three years after her 1917 conversation with PW had four of her stories made into silent films, two of them in 1919. Possibly through channels opened by Hurst, the Currans negotiated film rights for "Rosa Alvaro, Entrante" with the Goldwyn Studio, whose copyright to *What Happened to Rosa?* is dated November 22, 1920, with the film's release coming on April 23, 1921.[11] Fannie Hurst's *Humoresque,* based on her 1919 *Cosmopolitan* story of the same name, had been released in September

1920 and *What Happened to Rosa?* followed the same succession from popular magazine (*Saturday Evening Post*) to movie in the same span of years.

The delay in releasing *What Happened to Rosa?* until April 1921 has been attributed to Goldwyn's concern over visible traces in some scenes of actress Mabel Normand's alcoholism and drug abuse. A major silent-film star, Normand played the dual part of Mayme Ladd and Rosa, lending importance to the film as the only surviving representative of sixteen Goldwyn-Normand collaborations. A recent retrospect on Normand's performance as Rosa calls attention to her dark, sunken eyes as signs of her depression and addiction but concludes that "given good material to work with," her "delightful pantomimic ability" shone through. A popular biography of Normand, unaware of the film's derivation, describes the *Rosa* plot as incoherent and its Spanish Cinderella figure as "schizophrenic."[12]

What Happened to Rosa? is played for laughs, and for heightened romance. The fictional Mayme Ladd's ambiguous sense of dual identities, summed up in the original story's concluding question mark, is erased in favor of a Mayme more obviously determined to bring out her inner Rosa by dressing herself in Spanish costume. The story's analytic Dr. Drew is promoted from observer to love interest, smitten by the beguiling Rosa at a costume party on board the *Mandalay*, then losing track of her after she swims ashore and makes her way back to his office, disguised as an injured boy, to claim her Spanish costume and his heart. As if to suggest that Curran's entrepreneurial career should remain the less-told story, the PW Record makes no mention of the film or the publicity that presumably would have accompanied its showing in St. Louis; nor is the film mentioned by Prince or Litvag in their studies of PW.

Privately, Curran revealed that after "a good deal of corresponding" she had sold her story to Goldwyn for "FIFTEEN HUNDRED DOLLARS! . . . Oh my dears can you imagine!" she wrote to unnamed friends she had recently visited in New York. The future could well belong to the living writer, she probably thought, even as she granted that "the Patience Worth stuff has been wonderful of late." A theater company preparing to turn "Rosa" into a one-act play had expressed interest in "any and all" of her stories—"if I can just deliver the goods," and she had sent a new story, "Sprig O' Heather," apparently never published, to the *Post*. Behind the excitement, Curran's precarious balancing of determinedly conscious against automatic agency remained even as she wrote her friends, telling them that she must assure herself that her own writing "has been a boost rather than a detriment" to PW, she must "keep humble" and "not get foolish," and she must remember "that God gave me an angel to help me," confessing, "Theres [*sic*] no telling how much she has done of my stuff and I know that." And there was unease about John, who had begun a new and struggling business at a shale plant in Colorado—referred to in the Record as a "long siege" and "the hard fight in Denver"—in the year before he fell ill (PWR 14:2606, 2657). Pearl's diagnosis was ambivalent. Though "Jack" was doing quite well, he was "not himself at all." Adding his name to her own she ended a mostly celebratory letter by hoping that their recent hard times are over and that her good news "will be the means of restoring him to his health."[13]

The Nun and the Knight

What neither Pearl nor Patience could foresee in the year following Reedy's death was the death of John Curran two years after, in the summer of 1922. His steady support of the PW project would be partly replaced when, after his death, Pearl ambitiously widened her scope of performance, but his absence from the Record as enthusiastic witness to PW's table talk can be felt in the minimal, irregular stenography that followed. No Svengali or Westervelt, John Curran had in a sense been co-manager with Pearl of PW enterprises and first among her audience of defenders. In the four years before Pearl remarried, her ambition became more publicly visible, and its income, however irregular, more necessary, but the birth of her first biological child six months after John's death raised a question whether the figure of Patience the handmaiden had not been more mask than expression. With David Copperfield, Pearl's daughter might have said, "My father's eyes had closed upon the light of this world six months when mine opened on it."

In the spring of 1921, more definite signs of John Curran's illness began to appear. In March the Record reports a "recent sickness," perhaps only a "bilge belly," PW suggests, while John calls for "a little sympathy" (PWR 15:2815). On April 7 he is reported to be at Barnes Hospital but by the end of the month has returned home, where PW addresses him with a nickname to be repeated in the series of get-well poems she addresses to him over the coming year: "Thee art mouthin' o'er smooth pebbles, laddie, Swallow 'em" (PWR 15:2871). The PW poems resemble previous attempts to pledge troth to male members of her audience, but more pointedly now, repeating a metaphor of "tryst," they reflect Pearl's anxiety for her husband: "Laddie, Laddie, oh the trystin', / . . . Be it not / A pledge o' lovin'?" (PWR 15:2890). St. Luke's Hospital becomes John's new address, and in June he is described as "recovering from a relapse which had cost Mrs. Curran many anxious days." PW tells him, "I cannot sing unto pale stars. . . . I need thee that I may sing" (PWR 15:2932).

At intervals, John was able to return home. In October, several PW followers gathered upstairs with him when he was unable to leave his bed. As relief from his complaints, "Patience gave Mrs. Curran a picture of him riding the long narrow bed as though it was a nag" (PWR 16:3012). In a matter of weeks both Pearl and John would be at St. Luke's, she for an emergency appendectomy, he presumably from another relapse, their rooms across the hall from one another. The Record is written to reflect John Curran's point of view as he learns that Pearl will be operated on by Dr. Harvey Mudd, "the great surgeon," and the couple is allowed to speak for a few minutes before the operation. "Each was strengthened by the sight and touch of the other," reflects the record-keeper, "and at 10.35 Mr. Curran, standing at his door, said 'Good luck, pal' and watched the nurses wheel the white figure down the hall and into the elevator." Patience was with her, Pearl told John after the operation, the familiar voice a "croon" above the murmur of a brook and images of hyacinths and daisies (PWR 16:3019).

John Curran's decline is irregularly reported from the winter of 1921–1922 to his death in June, but its direction is clear. Two weeks before Christmas his illness is "severe," following "a stroke of paralysis in his right hand." A week later, at rest "in a bedroom above," he is described as in "critical condition" (PWR 16:3054). In the absence of its experienced reporter, the Record is dutiful but spare, and it is possible that others had quietly substituted for him in the seven years since he took the Record into his own hands. The language of the Ouija board had woven together love and atoms and cosmic harmonies, but John's reporting evoked the urban, domestic setting of the "hut," as when, with the temperature at twelve below and daughter Julia at the movies, the January snow "sifts into crannies" at the site of the Currans' communications with the beyond (PWR 6:1159). At times, the record-keeper could seem outside the action. When "Mr. and Mrs. Curran 'put on' one of their quarrels," the text moves to PW's weariness at "the babes that set them at fool's gabbin'" (PWR 6:1068). But John had pledged himself to the idea of PW, even adopting her spelling as he signed off from one evening's session: "I am loth to leave even the writing of this record, as loth as we all were to say good night. But this night will be lived over and over again in the memory of those who were there, each one of whom came and went with heart tuned with that of the little gray dame who reached out of the dark to soothe and comfort and heal" (PWR 6:1004). More orgasmically than Casper Yost would have worded his bond with Patience, John could say of the voice he heard in his wife's voice, "We simply groaned out our love for her" (PWR 4:628).

On June 1, 1922, "after an illness that confined him to his bed for over a year," the *St. Louis Globe-Democrat* reported that John Curran was dead at the age of fifty-four. The obituary, moving quickly to his association with the "matter known as the Patience Worth Writings," was probably written by Editorial Director Casper Yost since it assures readers that little profit was made from the sale of the writings and "no profit whatever" from any related boost in Ouija-board sales. Secondarily, Curran's public life receives attention, including his brief political career as Populist candidate for secretary of state in Kansas. The new Colorado business spoken of in the Record is given as the Process Engineering Company, with Curran as its secretary until the previous year.[14]

In the time leading up to John Curran's death, PW's commentaries serve as an index to his wife's state of mind. "I hae e'en lied a whit," the poet admitted, acknowledging that she had sometimes counseled hope against others' despair, even when there was little basis for it, as the task of her "ministration." "I hae sayed hope sails a bird hither, and I kenned that the eagle sought its prey" (PWR 17:3149). For two months, from April 13 until shortly after John's death, there are no entries in the Record, until finally PW's memorial poem is recorded. After services in the Curran home by an Episcopal clergyman, John's body was taken to Mound City, Illinois, for burial near Pearl's father, George Pollard, and a PW dedicatory poem titled "The Triumph of Death" was read to the mourners, whose names are not given in the Record. The triumph belongs to a young eagle, "Unfettered of the day / Freed for the heights," PW having transformed the predator to an ascendant soul (*SS*, 230). A later PW manuscript titled "The Eaglet" might suggest a continued attempt to work out the figure's valence and the experience that gave rise to it, but that question is subordinate to another, more challenging puzzle.

As both Litvag and, much earlier, Walter Prince report without comment, Pearl Curran, then thirty-nine, was pregnant at the time of her husband's death. Eileen Curran, who would have been conceived somewhat more than two months before John Curran died, was born on December 21, 1922. The improbability that the Currans, married since 1907 and readily compliant with the Ouija board's instruction that they adopt a child in 1916, should finally conceive on John's deathbed was surely a subject of discussion within and beyond the PW circle but has not appeared in any related documents including, unsurprisingly, the PW Record. Eileen's birth certificate gives her as the daughter of John and Pearl Curran while noting John as deceased and Pearl as "authoress" returned to Kingsbury Avenue, only a few blocks from the site where PW originally spelled herself. A 1943 revision of Eileen's St. Louis City birth certificate, when she was twenty, indicates that her name had mistakenly been entered as "Eilene Elnore" rather than "Eileen Lenore." The surname is clearly *Curran*.

Whether Eileen had information directly from her mother or after 1937 from surviving friends of the family, it is clear that as an adult she did not believe herself to be John Curran's daughter. Ruth Duell, whose preliminary inquiries into the case of Patience Worth began in the late 1950s, cast a wider net than Walter Prince when she interviewed or questioned by letter persons close to the Curran family, and at one point Eileen herself. In its frankness concerning her mother and older sister, the sketchy interview with Eileen provides a less reverent portrait of Pearl than had earlier accounts, passing on the comment of a local "church lady" who told Eileen, "Your mother was drunk," after Curran had gone to a dinner whose attraction was its apple brandy. Apart from stating that she had been born in a Catholic hospital—her birth certificate names St. John's—and was baptized Catholic, Eileen confided nothing about her birth in the interview except to say that when a boy's name, *John,* presumably chosen by Pearl in memory of her late husband, had to be set aside, a nun had suggested, in the fragmentary language of Duell's notes, "why not Eileen, so was."[15]

Nor is another item in the American Society for Psychical Research's Patience Worth Collection, a letter from Eileen's second husband, Ralph Kleymeyer, any more helpful. Writing Ruth Duell in advance of her interview visit to New Orleans, Kleymeyer said only that Eileen's birth "was, of course, something of a surprise."[16] More recently, in an unsolicited letter to the author, Kleymeyer stated unambiguously that Eileen's father was a married man with whom Pearl was having an affair. Though Kleymeyer said he was unable to remember the name of the man Eileen believed to be her father, he claimed to have once called a nephew of the same name out of the St. Louis phone book, with Eileen's knowledge, awakening more interest from him than he had expected but gaining no further information. The alleged father had died earlier, Kleymeyer came to believe, the widow at that time was still living, and no further inquiries were made.[17]

Only one name has been suggested. Its source, appearing in a Ruth Duell interview from 1957, was the eighty-four-year-old Mrs. A. P. Holland, the family friend who had also suggested that Patience Wee might have been the daughter of John Curran's sixteen-year-old daughter, Julia. While the question of Eileen's paternity is unlikely ever to be established with certainty, Holland's gossipy recollections accord well with features of the PW Record in the period just before and following John Curran's death. According to Holland, who recalled that at one point she "took care of Eileen," Pearl was "very much in love with" John Cashman (sometimes spelled "Cushman" in the Duell notes), a "prominent and attractive St. Louis lawyer married and of staunch catholic family."[18] Cashman's prominence is suggested by a 1918 profile in *Reedy's Mirror* that describes him as "one of the busiest lawyers in the city," first as an attorney for the Missouri Pacific Railroad, then as partner in a downtown law firm. He addressed juries, according to the *Mirror,* "in such a forceful, clear, perspicacious fashion that it is hard for them to escape accepting his contention. He always has the law and he always appears to think he has the facts as well, on his side."[19]

While speaking of Cashman as "purported to be the father of Eileen," Holland went on to say that John Curran's "handsome funeral" was paid for by Cashman—"rather shoddy," she continued, "because of the scandal," and a jarring note set next to her assertion that "at Curran's funeral [Pearl] became almost hysterical." If a scandal circulated, no other source reports on it, but Holland enlarged on her suggestion with an anecdote that has Pearl, "without letting her mother know," going to visit Cashman in Chicago "for an early assignation" and added that Pearl was later urged to marry Cashman's brother "Jo" in order to "make Eileen legal. Said no." Whatever the trustworthiness of Holland's memory, or intentions, twenty years after Pearl's death, she delivers information to the interviewer in the manner of a family insider, commenting bluntly on drinking habits, divorces, and enmities (Curran and Emily Hutchings "fought like cats"), while never referring to the Curran/PW writings.

In the relevant years, John Cashman is very much in evidence in the pages of the Record, sometimes appearing at PW sessions with his wife and daughters. On the increasingly rare occasions when John Curran was able to keep the Record, he and Cashman would have spent time together, and they certainly knew each other. Cashman also seems to have been acquainted with Emily Hutchings since their names are entered together for a session of August 18, 1921, four months after John Curran's first hospitalization. With characteristic fullness, John Curran describes PW responding to a ribbon in the colors of the new Irish Republic, given Edwin Hutchings by Eamon de Valera. To a PW poem on a "newer day" for Ireland, Cashman explains authoritatively that the ribbon's golden sunburst was "the symbol of the Irish nation and its fight for freedom." He is rewarded by PW with a chilly bow to the "legal light." "What be it then, sirrah? Is justice law, or be law justice? A wiser head than thee needs ponder o'er it." A prose-poem, "The Lawyer," then follows, as if Cashman were defending his profession, tasked with the "cajoling of wisdom against folly" while "days shriek their complaints." Meanwhile, "beloved," continues the poem, "I turn to thee and the depth and surety of thine eyes, / And the soft touch of thy hands, and the gentle / Cadence of thy voice . . . " (PWR 16:2983).

Casper Yost and others had been "beloved" long before Cashman made his first appearance. Since PW regularly chided human folly, her observations on "Treachery" in the following month do not necessarily have personal implications, as when the medium sketches a deceptive lover "who lays his cheek to thine and sweareth troth." But the charge is insistent. "I love liars," says the dialectally unadorned prose of a September 1921 record. They are after all "such a common lot. All men are liars and bred of women who first begot lying" (PWR 16:3005). If PW was Pearl's inner eye, it shifted back and forth during this period from John Curran and the state of his health to John Cashman and the question of constancy. The Record entry of October 27 from the Currans' joint hospital stay has the PW voice jauntily describing Pearl "half a-dream" as she "slip[ped] *ether*ward" for her appendectomy. Returned to consciousness with Pearl, PW addresses a poem to John that acknowledges "secret longings" and "betraying words wherein / My confession may be read," but promises, "Ne'er shall I / Betray and ne'er forsake my plight. . . . This be a troth" (PWR 16:3020). In early November 1921, the Record notes that Curran has had "a good cry" at her husband's decline while PW attempts to bolster her faith. The poetry already contemplates the Currans as "Parted," voicing Pearl as she labors with "sore-laggard days," which would include a tonsillectomy for Patience Wee in November and the stroke in December that left John Curran's right hand paralyzed (PWR 17:3042, 3052).

As John Curran declined and John Cashman's attendance became increasingly regular, variations in PW's use of the figure of wine provide glimpses of the medium's more than instrumental presence in what she dictates. As the new year of 1922 begins, PW resolves to hold her mug for each day's offering, bitter or sweet, supping it "to my valor" if sweet, but if bitter, "I shall spread my legs and spat" (PWR 17:3069). On January 16, a wry tone of stoicism drives out poetry in a couplet titled "Fickle":

> Yesterday I wept and today I forgot it.
> Today I smiled and tomorrow I shall forget it.

On January 23, Mr. and Mrs. Cashman and their daughters Alma and Mary join "the Family" for a session. One daughter is given a lighter poem, "My Friend Day," the other is instructed on Earth's cloak of compassion (PWR 17:3073–78). In two weeks Mrs. Cashman revisits with her husband and daughters to receive a poem on spring (PWR 17:3087), while a poem for John Curran has PW presenting herself as a "Mither" asking forgiveness from her babe if she has misrepresented love and faith as "golden." "Mither" then asks, "Did I betray thee then, Beloved?" (PWR 17:3081).

Looking past mid winter, the poet finds that yesterday's dust has been "[m] ade sweet for spurting new things" (PWR 17:3097). Three days later, after forewarning a questioner that her loosed tongue "would sip seductively at the nectar of expression," PW responds zestfully to his request for a poem on Sappho: "I would sing of flesh and love which drank / Its wine from out the cup of flesh" (PWR 17:3100). With the Cashman family again present on March 20, PW claims the eaglet, before it becomes John Curran's memorial, as a figure for "my soul," this eaglet surveying heights "with an hunger that consummeth [*sic*] it . . . fed of desire for flight." In a poem she addresses to Cashman, PW suggests a happily shared secret: "And life winked and I winked, / For life and I had a jest" (PWR 17:3117–19).

At the same sitting, Mrs. Cashman hears her own voice sympathetically represented in a poem by PW that, again stripped of dialect, has begun to question justice:

I wonder how just day is?
. . . .
I am doubtful. I become confused.
I am sure of my faith and yet I wonder wherein
The tipping of the beam is justice.

The dimension of Curran that winked at life's jest while attempting to read Mrs. Cashman's mood concerning her lawyer-husband had much to sort out that evening. Whoever was Eileen's father, conception would have taken place at approximately the time of these late-March entries.

As much as anyone in the PW circle and more than most, Casper Yost as spiritual "brother" to Patience would have been aware of any growing relationship between Pearl Curran and John Cashman. As 1922 began, PW, speaking prose, felt it necessary to address the "deep wound" she read in the "scarlet script" of Yost's heart, aware of his "wonderment." He has "watched the shadows," she knows, but is asked not to number their hours or count their nearness. Instead, in a petition rare for the sharp-tongued control, PW implores, "Remember how the vessel thirsted for the wine. The flesh cries out for sup and there is no sup save rest" (PWR 17:3069). With John Curran's death now all but certain and grieving already begun, PW's imagery lends itself to a sympathetic reading. Still, in the past, Yost's relationship of sympathy with PW had needed no petition.

The language of "spurting" desire and green new growth that runs through the PW poetry in early 1922 is as clear, and conflicted, as Pearl Curran's grieving in the months after her husband's death, months that would have made her pregnancy increasingly visible among friends and family. PW's metaphors are correspondingly ambivalent. With only Casper Yost and Pearl's mother, Mary Pollard, present at one session in July, Yost records a prose communication for Pearl that the three understand as coming from John through PW: "Behold I have left a taper burning." The import of the metaphor, Yost comments in the Record, was not evident immediately but became clear "a little later." When PW's verbal fashioning of a spirit-husband pledges to "keep the wick" as a "tryst and a trust," describing the "holy taper" for his widow as "the flame of thy desire," Yost observes, "Mrs. Curran was so touched she could hardly go on" (PWR 17:3157). For the Record, Yost calls the "benediction" of John Curran's translated spiritual visit "one of the most beautiful records Patience ever made in its tenderness and understanding." If not for one of the Duell-Holland interview notes, there would be no basis for speculating who, including Pearl herself, might have confided his wife's infidelity and pregnancy to the dying John Curran. Before the phrase "Been told of John Cushman's [*sic*] child,"

Duell wrote "Curran." As a fragment, using the passive voice and derived from a single source, Duell's memo to herself twenty years after the death of Pearl Curran can only qualify as hearsay.[20]

In the period just before and following Eileen's December 21, 1922, birth, the PW poetry began to darken its portrait of law and justice as metonym for a then regular visitor. As Curran neared the end of her term, the Record referred twice to an "illness" of five weeks but said nothing of pregnancy when a PW session of December 5 took place with a nurse present and in the joint company of Yost and Cashman. PW's first poem that evening, directed to no one in particular, may only be, as the Record suggests, "suspiciously apropos to the situation of sorrow" the group had shared for months. In the night through which they were passing, claims the PW voice, "My dreams are stifled" and a "cocksure knave rides rampant upon a coal black steed," until the night becomes a nun and the knave a black knight—Cashman was a member of the Knights of Columbus—who "rides dayward in defense / Of her quietude and sanctuary." The poet makes her way toward identification with the nun.

> I have known her quietude, her solitude.
> I have counted her beads and I am sure
> That night is a nun and hath no part with him,
> Upon whose flank the moon swings. (PWR 18:3171)

On the same evening, a poem intended to be in Mary Pollard's voice casts oblique light on a prominent visitor. "Who is the judge," begins the poem, instructing that person to acknowledge that "he is a fool," proud of "the justice of his own conviction," while the speaker learns to "frown upon the judge . . . ." In his uncomfortable turn, Cashman, "who had known a recent sorrow" not described, receives what the Record describes as "a beautiful tribute." As if plucked from the subject's name, "ash" spells "the dust of a cherished memory" or—like a Catholic on Ash Wednesday—it is a day "in sackcloth with a cross of ash upon / Its brow . . . " (PWR 18:3174). If the voice of PW is now the medium between Curran and Cashman, it represents their relationship as one in which the expectant mother sees her black knight as sometime hero, sometime knave, the pair drawn into a ritual of shared ashes known better and longer by her nunnish hand than his. In the new year of 1923 Cashman made no appearance until September 3 as one of a small group of intimates that included the Yosts and Curran's friend Dotsie Smith, who would hear the baby Eileen described as the "holy flame" of a communion's "inward grace" (PWR 18:3267). Following a poem that claims in Cashman's voice "My God is a God of justice," PW remarks, "The justice of God and the justice of man are like unto a monk and a knave. I laugh at the twain for they never meet" (PWR 18:3263). Curran began to travel in March, hoping to present PW in

Chicago "on a larger scale," repeating sessions at the home of Eugene Garnett in Evanston well into August, and giving poems spontaneously on subjects from the Rocky Mountains to patriotism to Theodore Roosevelt to the *Lusitania* (PWR 18:3190, 3194).

In practical ways, Cashman became a member of the inner circle. The most telling evidence of his place in the reduced Curran household is his inclusion in a curious session recorded for September 14, 1923, and held at Lake Villa, Illinois, where Curran's untrustworthy Spiritualist uncle, George Cordingley, appears (PWR 19:3292–93). Throughout the superficially harmonious session, Cordingley's presence is felt in questions about auras and "illumination," but the occasion for the gathering was in fact a property dispute, which demanded an attorney. As Curran recounted the story to Prince four years later, with no mention of Cashman, Cordingley had wired his sister, Mary Pollard, to propose a transfer of his property fifty miles northwest of Chicago to her in exchange for her coming to care for him in his final days, a move that would also have involved Curran and her daughters. Pearl and her mother agreed to the proposal, but the unexpected death of Mary Pollard left the property in Pearl's name, requiring her signature for any sale, while Cordingley retained a "managing right." There followed, according to Pearl, "a series of *threats* and abuse" from her uncle, including a letter to Chicago newspapers appropriating PW and the family's Spiritualist tradition to the Cordingleys. Curran's conviction that her uncle could not be trusted in any legal negotiations, which she held before the agreement that her mother made with Cordingley, would alone account for Cashman's accompanying her on the trip.[21] The Record contains no further references to the property, suggesting that it reverted to Cordingley, perhaps from Curran's desire to disentangle herself from any relation to a known confidence man.

With Curran's return to St. Louis, PW is at times sharply aggressive, at others intimate or generous. When the circle expresses its "wishins" to PW, Cashman asks for something sterner, and receives it. "A sterner stuff, eh sirrah? Weel, were I to wish thee justice, 'twould be vain. Should I wish thee understandin', 'twould be the same" (PWR 19:3299). The record-keeper at this session, somewhat atypically, then introduces an "intimate remark" from PW to Cashman, actually a set of rhetorical questions: "Who sets a bar upon love? Who swings a door or says it nay?" (PWR 19:3309). Ordinarily not a questioner of PW, Curran asks whether "a life as fine and good as one can make it" is nevertheless "sinful or mistaken" if "we seem to be in the grip of something we don't seek . . ." PW is reliably Emersonian when she responds helpfully: "The law be within thee; not spaked with the lips of thy brother" (PWR 19:3312).

With "Samuel Wheaton" staggering toward completion after five years, Patience Wee at seven an increasingly troublesome child about to be entrusted to Dotsie Smith for schooling in California, and with a continued prospect of reduced income, PW observes pragmatically of her medium, “the harp wert breaked . . . and if it wert breaked asunder, then must I cease to sing” (PWR 19:3312). Well prompted, PW consoles Pearl in one of several poems addressed to Cashman in his absence, claiming that “love is never done,” even with desire consumed and “stand[ing] in the ash of my disappointment” (PWR 19:3316).

Ashes to ashes. On January 16 of the new year, 1924, little more than a year after the birth of Eileen, the harp’s resilience would be tested further—by the unexpected death of John Cashman at the age of sixty-six.[22] In the final months of 1923, PW had advised Pearl to keep to her work: “Repentance is a tattered cloth. Let thy hands at the weaving rather than repent. Make whole the tatters ere thou dost let remorse to gnaw thee” (PWR 19:3321). Cashman’s final visit to a PW session had been on November 29. After a flurry of Christmas poems, and then undone by January, the PW voice remained silent until February 20, a month after Cashman’s death.

John Cashman is not mentioned again in the Record. When “Samuel Wheaton” was completed the previous October, PW had instructed that the work be dedicated to “Dame and Laddie” to honor the devotion of Mary Pollard and John Curran to a “story they adored.” Six months after Cashman’s death, PW waded into a purplish fountain of romantic imagery in search of an adequate lover but had to conclude, “This is a jest.” The jest may be futile, frothy poetry, but even more it is men: “So these are men—The jest!” Even more, it is the jest in antique romance of the swaggering lover, of which both John Curran and John Cashman may have been pale imitations. The Pearl Curran later described by Eileen might never have conceived her: “Not a sexual woman. Everything in head. Romantic, idealistic. Not physical.”[23]

The session that made a jest of men, held June 12, 1924, was attended by Emily Hutchings, recognized by PW as continuing to seek a lute and a hand for her song. Hutchings may have noted that competition had become pointless for the latter-day PW: “What are words to the universe?” PW asks; and, “Do the stars know singing?” No longer patient, and speaking on Curran’s behalf, the poet erects an icon of rare masculinism and, surveying the mass of men, laments a divine failure of invention:

> God, could I grasp the hand of one
> Who had a mighty throat;
> Who swore in a rage hot oaths,
> Steaming fresh from the pot of his anger.
> Could I click my cup with his and laugh, . . .
> And hear him lie and know that he was lying,
> Rather than listen to the wisdom of this day.

This wry-bought wisdom, this mimic truth,
This mincing day. God, to know a man. . . . (PWR 20:3395–96)

At the last instant, PW prescribes divine mercy as a way of coaxing a final farewell from Curran to the man of law as raging lover, but Curran had already taken down "a poem of comforting one lonely night" that dwelt on an image of "the little green house where you lie," figured prayers as "whimpering babes," and recalled an Arcady of "golden fetters" and "dear lips on mine . . . the ecstacy [*sic*], the bliss" (PWR 20:3397–98). Tilted toward the matrimonial by eternal pledging, and defining heaven as "where thou art, beloved one, for me," the poem's generalized sentiment nevertheless preserves the anonymity of the dead lover, PW disdaining what would have been the outright deception of addressing him as "John."

Patience on Tour

Pearl Curran's marriage in November 1926 to Dr. Henry Rogers after a month's engagement may have been the least important event of the years between John Curran's death in 1922 and her move to California in 1930. Ending Pearl's four years as a single mother, marriage provided her with a platform of respectability for launching the next stage in her career and seems not to have interfered with her increasing travels on the lecture circuit or with her intense relationships with friends, such as those she had formed in the company of Williamina and Grace Parrish. Headlines about the wedding featured the bride's more celebrated companion—"Mrs. Curran Receives Wedding Day Poem from Patience Worth"—but stories of her marriage to a retired physician had difficulty making a major event of what seemed a marriage of convenience. For the suspicious Mrs. A. P. Holland, it was Pearl's need for "a permanent escort" on her increasingly frequent lecture trips from St. Louis that prompted the marriage.[24]

The groom, an old family friend, was at sixty-eight the bride's senior by twenty-five years. As Rogers told Walter Prince with the wedding in prospect, his first wife had taken an early interest in Pearl's musical career and had suggested, then supervised, her work and training in Chicago. At sixteen, he said, Pearl had been a "pretty, becomingly dressed girl of pleasing manners," but he had not been aware of any "outstanding qualities to report until the 'Patience Worth' work began" (*CPW,* 29). Prince chose not to quote from Rogers's further statement, "So that all along I have considered 'Pearl' one of my good friends and she has addressed me as 'Uncle Henry.'"[25] For the no more than amiable couple, PW dutifully wrote "A Marriage Song." The ceremony, performed by an Episcopal clergyman at the groom's house on Lindell Boulevard, appears to have been entirely conventional. In correspondence with Prince after the wedding, Pearl was fully aware of the sensation she represented as she took the arm of Dr. Rogers: "Lordy, being a spook makes lots of folks know lots of things about one that amazes me! Dr. Rogers was a brave man to marry a 'bug'—taking on one normal woman with one normally complex personality is bad enough—but a woman with a two personality complex—ye gods! . . . Perhaps he should have taken out two marriage liscences [*sic*]—who knows?" After a honeymoon of three weeks, the new Mrs. Rogers, it was reported, would continue her writing and lecturing career.[26]

Until her move to California, Pearl Curran Rogers continued her correspondence with Prince, confiding details of PW's increasingly public career and the changes that marked time for the medium: "I weigh 133 and ½ pounds—getting fat and forty *plus.*" Already her defender, Prince became a second conscience to whom she could turn for approval. In the spring before her second marriage, she told him she was looking forward to the end of her current tour "as I'm tired of crowds and need a rest." With a "Get thee behind me Satan," she had resisted temptation, she told the former clergyman, turning down an offer from a booking agency as inconsistent with "all your labor." The resolution to keep PW free of commercial taint was not to last, and Prince was prepared to see in the affair "the old story of commercialism barring science."[27]

The sinking of the market for PW literature and Pearl's need to establish an independent economic base as a lecturer and public medium had been in process in the years preceding her marriage to Dr. Rogers. Audiences wishing to spend "an evening with Patience Worth," as Pearl titled the performances, were rewarded on a circuit that included Chicago and Lake Forest, Illinois; Detroit, Michigan; Orange, New Jersey (*SS*, 252–53); and Concord, Massachusetts, where she had an April 1924 reunion with her Episcopal pastor in St. Louis, the Reverend David Garrett (PWR 20:3383). PW sessions followed in New York in February and April of 1925, with Mrs. Walter Damrosch, Mrs. Hamlin Garland, John Ticknor, and Mrs. Arthur Scribner named as guests, as well as meetings at the Prince George Hotel with sponsor Herman Behr and other New York appearances at the Town Hall and Writers clubs and the Hotel Martha Washington.[28]

Walter Prince, promoting the PW cause as his own after publication of his book, invited Pearl to speak before the Boston Society for Psychic Research, of which he was an officer, and in New York, again through his intervention, at St. Marks in the Bouwerie, where he introduced her. Reporting on that appearance as "an earthly comeback" for PW, with Pearl as her "mortal literary press agent," a United Press story in October 1928 described Pearl reciting verses "as fast as most persons could talk through the telephone." Pearl's enthusiasm for large-audience appearances rose and fell with a temperament she felt she could not control. To Prince, she confided that the St. Mark's appearance was "not at all" PW's best and suggested that, confronted "with a *public*," her control became "*perverse* and less inclined to shine." In reply, Prince wrote to say that while "the Patience Worth delivery" was not equal to what he had previously heard, "any poet that ever lived" rose and fell in excellence. "I do not mean that it was bad, but it was not so dazzlingly good as it is sometimes." Relying on an inexperienced stenographer, Pearl found disparities between what PW had given her on "first delivery" and what was recorded. A need to "re-do" what had been communicated could suggest a kind of tampering, she feared, "not fair to me or to Patience," but despite her tears, she told Prince, the "omitted lines and mistaken words" resurfaced: "*Patience* saved me!"[29]

Rogers's eventual discovery that PW could be counted on even before large, intimidating audiences may have had the ironic effect of bringing Satan forward in the shape of the Alber Bureau ("Bringing the World to Your Door") of Cleveland, which was "old in the business" of managing lecture circuits, she assured Prince after she signed up. The agency advertised its new lecturer acquisition as "The Most Baffling Psychic Phenomenon of All Time" and promised, "A session with this delightful personality is a refreshing and unique adventure in the uncharted realm of mystic revelations." No longer embattled, the medium was delighted to send Prince clippings of a "*very* successful lecture" in Detroit and to test the former clergyman's tolerance for unveiled ambition: "I love lecturing—I've smelled raw meat and the 'animals [*sic*] eyes are out.' Alber says I'm a distinct success."[30]

Something of Pearl Curran Rogers's late manner is suggested in a 1929 newspaper report of her appearance before the St. Louis Theosophical Society. After describing the sudden emergence in 1913 of her "ghostly whisperer," the medium, described as a "tall woman, blue-eyed and with graying hair," covered in a "shimmering white robe" and occasionally raising a green lace handkerchief to her forehead and lips, would chat with the audience, passing on examples of PW's humor before taking suggestions for extempore poetry: "'Success. Success,' Mrs. Rogers intoned. 'She closed her eyes and swayed from one foot to the other.'" Referring to "Patience's Prohibition Joke," Rogers recalled the request of a previous audience for a poem on spirits with PW replying, "Distilled or deceased?" Rogers continued: "Don't you love that? I like her when she's saucy."[31]

Rogers's economic needs were growing in the late 1920s. She had two children by then, and Henry Rogers was in failing health shortly after their marriage and is described as an invalid after their move to California. Herman Behr, editor and publisher of *Telka* and the poetry volume *Light from Beyond*, was supplementing her earnings by this time, ten years after his "conversion" to PW. In 1919 Pearl had called him a "German philosopher of N.Y. who has been an Atheist," now come into spiritual enlightenment "by the words of

Patience."[32] Behr was also wealthy and generous, already providing $400 support each month (*SS*, 231) when Pearl wrote Prince to say, "Mr. Behr raised my income $100 per month which helps some with my growing up young ladies," adding that she was "putting both children in convent for the winter." Herman Behr's son, Max, would also play a major role in the lives of Rogers and her daughters—he was both piously supportive and needy—after their relocation to California. A hint of her ambivalence about what would prove a Behr family trait is already suggested when she complains to Prince about "Father Behr's" having written the introduction to *Telka,* a perquisite of his patronage, and worries aloud about her patron's relation to "spooks." "He is so good and wonderful but a couple of mediums in California have gotten him loco," she concludes, with her own move to Los Angeles in prospect.[33]

Patience as Pierrot

In the 1920s, when no new PW fiction was earning critical attention, Pearl Curran was taking lessons from a local culture of aestheticism that had been to school abroad. The entry of the Parrish sisters into the PW circle after the disbanding of the Potters, the St. Louis women's art club they had started after the 1904 World's Fair, brought Curran into relation with their experience of a new art and their history of world travel and recognition by English and European judges. Having exhibited their pictorialist photography in London and Dresden, Williamina and Grace Parrish were among the organizers in 1903 of the Salon Club in New York, then the Potters in St. Louis, and then they worked for the Red Cross in Europe during the war, and at the time of their relationship with Curran in the 1920s were major contributors to the Tenth Open Competition of the St. Louis Artists' Guild.[34] For the widowed Pearl Curran and more perhaps for the new Mrs. Rogers, the Parrish sisters were an initiation into the great if fading world of late nineteenth-century aestheticism that made an antibourgeois saint of a clown whose melancholy lute may have reminded Pearl of her own.

Continued interest in PW may also have reawakened some of the original energies of former Potters in the years from 1924 to 1928. Sculptor Carolyn Risque's daughter recalled that for PW sessions at the Parrish house, the sisters restaged for their visitor by creating "a special table made with zodiac sign decorations for use in the séances." Curran's self-presentation at PW appearances closely resembles a description by Vine Colby of Potter associate Susan Williams's performance: "Do you remember how she stood swaying with the long portieres, and seeing visions away off? It is lovely to feel yourself yielding to witch-craft and enchantment, as you do when she whispers, 'My souls are nine.'"[35] Increasingly, Curran absorbed something of the culture of local women who wrote what pleased them and who were pleased most by exotic dreams of all that was not St. Louis.

Become temporary editor of the PW dictations, Williamina Parrish involved herself with Curran's publishing efforts while also, like John Curran, noting the occasions and personalities that were the Record's context. In return, PW broke her vow not to traffic with the dead by giving Curran a dream in which she saw Parrish's mother, "Aggie" Parrish, running into the arms of her late husband, "Dinks," the dream preceding the mother's sudden death by two weeks (*SS*, 239–40). To PW, Parrish was "mine Owlet," frequently "Will," and sometimes "Willie" in the Record, a "wee witch wi' wit as wing, wi' fancy as mart, and all chaos, egad, o'er which to reign" (PWR 25:3986). Beginning in 1924, Parrish gathered poems written for her by PW into a typewritten book that begins with an echoic response to her mentor and "sister": "And I sayed me unto me, / How may I sing too?"[36]

A moody young man who appears as "Sasha" in several of Parrish's posed portrait photographs is styled a young Russian "in whose brooding eyes are dreams of liberty and revolution," but he was most likely the Italian Nino Ronchi, whom she had first met in 1915 while acting as a governess to his family in Milan and whom she "installed" in her house in St. Louis in 1924.[37] Ronchi acquired a studio during his visit to St. Louis, which Parrish recalled as the site of her first meeting, in the spring of 1924, with Pearl Curran. When Walter Prince undertook his study, he detailed an elaborate relationship of telepathy between Curran and Ronchi on the basis of what Parrish told him of the origin of a 2,700-word "masque," "Lamento Doloroso," dictated by PW in the summer of 1924 after Ronchi had gone to New York.[38]

In Parrish's account of the origin of the unpublished "Lamento Doloroso," PW was writing poetry within a month of Nino Ronchi's departure memorializing him as "Falcon" and complaining, "My lute, my love, is in my hand, / But I may not strike it." When Parrish forwarded the poem to Ronchi—recommending its "spirit-voice" as a possible aid to his English—she received in reply "a long, dolorous letter (in Italian)" that included a pencil sketch "of a Faun and a Nymph under a sort of dream-tree" with the inscription "To Patience Wordt, my lute, my love, Nino." The remainder of his letter, she believed, contained the "seedlings" of a dialogue PW had recently dictated, featuring a Nymph who dances wearing only garlands of myrtle, a Faun lamenting his broken lute, a Punchinello, and a Friar. Yet Curran knew nothing of Ronchi's letter, Parrish reported to Prince, in which he described himself as a monk shut up in his room who would emerge onto the street only to become a Punchinello for New Yorkers who laugh "and call me Valentino." Prince, straining to justify his attention to the masque as an instance of telepathy, is anxious to report that PW began dictation of the dialogue within a few hours of Will Parrish's private reading of Ronchi's letter (*CPW*, 312–14).

As much as *The Sorry Tale* and *Hope Trueblood*, "Lamento Doloroso" was delivered by literary fashion. Typically too the fashion was not a new one. Curran had been acquainted with commedia dell'arte themes and figures at least since she sang Sara Teasdale's poem "Pierrot" in 1912. What was new was Curran's introduction through the Parrish sisters to a more sensuous art than her memory's canonical literature, and in Nino Ronchi's melancholy and ambiguously gendered sexuality an embodiment more immediate than her early reading of Whitman. Whether Curran's piano had ever played Claude Debussy's *Prelude to the Afternoon of a Faun* (1894) is less relevant than the popular currency of fauns, nymphs, Pierrots, and Punchinellos, a collection of types that took its tone from aestheticism's divinizing of the artist as pagan, alternately celebrating sensual beauty and, in the sad-faced clown, lamenting its loss.

Given the proliferation of resuscitated commedia dell'arte figures among her contemporaries, Curran could plausibly maintain that "Lamento Doloroso" was dictated to her from the air. A modern commentary on Arnold Schoenberg's soprano-declaimed *Pierrot lunaire* (1912) describes the Pierrot character as "an archetype of the artist" in the late nineteenth and early twentieth centuries, transformed from the "uncaring prankster" of his commedia origins "to romantic *malheureux* . . . tormented figures submerged in a bizarre, airless inner world."[39] With her vocalizing of poems by Sara Teasdale and Zoë Akins in 1912, Curran would have breathed in the Pierrot ur-plot as well. In that year, Akins had published her first book of poetry, which included a poem titled "Pierrot and the Parasol."[40] Williamina Parrish's sketch of a young man in "The Faun" had been awarded second prize at the Wanamaker American Exhibition in New York in 1915, the year in which she met Ronchi. In a 1917 collection of reprinted poems, *Mon Ami Pierrot,* Teasdale and Akins evoked a "half merry, half melancholy little lad above whose head ever hovers the halo of a lost love."[41] Teasdale offered three poems, including one titled "Pierrot's Song"; Akins contributed "Pierrot and the Peacock's Feather."

Three years later, on March 18, 1920, William Reedy published Edna St. Vincent Millay's play *Aria da Capo,* in what would prove to be one of the final issues of his *Mirror.*[42] Millay's treatment of paired Pierrot and Columbine figures is satirical, but their effete indifference to the casualties of war, suggesting the idiom's versatility, would have drawn attention as a local publishing event. Nino Ronchi's performance of art and melancholy as a self-styled Pierrot had already made its impression on Curran during his St. Louis stay. In the June of his 1924 departure for New York, PW describes him as

> Child of the fays, consorter with the gods,
> Consort of goddesses, to whom
> No mysticism is evasive. . . . (PWR 20:3391)

The more closely Curran's imagination approached a figure of art ready to speak what the PW idiom could not, the more a pattern of attraction-repulsion set in. When Prince later asked about the portrait of Ronchi done by Parrish (*SS*, 248), which in 1926 he had seen hanging in Curran's hall, Curran responded by describing swirling images that resisted what PW was bringing to vision. She may well have known a series of photographs done by the Parrishes that identified Ronchi by name as the young man holding a cigarette, wearing a polka-dot tie, costumed totally in black. Other photos show an unnamed male nude, sometimes lying, sometimes standing, by a stream or beside a waterfall.[43] Ronchi's own drawings and paintings had fascinated Curran with their "mystic quality," according to Parrish, but invaded by images mindful of the Italian visitor, Curran's words balk at what they are asked to express.

As described for Prince, the image of a yellow-green liquid in a cup or wine glass gives way to a feeling of revulsion when Curran announces that she does not like what she sees, though yes, it is a pretty picture; she says it is pretty even as, gripping the stem of the glass, she feels it as a thorny branch, "full of thorns. It pricks my fingers. It seems to be growing, and this bowl is attached to it." The eroticized picture finally excludes her when she finds her lips dry "like corn husks," then is made grotesque as she becomes aware of a green smoke issuing from her, "and I want to get rid of it—just spit it out; it almost stifles me and I am sick all over and I want to speak, but the speech is an effort." A sense of unspeakable knowledge then climaxes with an image of her eyes dropping out "like a doll's eyes." Curran draws her own inference: "I think it is a sense of seeing wrong." As if her two eyes were guilty of taking in, deeply, the portrait Prince had inquired about, she continues: "The thing I feel in this is as though I had moved up to a wall and couldn't get past—just as though it were no use trying" (PWR 23:3718; *SS*, 248–50).

With Curran in retreat, PW attempts the task of at once censoring and shielding her medium. The cup is fantasy indeed, a "mocking dream," says PW, that leaves her a "famished . . . she-wolf" needing to suckle her "brats of fancy" when she hungers only for "REALITY," a desire she addresses heavenward:

> God, what a sup!
> Green as jade;
> Poisonous as the venom of an asp. (*SS*, 250)

Two years earlier, at the time of Ronchi's visit, PW had armed Curran against herself by trumping desire with punitive memory. When one of the Potters "begged for the pagan Faun" in a poem, PW told her,

Such love is a myth,
A frantic being
Plunged in a thicket of desire, . . .
Caressing with hands,
But the hoof trods . . . (PWR 20:3439)

A Puritan maiden would need to enter a moonlit glade with care. Strains of homoeroticism, bisexuality, and androgyny were part of the lute's music both in the expressed tastes of the Potters and the unexpressed sexual preferences of some. Nino Ronchi's sexuality figured multiply in the characters Curran transcribed. When the Parrishes invited a reader of past lives to their house, a person identified only as "Jean," the visitor pronounced Nino a "Brahmin Reader" in a previous incarnation, saying he "[u]sed to hide behind the tortuous, gnarled trees and look at the nude young boys taking their exercises of purification."[44] Williamina is described as "a polish [*sic*] man-child of the time of Stanislaus. . . . Very fond of the ladies and treacherous in his dealings with them." Commenting on "Lamento Doloroso," Williamina suggested to Prince that the masque's dialogues might be understood as attempts to delineate one personality, presumably her friend Nino's, in "three of his moods," the Faun, the Monk, and the Jester (*CPW,* 312). The representing of psychic fractions would have come readily to Curran as she initiated a Pearl–Patience dialogue in which desire and denial are finally synthesized into a tearful joke, a plot as familiar to the local medium as to her widely traveled friends. Williamina's regard for "Lamento Doloroso" and its faun was evident when she made the manuscript into a book for Curran's patron, Herman Behr, but the effort also signaled the widowed Curran's arrival in a sorority of artists. When the Parrish sisters initially proclaimed their calling following the World's Fair of 1904, they published photographs taken by Williamina of the nine muses, Grace posing for each of them in Greek dress.[45] Two decades later, the group's alumnae had in Patience Worth their tenth muse. For Williamina Parrish, the "little Idyll" was not "too pagan" for the spirit of PW, only another example of her "many-sided genius" (*CPW,* 315).

As a local scripting of the commedia fund of figures, "Lamento Doloroso" adds to the impression of a writer become discursive chameleon with the aid of an endlessly adaptive talent for mimicry. The stock characters obey their traditional casting—the naked Nymph as nature's only unconflicted representative; the Faun, her companion in the glade, who complains fashionably of his "half-man, half-beast" doubleness ("wild of intent, yet with reason cursed"); love's fool, the Punchinello, also called a Pierrot in motley; and the Friar, "his belly bound of a thong," who knows painfully well what he sublimates:

The Holy Virgin's love was consummate,
And love unconsumate [*sic*] is agony.
The night is but a deathly sweat of reasoning,
Of wonderment and prayer. (6)

At this, the Punchinello "stands dismayed and crosses himself." The Faun's "lute is breaked," as it must be, and he caresses its "sagging strings" while he asks the celebratory Nymph, "Why dance? Why sing?" The trio of males commiserate with each other *au claire de la lune* while the Nymph is left to carry the presumed theme:

For every king a vassal is,
And every vassal is a king,
In love, dear Faun, in love! (11)

The last available text from Curran's hand is delivered more directly from recent experience than any of its predecessors and seeks approval from an audience no longer typified by Casper Yost. A prominent refrain condemns reason and praises wit, which it sometimes achieves, as when the Punchinello asks, "For know ye not that even wit is holy? For holy writ of wit unlit is dull . . . " (5). The Nymph is free to sing mockingly of love while greeting the fresh appearance of two lovers at dawn. By contrast, the sorry male trio looks to a single night's passage to resolve their crises, each one eying the identity of another as a mode of escape—the Faun preferring outright clownishness to his hybridity, the Punchinello wishing he were a friar, the Friar joining the Faun in citing his "itch to break the holy Image / That the fancy let me free" (6). Even the plot PW has inherited reads and rejects itself when the Punchinello turns against his instructions: "A new script to read! . . . I will not own the brat!" (9–10).

It is finally the witless Ass, wandered over from Shakespeare's midsummer, that overcomes the masque's objections to itself. Finding dawn's pair of lovers too trite an answer to his quest, the Faun ("and yet a myth am I") is relieved to discover the Ass browsing behind them. For the medium, the song of love becomes bearable when the Faun, now allying himself with the Punchinello and the Friar, can laugh at the reward for a night's vigil: "The Day doth send but Lovers . . . / And the Ass!" (11).

No further communication remains from Nino Ronchi to suggest whether PW's "whimsical lyric," as Will Parrish called it, had moved him to the risk of irony. He may however have helped Pearl extend herself beyond the shadow of PW. In the summer of 1925, as Pearl later wrote Walter Prince, she had completed a story titled "That Pietro" about "the Italian boy whose picture you so disliked and *admired*." The story has not survived, but, with no reference to

PW, she describes a writer's determination in her use of the first person: "It is the story I worked *hardest* on," she tells Prince, "and is about my utmost *best.*" By granting that the story was "*faulty* and needs rewriting," she has shifted attention to conscious agency, a change that will become more pronounced in her later work on the "Elizabethan" manuscript in California.[46]

As pursuers of their own art, the Parrish sisters eventually left Mrs. Rogers to her marriage and newfound zest for the lecture circuit, a loss that may have added to the accumulation of motives that turned Pearl toward California. Wishing "Gracie" well and enclosing a handwritten PW poem in a letter in April 1927, she reflected, "You too are gone—somehow the anchor seems really pulled up. . . . I can't write much. I'm all 'cut up' today."[47] In the new surroundings of California, PW would gradually draw Mrs. Rogers, soon to be Mrs. Wyman, into quieter settings and almost until the end would little by little lapse into textual silence as Pearl's final years alternated between the mock fulfillment of brief celebrity and new domestic opportunities to test her muse's poetry of consolation.

Chapter 8

THE CITY OF ANGELS

The story of Pearl Curran Rogers Wyman's seven years in Los Angeles, inconstantly recorded and only intermittently public, may always be incomplete. Only scraps of biography rather than a coherent narrative can be constructed from newspaper sources, the recollections of family and friends, and the patchy record of PW sessions. Curran never stated a reason for her move to the West Coast, but she had evidently surrendered to the earnest invitations of her friend Dotsie Smith, and, with no recent publishing successes, she began an energetic search for another plane of fame in public appearances. It is proportionately difficult to make out what happened to Patience Worth. That energy appears to have responded glowingly to initial celebrity in movieland, visiting Mary Pickford and Douglas Fairbanks and attracting the attention of Los Angeles columnists. Like other California-bound performers before and after, PW at times misplaced the identity she had arrived with. In new surroundings, the anachronistic voice at times gave way to another more like Pearl's when it strained for insider hipness and the tone, after 1929, of a world-weary flapper jaded by failures in love and on Wall Street. Perhaps in recoil, the voice that had sought its body in timeless text fell silent for almost two years during a period when Pearl's domestic life alternated between conflict and depression.

At the outset, the security promised by Dr. Henry Rogers as an aging bystander-husband was quickly lost when his invalidism coincided with the 1930 move to California. When Pearl resumed a relationship with Robert Wyman, the suitor rejected before her marriage to John Curran, the elderly Dr. Rogers urged his wife to divorce him, giving her the freedom to marry her first love, an offer she had accepted by December 22, 1931, when she and Wyman were married (PWR 28:4242). Increasingly, too, the care and education of her two daughters demanded more attention than in the period of their St. Louis childhoods. Patience Wee, now "Patty," became a wayward adolescent. Her mother watched with apprehension as the child entered a difficult puberty, while the spiritual mother hopefully indulged her heaven-sent gift: "Slothful, eh, Laggard, eh, . . . I bid ye nought, / Nor chide ye ne'er, but I ken ye" (PWR 27:4207).

For the reverential support she received from Dotsie Smith and a new parlor of devotees, Rogers paid with regular, increasingly routine deliveries of what her new congregants had come to hear. After Pearl's death in 1937 at the age of fifty-four, PW suffered the indignity of being asked to speak to them in continued transmissions through the medium's daughters and miscellaneous others, variously accomplished. Near the end, PW demonstrated that she would not be silenced prematurely. The stress of being obliged to uplift without stint and the divorce of the medium's graying experience from a formerly gilded text made their contributions to PW's silence. The reserves automaticity could call on appeared at first to have been exhausted, then responded to what Pearl believed her most fully authorized ambition. Persuaded to accept editorial guidance, she taught PW the arts of laborious revision. The most important product of that changed relationship between creative source and conscious recrafting, "Elizabethan Mask (Three Days in the Life of William Shakespeare)" (*SS*, 259), may never come to light. But at the end of a process that in 1913 had begun as dubious experiment, the manuscript's real importance for Pearl was as evidence, if only to herself, that she could command her own text and dance compellingly, not for an historical Caesar, but with young Will.

Patience in the Papers

Even before Pearl Curran Rogers's move to California, which was promoted for some time by Dotsie Smith, there were signs that she intended to seek a larger arena for her voice. The national scope of her public, agent-sponsored appearances is reflected in a 1928 *Los Angeles Daily Times* story, printed as an "Exclusive Dispatch" from a recent PW appearance in Chicago but repeating the terms in which the PW phenomenon had been regularly headlined. Against the dispatch "Spook-Poet Performs," the casually iconoclastic medium protests, "I never saw a spook, and I never want to. . . . I'm not a bit psychic; in fact I'm so normal that I can eat cabbage, or curl my hair, as I receive Patience Worth's messages from the other world." The story includes spontaneously delivered poems "Insight" and "Recapitulation," but their mode of delivery was what caught the reporter's attention, as Rogers dictated a "rush of words and syllables" to a stenographer for punctuation, "sometimes spelling the words first, and then pronouncing them." As evidence of her claim that she did not require a trance, her audience observed the medium carrying on a conversation with them, withdrawing only to fix her eyes on some unseen vanishing point as she begins a poem.[1]

A new audience of reporters was now receiving variant, shorthand accounts of the coming of PW, whose earthly life had evolved into a narrative adding color and conflict to the genesis myth assembled incrementally during the St. Louis–Casper Yost years. Following Rogers's lead, a reporter was able to secularize PW by linking her to a pinochle game. "Eight [*sic*] years ago," recalled the medium, asking that she not be called a medium, "my husband was devoted to pinochle and I was forced to amuse myself with a ouija-board. One night a message came, signed Patience Worth. A few days later this quaint character told me she had been born in Dorsetshire, had come to this country when she was about forty, and had always rebelled against being a Puritan."[2]

A Sunday supplement writer had it that PW was the only daughter of a weaver, her thumb thick "from twisting the flax." The father having left for America, Patience—at age thirty-five—followed him after her mother's death.[3] A retrospective published after Pearl's death again directed attention to the swollen thumb and appeared to diagnose PW's childlessness as a work-related injury, describing her as "a Puritan maiden who worked so hard spinning flax that her thumb had become enlarged and she had died without experiencing the joys and sufferings of motherhood."[4] Rogers's arrival in California coincided, perhaps by design, with a national convention of "Psychic Science Churches" reported by society columnist Alma Whitaker as a major social event honoring British visitor Dr. Arthur Ford, a friend to "all the spiritualistic nabobs" in London. Dr. Ford, Whitaker could report, had psychic information that "Dwight Morrow will be the next President of the United States."[5]

Before a Southern California audience accustomed to masks and costumes, Rogers enhanced PW's antiquity by her own modernity of dress and attitude, while also signaling an openness to psychological explanation that her spiritualist followers would not have welcomed. Detected by the sensors of a fantasy-nourished culture, Rogers was interviewed by a Miss Chandler almost immediately on her arrival in Los Angeles and, with photo, presented to readers as an "amanuensis of spirit author" and a "real 'ghost writer.'" Describing the "wonderfully sweet voice" that speaks to her, Rogers makes it clear in the Chandler story that she wants to be understood as "normal" and supplies PW with a familiar motive for her return to the world: "in order that she can do the things she wanted to do and could not when she lived." By the end of the interview, a naturalized Rogers is holding out the possibility that "science is just now getting a few faint glimmerings of new revelations and knowledge of the powers and functions of the human mind . . . crawling toward new discoveries," for which PW might constitute helpful "data."[6] Columnist Alma Whitaker demonstrated the seriousness of Rogers's newfound enthusiasm for science by informing her readers that Rogers had recently promised to will her head to Dr. Cecil Reynolds of the Royal College of Surgeons, but the promise seems not to have been kept.

The columnist, after attending a reception at the home of Dotsie and Alexander Smith, assimilates the midwestern medium to her new environment with sharp-eyed attention to costume, character, dashes of slang, and a lilting voice in her column about the event. A cartoonish Pearl surrounded by party onlookers precedes the list of guests; Whitaker describes Pearl "Rodgers" as dressed "in long, clinging black, with angel sleeves caught with silver. Her hair is gray, bobbed and curly. She wears longer ear-rings and she has tiny well-shod feet." Whitaker reverses previous rankings of medium and control when she shares her own and other guests' estimate of Pearl as "undoubtedly a brilliant woman" and therefore more interesting than PW, the "intellectual spook." After an evening of "corking good entertainment and high-grade literature," why, Whitaker wonders, should the audience credit a "suppressed damsel of the Middle Ages" over the woman whose "engaging personality makes every line sound like piquant wisdom." Dazzled by instantaneous PW responses to subjects proposed by guests (hell? "Man's full consciousness of self"), the columnist quotes Rogers's comparison of receiving PW dictations to "turning on the spigot."[7]

Scrutiny of Pearl's doubleness appeared a year later in a Sunday section called "Home, Club, and Civil Interests of Women." A reporter notes that in deferring to the source of her poetry, Rogers "used the impersonal pronoun 'she'" but in the second part of her presentation used the first person exclusively, "which was, to me, a significant psychological study." The story's implication continues into the news that in a poetry contest of 40,000 entries, one of the 100 prizes was awarded to Pearl Rogers—"or Patience Worth."[8]

If Pearl began to distinguish herself from PW when she first wrote fiction under her own name, in California she arranged her alternative modes of self-presentation spatially. Dotsie Smith, according to the Record, had already looked forward to PW's arrival in Los Angeles by preparing in 1929 a site for the spiritualist faithful to hear her, "a home in the mountains, which she named Patience Worth's Sanctuary" (PWR 26:4086). The house in Montrose would earn its title over the next eight years and beyond as the gathering place for Patience-seekers even as the Pearl Curran Rogers represented in society columns housed herself in a Santa Monica beach house at 917 Ocean Ave. In September

1930, Alma Whitaker, noting the superstition of members of "the acting profession" and naming Mary Pickford among them, includes PW in a story about fortune-tellers, but only to cite again her epigrammatic "swift retorts" to audiences. Whitaker registers an audience's impression of automaticity, if not the term, in her image of Rogers "apparently not waiting to think. It's like touching a button and the light coming on."[9] A news story in 1932 records that Pearl Curran, not Mrs. Rogers, will be joining Hamlin Garland and Mr. and Mrs. Upton Sinclair at a reception for honorary members of the Los Angeles American Society for Psychical Research, Sinclair having already questioned PW in a session on November 20, 1930 (PWR 27:4171). By 1935, the disruptions in Pearl Curran Rogers Wyman's life are obliquely reflected when Whitaker submerges the unnamed medium in her role, referring only to "Patience Worth," and confers full Hollywood citizenship on the merged entity by observing that her "two or three marriages (I've lost count, but there was a Curran and a Wineman [*sic*]) do not appear to have impaired her spirituality."[10]

When, shortly after her arrival in Los Angeles, Rogers was invited to "Pickfair," the Acropolis of stardom, she could well have imagined that PW's writing might gain entrée at the top. The commodity sought by Mary Pickford and Douglas Fairbanks when they invited her to their home, however, was not literature but advice on careers and a marriage in jeopardy and, for Mary Pickford, communication with a lost parent. In the summer of 1930, Pickford was more likely than her husband to have sought out Patience Worth. Her high-minded mother, Charlotte Smith Pickford, who had managed much of her daughter's personal life as well as her business interests, had died in 1928. Aware that her mother's stringent piety would not have welcomed an effort to make contact with her in "the other life," Pickford at first dispensed with mediums and, she said, conversed with her mother in her dreams, claiming to "communicate with Charlotte almost nightly."[11] PW's long experience in the art of the persona, which often had her speaking as mother characters in poetry, then made a genial substitute for spiritualist channeling when she brought it to Pickfair on August 13, 1930. Cast as disembodied stage mother, "Charlotte" first identifies herself, though in a recognizable PW poem, to her daughter: "Behold I have loosed a lark unto the day! A lark that ever sings of May," before she concludes pointedly, "Oh, my beloved, that lark is thee." In a series of nineteen poems or epigrams, PW repeats from St. Louis days her formula for the soul as "Once uttered, ever uttered," and briefly fetches up her Scots to say,

> There be nae sic 'n thing as time. . . .
> Who measureth time hath been
> On tiptoes to bump his nose
> Upon a star.

The Charlotte voice offers unending support in language mindful of the medium's own losses: "Have I not trimmed the wick and left thee oil? . . . And would I for one instant leave that beloved task?" (PWR 27:4116–19). But in their western translation, the pledges failed to secure further visits to Pickfair.

The Pickford-Fairbanks marriage would soon be over as well. In the year before Rogers's move to Los Angeles, the couple had made *The Taming of the Shrew,* a film Pickford later described as "my finish," convicting Fairbanks of shattering her confidence by his selfishness and indifference so that she "was never again at ease before the camera or microphone." When PW made her appearance at Pickfair, Pickford had already begun a new film, *Secrets,* but would later burn the negatives and write off a $300,000 loss, taking up the project again only after playing a French singer-dancer in *Kiki,* yet "another misadventure." Biographers have suggested possible reasons for her abandonment of *Secrets,* including the director's alcoholism, Pickford's own secret drinking, and her apparent mismatch with a younger leading man.[12]

The Record has Pickford questioning PW bluntly, "Should Mrs. Fairbanks Go On With Her Picture?" The response suggests some awareness of a thirty-seven-year-old star's late-career investment of reputation but makes an issue of the artist's sense of dignity and its potential loss. Speaking through her moviegoer medium, PW enacts a Mary Pickford who spies falsity in her new script. "May I utter with a hand of ice upon my heart?" is the rhetorical question America's Sweetheart is made to ask herself. "May I utter fool's words which reflect not the thing which is myself?" (PWR 27:4118). Given the film's theme—"the indomitable strength of a woman in preserving the family"—Pickford's apprehensions could be made to feel both plausible and flattering.

The greatest challenge for PW during the session would have been to negotiate the space between Douglas Fairbanks's vanity and his wife's growing conviction that, as she later said, he "no longer cared apparently about me or my feelings." At third hand, Eileen Curran Kleymeyer's husband, Ralph Kleymeyer, recalled Eileen's memory of her mother's version of the meeting with Fairbanks, who "told Pearl that he would jump for her, but he had a cold."[13] It is folly, PW comments during the session, for her host to ask, "Does Douglas Fairbanks Work Under Inspiration?" as she struggles to find a didactic response that could do without her staple term, *egotry.* The actor should at least understand that he cannot count on inspired "inflow" with a throat "not wide nor deep enough" and with "ears too shallow for to hear." Artist to artist, she tells him that he can be assured that one who creates "hath touched the fringe of the raiment of God." But when PW sketches a brief first-person portrait of the hero of *Zorro* and *The Three Musketeers* "sup[ping] a full mug" and taking up blades and broadswords, the voice is made to settle for less than art: "I have paid in blood and labor, / And learned understanding. A slow lesson, egad!"

As the session nears its end, PW appears to be passing the sword from militant Fairbanks to vulnerable Pickford with two lines on the subject of "turning the other cheek," a habit Pickford had occasion to cultivate, by advising a familiar defense against the knight as knave: "When thou hast received a wound, / Unsheath thy blade and keep it nigh." More peaceably, the visitor as village maiden bids good-bye by remarking her hosts' hearth and asking them in future to imagine her seated, weaving, beside its glow. Mary Pickford effectively ended her film acting career in 1933, filed for divorce from Douglas Fairbanks in December of 1934, and in 1935 wrote a novel, *The Demi-Widow,* and a "spiritual self-help manual," *Why Not Try God?*[14]

The Daughters of Pearl and Patience

Pearl Curran Rogers should not have been surprised when her adopted daughter, known as the "Ouija-board baby," who had grown into adolescence by March of 1931, became the subject that dominated the Sunday coverage of PW. The original St. Louis coverage of Patience Wee's adoption was revisited in a story in the Los Angeles publication *Every Week Magazine,* along with photos of an infant dressed in storybook Puritan costume, but the story could now also report on the life of Patty Curran, a Southern California high school girl. The career of her earthly mother, grayed and respectable in a fur-trimmed coat and serious expression, is familiarly summarized, while Eileen, the eight-year-old biological daughter, figures least in a two-page feature that has difficulty deciding whether to emphasize most the normal or the precocious in her fourteen-year-old sister.[15] By 1943, only Eileen would still be living, her relative ordinariness a saving grace.

In 1931, both daughters attended Catholic schools, a choice their mother explained by recalling that some of the nicest comments on her communicated writing had come from Catholic nuns. And PW, immune to anti-Popery, made it known that she had no objection to her godchild's being baptized into a religion her medium believed would be good for her. When asked by Patty for a poem on her Arcadia Convent School, PW idealized it as "Arcady, a sacred spot" (PWR 26:4023). In adolescence, Patty appeared to the reporter to have lost the early signs of preternatural influence that reputedly had her singing and speaking at two "in a new and novel manner . . . way above that of the ordinary infant." Her red hair gone chestnut, she was "robust and plump, and healthy," dressing like her schoolmates though "inclined to be tomboyish," and wearing "all the ornaments and jewelry so dear to the hearts of girls." Nothing about her love of sports and interpretive dancing or her interest in journalism would reveal "that she is being brought up under the guidance of a 'spiritual godmother.'"

Eileen's recollections of her mother and sister, conveyed in a letter from Ralph Kleymeyer to Ruth Duell rather than offered to the press, are the most useful basis among few choices for considering the disarray in what remained of Patty's mature life. As Eileen recalled, their mother settled first in a large house in Venice, California, with her new husband and the invalid Dr. Rogers, whom she continued to care for in his terminal illness. (The date of Rogers's death does not appear in the Record.) Eileen, enrolled at the Flint Ridge Sacred Heart School, soon announced that "she had two daddies" at home, news that provoked a meeting with members of the Parent-Teacher Club, who then found themselves charmed by the talented, newly divorced, and newly married Mrs. Wyman, whom they invited to address their next meeting.[16] At times, both sisters had been cared for outside their mother's home, Patty by Dotsie Smith in advance of the family's move to California and Eileen at some point watched over by family friend Mrs. A. P. Holland, who maintained that Pearl "had nothing to do with [her] children."[17]

If neglect prepared Curran's daughters for unusual living circumstances, it proved successful. Patty and Eileen, twenty-one and fifteen at the time of their mother's death in 1937, made a new family unit with PW acolyte Max Behr as guardian and gave an interview to the *Los Angeles Times* that adds to the scarce information on their life with a medium-mother. Gathered in Behr's bungalow on Palisades Avenue for the interview, the "two comely girls" were quick to adopt their mother's denial of spiritualist practice, but they also denied she had been a member of any church or had ever read Shakespeare. Behr came forward as family spokesman, ascending to hagiography when he asserted that what PW knew derived from a higher realm, as when that voice once repeated a prayer that Behr had formed in his mind. In short, said Behr, PW "had developed into a state of omniscience," an assertion that left the reporter gasping and "bewildered."[18]

Unmentioned in the story is Patty's 1934 marriage, following which, at the age of nineteen, she made Pearl a grandmother, naming her child Hope after the "brat" of PW's second-published novel. Called on for poetry to celebrate family weddings, Patience obeyed convention but also advanced proprietary views. At the wedding of Pearl Curran Rogers to Robert Wyman, PW seemed to take credit for effecting the reunion: "I with my cunning fetched the goblet" (PWR 28:4242). Two years later, writing to her godchild as "THY MITHER," PW moved to the edge of dark prophecy but settled for tender admonition. The man who takes a bride "nurtured o' love" from above—Patty's sign-painter groom, Gerald Peters—"needs take thee in love or his day shall fall short" (PWR 29:4326).

Pearl, sensing disaster, had already attempted to talk Patty out of the marriage. As Eileen later recollected, the "ratty little man," Peters, "supposedly studied art" but in fact "lived from hand to mouth." Perhaps petitioning for entry to the family of Patience Worth, he claimed psychic experiences, but Eileen remembered him for killing a puppy with a hammer, then for hitting Patty when she was pregnant. The household included Peters's mother as housekeeper, "a tiny woman with a Cockney accent." Not long after the birth of Hope, Patty sought a divorce. When in 1939 Patty married Max Behr, thirty-three years her senior and still on the scene two years after Pearl's death, she may have preferred not to recognize that he was marrying the daughter in the mother's stead. In the best of spheres, Behr would have preferred to join with PW, the sanctum sanctorum, had she been approachable. A "generous but domineering man," Eileen recalled. "Max thought he was Christ." He was also alcoholic, as Patty may have been as well by the time of their marriage, when Eileen, transferring to Santa Monica High School, became the couple's caretaker. Rarely sober, frequently violent, Patty "broke Eileen's ribs" on one occasion, Eileen told husband Ralph Kleymeyer.[19]

The couple required so much attention that Eileen was eventually expelled from school for numerous unexplained absences. When Eileen finally left the Behr household in 1941 after finding that Patty had brought home a party of soldiers, her sister had only two years to live. In November of 1943, police summoned by Max Behr found Patty dead in bed following an evening of drinking and an overdose of sleeping pills. She was twenty-seven. An autopsy surgeon reported that "a heart condition rather than the sedative might have caused her death." Eileen doubted the overdose was instrumental in her sister's death since she "was always taking them by the handful." Behr told police that his wife, drawing on some of her adoptive mother's psychic gifts, was convinced she would die early in life.[20] Risking prophecy in the month before Patty's 1916 birth, PW had caused her circle to marvel at a "first real attempt to forecast the future of anyone" when she reacted to speculation that an adopted child "might turn out badly." "Yea, but this shall never be!" the board spelled reassuringly (PWR 4:670).

In Behr's case, alcoholism exacted its penalty less mysteriously but more gradually. Sixty at the time of Patty's death, he continued to make demands on Eileen, threatening to get drunk if she broke off relations. Deaf, a danger to himself and a frequent patient at sanatoriums, Max called on Eileen's indebtedness for past support and on her love for him "as the only father she ever knew." Her freedom came only with marriage to Kleymeyer and Max's marriage to a woman described by Holland as "a beautiful Italian countess" and by Eileen as someone interested in his house and fortune. That wife too predeceased him, but Eileen and her new husband, who, as he wrote Ruth Duell, was convinced that Eileen failed to "realize how really monstrous [Behr] was," did not respond when Max attempted further communication.[21]

Pearl and Patience at the End

Supernormal counseling of Hollywood stars did not become the staple of Pearl's final years. Increasingly, her private life drew her from the public scene, and PW appears not to have been an important reserve for managing a household in continual flux. Pearl's reunion with Robert Wyman promised a California recovery from the truncated relationships of the past eight years. But a series of disappointments mentioned by Eileen in her 1957 interview with Ruth Duell resulted from Wyman's "many business ventures," possibly funded by Max Behr, which "never turned out." If, as Eileen recalled, her mother had no interest in reading the PW novels—in his 1937 interview Max Behr claimed that Pearl had never read *The Sorry Tale*—she also seems not to have lingered over PW's late-season advice on marriage and parenting. To a direct question from a Dr. Bell in the year after her 1931 marriage to Wyman, she answered flatly, "No, Patience never intrudes in my life or affairs" (PWR 28:4274), and did not entertain the possibility that her other voice had been a therapeutic form of dissociation whose chidings vented unease while amusingly deflecting criticism. In the months before the Wyman marriage, PW intruded far enough to say that in her "scarlet pettiskirt" (a red dress) Pearl "looketh like unto a town fool with his nose abust" (PWR 28:4221), noting as often before the medium's brazen folly. On the fall into dowdiness that Eileen recalled as the note of her mother's longest California years—"became terrifically drab—got hunched up. Not care about hair"—PW refrained from saying anything, not even to celebrate a triumph over vanity.

Pearl L. Wyman, as she signed herself, wrote Walter Prince a final letter dated February 24, 1934, containing the only inside narrative of her California years. His inquiry through a mutual friend drew the admission, as Pearl looked back to St. Louis, that "I seem to have lost myself to my friends and dropped off the earth!" Slightly more than a year into her third marriage, she evokes the Hollywood ending of reunion with her "first sweetheart" while making herself seventeen rather than nineteen at the time of their original engagement. As if it were a familiar topic, she also describes two years of "miserable health," ailments unspecified, and "the dear old depression." The result was that "I simply came a cropper as to health—for a time feared my ball of yarn was about wound up," and if not for the "good and perfect" love of her friend Patience, "I think I would have just waved bye bye to this old world." Of this dark period, Duell's jotting from Eileen's 1957 interview recorded: "Had miscarriage Wyman—so soon," but Pearl makes no mention of a pregnancy, waving away problems as "the bad part of things." The qualifying negatives and past tense of her denial make their own assertion: "I may only say I was not unhappy in my marriage but life in general was rather rotten."[22]

The circumstances of the Rogers-Wyman reunion do not appear in the Record, but the suitor redux was already on the scene in August of 1930 (PWR 27:4130), was counted as present at a session with "Mrs. Rogers" on July 8 of the next summer, and thereafter, with his adopted daughter, Roberta, was a regular among PW audiences. In the month when Wyman made his appearance in the Record, Rogers rewrote romantic smittenness using her own voice in lines that appeared among the numbered poems of "Odds and Ends":

I never swore until I met dear love,
I never uttered bromides such as "Dove"
Until I met that clever fetching man,
And then I swore—I simply murmured DAMN! (PWR 30, poem XI)

Wyman earns PW's compliment for his willingness to be "a-tethered / For her way is light and free" (PWR 28:4237). But there are darker notes. After speaking with a double voice of lyricism and wry fatalism in "Lamento Doloroso," Pearl Rogers had responded to her new environment by composing "Light Wines and Cocktails," a set of poems whose knowing jingles and gum-chewing rhymes could have been the work of a Mayme Ladd, given new life as a down-at-the-mouth casualty of the Great Depression ("Hoover's in the White House / Counting out the money . . . "). In these jottings, the PW voice is silenced by what would sound like a Dorothy Parker imitation were it not so clearly Pearl, emerging to speak for herself, as in "WHATHAP," dated August 1930:

They told me God was in the sky,
I believed it then—I know not why.
And now they say that love is hell.
And I'm in love again—Oh Well![23]

Looking ahead to the December 22, 1931, wedding at the home of Dotsie Smith, PW was free to pipe away yesterday as "a worn toy and well lost," yet tomorrow was no more than "a bauble yet to be," a caution against overinvestment. The Rogers voice, gone naughty poet, suggests that what audiences heard as frankness from PW was really euphemism:

If I should write the naughty things
I really truly think. . . . I'd have to burn the paper,
Or print it in red ink.

With marriage to Wyman still in prospect, artless poetry deleted romance from the plot. Rogers's thick-headed lover in this poem renders the "OLD STORY" wearier than wisdom:

She studied lore,
And store on store
Of knowledge did she
Lay away.
He didn't know the atom
From the molecule they say.
And yet she flung
The garment of drear
Wisdom for a veil . . .
And just a little later
Why, a baby came to wail. (PWR 30, poem XIX)

Pearl's conflicts in her new environment continued to be reflected in separate voices, one deriving from leather-bound texts, spiritually optative and romantic, the other attuned to celluloid novelty and jaded, smart-set convention. With her medium settled in Los Angeles, PW praised Dorothy Parker ("A wench egad, wi' a touch o whimsey / And I hae a lo'in o' her"). The medium had either forgotten Parker's taunting of spook writers or, belatedly, was discovering what they shared (PWR 27:4157). While PW continued to authenticate herself as seeress of love at the Montrose retreat, that voice could be teased by other audiences into wisdom on jazz ("Folly to the toes and whimsey to the head") and television ("All things be held by the law of rhythm"), Mickey Mouse, Mussolini, and flappers.[24]

Pearl was now, in another of the PW writings in "Odds and Ends," convicting herself, not her mother, of breaking off the engagement to Wyman before her marriage to Curran: "Beloved I did stab thee in thy youth," she confesses, while present illusion—"through all the years he sees no change in me" (PWR 30)—predicts recovery. In the first year of marriage, PW addresses Wyman ("oh bonny one") with a compassionate series of "I kens," referring to his "leaden hours" and the "silent anguishes thy tongue will never say." Business failures earn sympathy, and the image of Wyman's "river of love" uselessly ebbing into an open sea stirs an assurance that his suffering will not last. Hymning Wyman as builder, his literal occupation, Pearl's voice replaces PW's: "He is a builder now—the irony!" The story's failure remained to be played out, but the medium was temporarily able to ignore PW's hint that her argument against reincarnation might apply to romance as well: "It be nuff ' that ye stumble once" (PWR 27:4169).

Nearly a year again later, PW is free to abandon ambiguity. A September 1933 dictation, spoken aloud we must recall by Pearl Wyman, draws laughter from a group gathered at the Melrose house when PW constructs a "Bob" who confesses that having "plucked a thorn" he has much to learn. Forced to his knees "for love's sweet sake," the fictive Wyman pledges to keep faith while he says "amen" to a lesson he had apparently ignored, "How could I know that love is learning–how could I know." By now, Wyman would have been a practiced auditor of his wife's double voice, enterprising enough to make PW his medium to Pearl by daring the cover-voice "to tell what Pearl *really* thought about Bob." In return he receives nothing like the whole truth, only PW's drifting wishfully into platitude: "Thou art the all I hoped and dreamed / And could not let to go" (PWR 29:4310).

The actuality of Robert Wyman and his failed business ventures, as against the builder-knight spun from Pearl's memory, was otherwise. Eileen remembered being taken to several hotels by her mother at times when the marriage appeared ready to break up. The couple were certainly separated at the time of Pearl's death and probably divorced. If, as Eileen recalled, there were "suitors after Wyman," no serious relationship followed.[25]

It was an index to the course of Pearl's last marriage that Robert Wyman figured least among the three men playing major roles in her final years. When Pearl Wyman recounted PW's resurgence as a writer for Walter Prince, she named only Max Behr and Gordon Ray Young, a *Los Angeles Times* book reviewer and writer of popular westerns, for their encouragement and editorial service. In two years, Wyman told Prince, she had written just eight pages, then three more during a retreat of six weeks in the desert—"sitting with the typewriter and writing patiently"—until Max Behr came to live at her Santa Monica beach house in domestic "circumstances" she did not elaborate on. Crediting Behr's orderly methods, she found PW producing a new manuscript in little more than a month, once dictating nineteen pages at a time. "I was giddy with it," she enthused, "it was like being a child with a marvelous tale being told every day." Without specifying Behr's role, Wyman credited him with doing "the most beautiful work with the manuscript." He "keeps everything in working order," she told Prince. Behr's devotion appears to have sprung from a need to validate his own "important work" with PW; he is recorded in the Record urging her to reveal the clue to his chosenness: "Why am I a fit vessel for this work? Is there anything peculiar as regards my mentality?"(PWR 29:4306).

Gordon Ray Young, born in Ray County, Missouri, in 1886, was prepared for Patience Worth's arrival in Los Angeles. He had reviewed both *The Sorry Tale* and *Hope Trueblood* enthusiastically for the *Los Angeles Times* and with his wife—also named Pearl—attended one of the early PW sessions in California (August 27, 1930) noticed by Alma Whitaker. His 1917 review of *The Sorry Tale* adopted the same tone of savvy skepticism that William Reedy maintained in his survey of spook literature and dismissed, among other "stenographers of the heavenly host," Emily Hutchings, who he concluded must have been in touch with "a singularly deteriorated Mark Twain" when she channeled *Jap Herron.* Like Reedy again, he found himself moved suddenly to superlatives—"astounding," "remarkable"—when he discussed the *Tale*'s multiplicity of characters and the dignity and "biblical loftiness" of its narrative.[26]

Young's subsequent review of *Hope Trueblood* set aside PW as psychic phenomenon to argue that "by all the standards and requirements of literature she is an artist." As evidence he pointed to the "ironical motif" of Patricia Passwater's "God is Love" sampler as it recurs through the novel about a young woman's legitimacy and to the tone of intimation and suggestion by which the narrator, herself a medium for the "illimitable Patience Worth," establishes a cumulatively forceful character. As a winking figure for literary immortality, he noted, PW should alert contemporary mediums to possible calls for their service. If PW were "some Bronte from Spiritland" pressing her lips "to a tiny aperture through the bleak wall of death," would Marlowe, Chatterton, Byron, Shelley, and Keats, he asked, be far behind in seeking compensation for their abrupt endings?[27]

Young's intervention as an editor opened the PW dictations to a measure of conscious rewriting and did so without breaking automaticity's connection to its unconscious sources. Only if the "story of Shakespeare at 18," which Pearl titled "Elizabethan Mask," could be read in manuscript along with the familiarly titled but unfinished "The Eaglet" (Young called it a "knock out") would a reader be able to weigh the value of a Pearl-PW synthesis. Young found himself provoked to partnership when Wyman, as she told Walter Prince in her February 1934 letter, read him "all but the last three chapters or episodes I should call them. . . . After an hour or so he came over to me and said—'I'll tell you Pearl. You GOT SOMETHIN.'" Then followed an offer, contingent on her willingness to work hard over a year or two, that he would deliver "editing power gratis and all the time you need, just for the priviledge [*sic*] of having a hand in it. I think it is very great!"

Negotiations with PW began soon after. Young insisted that he would add nothing to her words but believed she could do better, "and I must have her very BEST." Consultation with PW found "the lady" not averse to "snippin a seam or puttin in a tuck so long as the pinafore were bettered." The metaphorical pinafore was significant in the context of PW's early stubbornness against accepting corrections from her audience, or medium, and in the light of Eileen's recollection that her mother, as a girl, had detested wearing pinafores.[28] In school, Pearl had once filled her pinafore with walnuts, which rolled down the aisle when she stood up, and she was punished by being made to stand on one leg, balancing a book on her head. Something of PW's defiance of authority emerges from Eileen's retelling: "Took book and threw it at schoolmaster's head." Resurrected, the image regathers what had been aimlessly spilled in recent years and promises a new version of the book as well-aimed revenge on schoolmasters. As scriptwriter, PW was now "fighting her battle bravely," Wyman told Prince, in editorial conferences of "the three of us," the retrieved "little Patience . . . sometimes meekly laboring like a beaver."

In her 1934 letter to Prince, Wyman was PW's delighted audience and therefore her own enthusiastic reviewer. The new story takes place, she said, during a May fete in England. A reader scanning her précis for gleams of brilliance will need to be prepared for disappointment, though the project's concept faintly foreshadows the 1998 movie *Shakespeare in Love* by making the origins of several plays part of the action and coaxing text-enshrined bardisms from the young poet:

> a may-mad fantacy [*sic*], covering only three days—through it moves Will Shakespere [*sic*], with his best friend who is a swineheard [*sic*] meeting those who happen in the inn—taking part in the homely little town affairs, with the beauty of the poet budding—The manner in which small incidents take root and flower in his imagination is simply devine [*sic*]. Gordon now says there is nothing in the language so packed full of poetry in i'ts [*sic*] highest sense—it is baudy [*sic*] rollicing [*sic*], tender, beautiful[,] sentimental, and cold all rolled in one.

A typical typescript from Wyman, the letter suggests how formidable an editor's task would have been, but her account of Young's dialogues with PW suggests script conferences rather than proofreading for mechanical errors. Heaven-sent spontaneity surrenders to the labor of producing what Young called a "defined" copy. Punctuation and phrasing that mimic Shakespeare's are "fearful to do," she said, and she claimed to have worked over some chapters as many as nine times. The gap of dissociation is bridged and nearly closed in the dialogues between Wyman, as she translates Young's counsel, and PW, who rewrites accordingly. If saying, "Fancy hath no power" fails to picture powerlessness, PW must "define fancy for us," as she does in "Mug hazed fancy." If a couplet mentions an ale song, the song needs to make an appearance. "Aye," says PW—"and bingo comes the song to order," says Wyman. If a character seems too young, PW will at most "argue a bit" then "recreate the whole character." For no better reason than "because she liked their rythm [*sic*]," PW had chosen Italian names for the Shakespeare story, then had "balked over it much" when Young, and Wyman in her editorial mode, argued for English names.

What was abandoned—remunerative public appearances and an adoring social circle—counted for less than what Wyman could claim as her own: "I have not the strength to waste . . . and do this too and I preferr [*sic*] this!" PW came forward with a preference for writing in "a rhyme never used," described as "a Rhythmed song sprawled as a briar." The confidence of the dramatic text earned Wyman's esteem, and setting aside the first person she urged it on Prince, promising to send him an episode. "You will find a very SURE Patience in this work—concretely laying hold upon it with a firm hand. Some of the episodes are as tender and lacy as down—some are rough and vulger [*sic*]." The aesthetic dichotomy Wyman cited, mindful of the contrast between Franco and Telka, continued to divide the agency that was its source, but it was a single-minded writer who reported from the brain's hidden processes, "My life is just my work now."

Even if the "Elizabethan Mask" failed to find its audience, Young assured his coworker, "Patience will be the greatest Poet living or dead when it is out." Accordingly, PW went beyond any hoaxer's claim to have channeled Shakespeare—"Who stirreth this pudding?" she asked defiantly—to tell a questioner that Shakespeare was of course Shakespeare but that she was free to improvise: "Weel, since he wert, need I for to create a-new? I hae loosed his tongue and wi' cunning pettiskirted the word in mine ain fancy." The temptation to outlandish claims was spelled glaringly large by Gordon Young's New York agent, who said of the manuscript that "it out Shakespears Shakespere!" [*sic*], but Wyman and Young agreed that the manuscript become book would have its most objective reception if published anonymously in England—Young having "his eyes on the Oxford Press," Wyman concerned that the bare mention of "psysic [*sic*]" would "start a gabble and hurt the work." Should the nine episodes of "thirty or there abouts pages each" ever come to light in the twenty-first century, they would at a minimum suggest what automaticity in harness was capable of when PW welcomed second thoughts.[29] Or those pages might strike a reader familiar with *Telka* as little more than a stylistic sequel, the eighteen-year-old "Will Shakespeare" supplying yet another version of the kind of poet Pearl Pollard knew best, risen from rural mire, "Stratford" an honorific renaming of a Texas or Ozarks village. For the demotic poet, Shakespeare needed no title to have written Shakespeare: the language of dreams, she knew, "be not in the hand of the Lord Mayor" when we see that its "eerie ghostlike quality . . . slippeth like a keen blade 'twixt the ribs o' hungered bumpkin or a lordin' a-puffeth past his be" (PWR 27:4141).

Nearing completion of the Shakespeare text in September 1933, PW had enthused to her coworkers, "Soon shall the nag jog to the mart, eh?" (PWR 29:4312), but there is no record of manuscript submission to a publisher. Aging with her medium, PW repeated herself by giving "almost verbatim" a poem that had been dictated once before (PWR 29:4330). Perhaps distracted by Patty's stormy marriage and its unhappy facsimile in her own life, Wyman had not seen Gordon Ray Young and his wife since May of 1934 when in April of 1936, with Eileen and Max Behr, she met them for an Easter reunion at the Patience Worth Sanctuary (PWR 29:4347). A week before Thanksgiving 1937, Wyman appeared at the Query Quest Club in Santa Monica. At about the same time, as Irving Litvag recounts in *Singer in the Shadows* the succession of events that led to her sudden and unexpected death, she told Dotsie Smith, "Oh, Dotsie, Patience has just shown me the end of the road and you will have to carry on as best you can" (*SS,* 263). A cold caught on Thanksgiving Day was followed by lumbar pneumonia, the illness given as the official cause of Pearl Wyman's death at Wilshire Hospital on December 3, 1937.[30] Fragments of information gathered by Ruth Duell suggest other complications. Eileen twice cited her mother's smoking, once for its damage to her voice, then again in direct connection with her pneumonia. Eileen also speculates about other possibilities—which Duell noted as "Tumor? Uterine?"—recalling only that her mother had talked worriedly about dying. Duell's telegraphic notes reporting Holland's diagnosis make little sense—"Scaled foot. Caused lumbar pneumonia"—though another respondent also mentioned "Skin disease foot."[31]

The PW voice had evoked eternity often enough to make it seem a familiar neighborhood and death a dozy transition, as in a characterization of June 1933: "A bit weary wi' the fetters, a yawn, a blink and the wakin'" (PWR 29:4302). In the Record, the PW "Family" registers no shock at Pearl's sudden death, whatever may have been her intimates' sense of loss. Max Behr, described in the Los Angeles obituary as a "Spiritualist minister," officiated at a service held, appropriately enough, at the Wee Kirk o' the Heather in Glendale's Forest Lawn Cemetery, and his sermon in honor of the "snuffed candle" appears in the PW Record (29:4372–74) along with the only remnant of the Shakespeare manuscript, the poem "The Mire Song." According to Eileen, music at the ceremony included "Because, Because," the song sung at Pearl's wedding to Wyman, though he is not mentioned as one of the mourners.

An endnote to the chronological PW Record directs the reader to the Pearl-Patience burial site in the Sunrise Slope section of Forest Lawn, Grave 3, Lot 5778 (PWR 29:4375). On her burial marker Pearl Curran became legibly ascendant over "Patience Worth," a name bound by quotation marks. While it had been characteristic for the PW voice to cite the medium's "wry wit" while pointing out "thy wit be borrowed" (PWR 25:4011), it was probably inevitable that Pearl would perform a public cross-examination to retrieve herself from what she had often conceded as PW's autonomy: "Out of naught save word and wheedle hae I built flesh" (PWR 14:2695). As happily as her annihilators, Curran's PW would deconstruct herself, but still with a distinction: "I have caused tears, agonies, and bloody sweats. This is creation. Lo, that that is me is but a myth; yet that which IS me is before thee, for the flesh is nothing" (PWR 25:3970). Addressed to Curran by Curran the voice would ask, *what in you am I?*

In a testy exchange in the summer of 1932, a dialectic of identity took place in which the medium challenged the control to define its authority, PW revising the terms of her defense several times. In their territorial debate, Curran spoke of hearing the characters of her novels directly, not mediately, while PW, unwilling to be abolished, argued that what Curran had received was her control's deep knowledge of once-living persons, transformed by "fancy." But, protested Curran, when delivering PW's redactions of the Gospels, she heard a voice that was not PW and that sounded like "the voice I heard when writing the words of the Lord in the Sorry Tale." Increasingly, the pair articulated both their authority and their interdependence in ways that describe what Mary Austin called the experience of any fiction writer. PW had borrowed the spirit of the scriptures, then had "musiced" the words according to her own "inclination," or had drawn on the phantoms of once-living persons who "breathed, suffered, hoped and despaired, e'en as ye" and then unleashed them to "trek the page," becoming in relation to those sources "what my harp be unto me." Curran then was medium to a medium, or was constructing a redundancy, since PW processes had to be defined as some version of her own. Though "she felt rather fresh in asking this question," Max Behr said of the conversation he recorded,[32] Curran wondered whether PW's personages were not already impending fictions, acting "as mummers, the word you use to characterize the actors in a fanciful play." If so, PW contended, they came to life only because they had been articulated by one who identified with "their whole human lot" and who "breathed new life into old atoms." But how otherwise might a writer of fiction define herself, Curran could have remarked as PW confessed her relation to those atoms: "They be unto me what I be unto you." Curran had impelled herself into quizzing a mirror that showed her hand and PW's moving as one.

"What a taskin'," the dictating voice almost breathed, appalled at the diminishing returns of signification enacted one day at the home of Gordon and Pearl Young:

> To dip the sea of imagination with the cups of finiteness.
> Words—little separate fellows—
> Lone, meaning nought.

Take, for example, the moon, infertile and overcolonized with signs "tethered" to it by poets' untranslatable urges, including the present poet's mixed urges to surpass convention while toying with language's in-house ironies:

> That age-old tryster, tawny, red-swollen,
> Gold, mellow, leprous, pale, pallid-pale, sickle, disked,
> Hauntful, blazing, ghost-like, eerily shuttling cloud,

Phantom-like, spreading mist of silver;
Retreated high wi' a shepherd star, lazy-hung, cumbrous,
Laggardly rising from a fruitful field—empty! . . .
Pantin' 'twould seem, as 'twere Eve's breast pulsin',
An' the gem a-glistenin' 'pon it.
Yet ye say *moon* wi' confidence. (PWR 28:4236)

The poem's contest against facile naming, while reveling in it, leaves PW undone as the moony signs that made her. As a strategy for escaping the orbit of her wraith made of words, Curran's California-cultivated "Light Wines and Cocktails" happily ignored the bounty she inherited from nineteenth-century poets and the publicity that brought the PW poetry greater attention than, for the most part, it deserved. In her final years, the medium could at least demonstrate that the term *control* had no application to a verse-maker who could go unpunished for rhyming *June* and *moon* and who could throw down *PISH* as her final word (PWR 30). Never single, the voice heard by Patience Worth audiences took its life from a contest whose imperative against one-sided dominance called for an echoic formula: "a worthy aggressor must be received with Worthy aggression."[33]

Chapter 9

THE NEURAL PEARL: AUTOMATICITY FOR ALL

> The function of consciousness must be in part to dummy up and shape a coherence from all the competing conflicting subsystems that processed experience. By nature it lied. Any rendition we might make of consciousness would arise from it, and was thus about as reliable as the accused serving as sole witness for the prosecution.
>
> —Richard Powers, *Galatea 2.2*

Mediums Quiz the Mirror

Although Pearl Curran told readers of "A Nut for Psychologists" that she would aid men of science "with all my power" by delivering the "facts" of her mediumship, her fatigue with familiar diagnoses was evident. When the "beautiful French story" (which was never finished and never titled) began to be dictated, she estimated that a mind-scientist would quickly conclude that not only the names of Villon and Basselin but the character of her story about them "must have slipped into my subconsciousness whole while I was not looking! Sly dog!" (*CPW,* 400). Suddenly become the reader of a "wonder book," the first person must assert itself, intending no disrespect for wonders, to claim some version of ownership. "If Patience Worth is a part of me, I auto-educated myself," Curran said (*SS*, 215–16). Well before the brain could be imaged in its magnetic resonances, the language of the introspective writer-medium found itself at a borderland of agency, between experience too glorious or threatening to be claimed as one's own and too familiar to be denied.

For James Merrill as poet-medium, double-mindedness became not simply a curiosity but a mandate: "to remain of two minds about everything that was happening."[1] After casually looking out and up to "that realm of, oh, cosmic forces," Merrill pointed to the "absurd, flimsy contraption" of the Ouija as "a hedge against inflation" (*CPJM,* 110), unembarrassed by "the degree of credulity" its dictations required (*CPJM,* 143, 168). Curran, too, greeting a rush of language from nothing more than the "dead wood" under her hands, was ready to settle for diagnostic formula when she told readers of *Patience Worth's Magazine* that the "average" Ouija-board sitting is "an insult to the intelligence," the board only an instrument for moving thought "from the subconscious to the conscious mind" (*PWM,* Oct. 1917, 9).

Probably everyone "wants to get beyond the self," Merrill granted, to some kind of "god" within, where the self is "stranger and freer and more far-seeing" (*CPJM,* 107–8). Yet even while playing the lesser self, the medium must eventually emerge to acknowledge that the natural he or she is the inexplicable event. Merrill is the performer being interviewed, not his first speaker, Ephraim. At times, Curran could not resist the temptation to demote *Patience Worth* to pen name. The mediums' polarity—a minimizing of originary circumstances and a sense of boundaryless inflation in the result—is as evident in Merrill's comments on the production of *The Changing Light at Sandover* as in Curran's attempts to crack the nut of her own experience. On any basis other than their dramas of doubleness and the paradoxical stakes of mediumship, there would be no point in speaking of Curran and Merrill in the same space.

The experience of mediumship must be spoken of as double both from within and from without. The board game, trivial in itself, points through its practitioner to possibilities almost but never quite beyond wording. The medium, performing as no more than an interested questioner, is aware of respondents numbering from one to dozens who speak as if from elsewhere but raise suspicions in their host that they come from within. Outside the game, from experimental and neurological perspectives adopted by psychology, the subjects are doubled again by being addressed in a different discourse. Or perhaps one should say that for psychological research the subjects are multiplied, because its questions—about dissociation, memory, automaticity, and subliminal self-representation—are open-ended. Stepping back from the Ouija experience, the medium takes introspection to its limits. Stepping into questions raised by the immediacy of Pearl Curran's and James Merrill's scorn or celebration, puzzlement and discovery, the voices of psychology will make their own contribution.

In practice, Merrill struck the note of ordinariness, with an overturned Blue Willow teacup as pointer, then by arranging the alphabet and Yes/No of the board on a cloth, or cardboard, or, for portability, he suggests, brown paper. Namer of the twentieth century's God Biology, his unseen interlocutor in their mind-bending conversations, Merrill confesses to little reading in the sciences ("The simplest science book is over my head" [*CPJM,* 86]) just as Curran made a point of professing even larger deficits. Self-described, the medium qualifies as little more than an instrument for centuries of talky peers. Cautioning against metaphysical airs, as had PW, Merrill's "Wystan" (Auden) advised the poet to look past childish autonomy "TO POWERS BEHIND THE THRONE. . . . THINK WHAT A MINOR / PART THE SELF PLAYS IN A WORK OF ART."[2] By the time of a 1982 interview with J. D. McClatchy, Merrill had moved past instrumentality to a more refined doubleness, suspended between an idea of the self as a gamer of language and point of origin for an unidentifiable alphabet emerging into partial legibility. Or he could turn around the values of that taut line of doubleness. Real as the powers behind the throne or beneath consciousness might claim to be, they would be "inconceivable," in a double sense, without the "costume box" of language (*CPJM,* 110). The signifying costume supplied by the poet makes real those "oh, cosmic forces," his three volumes and a coda taunting their multiplicity and his own with dependence on his naming-as-creation.

For both mediums the paradox of identity's immersion in self giving way to the emergence of some Other calls for a deeper etching of the line between first and third persons to preserve an illusion of the distance between them. Making a third person of his text, Merrill could say that he saw something in it that verged on an idea-swollen Shaw-like preface and was therefore "not at all the kind of page I could turn out by myself" (*CPJM,* 112). Though he did.

Curran could be tempted to immersion, temporarily making it a goal, as if language were an afterthought rather than a reification. Unconfined identity was PW's deep gift to Curran as she told John Livingston Lowes, "I *am* Ione . . . in `Telka.' I'm living, dying—not telling a story. The board has nothing to do with it."[3] In comparison with the "magic picture book" she had been given, the dictated text could appear shrunken, made plain and predictable by the imagery that held her in custody. Introspection alone has no devices to settle the priority or interdependence of visual and verbal processes; and the pictures threaten the medium with their inexpressibility. "Well, now I don't understand this," she remarked as visual imagery floated to the surface of cognition (*CPW,*

322–23). Within a wordless magic picture book, Curran could only dwindle to shipmate with Patience Worth on her Atlantic voyage or compete with the trance-mindedness of spiritualist celebrities. In the panoramas she recounted for Walter Prince, Curran as object appears as a "tiny figure," as if summarizing the history of little women's arrival at their art. But in a purposive dialogue, Curran described successions of "magnificent pictures" while PW continued to insist, "Song is born of thirst" and "I would sing." As Curran found her place among a "chastity" of vibrating silver threads, she announced, "I have learned MY ONE NOTE!" and PW responded, "Then I may sing exultantly." What Prince calls the *rapport* between PW and the medium as her word-seeking instrument has the look on his page of a double-voiced first person, summarized in PW's echoic announcement, "I am uttered" (*CPW*, 323–27).

Voices in the mind had a familiar sound for both Merrill and Curran. Many of Merrill's conversations with the dead in *Scripts for the Pageant* represent persons he had known, and for the first two volumes of *Sandover*, the material of the poetry came in an "unprecedented way" that was at the same time "like what a friend or stranger might say over the phone" (*CPJM*, 85). In Curran's mediumistic simile, the voice is like that of "any other friend gone into the great beyond." While the market babble of *The Sorry Tale* went forward in an unspecified foreign language, "over and above" that noise Curran said she could hear the voice of PW, which explained everything to her (*CPW*, 395). Later recalled by a visitor from the early 1920s, an audible version of that voice was part of Curran's engagement with PW, when Curran's "Let's have a little Patience" was followed by a "little tinkly voice," softer than the medium's and "with lilt," sounding "far off" despite its "Missouri twang" when speaking of England.[4] The explanatory voice has become the unexpected guest of automaticity, assuring the medium of the constancy, even easy familiarity, of immanent otherness. But automaticity is duplicitous, its generosity suggesting unlimited resources. The desire for an absence of limits took Curran beyond the skull's store of language when she found herself "kneeling on the edge of chaos," unable to pray or say a word to convey the brilliance, times ten thousand, she said, that permitted her to see "*infinitesimal* substance. . . . it might be new planets in creation; it might be *anything*" (*CPW*, 325–26). Wordless, a medium looks into nothing, or in a lighter mood at "length and looniness," as Merrill spoke of "The Book of Ephraim" in 1973. By 1993, Merrill was ready to describe the whole of *Sandover* as "an imaginative construct," as must be "the ineffable, unknowable universe" in whatever version (*CPJM*, 85, 168).

Past the counterpoint of their conversations with themselves, Merrill and Curran could not avoid approaching the oblique mirror implicit in their arts. As in Luigi Pirandello's *Henry IV*, the through-line of Merrill's extended performance consists in the *I-am-he, I-am-not-he* of what Henry-JM sees when he looks in the mirror. Whatever the gain for Merrill of hearing the God Biology speak beyond craft, he was unwilling to abandon his office as poet and could bear to speak of seeing himself in the mirror from which others clamored to escape.

> If only we were less free to reflect;
> If diametrics of the mirror didn't
> Confirm the antiface there as one's own. . . .[5]

The same difficulty, caught in the same metaphor, arose when PW in a conversation with her medium commented, "It be hard to reflect in a mirror, the mirror itself" (PWR 18:3265). By 1925, a PW poem would call the mirror "a jest . . . a phantomery," and ask of it, "Am I a myth, or you?" (PWR 21:3566).

Patience Worth would not have gone unemployed in the century that followed her first fame. Nor would her medium have failed to draw attention from a twenty-first century generation of cognitive psychologists, including neuropsychologists keen to reveal the very image of PW processes illuminated on a map of Pearl Curran's brain. Large as that leap might be—from the spiritual telegraph of a more technologically innocent generation to the registering of magnetic resonances given off by activity in the brain's prefrontal cortex or hippocampus—one continuity seems certain. The PW phenomenon remains a source of more questions than answers, even as the questions have become more focused and experimentally relevant and less drawn to the idea of a sleuthed solution than Walter Franklin Prince's term *case* implied.

As a new but also continuously revisable science of the mind-brain goes forward, psychology has complicated enormously the task it would have of describing to Pearl Curran how she was both *an* author and *the* "authoress," PW representing a schema in her memory, its processes multiple and overlapping with those she demonstrated as conscious writer and registering its unconscious intentionality in automatic writing. Curran may have expressed her inscape best, most in conformity with what experiment and neuropsychology would see retrospectively in her case, when she confided to readers of the *Unpartizan Review* in 1920 that "there seems to be no definite place where my consciousness ceases, and that of Patience comes in" (*CPW,* 398). Pearl and Patience, named separately, served contemporary observers as an example of dissociation, but the two were connected in ways that neither Curran's introspection nor invidious comparisons of their literary intelligence could articulate. Though limited now to a retrospective view, psychology, with its recourse to neural science, can do much to bring an author-medium out of the shadows and into an arena where nominal doubleness can be seen in the context of multiple features of the writing process.[6]

Had it been available before 1937, fMRI testing might have made PW resonantly visible as a property of her medium, not simply for debunking's sake but as a demonstration that Curran herself contained the wonders so often celebrated in PW. Illuminating PW activity on the brain scan of a recumbent Pearl Curran as she read or dictated PW text, a neuropsychologist would be particularly attentive to activity in the Broca's and Wernicke's areas of the neocortex, "the former largely focused on creating speech, the latter on processing incoming words."[7] The investigator might be interested in comparing the location and intensity of brain activation registered under such trials as: Curran singing the words to a Thomas Moore ballad, then calling on PW to recite a speech by the heroine of *Telka;* Curran reading a passage from "Rosa Alvaro," followed by one from *Hope Trueblood;* and finally, asking PW to dictate a poem on a subject of the experimenter's choice. The comparative results of such tests could not be expected to provide fully nuanced portraits of the medium and automatic writer, but the commonalities and relative differences in brain activations between writings either known to or claimed by Curran and those calling on identifiable PW processes would have provided distinguishable images proceeding from a single brain. As in the experience of author Steven Johnson when he offered himself for fMRI experiment, the brain's relative intensity of illumination ("hotter," "more yellow") in language-related areas registered at one point that he was reading his own prose. Moreover, Johnson's hippocampus, the seat of memory, gave bright red evidence, brighter than when he read from a neuroscience textbook, of false starts and revisions he recollected from earlier versions of his work.[8]

Common-sense questions accumulate all the same. What account of perception, attention, and memory amounts to a formula for the association of uncommon historical idioms and imagery into unconscious, automatically delivered patterns of language that, articulated as poetry and fiction, belong to a process substantially more complex than recall of the meaning of miscellaneous historical words or the names of authors? If PW is taken as the sign for enabling cognitive processes that registered the fullness of Pearl Curran's talents, should an observer then join the medium in denying her primary agency? If Pearl Curran, represented as Ouija-board automaton, must be distinguished categorically from writers (whatever their talent) who speak of their craft, her example has the interest only of a career ventriloquist whose dissociated blithe spirit by some means quietly entered and returned from the House of Literature at whim. To set aside cognitive questions raised by the PW text simply on the grounds of its automatic production seems less reasonable—when inquiry into those questions can be reasonably interesting—than a flat declaration of boredom after literary taste has sampled the product.

Stephen Braude, whose interest in the case of PW led him to edit selected poems for modern publication, has argued that the persona's writings were the "dissociative unleashing of prodigious latent capacities" in Pearl Curran. His thesis attracted two interested commentaries, published simultaneously with his, from faculty in psychiatry and philosophy. Psychiatrist Jean Goodwin asks: if PW represents an extreme case, "Do we know what we mean by normal dissociation?" and "What is the relationship of normal dissociation to creativity in general?" More critically, philosopher Jennifer Radden finds the alternatives of communication with a spirit and latent capacities "equally unpalatable" and suggests that "knowing deception" by Curran be considered. Radden nevertheless paraphrases the latent-capacities argument sympathetically and offers a compactly stated summary of influences from Curran's youth. Goodwin's questions about the applicability of "normal dissociation" to extraordinary PW performances still linger. Braude offers Patience Worth, in need of "empirical" elaboration, as "a partial answer" to the question, "What are the limits of our subconscious, latent, creativity?"[9] Clearly, the aim of normalizing the dissociative features of the PW phenomenon is both consistent with and a necessary precedent to speculations on an unleashed Pearl Curran.

The project is inherently interdisciplinary. Confessions of vulnerable methodology, too, can extend across disciplines, as when a psychologist grants, "It is in the nature of the laboratory to simplify conditions."[10] Moving across the discursive divide between one disciplinary tribe and another makes clear that the core term of the literary domain's complaint against psychology as snapshot, qualia-challenged experimentalism—its reductionism—has a quite different and positive valence for the researcher seeking to build increments of discovery on progressive discovery, as in the admittedly "utopian" hope expressed by a distinguished experimentalist in 1997 that "in a decade or so we may have an early biophysiology of consciousness."[11] As intellectual standard, reductionism can detect unprofitable labor on either hand. While sociobiologist-entomologist-fictionist Edward O. Wilson observed in 1998 that the absence of empirical foundation had clearly not inhibited postmodern literary theorists ("blissfully free of existing information on how the mind works"), Henry Roediger III, surveying experimental progress at about the same time, could find some early claims for the neural bases of cognition "not just wrong but completely far-fetched today."[12]

Set against the trope of reductionism as a self-devouring serpent, with cognitive psychology disappearing into biochemical neurology, those processes in turn disappearing into the maw of physics—metaphysics and mathematics no doubt the abstractly delighted spectators—there is such a thing as Steven Pinker's "good reductionism," notes Steven Johnson, not an attempt to reduce one discipline to the terms of another but to connect them by inspecting each other's results.[13] For Nancy Cartwright, that comparison is better expressed as surveillance of a negotiated "patchwork" of loosely related territorial laws rather than as the construction of a "pyramid." For Carl Craver, neuroscientific research into specific cognitive processes and functions, proceeding both downward and upward in complexity, can demonstrate "how myopic reductive models are when it comes to describing the unity of science." Increasingly, literary theory has drawn on cognitive psychology to articulate and respond to questions in its own domain while neural science, often working within the artificial simulations of the computer, has given attention to emergent or synergistic properties belonging to a whole that cannot be derived from the sum of its constituent parts. To complete the discursive circle, Manuel DeLanda has observed that awareness of holistic phenomena emerging from interaction among contributing formal properties "must be as old as art itself."[14]

More or Less Dissociated

Current diagnostic profiles of dissociational disorders do not match well with what is known of Pearl Curran's experience and behavior. The term *dissociative identity disorder,* widely applied in cases of post-traumatic stress, often involves childhood physical or sexual abuse and is manifested in sudden personality switches from a primary self to an alter. While Curran occasionally mentioned headaches accompanying her PW dictations, an observed but not universal characteristic of DID personality switches,[15] the PW board writings were part of a familiarly social, scheduled routine rather than unexpected changes of identity and were not characterized by the kind of trance state entered into by spiritualist performers whose much-publicized lives bristled with symptoms. PW conversations and literary dictations do not resemble a pattern of surges from traumatically amnesic experience,[16] even if one finds Walter Prince an incurious clinician when he accepts at face value Curran's assurance, "On the whole, my childhood was happy" (*CPW,* 321).

While Curran's was not an instance of pathological dissociation, the popular version of a "control" consciousness that chooses an automatic medium as instrument of its remarkable productivity had from the beginning implied some form of doubleness at the heart of things. With broad continuity, psychology has continued to generate versions of cognitive dual processing that carry forward while refining and complicating the rubric of "two minds in one brain," as Jonathan Evans has called it. Given the multiplicity of mental processes the distinction is understood to involve, dual categories cannot reflect the sort of clean dissection that would wholly identify PW with Pearl Curran's unconscious cognitive processing. Under his choice of the headings "Intuitive Mind" and "Reflective Mind," Evans lists familiarly contrasting attributes of Unconscious and Conscious, Implicit and Explicit cognition. Attributes that psychologists have associated with each of the "two minds" appear in an accompanying table, including Evans's view of the evolutionary "old mind" as the source of intuitive cognition and the evolutionarily recent "new mind" with its capacity for conscious reflection and language. Flattering as it might be to the language-proficient, consciously reflective mind to discover itself in control, such control is largely illusory, Evans argues, requiring unconscious support and characteristically rationalizing its intuitive promptings to maintain the illusion of control. In a comparable way, rapidly deployed experiential intuitions that could not be corrected by the intelligence of the reflective mind would be regularly subject to frustration of long-term goals. Arguing that neuropsychological research continues to support a dualism of interactive minds in whatever cognitive domain, Evans describes their relation in terms that would not have surprised Pearl Curran: in a great multiplicity of interactions, the two minds qualify both as a "partnership" and "a somewhat uneasy alliance."[17]

Had Curran in her later years sought a professorial psychologist to address the question of control between PW and herself, she might have identified Ernest Hilgard (1904–2001), who hoped to qualify the idea of a dissociated second personality when he adopted the metaphor of "hidden observer" to describe in hypnotized subjects an unconscious "form of parallel information processing" that provides covert access to "matter-of-fact, reality bound" experience. A member of the Stanford University psychology faculty for four years when Curran died, Hilgard had grown up in Belleville, Illinois, across the Mississippi from St. Louis, and was fourteen when *Hope Trueblood* was published. As late as 1977 he was citing Charles Cory's 1920 study of the woman whose B personality, like Curran's fictional Rosa Alvaro, spoke broken and crudely imitative Spanish. Hilgard's applications of hypnosis to unconscious cognition carried forward the work of William James and Morton Prince, and with others he made automatic writing the basis of newly experimental studies of dissociation. In a brief glance at Litvag's *Singer in the Shadows,* he comments on the "St. Louis housewife" as an example of the automatic writer's readiness to abandon the Ouija board when it had served its purpose as an initial prompt.[18]

With his predecessors, Hilgard argued that hypnosis and automatic writing make it possible "to converse directly with the dissociated consciousness,"[19] a conversation familiar to PW's interlocutors. Correctly anticipating criticism, he was quick to explain the hidden observer not as another version of the logically recessive homunculus-self within the self-to-be-explained but as "a convenient label for the information source capable of a high level of cognitive functioning, not consciously experienced by the hypnotized person."[20] To describe the subconscious ordering of information sources under a single term, whether *PW* or *hidden observer,* locates the covert assembling of a lengthy biblical novel under a single, large tent, but Hilgard's interest in Cory's 1920 study and his glance at Curran's secondary personality may have energized the experimentalist's overreach, as when he asked facetiously of writer Jessamyn West, "Does she perhaps have a hidden observer to organize the material for her?"[21]

Studies that have identified quite ordinary forms of cognitive multiplicity would now support the petition for normalcy implied when Curran assured Walter Prince that she'd had no invisible companions as a child. Assessing a broad range of normalcies, experimentalists observe a general "dysunity [*sic*] of consciousness" and the "inherent multiplicity of the brain," minimally evident in the mind's success at undertaking quite different tasks at the same time.[22] Attempts to sort out Pearl matters from Patience matters today would need to draw on research dealing with variously networked processes of association and dissociation, decentered, though never entirely separated, from versions of a sociocultural "I." While granting that a galaxy of terms swirls about the Western idea of the self, Matthew Erdelyi articulates the widely held view that "the unitary *self* is an illusion," stipulating that dissociation necessarily results from states of "polypsychism" where "self" may alternately be composed of multiple modules, serve as one module among others in a social "suprasystem," or experience contradictory instructions ("GO, NO") at the synaptic level.[23]

For philosopher Daniel Dennett, the sturdy singular self from which an additional self might become dissociated is the original fiction, a presumed center spied as we look back from a circumference of phenomenal reports only, which constitute "multiple drafts" but never identity's fair copy.[24] The real "bogey tale" view, according to Daniel Schacter, is that dissociation somehow disrupts a foundationally unitary self. Instead, dissociation should be seen as "a natural consequence of the basic architecture of normal cognition," susceptible to disruption between "parallel interacting systems" of memory.[25] As often observed, the traditional normalist architecture of the first person, become a tent city of selves, might be described as the meta-subject of much postmodern fiction.

In a parallel effort, psychology has been prepared for some time to characterize dissociation as the writer's means of grace. In a recent "quest for Xanadu," as Nancy Andreasen, an MD and English PhD, describes her inquiry into Coleridgean mysteries of creativity, the bibliographical approach of John Livingston Lowes would give way to neuroscience, with creative individuals from Tchaikovsky to Neil Simon described as less likely than others to filter their floods of sensory input, understanding themselves as detached observers capable of slipping at times of production into a dissociative state.[26] In the metaphorical resonance of one account that links features of dissociation and imaginative activity, a hypnotized subject's bypassing of executive-level "planning, monitoring and coordination" has the sound of a creative revolution, a tale of two cognitive cities: "lower subsystems . . . enact specific behavior sequences" but with a supervisory system weakened, "inappropriate or irrelevant associations and behavior" flourish.[27] To be sure, the psychologist's use of the terms *higher* and *lower* points to levels of cognitive complexity rather than a scale of cultural values, but talk of unconsciously triggered subsystems and unplanned associations negotiating with conscious deployments evokes a long-familiar pattern, Bohemian to Beat, of creative process.

Studies of exceptional performance describe a "dissociative style" in subjects whose responses did not suggest a "disturbed function" but showed "an enhanced ability to direct and divide attention." Already in the mid-1920s, experiments with hypnotically divided attention in automatic writing were providing evidence of "interference or leakage between conscious behavior and subconscious tasks." At the end of the century, Yves Rossetti and Antti Revonsuo prefaced a volume of studies aimed at looking "beyond dissociation" to consider how "dissociated modules interact to contribute to the whole mind brain function."[28]

To locate PW within a pattern of neural processes apparently dissociated from but actually interactive with the conscious Pearl Curran displaces a radical dichotomy of selfhood and acknowledges mutuality and simultaneity in processes too interdependent over time to be named other to each other. A new study of imagination and creativity by Jonah Lehrer, drawing on neurological experiments by Mark Jung-Beeman and John Kounios, relates the "Eureka!" or "Aha!" experience to an electrical surge of gamma waves from the anterior superior temporal gyrus (aSTG), a fold of tissue on the surface of the brain's right hemisphere. Previously dissociated functions of the brain come together in a moment of insight after a period of conscious searching has yielded nothing—save that the "prepared mind" was necessary for the instant of discovery. Curran's breakthrough moment, too, had followed a year of apprenticeship at the board when the PW voice and vocabulary began "solving verbal problems with insight," as the experimenters described their subjects' epiphanies. Respelling PW as aSTG, however, would not conclude experimenters' questioning what sequence of unconscious memory processes developing in what emergent relation to one another might finally consolidate in the moment of "Eureka."[29]

Memory: The Implicit Word-Hoard

> The way memory can resemble steeple bells,
> the play of them, the bell ropes having left
> our hands
> —Carl Phillips, "The Smell of Hay"

Diligent or lucky research may someday reward a suspicion that Pearl Curran regularly consulted historical sources. The researcher would then need to address the difference between consciously strategic enrichment of a text within the limits of working memory and the fluent dictation of poetry and fiction from schematically linked storages of unconscious long-term memory. If never dispensable, skepticism should not be based on the assumption that in no circumstances could human memory retain and put to fluent use the arcana, long since attended to and encoded, that appeared in the PW dictations. As anyone might, Pearl Curran benefited at some level of memory from more resources than she could consciously summon into conversation, and the content of what she drew on existed in patterns of association somehow adaptable to a distinct idiom of poetry, fiction, and declamatory table talk.

Distinguishing Pearl from Patience benefits from an inquiry into the relative contributions of implicit and explicit learning and memory, subjects that psychology continues to debate and qualify. Emphasizing "the primacy of the implicit," Arthur Reber sees "no clear boundary" between implicit and explicit learning and instead emphasizes "cooperative processes" between them. Implicit learning, Reber argues, takes place when "encoding occurs without the subject's intention to learn" and "is measured by the influence of that knowledge on another task."[30] Implicit learning therefore defies direct interrogation, as when Walter Prince questioned Curran on her reading, since while subjects may have "a 'feeling of knowing,'" they "do not, by and large, know what it is they know."[31] Unconscious accrual of associated patterns of language and imagery would not be recognized by Curran as her own since, according to Reber, the raw knowledge acquired from implicit learning "is always ahead of the capability of its possessor to explicate it." In a study of implicit memory, Daniel Schacter points out that early psychic researchers were the first to document the emergence of knowledge in subjects who believed that what they spoke was "foreign to their own conscious personalities."[32] That Pearl Curran believed Dickens had written *The House of the Seven Gables* would not have prevented automaticity's deploying of Dickensian patterns of language or stylized characterization from implicit memory with no need to credit their source.

For the literary medium astonished at her output, unconsciously acquired information would have developed precisely in "the absence of a link to the self," a capacity, though a dissociated capacity (or negative capability), which is then capable of drawing upon other resources of memory. The very premise of the Ouija board—its spellings cannot be traced to the conscious intention of either participant—creates an efficacy of dissociated production for both. Texts seemingly long forgotten by Curran need not have had for her anything of conscious "me-ness" about them even as their associations were being formed within memory processes over time. A characteristic basis for the wide variety of unconscious structures and processes, including automatically acquired skills, John Kihlstrom argues, is "memory without the self . . . reference to the self as the agent or patient, stimulus or experiencer, of the event has not been preserved."[33] As William James was aware in setting forth his stream-of-thought metaphor, an earlier "state of mind," when unapprehended by later states of mind, "is as if it belonged to another stream of thought," the qualifier "as if" serving to reassure polite readers of their utter normalcy when encountering a stream alienated from them by time.[34] That a young woman entering the twentieth century might at one point dictate sentences containing authentically historical or pseudo-archaic English, unaware that they were her own acquisitions and improvisations, then consciously recall her admiration for Tennyson could readily be addressed as separate but parallel mental processes or be seen as alternating in a general system of implicit and explicit memory, now one process, now the other, predominating.

However rashly, biography seeks entrance where neuropsychology will not since, according to Howard Gardner, the latter must disclaim an ability "to model events or processes unfolding over many years." Connecting the death of George Pollard to subsequent retrievals from Pearl Curran's memory at the prompt of a Ouija board has become routine but left to speak for itself, as when Leonard Zusne and Warren Jones observe that "the trigger" for the 1913 onset of PW dictations was the father's death.[35] Both narrative and experiment have reasons for converging on the metaphor of a trigger for events in consciousness. For memory researchers it is not enough that an original perception make its way, however surreptitiously, into the brain. For retrieval, a memory trace must be activated by an appropriate cue, defined as "the information present in the individual's cognitive environment when retrieval occurs."[36] At a minimum, one can say that before George Pollard's death on September 6, 1912, no results comparable to the PW dictations had been triggered for Pearl Curran in the time since July she had spent at the board with Emily Hutchings and her mother. Curran was, however, accustoming herself to a habit of dissociated passivity, a cognitive reaction against Emily Hutchings's interest in coaxing talk, racy or edifying, from the dead. Somewhat surprisingly, there are no expressions of grief from Pearl recorded in either the Hutchings or Curran transcripts following George Pollard's death. If, as reported by Emily Hutchings, Pearl had been shaken when the board predicted her ailing father's death, the event removed her further from any consciously willed connection to its unpredictable devices.[37]

Curran may not have retrieved at once memories that would serve as a library of resources for the PW dictations. But the strong conjunction of then and now at the time of her father's death had the potential for establishing schematic coherence among neural processes that, unrelated, might only have summoned from a miscellany of long-term unconscious memories. The developmental array of grammar school anthologies, fiction and poetry read or heard, plays and music performed or witnessed, with the father's writerly and publicly pseudonymous role at its center, provided a context for the convening of potentially performative, re-enactive accumulations by an appropriate cue. In the conventional shorthand, "neurons that fire together tend to wire together." In Daniel Schacter's elaboration, the principle of "cue-dependent memory" derives from "the similarity or affinity between encoding and retrieval processes," a match whose contexts would have been the original codes of "subjective perception," including "whatever thoughts, fantasies, or inferences occurred at the time of encoding."[38]

What hovered above the table Pearl Curran sat at after the death of her father could have earned another name than *Patience Worth.* Schacter has traced the etymology of a figurative entity, a memory's *engram,* or memory trace, to proposals made by the German Richard Semon in 1904 and to later research on neuronal connections that made clear the significance of the "ecphoric stimulus," that is, "the hint or cue that triggers recall." PW would not have been constructed from a single encoding, the textbook image, say, of a woman languishing in a medieval tower. Continuing contextual information from the present, if "similar enough to a previously encoded pattern," would have combined with stored patterns in a unique, even creative, emergence. Over time, Schacter suggests, some memories can undergo consolidation, with the possibility that their repeated consultation may strengthen networks in the brain that can endure over decades.[39] As the scope of the PW literary project increased, the more complex habits of a medium-musician would make their own out-of-sight contribution.

The Music of Pearl Curran

Prior to and during the early years of the PW dictations, no other activity took precedence for Curran over her music ("I shall sing that thou shalt know what be within me" [PWR 5:801]). Though not a regular church-goer, as she told Walter Prince, she had dictated the first volume of the PW Record "while I was singing in the choir. The preaching did not seem to affect me; I was there to sing. . . . I wanted to go on the stage and sing" (*CPW,* 20). There is good reason to argue that minus Curran's talent for and developed training in music the PW text would never have existed in its present form. Evoked as performance, which required its own store of procedural memory for the exercise of skills become automatic, implicit memories became available in rhythmically voiced language.

Psychologists are cautious in addressing the question of which components of creative skills are "domain specific," with capacities for poetry and physics less likely to keep company at an expert level. Studies of the musical brain have made a point of distinguishing, but not totally separating, the neural structures engaged by music and language. While music and language have "independent pathways" and can sustain "functional independence" after injury to one or the other system, they also share "some common neural resources," Daniel J. Levitin points out.[40] Popular characterizations of left-brain analytical and right-brain artistic dominance do not accurately reflect findings that musical syntax and musical semantics are processed in both hemispheres near or overlapping with the language-related Broca's and Wernicke's areas. For the Ouija-board performer, previous training in the prosody of sung language and in the musical semantics that associate tone and meaning at the piano would have had value for the extended automaticities of dictated language. At any given moment, the pianist monitors the "ongoing development of a musical theme," a task for the left frontal lobe that, if not identical to that of textual production, could have contributed to an automaticity of likely usefulness for the future writer of poetry and cadenced prose. Aniruddh Patel cites "deep connections" between the cognitive and neural processes of the two domains and addresses work by sociologists and ethnomusicologists who observe "the use of music to *construct* self-identity," along with an anthropological view that listening to music affords an opportunity to become "another kind of person than one's ordinary, everyday self."[41]

Early in her tutelage, Pearl Pollard would have had to commit to practiced memory both the music to be performed and the more literary texts of art songs, while subvocalizing both. Cognitively, the young artist would have formed what John A. Sloboda describes as a "symbolic *internal representation*" of what she played, exercising at first the "receptive skills" that developmentally preceded "productive skills" that resulted in the making of her own music.[42] Associated with speech production rather than comprehension, Broca's area becomes a "music region" as well in the sense that musicians "silently speak music in their brains" as they read, and reading, play.[43] While words read—graphemes—would more likely be retained than words heard—phonemes—Curran's experience of rehearsing performances subvocally and of singing the poetry of song lyrics for her listeners would promote synaptic strengthening in relevant brain regions and create an early habit of attention, assimilation, and vocalization whose later productions could persist from piano to Ouija board to typewriter.

While the prosodic foot may have no precise counterpart in a musical measure, Fred Lerdahl argues, it is evident that both qualify as "sounds organized in time"—the sustained insistence of PW's unplanned iambics, for example, even though Emily Hutchings found Curran technically ignorant of common measures. Among the more interesting sharings between music and language noted by Mireille Besson and Daniele Schön is the establishment of "strong expectancies," by which in a specific context a given word—or notes and chord—either satisfies expectation by falling into place or creates "tension or surprise if not."[44] For her conscious art, a writer or composer would surprise no one by claiming manipulation of those expectancies. For Curran, streaming fiction at the Ouija board, the deployment of underlying expectancy patterns could readily have drawn on early automatisms formed by music performance, setting the stage for language that would speak them. The opening paragraph of *Hope Trueblood,* seemingly delivered impromptu, exhibits a musician's habit of announcing an opening theme while introducing a rhythm of expectancy in a temporal plot yet to unfold in detail.

In its cognitive sources and in performance, the process of vocalization ties Pearl the medium and Pearl the musician together most closely. Whatever wisdom visitors took in as they engaged PW in conversation, it was Curran's voice they heard as its physical medium. If by report the voice sounded somewhat different from that of their hostess, the difference registered not only the performer's staging of another identity but the inner speech of her subvocality. The character of a subvocal language of thought unconsciously arrived at is inevitably personal, "embodied in the history of an individual," and as inner voice is "a steady companion" in creative persons, who often remark their "inner speech writing" as "not simply the interior counterpart of external speech." Citing Anaïs Nin, Vera John-Steiner goes on to note the potential for ambivalence in a woman writer's voice divided between identifying with/appropriating or turning away from a lineage of male writers.[45] Richard Powers has made a point of advancing the vocal fictionist, revealing that his stenographer is speech-recognition hardware: "Speak the thing into being: as dreams go that's as old as they get."[46]

PW as Neural Control

For non-Spiritualist observers, what was most objectionable in the PW phenomenon was that Pearl Curran should be praised for activity that eschewed the disciplined and thoughtful craft characteristic of real writers. Telegraph operators, piano players, and mediums had already been characterized as engaging in "cerebral reflex action" by nineteenth-century British physiologist William Carpenter, who also viewed the operations of imagination and genius as "essentially automatic."[47] But it is inaccurate to describe the Ouija writer as lacking in intention. Despite psychology's predominant denial of "free" or conscious will, the presumed basis of the artist's choices, terms like *goal-minded* or *intentional* have remained to describe a coherently organized tendency in cognitive processes—in which case PW as "control" should signify the unconsciously assembling processes that came to constitute Curran's goal-mindedness.

> I would unloose them, like little wan-faced children
> Seeking some consolation, some familiar tongue. . . .
> Yea, it shall be my hand which shall unloose them from their prisons.
> Little memories which have become mute,
> Wringing their hands in supplication. (*CPW*, 288–89)

Dictated for Walter Prince in rapid alternation with several longer prose texts, these lines from PW declare only an intention to unloose, leaving it to the dissociated memories themselves to search for an appropriate language, a tongue familiar to them. The poet's implied division of conscious and unconscious agency reflects the assertion by a team of psychologists that "all task performance" is "a joint product of unconscious (automatic) and intentional (controlled) processes" and that when higher-level processes attend to a goal, such as that announced by the poet, the enabling lower-level processes "are largely automatic." The combination of intention's goal and automaticity's flourishing had already been described as a "dynamic orientation" or an experience of "flow" in an attempt to characterize the result of a perfect match between what an environment calls for and what an individual's talents can deliver. If nonconscious cognitive processes predominate in artists, it may be, Larry Jacoby suggests, because "people are especially susceptible to unconscious influences when they are 'in flow' and so are not analytically monitoring sources of influence."[48] In the medium's experience, as in the psychologist's terminology, *intentional* can actually mean in large part "controlled"—by the automaticities that come in the train of intention's goal, productive and purposeful in tendency as they are nonconscious, an "unconscious intention" being "just as 'intentional,'" according to John Bargh and Kimberley Barndollar, "perhaps even more 'rational' than the momentary conscious goal."[49] While a PW poem could plaintively acknowledge memory's search for "some familiar tongue," it was the inexplicable loosening of automaticities in response that nourished Curran's understanding of PW as a deliverance from silence. The memory-into-language event results from unwitnessed control—the very definition of Patience Worth.

The medium defers to her control. An association among neuronal systems enlists other systems toward an implicitly held goal. As control, PW is the moving of memory's reconsolidations into an enlarged series of rewritings, an activity that conforms to Marcel Kinsbourne's use of the term to stand for a "dominant focus of neural activity" or "network attractor state," which at a given moment of responses may include "verbal and imaged thought and expression." If Curran found it impossible to trace the activity of her discarnate control—constrained to metaphor as she was—a literal explanation of the difficulty appears in Ran R. Hassin's assertion that "working memory, the mental organ whose essence is cognitive control, can operate completely outside of conscious awareness."[50] The processes arriving at control suggest agencies as vigorous and invisible as the didactic handmaiden. In the "Global Workspace" of cognition, a "goal image" gains "uncontested access" to the "theater of consciousness," then is "globally distributed to recruit and organize unconscious automatisms needed to achieve the goal."[51]

What the well-named Patience then required was "duration" itself, perhaps the "crucial variable," suggests Kinsbourne in posing the question in his essay title, "What Qualifies a Representation for a Role in Consciousness?" An emergent PW could greet Curran only when an indeterminable number of unconscious processes from what Kinsbourne calls "the uncentered brain" converged in July 1913. The contents of a representation should not be seen clamoring for entry into a dominant pattern simply because of the "intrinsic nature of the[ir] contents" (like Poe's uncoffined Madeline Usher demanding vengeful entry to her brother's room of consciousness), but, Kinsbourne argues, according to "how amenable [the representation] is to being integrated into the dominant neuronal activity"—amenable, that is, to the "pattern of neuronal firing" that constitutes the subject's predominant brain state. Potentially amenable candidates become "competing 'drafts'" of representation, and if the drafts cannot be thought of as appealing to an executive editor, another figure, cycled through experiment and back to PW as cognitive control, will do as well. Once incorporated into a role in consciousness, observes Kinsbourne, the new representation "shapes or modifies the existing field of awareness, as the potter's fingers continually modify the artifact."[52]

Automatic *and* Smart?

Against characterizations of her as an instrument mechanically producing automatic literature, Curran could in time have discovered that automaticity's generous gifts follow a "top down" development from higher-order learning processes. But the idea would have been slow in coming. In 1997, Herman Spitz suggested that attributing organized, even creative, processes to a smart unconscious would amount to a "paradigmatic leap," and Elizabeth F. Loftus and Mark R. Klinger had already found a number of colleagues unwilling to take that leap. With *smart* defined as the ability to handle complex tasks, classify patterns meaningfully, and deal flexibly with novel situations, they reported a consensus that "the unconscious may not be as smart as previously believed."[53]

Still questioning whether unconscious processes were "routinized" or "flexible and adaptive," Rhianon Allen and Arthur Reber were willing to venture that complex learning and even "production of creative ideas" are not always "accessible to, or have their origins in, conscious contents or procedures," then asserted firmly that development of "a sophisticated unconscious"—given survival's harsh economy for leisurely planners—is demanded by "the basic principles of evolutionary biology."[54] Stirring discussion on a "new unconscious," James S. Uleman gathered colleagues to respond to his introductory question, "What, if anything, cannot be done without awareness?" The dare was taken up in the same volume by Jack Glaser and John Kihlstrom, who described a trend in research on the oxymoronic "volitional unconscious" that would argue its participation in "a full spectrum of mental life (i.e., affect, cognition and motivation)" that includes self-monitoring for such metacognitive goals as accuracy.[55] Long past a version of the unconscious as desire's dark harbor, research into a new unconscious sums up capacities that by definition do not speak for themselves directly, while placing them in a frame large enough to contain a credibly equipped Pearl Curran.

Activation of that nonconscious repository can bring forward a troop of what John Bargh and Tanya L. Chartrand call "mental butlers," automatic processes intimately aware of "our tendencies and preferences" and prepared to serve them without being consciously addressed. With no bow to a petitioning PW, Bargh and Chartrand suggest that the only remaining task for conscious awareness might be to select from or assemble automaticities, in service, one could imagine, to a career of performance: "people have the capability of building ever more complex automatic 'demons' that fit their own idiosyncratic environment, needs and purposes."[56] But rewording the old dichotomy of a dumb Pearl Curran and a smart Patience Worth is to ignore the conclusion of such psychologists as Arthur Reber that the processes of a "sophisticated" cognitive unconscious are "delicately intertwined" with more familiar processes of conscious control.[57] It remains impossible to estimate the number and kind of rejections and revisions Curran may silently have effected before and during the board's dictations, and at what level of awareness. As an intelligence, PW was not superior to her medium, but rather an extraordinary activation and proportioning of the conscious/unconscious dynamic in Curran as medium *and* control, an aggregate of processes she could neither have consciously designed nor denied herself.

Fugitive Agency

Misattributed agency—"something else is moving the planchette"—was psychology's epitaph for Spiritualism's discarnate legions of poets and orators.

No wonder, then, that an empirical PW has power to haunt the honorific figure of the conscious artist. Setting aside the ordinary and universal experience of conscious willing along with Spiritualists' readiness to attribute agency elsewhere, Daniel Wegner has introduced the term *virtual agency* to describe one's felt agency as a personal fiction.[58] Wegner's review of earlier work on automatic writing, including that done at the Ouija board (103–13), makes only brief mention of PW (112n5), but that figure is unobtrusively stationed at an entrance already traversed by mourners and celebrants of the death of the Author. If conscious will as "a kind of authorship emotion" (325) is the most common of our illusions (143), authors themselves must be understood, not just culturally or theoretically but cognitively, as virtual agents, variously brilliant or ordinary, but afloat always on a deep that harbors numberless unnamed automaticities.

Drawing on experiments by Benjamin Libet and others, Wegner points out that the feeling of conscious willing—the experiencer's only source of information on causality—arrives *after* the brain has silently begun its preparations, so that in this single, time-constricted instance, at least, the complacent cause-effect logic of conscious will producing its intended result has been seriously undermined (50–55). Wegner's reviewers have also cited the qualification introduced by Nobel laureate Eric R. Kandel, who concurs that awareness follows rather than precedes the choice of an action but cites evidence that a conscious freedom to "veto the action" is observable in the final milliseconds—for the constantly revising writer, a definitive change capable of provoking other changes in its train.[59]

Wegner's quotations from the naturalist determinism of writers like Ambrose Bierce and Mark Twain echo his argument nicely, but his introduction of Gertrude Stein on the issue of agency suggests the difficulty of estimating kinds and degrees of automaticity either from authorial testimony or from the textual product. Repeating an earlier claim by B. F. Skinner,[60] he suggests the possibility that Stein's writings, "not noted for their content but rather for the use of sounds and rhythms of words," may have been produced automatically (105n2). As an icon of consummately conscious art, Stein serves as an inviting target, the more so because of her affiliation with William James's early investigations of automatic writing. Discussing Skinner's 1934 assertion, Steven Meyer has established that Stein's participation in James's laboratory experiments on automatic writing convinced her that, unlike the subjects whose suspended arms she coached to write without forethought, her own achievement came by "xtra consciousness, excess." To practice automatic writing of the kind she described in an 1898 report on her experiments would have been to write without conscious awareness, a meaningless act.[61]

As a further personal report, Stein did concede that a writer might enter deliberately into "a certain amount of distraction of attention . . . to ease the act of creation." The amenability of automatic writing to Stein's goals and convictions would have been its promise of freeing attention from canonical prose models and the conventional literary and social environment a subject would have assimilated "in a manner in general accord with the previous habits of the person," as Stein's coinvestigator, Leon Solomons, put it. As experimentalist in charge, Stein had taken conscious pleasure, as she watched her subjects' arms and cultural identities in suspension, in observing young New Englanders freed into automaticity, having noted their "habit of self-repression, the intense self-consciousness, the morbid fear of 'letting one's self go . . . '"[62]

To the general reader, the strings of automatic writing generated by Stein when she acted as an experimental subject in Solomons's study will sound more "Steinian" than the analytic prose in which she reported her laboratory experiment with others as subjects. Readers unacquainted with Stein's laboratory experience would have no reason to discover her in the prose of her commentary as experimenter, while a sample of her writing as experimental subject in the Solomons article evokes a dimly remembered acquaintance: "Hence there is no possible way of avoiding what I have spoken of, and if this is not to be believed by the people of whom you have spoken, then it is not possible to prevent the people of whom you have spoken so glibly."[63]

When Stein maintained that "[w]riting for the normal person is too complicated an activity to be indulged in automatically," she spoke, as Pearl Curran could not have, from intensive and extensive knowingness about the act of writing, yet neither the acclaimed conscious writer nor the automatic medium had direct sight of the interactive cognitive systems, the unobservable processes, many of them as yet unnamed, involved in the act of writing. When Stein drew a firm line it was not to mark an experimentally derived proportion between conscious and unconscious literary production but to set a limit to "foolishness," excluding what she judged extrinsic to her, that is, "being mystic or impressionistic"—"Everything I write means exactly what it says." The literal loopiness of freehand writing well behind her, Stein was prepared, in her continued attention to her writing processes, to make out a blinking on and off of conscious intention, a preference for the open geography of fluent directionality punctuated by a conscious negative: "I do not know where I am going but I am on my way and then suddenly well not perhaps suddenly but perhaps yes I do know where I am going and I do not like it like that."[64] The unremitting artist was also ready to grant, "I take things in and they come out that way independent of conscious process." Stein's study of her own acts of writing bridged the half-century from Solomons's thesis that "we underestimate the automatic powers of the normal subject" to the beginnings of experimental attempts to describe the extent and character of those powers. For his part in this genealogy, Solomons, according to Ulla Dydo, had begun his inquiries out of an interest in "mediumistic visions."[65]

The Writer's Inner Eye: Representation's Dreamer

To observe oneself is to develop a body schema, a mental representation of the owner's body that can form itself with or without conscious attention in a continuous process of cognitive mirroring.[66] Curran's internal mirroring of herself as musician and medium would have included the hands schooled by training and habit, through which she could feel art had passed, and as the hands' accompaniment, an audible mouthing of inner speech, the habitual "covert activity," as Allan Paivio notes, of a pianist like Glen Gould.[67]

Fashioned from some of the same ingredients as the medium's schema, PW fully qualifies as specter, but a specter mothered by cognitive body, an enhanced form of schematic self-recognition on the part of Pearl Curran. Current research into mirror neurons that imitate and feel with the actions of others has demonstrated how closely imitation of the other and self-recognition go together. Repeatedly, according to Marco Iacoboni, while brain mappings register neuronal firings for both self and another in relation, they show "a much stronger discharge for actions of the self than for actions of others." In a relevant linkage, research indicates that the Broca's area of the brain "is essential not only for language but also for imitation."[68] As neuronal activity, the movement in Curran from taking in Emily Hutchings's attendance on revelation, to feeling with that other but with even more of herself, could well have established the network of dynamic mirroring that would eventually call itself Patience Worth.

For a sighting of PW as schema internal to Pearl Curran, an early investigation of the subjectivity of artists by pioneering psychologist June Etta Downey deserves renewed interest, while Antti Revonsuo, professor of cognitive science at the University of Skövde, Sweden, has more recently taken biology to limits that could invite the discourse of phenomenology into thinking about PW as an introspective phenomenon for Pearl Curran.

Interested, like Gertrude Stein, in the character traits of automatic writers, which she discriminated through a technique of "muscle reading," June Downey sought experimental ways of examining the inner landscape of writers from Coleridge to Jack London and Mary Austin and including Pearl Curran, whom she considered briefly in a psychological study of the creative imagination published two years after Lowes's *Road to Xanadu.*[69] Herman Spitz has cited Downey's early awareness of the extent of unconscious, automatic movement, her experience of how difficult it is to make subjects consciously aware of their own automatisms, and her observation that unconscious processes may "actually exhibit intelligence, as we usually rate intelligence."[70] In effect, notes Spitz, Downey anticipated later experimenters Loftus and Klinger in their 1992 attempt to distinguish between a "smart" and "dumb" unconscious. In her study of the writer's "inner world" Downey was less interested in Curran's "writing in automatic fashion" than she was in her report of the internal imagery that accompanied the dictations of PW and that created as surplus an extratextual field for projected self-images.

Citing Curran, whose "Nut for Psychologists" she appears to have read, Downey supplies all but the term *body schema* when she suggests that for some writers and artists the process of creative imagining includes a self-visualization, an image of the self projected into the work whether or not that image finds explicit representation in text or canvas. Indicating no interest in a discarnate PW, she attends to the "tiny panorama" Curran had reported on as part of a PW event in which the subject saw herself "small as one of the characters" and could report sensations of smell ("flowers in the garden") or touch ("the texture of a foreign fabric"). Appointed chair of a combined philosophy and psychology department at the University of Wyoming in 1915, Downey was aware that in relating an artist's cognitive subjectivity to her work, she had entered an arena already warmed by critical debate, most of all when she cited Leonard Stein's modernist view—with no mention of his sister Gertrude—that the "rhythmical whole" of a work of art simply "*shuts* one out." Against claims for aesthetic autonomy, and anticipating the relational language of mirror neuronists, she argues for two deployments of the representation in consciousness of its owner's "self"—the "observing-self as well as the self-observed." In her own experiment, Downey draws attention to an oddly "schematic figure" projected by a subject she names "J" (as in June) and identifies textual "apparitions" of similarly projected doubles as she finds them in Goethe and Shelley. Deploying her own initial as sign, she invites discovery of her apparitional citizenship in the artistic subjectivities she describes, just as the "D" of her earlier study of automatic writing had quietly distinguished Downey from coauthor John E. Anderson.[71]

While devolving from psychological studies of multiplicity in the previous generation, Downey's interest in doubleness, one part of which roams an internal and socially unnamed territory within the artist, characterizes her in brief space as the most resourceful early inquirer into the Pearl-Patience relationship. Her awareness of Mary Austin's writing, perhaps including Austin's self-division into Mary by Herself and I-Mary, further suggests that a notion of the unspoken gendered self underlay several of her empirical inquiries. In the visualizations of Curran's essay, Downey found evidence that as object, the writer as woman is seen in miniature, while as the PW schema, an invisible subject, the artist's eye creates an entire panorama.

The inky dream that is literary text, understood as generated from the brain's original dreaming, situates Pearl Curran firmly among all those whose drafts of what is external derive from the internal sense messengers of elusive cognitive processes. Except internally and imaginally, Pearl Curran never saw a Patience

Worth, any more than Mark Twain's August Feldner sees the shimmeringly satanic No. 44, his "mysterious stranger." Nor in the recent work of an experimentally and metaphysically ambitious "biological realist" would Curran have seen herself, except phenomenally. Rejecting previous metaphorical models, beginning with James's stream, as a basis for research into how consciousness works, Antti Revonsuo argues that just as the fruit fly's rapidly successive generations can model research on evolutionary processes, our experience of dreams could serve to model research on consciousness since "the objects and events in a dream are transparent surrogates of the real thing, closely similar to those transparent surrogates constructed in the brain during waking perception."[72]

No more than her discarnate control would the medium's own physical organism have been available to her immediately but only as presented to her by her own cognitive systems. For Revonsuo, Curran would have been, as we are to ourselves, a cognitively phenomenal body, a fit companion for the imaginal PW whose physical appearance she grew into describing. In Revonsuo's description of "representative realism" we too in our mediumship are immersed in a cognitively virtual world in which perception is "a 'telepresence' experience created inside the brain, as the internal world simulation engages in real-time resonance with sensory information." Such news from the brain "flies in the face of our naïve ideas about perception and awareness," Revonsuo immediately grants. Anticipating objections to his fully elaborated study as a simplistic "internalism," Revonsuo does not to be sure deny the existence of an external physical world or argue that the material components of cognition are themselves virtual.[73] But the brain in his account is unable to use itself to perceive itself from within (*hmmm, so that's what my oubliette looks like*) and therefore can only be composed of its own virtual cognitions.

If representation is what we are left with, as critical theory and Revonsuo's extrapolations from neurobiology would have it, Curran was quite right to resent her slippage from "the firm ground of respectability" when those who disdained her productive cognition assumed that she was "an instrument differing in any manner from the masses" (*CPW*, 392). Between the internal circularity of consciousness studies and the externality of what the physical sciences examine, the challenge of building bridges seems daunting, as Revonsuo readily admits while seeking prospectively to fill in "the explanatory gap." Looking ahead to continued exploration of the "neural correlates of consciousness," he offers his "world-simulation metaphor" with the caution that succeeding studies that fail to focus on levels of biological organization relevant to phenomenal cognition could still, he fears, accumulate only as a miscellany of brain-mappings.[74]

To address a new century's PW might still qualify as an act of the imagination. The enterprising researcher would work toward resonance imaging of something like a panoptic, clock-watching super-neurode that reported instantly on interactions among the medium-writer's networks of memory and automaticity and on simultaneous cognition of the growing textual product, its alphabetical stimuli under continuous change that in an instant could either be ignored, or provoke some previously quiescent system into a new flow of elated automaticity, or be felt setting off alarms for course correction, with resulting activities free to obey alternative "no" instructions, or, as with the great tribe of writer-cognizers, unsettling the neurode and its networked companions by initiating well-practiced rituals of literate self-reproach.

In the end, the language of a "case" as a container for the phenomenon of Patience Worth is best set aside. Cases can be closed. Experiment remains open, its book notable for the absence of any claim to having the last word. If Patience Worth had claimed that she never slept, the claim could now be supported on behalf of her physical medium by research into the brain's default mode and what has been called its "dark energy." The metaphor may recall alarms once raised about Ouija-board activity but in fact alludes to what Marcus Raichle has described as the constantly active signaling carried on among the brain's different regions when apparently at rest.[75] Not only is the brain never at rest, its dark energy constitutes "from sixty to eighty percent" of the brain's activities and "in circuits unrelated to any external event" although, in its patience, the default mode may be critical in organizing memories and as a basis of preparation for future events—the instant readiness to swat a bothersome fly, Raichle suggests. Or perhaps to burst into the fluent dictation of a fiction. It is not just that the PW of a story told now for almost a century also exhibited a depth of unobservable energies crucial to important activities and ready to deliver instantly. It is no story at all that Pearl Curran was possessor of the same neural wonderbook of dark energies as those who read Patience Worth.

Notes

Introduction: From Spiritualism to Vivisection

1. James Laughlin, Peter Glassgold, and Frederick R. Martin, eds., *New Directions in Prose and Poetry 40.* PW poems were selected and edited by Stephen E. Braude, who has since published a study of the PW "case" in *Immortal Remains: The Evidence for Life after Death* (133–76), concluding that PW was a secondary self of Curran's subconscious. Pamela White Hadas's poem appears in *Beside Herself: Pocahontas to Patty Hearst: Poems.*

2. See Peter Washington, *Madame Blavatsky's Baboon: A History of the Mystics, Mediums, and Misfits Who Brought Spiritualism to America.*

3. David Abbott, *Behind the Scenes with the Mediums;* Deborah Blum, *Ghost Hunters: William James and the Search for Scientific Proof of Life after Death.* For the Metropolitan exhibit see Clément Chéroux et al., *The Perfect Medium: Photography and the Occult.*

4. "A Nut for Psychologists," in Walter Franklin Prince, *The Case of Patience Worth,* 393. Curran originally published the essay in the *Unpartizan Review.* Prince's study, first published in 1927 by the Boston Society for Psychic Research, will hereafter be cited as *CPW.*

5. Amy Tan, *Saving Fish from Drowning: A Novel,* xii.

6. Patience Worth Record 1:98 (hereafter cited as PWR), quoted in Irving Litvag's *Singer in the Shadows: The Strange Story of Patience Worth,* 86 (hereafter cited as *SS*).

7. Pearl Lenore Curran, *Hope Trueblood,* 3.

8. Curran, *Telka: An Idyll of Medieval England,* 16.

9. See Joseph Jastrow, "Patience Worth: An Alter Ego," in *Wish and Wisdom: Episodes in the Vagaries of Belief,* 78–92; John Hix, "Patience Worth—An Unsolved Phenomenon," 83–88; Rosalind Heywood, *Beyond the Reach of Sense: An Inquiry into Extra-Sensory Perception,* 107–11; and Robert Goldenson, *Mysteries of the Mind: The Drama of Human Behavior,* 44–53.

10. Mia Grandolfi Wall, *Rediscovering Pearl Curran: Solving the Mystery of Patience Worth.* Wall's study includes previously unpublished correspondence between the Currans and a Connecticut admirer of PW, Milo Leon Norton.

11. Gioia Diliberto, "Ghost Writer."

12. With others who have written on this subject, I reserve capitalized *Spiritualism* for the historical movement. See Sheri Weinstein's "Technologies of Vision: Spiritualism and Science in Nineteenth-Century America," 138n1.

13. Ann Braude, "Women's History *Is* American Religious History," 87–107. For the close interweaving of literary, political, and culturally gendered strands in the history of Spiritualism, see Molly McGarry, *Ghosts of Futures Past: Spiritualism and the Cultural Politics of Nineteenth-Century America;* Helen Sword, *Ghostwriting Modernism,* 5, 22–24; Ann Braude, *Radical Spirits: Spiritualism and Women's Rights in Nineteenth-Century America;* Caroline Field Levander, *Voices of the Nation: Women and Public Speech in Nineteenth-Century American Literature and Culture;* Susan Danielson, "The Woman Question, Free Love, and Nineteenth-Century American Fiction"; Daniel Cottom, *Abyss of Reason: Cultural Movements, Revelations, and Betrayals;* Russell M. Goldfarb and Clare R. Goldfarb, *Spiritualism and Nineteenth-Century Letters;* and Howard Kerr, *Mediums and Spirit Rappers and Roaring Radicals: Spiritualism in American Literature, 1850–1900.*

14. Elaine Showalter, ed., *The New Feminist Criticism: Essays on Women, Literature, and Theory,* 137–39.

15. On the origin of the white crow metaphor used by James to express his interest in the possibly "supernormal" powers of the Boston medium, Leonora Piper, see R. Laurence Moore, *In Search of White Crows: Spiritualism, Parapsychology and American Culture,* 146–47.

16. See Alan Gauld, *A History of Hypnotism;* Eric T. Carlson, "The History of Dissociation until 1880," 8–9, in Quen, ed., *Split Minds/Split Brains;* and Ernest Hilgard, *Divided Consciousness: Multiple Controls in Human Thought and Action,* 133–35. For a history of the Ouija board in America and copyright claims to the name, see Stoker Hunt, *Ouija: The Most Dangerous Game,* 5–6.

17. Morton Prince, *The Unconscious: The Fundamentals of Human Personality Normal and Abnormal,* 204–10. See Eugene Taylor, *William James on Consciousness beyond the Margin,* 106. For Janet on dissociation as a "failure (in the face of disturbing events) to synthesize" vs. later assertions of nonpathological capacities for dissociation, see Stephen Braude, "Memory: The Nature and Significance of Dissociation," in Jennifer Radden, ed., *The Philosophy of Psychiatry: A Companion,* 106–8. Adam Crabtree, in "Explanations of Dissociation in the First Half of the Twentieth Century," in Quen, ed., *Split Minds/Split Brains,* 85–93, situates Prince's work among the explanations of dissociation.

18. Morton Prince, *The Dissociation of a Personality: A Biographical Study in Abnormal Personality.* Prince also wrote an introduction to *My Life as a Dissociated Personality,* the account by a widow, Nellie Parsons Bean, of her experience as B.C.A., the initials Prince assigned to her depressed, carefree, and balanced identities. Her relation to Prince has been described as both mirror and, from her private writings, source of his theories of dissociation. Also see Robert W. Rieber, *The Bifurcation of the Self: The History and Theory of Dissociation and Its Disorders,* 89, and John Barresi, "Morton Prince and B.C.A.: . . . Dissociation Theory and Freudian Psychology in a Case of Multiple Personality," 94–129.

19. Deborah Coon, "Testing the Limits of Sense and Science: American Experimental Psychologists Combat Spiritualism, 1880–1920," 121–39 (Hall quoted on 131). On Sargent's *Planchette; or, The Despair of Science,* see the young James's skeptical but experientially curious "Review of 'Planchette,'" 19–23. On Stein and Solomons, see Chapter 9.

20. William James, quoted in John C. Burnham, "The Fragmenting of the Soul: Intellectual Prerequisites for Ideas of Dissociation in the United States," in Quen, ed., *Split Minds/Split Brains,* 79.

21. Drawing on the Patience Worth Record, Litvag reprints the interview, presumably recorded by John Curran (*SS,* 96–102).

22. See "'Patience' Refuses to Undergo Vivisection," *St. Louis Post-Dispatch,* Nov. 13, 1919

(cited in *SS*, 209). For Farrell's reply to "Young Barbarian," see *Reedy's Mirror*, July 29, 1919, 530. The gendered implications of the vivisection issue appear in Phelps's *Story of Avis*, as noted by Carol Farley Kessler, ed., *The Story of Avis*, 83, 258n, and in Kessler's *Elizabeth Stuart Phelps*, 110–12, 116. See also Lori Duin Kelly, "Elizabeth Stuart Phelps, *Trixy*, and the Vivisection Question," 61–82.

23. Kessler quotes Phelps from her 1908 novel *Though Life Us Do Part* and cites her *Trixy* (1904) and her three anti-vivisectionist addresses to the Massachusetts State Legislature in linking Phelps's feminism to her protests against laboratory use of animals (*Elizabeth Stuart Phelps*, 111). Claire Kahane, *Passions of the Voice: Hysteria, Narrative, and the Figure of the Speaking Woman, 1850–1915*, xiv.

24. David A. Zimmerman, "Frank Norris, Market Panic, and the Mesmeric Sublime," 61–90; Sword, *Ghostwriting Modernism*, *x*, 5. On Stein see Steven Meyer, *Irresistible Dictation: Gertrude Stein and the Correlations of Writing and Science*, 221–29. Meyer's unfolding of the significance of Stein's laboratory experiments on automatic writing informs part of my discussion of experimental approaches to the medium as author in Chapter 9.

25. Bette Lynn London, *Writing Double: Women's Literary Partnerships* (see 155, 171 for references to Curran's PW).

26. Sword, *Ghostwriting Modernism*, 25.

27. See London's chapter "The Scribe and the Lady," 150–78. On the High Court's decision, see the article in the *Virginia Law Review:* Blewett Lee, "Copyright of Automatic Writing," 22–26. I wish to thank Erika Dyson for calling my attention to the review by Lee, an attorney who published a series on the legal implications of fortune telling, conjuring, and other psychic practices. On Bond and psychic archaeology, see William A. Kenawell, *The Quest at Glastonbury: A Biographical Study of Frederick Bligh Bond.*

28. Sword, *Ghostwriting Modernism*, 23, 162–63; London, *Writing Double*, 174n33.

29. References to *The Changing Light at Sandover* are to the 1993 Knopf edition. The first edition (Atheneum) bringing together Merrill's three individual volumes and a coda was published in January of 1983, though its title page reads 1982.

30. "An Interview with J. D. McClatchy," in *Collected Prose: James Merrill*, ed. J. D. McClatchy and Stephen Yenser, 105–7. See the unbroken, unpunctuated series of letters in transcriptions of the Merrill-Jackson Ouija sessions from which the volumes of *Sandover* derived: *type/script: notebooks: an examination* (exhibition guide), 26, Special Collections, Washington University Libraries, St. Louis, 1996. Other samples of autograph and typescript transcriptions from the Special Collections of Washington University appear in the catalog *James Merrill: Other Writings*, 32–33. The Finding Aid for Merrill's *Papers* (WTU 00083) can be viewed through the university website: http://library.wustl.edu/units/spec. Mark Bauer, studying *Sandover* in the context of Yeats's use of Ouija revelation from his wife, George, follows Merrill's "shaping hand" by comparing published versions of two of the *Sandover* books with manuscripts sent to poets J. D. McClatchy and Alfred Corn. He describes most differences as clarifications, but says a few "suggest fundamental reconsideration." See Bauer, *This Composite Voice: The Role of W. B. Yeats in James Merrill's Poetry*, 197–200.

31. Helen Vendler, "*Mirabell: Books of Number*," in Robert Polito, ed., *A Reader's Guide to James Merrill's "The Changing Light at Sandover*," 164–67 (originally published in the *New Yorker* on Sept. 3, 1979, and reprinted in Vendler, *Part of Nature, Part of Us*, 220–32). In his afterword, Polito echoes the discourse of mediums to underline the question of agency: "*who's* controlling or in control of the poem" is its "most resonant subject" (231).

32. Frederic W. H. Myers, "Automatic Writing; or, The Rationale of Planchette," 233–34.

33. Harold Bloom, "From `The Year's Books,'" in Polito, ed., *Reader's Guide*, 133 (originally published by the *New Republic*, Nov. 20, 1976); Denis Donoghue, "What the Ouija

Board Said," in Polito, ed., *Reader's Guide,* 181; Stephen Yenser, *The Consuming Myth: The Work of James Merrill,* 259. Bloom's lesser enthusiasm for *Mirabell: Books of Number* and *Scripts for the Pageant* appears in his introduction to *Modern Critical Views: Merrill* (6).

34. Alison Lurie, *Familiar Spirits: A Memoir of James Merrill and David Jackson,* 92, 135.

35. Ibid., 63, 177, 181.

36. Ibid., 179–81, 177.

37. Anita M. Mühl, *Automatic Writing,* vii–viii, 39. For the Merrill letter, see Hunt, *Ouija,* 50.

38. From a catalog entry for Mary Johnston, *To Have and to Hold,* with illustrations by Frank T. Schoonover, Washington University Special Collections, Olin Library.

39. Lurie, *Familiar Spirits,* 52.

Chapter 1 The Domestic Oracle and Her Genealogy

1. *Patience Worth's Magazine* will hereafter be cited as *PWM.* Complete holdings of the monthly magazine's run from August 1917 to May 1918 are rare. Volumes consulted at the Pasadena, CA, Public Library have since gone missing, as have those at the University of Chicago's Regenstein Library. MHM has only two issues. For complete runs, see the New York Public Library and the Watkinson Library of Trinity College, Hartford, CT.

2. PWR 21:3478, italics in original (quoted in *CPW,* 210, and *SS,* 242).

3. Eugene Taylor, *Shadow Culture: Psychology and Spirituality in America.*

4. David D. Hall, ed., *The Antinomian Controversy, 1636–1638: A Documentary History,* 339. For a carefully argued proposal that Hutchinson's "spiritism" involved a condemned form of biblical divination rather than a claim to unmediated spiritual communication, see Michael G. Ditmore, "A Prophetess in Her Own Country: An Exegesis of Anne Hutchinson's 'Immediate Revelation,'" 349–92.

5. As a young woman, Cora L. V. Scott rose to fame as Cora Hatch, the wife of a Svengali prototype, Benjamin Hatch. She eventually divorced Hatch, and her later work carries the name of her last husband, William Richmond. Cora Richmond's writing and lecturing career spanned much of the history of American Spiritualism and deserves new treatment to replace Harrison D. Barrett's 1895 biography, *The Life and Work of Cora L. V. Richmond.* For a recent treatment of Hatch and the "Performance of 'Ouina,'" see Amy Lehman, *Victorian Women and the Theatre of Trance: Mediums, Spiritualists and Mesmerists in Performance,* 115–32.

6. Jane Kamensky, *Governing the Tongue: The Politics of Speech in Early New England,* 151.

7. Jane Kamensky, "Female Speech and Other Demons: Witchcraft and Wordcraft in Early New England," 32. Kamensky is quoting from Mather's 1693 *Brand Pluck'd out of the Burning.*

8. William Reedy, *Reedy's Mirror,* Oct. 8, 1915, 239.

9. Emma Hardinge Britten published the Seven Principles, as channeled from deceased socialist-communitarian Robert Owen, in her magazine *The Two Worlds* Nov. 18, 1887, and they have continued to reappear in Spiritualist publications.

10. Nathan O. Hatch, *The Democratization of American Christianity,* 20.

11. From Emerson's "Demonology," quoted in Goldfarb and Goldfarb, *Spiritualism and Nineteenth-Century Letters,* 52, and Moore, *In Search of White Crows,* 25.

12. A. Braude, *Radical Spirits,* 174.

13. William Dean Howells, *The Undiscovered Country,* 255.

14. Charles Beecher, *Spiritual Manifestations,* 13.

15. Moore, *In Search of White Crows,* 105.

16. Cited in Vieda Skultans, "Mediums, Controls and Eminent Men," 17. Alex Owen initiated a generation of new studies when she argued that Spiritualist women, because seen as simply exercising their feminine nature, had received less historical attention. See *The Darkened Room: Women, Power and Spiritualism in Late Victorian England,* ii–iii.

17. Frank Podmore, *Modern Spiritualism: A History and a Criticism,* 2:268.

18. See A. Braude, *Radical Spirits,* 114, plate 5 (from a copy in the American Antiquarian Society, Worcester, MA). Braude describes the planchette's dual use, as pointer to an alphabet or, with an inserted pencil, as writing instrument (24).

19. "Planchette," *Watchman & Reflector,* Sept. 3, 1868. Phelps was writing six months before William James's March 1869 review of Epes Sargent's *Planchette; or, The Despair of Science.* On the *Watchman & Reflector* see Frank Luther Mott, *A History of American Magazines, 1740–1930,* 463.

20. *Three Spiritualist Novels by Elizabeth Stuart Phelps: "The Gates Ajar" (1868), "Beyond the Gates" (1883), "The Gates Between" (1887),* ed. Nina Baym.

21. Austin Phelps, *My Portfolio: A Collection of Essays,* 169–71.

22. Sargent, *Planchette; or, The Despair of Science,* 104–5; John Kucich, *Ghostly Communion: Cross-Cultural Spiritualism in Nineteenth-Century American Literature,* 71.

23. Kate Field, *Planchette's Diary,* 5–6.

24. *Kate Field: Selected Letters,* ed. Carolyn J. Moss, 29.

25. A recent treatment of Field's formative friendships in Florence is Gary Scharnhorst, *Kate Field: The Many Lives of a Nineteenth-Century American Journalist* (16–37). Scharnhost also cites evidence pointing to Field as the original for Henrietta Stackpole in Henry James's *Portrait of a Lady* and notes *Planchette's Diary*'s mixed reception among Field's friends (61–64).

26. Field, *Planchette's Diary,* 95, 29–34, 55, 69, 28, 18.

27. Ibid., 13, 94, 32, 91.

28. Ibid., 9–11; *Selected Letters,* xvii–xviii, xxvi–xxviii; *Planchette's Diary,* 10.

29. Field, *Planchette's Diary,* 9; *Selected Letters,* 193; *Planchette's Diary,* 28.

30. Kerr, *Mediums and Spirit Rappers,* 90–91, 99–107; David S. Reynolds, *Beneath the American Renaissance: The Subversive Imagination in the Age of Emerson and Melville,* 478–79.

31. Morton Prince, *Clinical and Experimental Studies in Personality,* 208.

32. Mark Twain, quoted in Goldfarb and Goldfarb, *Spiritualism and Nineteenth-Century Letters,* 133.

33. Alan Gribben, "'When Other Amusements Fail': Mark Twain and the Occult," 178, and John W. Crowley and Charles L. Crow, "Psychology and the Psychic in W. D. Howells's 'A Sleep and a Forgetting,'" 162, both in Howard Kerr, John W. Crowley, and Charles L. Crow, eds., *The Haunted Dusk: American Supernatural Fiction, 1820–1920.*

34. Nathaniel Hawthorne, *Twice-Told Tales: Centenary Edition of the Works of Nathaniel Hawthorne,* 306.

35. John W. Crowley notes that in 1903 Howells distinguished between "psychologism and psychic fiction" in urging realist writers to concern themselves with the "*in*spects" and "psychical physiognomies" of the Hawthornean tradition. After *The Undiscovered Country,* Howells broke no new ground, Crowley argues, citing the more "mystical" interest of stories like "A Difficult Case." See his "From Psychologism to Psychic Romance," 133–38.

36. Sargent, *Planchette,* 290.

37. Hamlin Garland, *Forty Years of Psychic Research: A Plain Narrative of Fact,* 136, 2.

38. B. O. Flower, "Garland in Ghostland," 86.

39. Garland, *Forty Years of Psychic Research,* 93.

40. Nina Auerbach, *Woman and the Demon: The Life of a Victorian Myth,* 8.
41. Hamlin Garland, *The Tyranny of the Dark,* 222, 439.
42. Richard Harding Davis, *Vera the Medium,* 130, 151.

Chapter 2 From Pearl to Patience

1. A non-experimental impression of the "bland, humdrum personality of Mrs. Curran" is contrasted with the "vivid" one of PW, who is "sharp witted, fluent, very observant," in Leonard Zusne and Warren H. Jones, *Anomalistic Psychology: A Study of Magical Thinking,* 104.

2. See by contrast Stephen Braude's apt description of the "psychogenesis of the Patience Worth persona" as Curran's "latent capacities" became accessible in maturity through the stimulus of the Ouija board (*Immortal Remains,* 154–55, 174).

3. John Livingston Lowes to Morton Prince, n.d., 1915, in the research folder of Ruth Potter Duell in the Patience Worth Collection, ASPR. This folder will hereafter be cited as Duell folder, PWC. Although both the Missouri History Museum Archives and the American Society for Psychical Research archives have Patience Worth collections, the abbreviation PWC will be used for the ASPR collection only, since PWR, for Patience Worth Record, represents the great majority of MHM references.

4. William Holmes McGuffey, *McGuffey's Fifth Eclectic Reader.* The series' more literary selections appear at the fourth, fifth, and sixth levels. See John H. Westerhoff, *McGuffey and His Readers: Piety, Morality, and Education in Nineteenth-Century America.*

5. Obituary of George Pollard, *St. Louis Republic,* Sept. 7, 1912. Collected in MHM's "Necrologies" 5 (1912): 45.

6. Pearl Curran Rogers to Walter Prince, Jan. 21, 1927, "Correspondence between Mrs. Curran and Dr. Prince," Duell folder, PWC. According to the DeWitt Historical Society of Tompkins County, NY, George Pollard does not appear among the "Officers and Students of Ithaca Academy" in the remaining but incomplete records for 1838–1874. Records for 1845–1860 are among those missing. Donna Eschenbrenner (archivist), letter to the author, Dec. 9, 2003.

7. Walter Franklin Prince, "The Riddle of Patience Worth." Along with photos of Curran in this magazine article, there is one of Prince at his desk following publication of his *Case of Patience Worth,* with fifteen volumes of typed records he had compiled.

8. Certificate of Death, Missouri State Board of Health. Pollard's address is given as 5210 Ridge Ave., St. Louis, where Pearl lived for two years after leaving Texas at age twelve.

9. Pearl Curran Rogers to Prince, Jan. 6 and Jan. 30, 1927, "Correspondence," Duell folder, PWC. *Bertha Clay* was the pseudonym of Englishwoman Charlotte M. Brame (1836–1884), who wrote such popular romances as *Thrown on the World; or, The Discarded Wife.*

10. François Delsarte (1811–1871) taught in France a theory of "applied aesthetics," intended to connect "celestial" principles and their expression in the gesture and emotion of dance. In American schools, many of the lessons taught in his name encouraged artificial posing and came to be applied to gymnastics and physical education. See Ted Shawn, *Every Little Movement: A Book about François Delsarte.*

11. Eileen Curran Kleymeyer, interview by Ruth Potter Duell, New Orleans, 1957, Duell folder, PWC.

12. Ruth Potter Duell (1912–Jan. 16, 2005) never completed a projected work on Curran and PW. An "In Memoriam" obituary on www.iBerkshires.com for a Lenox, MA, retirement home described Duell as a writer-editor who had reported for New York papers and worked for her husband's publishing company, C. Halliwell, Duell, Sloan and Pearce.

13. Mrs. A. P. Holland, interview by Ruth Potter Duell, n.d., 1957, Duell folder, PWC. A second interview of Holland, dated Feb. 12, 1957, records another spelling: "Mrs. Pollard and Pearl always 'at daggerheads.'"

14. Pearl Curran Rogers to Walter Prince, Jan. 30, 1927, "Correspondence," Duell folder, PWC.

15. Business card, filed in "Correspondence," Duell folder, PWC.

16. Fred Stayton Williams to Walter Prince, Apr. 17, 1927, "Patience Worth—Biographical," Duell folder, PWC. Any elisions are those of Duell's transcription of the Williams letter.

17. George V. Cordingley, *Impromptu Poems: By the Inspirational Poet* (1901?), 10. The date is a librarian's entry in a copy in the Brown University Library.

18. Ibid.; Podmore, *Modern Spiritualism,* 2:289–306; Cordingley, *Impromptu Poems,* 10.

19. Steinway Theatre pamphlet, July 16, 1901, Chicago Historical Society.

20. Charles A. Burgess, comp., *Pictorial Spiritualism.*

21. On January 1, 1899, Cora Richmond's Church of the Soul and Cordingley's Progressive Spiritual Church both assembled at Handel Hall, Richmond's at 11:30, Cordingley's at 3:00 and 7:30 (ProQuest Historical Newspapers, *Chicago Tribune,* 1849–1985).

22. Ruth Brandon reprints a drawing of an Indian spirit guide, arrow in hand, leaning on a bow, and notes the figure's currency among Shakers. See *The Spiritualists: The Passion for the Occult in the Nineteenth and Twentieth Centuries,* 38, 120, 214. Robert Cox uses the same drawing as an example of spirit guides dedicated to reconciliation in *Body and Soul: A Sympathetic History of American Spiritualism,* 198–99. From the 1850s, Spiritualists came to rely on the trope of a vanished people "as spiritual forebears and teachers" (McGarry, *Ghosts of Futures Past,* 70, 83), while, as Philip J. Deloria notes, the "spiritual experience beyond representation" of the Indian had to be sought through books and intracultural instruction (*Playing Indian,* 168).

23. Acting as Ouina's earthly medium, Richmond called herself "Water Lily" and titled a volume of inspirational poetry and stories *Ouina's Canoe and Christmas Offering: Filled with Flowers for the Darlings of Earth* (see pp. 8, 17). Amy Lehman, emphasizing the performative dimension of trance speakers, relates Richmond's career to her biography of Ouina while citing the cultural script enacted by such figures as Pocahontas and Metamora. See her *Victorian Women and the Theatre of Trance: Mediums, Spiritualists and Mesmerists in Performance,* 115–41.

24. Erika Dyson, "Having Their Way with Science: Nineteenth-Century Natural Theology, the Spiritualist Movement, and the Mediumship of Cora L. V. Richmond," 38.

25. Cora Richmond, *The Soul: Its Nature, Relations, and Expressions in Human Embodiments,* 155.

26. Ibid., 397.

27. Howells, *Undiscovered Country,* 417.

28. "Necrologies" 5 (1912): 45, MHM; Holland, interview, Feb. 12, 1957, Duell folder, PWC. Eventually, nearing fifty, Pearl would marry Robert Wyman, "her girlhood sweetheart," after moving to Los Angeles (PWR 28:4242). See Chapter 8.

29. The sheet music of Pearl Gildersleeve Curran (1875–1941), words and music, may not yet have been available as Pearl Pollard waited on customers at the Thompson Music Co. in Chicago in 1901, but her "sacred songs" and others with such titles as "Dawn," "Rain," and "Life" strike notes in moonlit settings characteristic of the PW poetry.

30. The Gould's City Directory for 1914 lists a "Rosedale Studio" at 6040 Delmar. See *Literary St. Louis: A Guide,* ed. Lorin Cuoco and William H. Gass, 254.

31. Emily Grant Hutchings to James Hyslop, Mar. 27, 1915, PWC.

32. Lowes to Morton Prince, n.d., 1915, Duell folder, PWC.

33. John Curran, "Patience Worth's Records," *PWM,* Sept. 1917, 15.

34. As John Curran assumed record-keeping duties, he described the roles played by Mary Pollard as amanuensis and Emily Hutchings as an editor who added and subtracted at will in preparing a final copy, keeping the original. Prince incorrectly dates record-keeping from June 1914 (*CPW,* 31).

35. Emily Hutchings's transcript of the early PW dictations, "PW Record (Book communications) 1913–1914," is contained in the ASPR's Ruth Duell folder.

36. On James and Astor: Hutchings to Hyslop, Apr. 27, 1915, PWC. On Whitman and Marlowe: Emily Hutchings to Gertrude O. Tubby, Aug. 2, 1915, PWC. On Emily Hutchings's early career see Litvag, *SS,* 21, and Anne Johnson, *Notable Women of St. Louis* (1914). Tubby was assistant to Hyslop at the ASPR and had rented her house in Montclair, NJ, to Walter Prince, who wrote about his adopted daughter's psychic experiences there. See Prince, *The Psychic in the House,* 257–58.

37. Curran to Prince, Oct. 25, 1926, "Correspondence," Duell folder, PWC.

38. Hutchings to Hyslop, Feb. 22, 1915, PWC.

39. Hutchings to Isaac K. Funk, copy forwarded to James Hyslop, June 23, 1913, PWC. Funk, a publisher of dictionaries and author of *The Psychic Riddle* (1907), died in 1912.

40. Hutchings transcript, Feb. 15, 1914, 55–57, Duell folder, PWC.

41. Daniel M. Wegner, *The Illusion of Conscious Will,* 137–39. Wegner briefly describes Curran as a "planchette speller" (112n5). On "counter-intentional automatism" he cites Daniel M. Wegner, Matthew E. Ansfield, and Daniel Pilloff, "The Putt and the Pendulum: Ironic Effects of the Mental Control of Movement," 196–99.

42. Hutchings to Hyslop, Aug. 18, 1915, PWC.

43. Hutchings transcript, 64, Duell folder, PWC.

44. Ibid., 66; John Curran to James Hyslop, Jan. 19, 1917, PWC.

45. In *White Crows,* Moore notes the currency among female mediums of "swearing sailors, strong Indian braves, or oversexed male suitors" as controls (111).

46. Emily Hutchings to Isaac Funk, June 23, 1913, PWC.

47. See letters from R. B. Quinn to Hyslop, Oct. 10 and Oct. 24, 1916; also John Curran letters to Hyslop, Dec. 14, 1916, and Jan. 19, 1917, PWC.

48. John Curran to Hyslop, Dec. 14, 1916, PWC.

49. Hutchings to Hyslop, Nov. 9, 1916; Curran to Hyslop, Dec. 29, 1916, both in PWC.

50. Hutchings to Hyslop, Mar. 11 and Feb. 22, 1915, PWC.

51. Hutchings to Hyslop, Feb. 22, 1915, PWC.

52. Hutchings transcript, 4, 5, Duell folder, PWC.

53. Ibid., 10, 13.

54. Hutchings to Hyslop, Aug. 18, 1915, PWC.

55. In flight from England, the heroine, Lady Jocelyn Leigh, gives her name as "Patience Worth," who was her waiting woman at home, to the narrator Ralph Percy, who has selected her as his bride from a shipment of young maidens to Virginia. Like PW, this Patience is at first misidentified when Percy remarks, "Her dress . . . would have cried 'Puritan' had ever Puritan looked like this woman." See Johnston, *To Have and to Hold,* 18–19, 24, 35.

56. According to John A. Bargh and Melissa J. Ferguson, "Thus far, the research shows that information processing goals can become active and operate independently of conscious control" ("Beyond Behaviorism: On the Automaticity of Higher Mental Processes," 935).

57. Hutchings to Hyslop, Feb. 22, 1915, PWC.

58. Hutchings to Hyslop, Mar. 11 and Aug. 18, 1915, PWC.

59. Hutchings transcript, 54, Feb. 28, 1914; 56, Feb. 15, 1914, Duell folder, PWC.

60. Ibid., 57, Mar. 2, 1914; PWR 1:40.

61. Hutchings transcript, 63, Duell folder, PWC.

62. PWR 1:1. Also see Litvag on the Currans' assumption of editing duties (*SS*, 28–29, 44–45).

63. Hutchings to Hyslop, Mar. 27, 1915. In a letter to Hyslop of Dec. 20, 1915, Hutchings claims to have kept "the only really authentic record" from June 9, 1913, to Mar. 1, 1915, and notes "a good many changes" in the Curran transcript, from misinterpretation of PW dictations to the insertion of "imaginary questions" to separate a single long transmission.

64. Hutchings to Gertrude Tubby, Aug. 2, 1915, PWC.

65. Hutchings to Hyslop, Apr. 27 and Mar. 11, 1915, PWC.

66. Hutchings to Hyslop, Mar. 27, Mar. 11, Feb. 22, and Mar. 11, 1915, PWC. "Laugh and the world laughs with you, cry and you cry alone," from "Solitude," are Ella Wheeler Wilcox's best-known lines. Wilcox, recently widowed, had also begun to experiment with the Ouija board and cited Curran's PW as an early encouragement. See Ella Wheeler Wilcox, *The Worlds and I*, 362. Curran does not mention Wilcox to Prince among poets she has read.

67. James Hyslop, review of *Patience Worth: A Psychic Mystery*, by Casper Yost, *Journal of the ASPR*, April 1916, 189–94.

68. Reedy, an admirer of the PW writings, if not a PW believer, defended the Currans' honesty against Hyslop's "ugly" charges in his *Mirror* on June 2, 23, and 30, 1916, printing Hyslop's rejoinders on June 16 and July 7. Litvag was unaware of the Hutchings–Hyslop correspondence, but see his treatment of the review's reception in his *Singer in the Shadows*, 123–31.

69. Hutchings to Hyslop, Apr. 26, 1916, PWC.

70. Hutchings to Hyslop, Feb. 22, 1915, and June 27, 1916, PWC.

71. Shelley Fisher Fishkin mentions *Jap Herron* as the "strangest" among claims to postmortem communication with Twain but makes no comment on the novel's provenance. See her *Lighting Out for the Territory: Reflections on Mark Twain and American Culture*, 151–53. For Hutchings's 1902 correspondence with Clemens, see David Lawson's "Mark Twain and the Ouija Board Lawsuit," www.twainquotes.com/japherron.html.

72. Hutchings to Tubby, Aug. 2 and Aug. 20, 1915, PWC.

73. Hutchings to Tubby, Sept. 30, 1915, and Aug., 1915 (parenthetical comment is Hutchings's), PWC. Partial transcriptions of *Jap Herron* from May and June 1915 are among the Hutchings–Hyslop correspondence in ASPR files, which also includes two short stories from the deceased Twain, "Furrow" and "Daughter of Mars."

74. See Lawson, "Book Review—Latest Works of Fiction—*Jap Herron*," *New York Times*, www.twainquotes.com/19170909.html, and "Spiritualism in Lawsuit" (includes Reedy quote), *New York Times*, www.twainquotes.com/19180728.html.

75. James Hyslop, "The Return of Mark Twain," review of *Jap Herron*, by Emily Hutchings, appeared in the *Journal of the ASPR* in July 1917 (361–66); Reedy, *Reedy's Mirror*, Aug. 10, 1917 (discussed in *SS*, 165–68).

76. Curran to Prince, Apr. 10, 1926, "Correspondence," Duell folder, PWC.

Chapter 3 Pearl vs. Patience: Medium vs. Control

1. A listing of the Currans' frequent changes of address appears in Cuoco and Gass, eds., *Literary St. Louis*, 254.

2. See Litvag for Yost's presentation of PW to *Globe-Democrat* readers in February and March 1915 (*SS*, 52–58) and for Reedy's critical speculations on Pearl Curran and "necromantic poetry" ("Enter 'Fatawide,'" *SS*, 59–83). In 1916, "The Phantom and the Dreamer" and "The Stranger" were published in *Patience Worth: A Psychic Mystery*, by Casper S. Yost (hereafter cited as *PWPM*).

3. *Reedy's Mirror,* Nov. 29, 1918, 612–13; Oct. 8, 1915, 239.

4. See Pierre Bourdieu, *Language and Symbolic Power,* 211. John Curran (PWR 5:875) was improvising on a PW claim that love can triumph anywhere.

5. Steven Connor cites the PW dictations as a striking example of "a kind of visible speech" when the alleged spirit's voice makes itself felt in "highly phoneticized" automatic writing ("Satan and Sybil: Talk, Possession, and Dissociation," 172).

6. See Howard Eichenbaum and Neal Cohen, *From Conditioning to Conscious Recollection: Memory Systems of the Brain,* 19.

7. In saying this, Hutchings was referring to a physician and psychotherapist, William S. Browne, who had begun addressing inquiries on PW to Hyslop (Hutchings to Hyslop, June 30, 1916, PWC).

8. Hutchings to Hyslop, June 18, 1916, PWC.

9. Pearl Curran Rogers to Grace Parrish, Apr. 9, 1927, Grace Parrish Scrapbook, Patience Worth Collection, MHM.

10. Susan K. Harris, *19th-Century American Women's Novels: Interpretive Strategies,* 20. Harris's study of individual writers develops her influential view that the potential for disruption of the conventional overplot is to be sought in the novels' middles (21).

11. The poem is also printed by Ralph Kleymeyer in a family history detailing his marriage to Pearl and John Curran's daughter, Eileen Curran, with accompanying photos of her. See Ralph T. Kleymeyer, *Ancestors and Descendants of Some Early Settlers of the Evansville, Indiana, Tri-State Area,* 294.

12. The PW figure comparing music unheard between individual lute strings and speech released by overturned stones may be compared with Phelps's challenge in "Guinevere" to read a woman's story that has been written "invisible, in hieroglyphs that blazed." Deborah Barker calls attention to the Phelps poem, which promises discovery of an "awful volume, hid, mysterious, / Intent, there lies the unseen alphabet—." See "The Riddle of the Sphinx: Elizabeth Stuart Phelps's *The Story of Avis,*" in Barker's *Aesthetics and Gender in American Literature: Portraits of the Woman Artist,* 92.

13. Pamela White Hadas, *Beside Herself,* 128.

14. Hutchings to Hyslop, Nov. 9, 1916, PWC.

15. Holland, interview, Feb. 12, 1957, Duell folder, PWC. An "Althea Holland"—not necessarily Mrs. A. P.—appears in the St. Louis City Directory from 1921 through 1926 and is listed as artist at and an editor of the Women's Page of the *St. Louis Times.* Anne Johnson, who had included Emily Hutchings but not Pearl Curran among her "notable women of St. Louis" in her book by that title in 1914, told readers of the *St. Louis Republic* (Nov. 21, 1915) in the year before Patience Wee's adoption that Curran had been treated for "various ailments—from a prospective visit of the stork, a tumor, consumption—which all failed to materialize" (*SS,* 106–7).

16. Litvag provides a brief version of the Currans' preparations for adoption and of events on the night of the child's birth on October 7, 1916, but accounts differ in important ways (*SS,* 138–40). Headlines make much of PW's pre-vision when she halted dictations ("This be nuff'") at eight o'clock, as if simultaneously with the baby's birth, but the Currans had only been informed that the mother had gone into labor: "At nine we were to call and find if the Patience Wee had been born" (PWR 4:698A). In the Record an impatient Pearl learns of the birth when she calls at ten minutes to nine. Litvag and the *St. Louis Republic* (Oct. 20, 1916) describe the board stopping at nine, news of the birth coming by phone at ten. The Currans retrieved the baby, weighing five pounds, on the next afternoon, Sunday, Oct. 8, according to the Record—not "a few hours" later (*SS,* 139). The *St. Louis Times* and *St. Louis Republic* for Oct. 20, 1916, describe the mother as "in poor circumstances," but only Curran's retelling after her 1930 move to Los Angeles claims that the mother died four

days after giving birth (Jack Campbell, "How Patience Worth's Ouija Board Baby Grew Up," *Every Week Magazine,* Mar. 7–8, 1931).

17. Henry Holt, "That Patience Worth Baby," 194.

18. Casper Yost and Mrs. Charles H. McKee became godparents, Dr. and Mrs. Frederick Woodruff were sponsors. Surrounded by forty guests, the baby was christened on Nov. 26, 1916, by the Rev. George W. King. See PWR 4:754, and *PWM,* Aug. 1917, 8–9.

19. *St. Louis Post-Dispatch,* Aug. 7, 1917. Describing her fall in a letter of Aug. 9, 1917, to Mrs. Halsey Ives, Curran says her hand is "perfectly all right" but her dislocated arm will need to be "splinted" for three or four weeks. At this point, she is referring to the new baby as "Faith," saying that Faith is "all broken up" when her baptism sponsor, Dr. Woodruff, is called to military service. The name *Faith* does not reappear in any other PWR entries ("Curran, Pearl Pollard," Box 6B.4.6, Patience Worth Collection, MHM).

20. Eileen Curran Kleymeyer, interview, 1957, Duell folder, PWC; Hutchings to Hyslop, Aug. 18, 1915, PWC.

21. Lowes to Morton Prince, n.d., 1915, Duell folder, PWC. The poem is also cited in *CPW,* 20n9. In "A Nut for Psychologists," Curran describes the unpublished PW story in which a red-haired orphan's singing earns her the eponymous title "The Madrigal" (*CPW,* 397). The "Red-haired Girl" poem has not survived.

22. PWR 15:2937–38. The poem is retitled "To Casper Yost" in *Light from Beyond: Poems of Patience Worth,* selected and compiled by Herman Behr (3). The appendix to *Light from Beyond* includes Curran's visualization of PW's departure from England and shipboard experiences.

23. Holt, "That Patience Worth Baby," 198. Litvag quotes from Curran's letter (*SS,* 144–47).

24. See Pamela Thurschwell, "On the typewriter, *In the Cage,* at the Ouija board," in her *Literature, Technology and Magical Thinking, 1880–1920,* 102–3. Thurschwell quotes from Friedrich Kittler's *Gramophone, Film, Typewriter* and Mark Seltzer's *Bodies and Machines.*

Chapter 4 What Patience Wrote

1. *Reedy's Mirror,* July 27, 1917, 484, italics in original.

2. PWR 6:1132. Reprinted with varied lining and punctuation in *CPW* (148) and in *New Directions in Prose and Poetry 40,* ed. Laughlin, Glassgold, and Martin (161–62). Walter Prince makes a selection of PW poetry from the Record under his own subject headings in his *Case of Patience Worth.*

3. *New Directions in Prose and Poetry 40,* ed. Laughlin, Glassgold, and Martin, 164.

4. Hadas, *Beside Herself,* 126, italics in original.

5. "I had a 'crush' on a handsome actor, J——S——, whom I never met . . ." (*CPW,* 14).

6. See Howard Pyle's *Lady of Shallot: Decorated by Howard Pyle.* For the larger context of Arthurian fictions by women, which the PW stories follow in time and manner, see Alan Lupack and Barbara Lupack, eds., *Arthurian Literature by Women,* which includes selections from Elizabeth Stuart Phelps, Sara Teasdale, and Dorothy Parker.

7. Lawrence W. Levine, "William Shakespeare and the American People: A Study in Cultural Transformation," 38, 40, 48, 42.

8. Percy MacKaye, *Caliban by the Yellow Sands: Shakespeare Tercentenary Masque,* 156.

9. A 105-page typescript of "The Merry Tale" is among the Patience Worth Collection holdings at the MHM Archives, but it is mistakenly covered by the title page and "Cast of Characters" of *Redwing.*

10. "*Redwing*—A Drama, by Patience Worth," *Patience Worth's Magazine,* 1. *Redwing* installments ran from September 1917 through March 1918, the magazine from August 1917 through May 1918.

11. Lowes to Morton Prince, n.d., 1915, Duell folder, PWC.

12. Prince also summarized and quoted extensively from the text of *Telka* in his *Case of Patience Worth* (224–40).

13. Prince mistakenly reads *Telka*'s chap. 6 epigraph on time's passage to mean it was three years after Telka's marriage when she gave birth, but the epigraph counts three years not once but "thrice" (*CPW,* 232; *T,* 66). Or he had not yet benefited from the published footnote, which states simply, "Nine years" (66n).

14. *The Sorry Tale: A Story of the Time of Christ,* by Patience Worth, communicated through Mrs. John H. Curran, ed. Casper S. Yost (hereafter cited as *ST*). A recent reprinting, not used for this study, is from Kessinger Publishing, LLC (2007).

15. For a summary of reviews reprinted in the 1917 *Book Review Digest* see Litvag (*SS,* 152–63).

16. See Annette R. Federico, *Idol of Suburbia: Marie Corelli and Late-Victorian Literary Culture,* 130, 1, 162. *Marie Corelli* was the pseudonym of Mary ("Minnie") McKay (1855–1924).

17. Marie Corelli, *Barabbas: A Dream of the World's Tragedy,* 98.

18. Henryk Sienkiewicz, *Quo Vadis: A Narrative of the Time of Nero,* 431.

19. Lew Wallace, *Ben-Hur,* 488.

20. The durability of a white-camel myth, historically associated with Ali, an early Islamic leader after Mohammed, is suggested in a children's story by Eden Phillpotts, *The White Camel* (London: Country Life, 1936).

21. See Irving McKee, "*Ben-Hur*" *Wallace: The Life of General Lew Wallace,* 178–88, and Robert Moresberger and Katharine Moresberger, *Lew Wallace: Militant Romantic,* 460–64.

22. For a history of comparable silent films, beginning with an American version of the Oberammergau Passion Play to 1919 and beyond, see Roy Kinnard and Tim Davis, *Divine Images: A History of Jesus on the Screen.*

23. The biblical film originated, according to its video documentation, as a byproduct of the Kalem Company's dispatching a crew to the Middle East "to produce a quick series of Arabian potboilers" (VHS slipcover, Kino International Corp., 1994). The video is taken from an archival print of the 1917 rerelease.

24. *The Mirror* [renamed *Reedy's Mirror* in 1913], Nov. 28, 1912, 21.

25. Toni Bentley, *Sisters of Salome,* 40, 42.

26. Rhonda K. Garelick, *Rising Star: Dandyism, Gender, and Performance in the Fin de Siècle,* 101, 105.

27. Quoted in Richard Nelson Cullen and Marcia Ewing Current, *Loie Fuller: Goddess of Light,* 33, 35.

28. Elizabeth Kendall, *Where She Danced,* 23–24.

29. Isadora Duncan, quoted in *The Art of the Dance: Isadora Duncan,* ed. Sheldon Cheney, 63.

30. Charles Dickens, *The Personal History of David Copperfield* (Oxford Illustrated Edition), 13.

31. The English edition, published by Skeffington and Son Ltd., deletes the introduction by Casper Yost and the phrase "Communicated through Mrs. John H. Curran." Among English reviews, Yost found only a trade publication suggesting that the author was an American (*SS,* 189–90). The London publisher reported that an Englishwoman had written to "Miss Patience Worth" to inquire whether the novel was set, as she believed, in her own village (*CPW,* 374).

32. Litvag quotes the entirety of the rejected ending but is incorrect in stating, "And so the book ended" (*SS,* 186). The first-written ending (PWR 6:1072–73) is followed in the

PWR by the revised version (6:1075). A typescript of *Hope Trueblood* in the MHM collection of Patience Worth Papers, Patience Worth Collection, also gives the revised ending, but the cover sheet has erroneously mistitled the contents as "The First Book of Panda."

33. Pearl Curran, *Light from Beyond: Poems of Patience Worth,* selected and comp. Herman Behr. See Litvag, *SS,* 233.

34. *PWM,* Feb. 1918, 12. Villon, the fifteenth-century French poet, had been translated by Dante Gabriel Rossetti. Olivier Basselin was best known for his drinking songs, whose collective title, "Vaux de vire," may have evolved into the term *vaudeville.* He is also remembered as a poet of forgotten songs in Longfellow's *Birds of Passage.*

35. Ruth Duell noted a "Mrs. Thompson" as repository for the "Samuel Wheaton" manuscript (Duell folder, PWC). With her daughter Mabel, a Mrs. Walter Thompson was among frequent guests at PW sessions and among the group discussing trusteeship for the Dorset Press. See PWR 13:2531 and 14:2759.

36. Near Chesil Beach in Dorset, Yost found the ruined abbey of Abbottsbury, a St. Catherine's Chapel on the hill above it, and further inland the village of Portesham, which he took to be that of Patience Worth, with its Parish Church of St. Peter (PWR 16:2986). See *Portesham: A Peep into the Past* (Portesham Women's Institute) and Jack Elwin, *The Parish Church of St. Peter, Portesham: A Tour through the Church.*

37. Katharine T. Corbett, *In Her Place: A Guide to St. Louis Women's History,* 207–9, 232; *The Potter's Wheel* Collection, MHM; Pearl Curran, *The Pot Upon the Wheel,* 123, 127; Casper Yost, introduction to *The Pot Upon the Wheel,* vii.

38. Beverly D. Bishop, "The Potter's Wheel: An Early Twentieth Century Support Network of Women Artists and Writers," 86.

39. "An Evening with St. Louis Poets of Power," Apr. 17, 1912, Papyrus Club file, MHM.

40. Papyrus Club programs, May 12, 1914, and Nov. 2, 1915, Papyrus Club file, MHM. See also *SS,* 81–82.

41. Frances Porcher, "The Potters and the Potters Wheel," *The Mirror,* Apr. 5, 1906, introduced the public to the group's work and described the talents of each member in detail. See Margaret Haley Carpenter's *Sara Teasdale: A Biography,* 86–87.

42. Carpenter, *Sara Teasdale,* 91–92, 63; Bishop, "The Potter's Wheel," 13–16.

43. Bishop, "The Potter's Wheel," 3; Sara Teasdale, comp., *The Answering Voice: One Hundred Love Lyrics by Women;* Parrish, quoted in Carpenter, *Sara Teasdale,* 110. Emily Hutchings cited Curran's appreciation for Wilcox as evidence of her uneducated taste in poetry.

44. Watson's repentant "thief of the cross" in his *Companions of the Sorrowful Way* (134–35), together with his mention of Barabbas, suggests another context for fictionalizings of Christ's passion like *The Sorry Tale.*

45. Dotsie Smith to Charles van Ravenswaay, June 4, 1957, Patience Worth Papers 1916–1928, Box 1–2, Patience Worth Collection, MHM.

46. Edward FitzGerald, trans., *"Rubaiyat" of Omar Khayyam,* 64.19, 41.15. Among other FitzGerald usages, *ta'en, ne'er,* and *a-creaking* have counterparts in the PWR.

47. Yost, introduction to *The Pot Upon the Wheel,* xi; Curran, *The Pot Upon the Wheel,* 98.

Chapter 5 An Occult Vocabulary and the Problem of Knowledge

1. Prince treats the issue in "The 'Dialect' of Patience Worth," citing Barnes, in *CPW* (336–44). Similarities to Dorset dialect are rare and inconsistent in "The Merry Tale," but compare PW's "'Ees achin o' the lovin o' ye" and Cato's "'Eed best for to off 'ee!" with John Cowper Powys's characters in *Weymouth Sands:* "Do 'ee want John to lend 'ee naught?" (259). See the "Merry Tale" typescript (58), Patience Worth Collection, MHM.

2. In Yost's printing of "The Stranger," Lady Marye says, "I've played the jane-o-apes till the earth doth seem awry" (*PWPM,* 131). Historical usages and citations are taken from the *Oxford English Dictionary,* 2nd ed.

3. "Mrs. Curran's Library," *CPW,* 417–20.

4. Prince would have been inspecting one title in a twelve-volume series, *The Old-Spelling Shakespeare: Being the Works of Shakespeare in the Spelling of the Best Quarto and Folio Texts,* ed. F. J. Furnivall and W. G. Boswell-Stone.

5. Curran, "The Merry Tale," unfinished typescript, 24, Patience Worth Collection, MHM.

6. Ibid., 5.

7. "Theoi Greek Mythology: Exploring Mythology in Classical Literature & Art," The Theoi Project, http://www.theoi.com/.

8. A critic had objected that in naming the character Hermann in *The Sorry Tale,* PW could not have been thinking of an historical Arminius, a Romanized version of Hermann, given Hermann's status as enemy of Rome. After examining the relevant dates, Yost argued that PW's deep knowledge of Hermann is indicated by her nearby use of the name *Flavius,* "the Roman name given to the brother of Hermann" (*CPW,* 387).

9. Thekla Bernays attended a PW session on Mar. 24, 1921, along with Yost and a visitor from India (Bernays Collection, MHM). Bernays translated but did not publish *The Judgement of Salome,* a drama by an anonymous German woman, and wrote a highly praised memoir of her brother, Augustus Bernays, a famous surgeon. See Johnson, *Notable Women of St. Louis,* 20–24.

10. Corbett, *In Her Place,* 211. See also the Anna Yost obituary, *St. Louis Globe-Democrat,* May 5, 1960.

11. See "Time to Greet," David Clark's translation into Scots of a Galician poem by Celso Emilio Ferreiro, which begins, "Ah maun greet sair wi'oot tears . . ." (*Edinburgh Review* 106 [2001]: 62).

12. Curran, "The Merry Tale," 16, Patience Worth Collection, MHM.

13. Burns Club of St. Louis, *St. Louis Nights wi' Burns,* 1913, 37, Washington University Special Collections.

14. Burns Club of St. Louis, *Minutes, Notes and Speeches MCMXXXI–MCMXXXVIII,* 1–3. See portrait of Yost (12) and his address "The Story of a Book" (48–54).

15. Cuoco and Gass, eds., *Literary St. Louis,* 254; St. Louis Directory, 1918, MHM.

16. Carpenter, *Sara Teasdale,* 69.

17. So spelled in PWR. A dictionary spelling would have been *wain,* "a large open farm wagon."

Chapter 6 Dissecting a Specter

1. Wall, *Rediscovering Pearl Curran,* 150.

2. Reprinted in Wegner, *Illusion of Conscious Will,* 110.

3. Litvag, *SS,* 204 (from PWR 10:1973).

4. Morton Prince, *Clinical and Experimental Studies in Personality,* 357–74 ("Pandora's box" quote p. 367).

5. *CPW,* 414–15. Cory's "Patience Worth" was originally published in the *Psychological Review* (397–407) and was reprinted in *CPW* (428–37). Cory was a visitor to PW sessions on Mar. 14 and Apr. 8, 1918, and recollected a visit "one or two years" earlier (PWR 7:1223–27, 1279–80). On Cory's participation in PW sessions, see Litvag, *SS,* 275–79.

6. Walter Prince refers to Cory's "A Divided Self," describing it as the case of "Mrs. O," but only to argue that there is no comparison between B's counterfeit Spanish and PW's literary dialects (*CPW,* 447, 463); Cory, "Divided Self," 287–88.

7. Cory, "Divided Self," 283.

8. Walter Prince, "Psychometric Experiments with Señora María Reyes de Z[ierold]."

9. *The Mirror,* May 27, 1909, 1–2. Reprinted in *The Stories of Fannie Hurst,* ed. Susan Koppelman.

10. "The Gropers," *The Mirror,* May 26, 1910, 6–7; "Old Scotch," *CPW,* 413.

11. "Fannie Hurst and Patience Worth," *PWM,* Oct. 1917, 6; and see PWR 5:867–68. Hurst's visit and subsequent letter are not referred to by any of her biographers.

12. *Smart Set,* Aug. 1920, 105.

13. Jim Allee Hart, *A History of the "St. Louis Globe-Democrat,"* 192–95, 216, 248.

14. Clarence E. Miller, "William Marion Reedy: A Patchwork Portrait," 4, 49.

15. Walter B. Stevens, *Centennial History of Missouri, 1820–1921,* 674–77.

16. Porter to Breckenridge, Dec. 3 and Dec. 18, 1915; Breckenridge to Porter, Dec. 24, 1915, all in Breckenridge Papers, MHM.

17. Litvag also reports a conversation with a friend of the Yosts' who believed that Pearl Curran had lived briefly with them before her marriage, but he could not confirm the suggestion (*SS,* 52).

18. Yost, *The Making of a Successful Husband: Letters of a Happily Married Man to His Son,* 150, 187, 34.

19. Yost, *Making of a Successful Husband,* 149, 186.

20. Yost to Prince, Sept. 27, 1926, PWC.

21. John Livingston Lowes, *The Road to Xanadu: A Study in the Ways of the Imagination,* xi.

22. Hutchings to Hyslop, Feb. 20, 1917, PWC. Characterizing "the Washington University crowd," Hutchings does not extend her contempt to Lowes, whom she describes "giving dinners to his friends and reading them examples of the P.W. literature."

23. Christopher Norris, *The Deconstructive Turn: Essays in the Rhetoric of Philosophy,* 182.

24. Ibid., 135.

25. Lowes, "Burns and English Poetry," in Walter B. Stevens, comp., *Burns Nights in St. Louis,* 11, 13, 17.

26. Hutchings to Hyslop, Apr. 27, 1915, PWC.

27. Ruth Duell gathered and marked letters from Lowes to Morton Prince from April through November 1915 as part of the ASPR's Patience Worth Collection. Letters from Lowes to Prince of Nov. 19 and 23, 1915, respond to what Lowes called in a later letter to Hyslop "the ill-starred visit of the Currans to Dr. Prince" (Apr. 10, 1916, Duell folder, PWC).

28. Hutchings to Hyslop, Feb. 20, 1917, PWC.

29. Lowes, *Road to Xanadu,* 59.

30. Lowes to Morton Prince, Oct. 29, 1915, Duell folder, PWC.

31. Lowes to Morton Prince, n.d., 1915, Duell folder, PWC.

32. Norris, *Deconstructive Turn,* 134–35; Lowes to Morton Prince, Oct. 29, 1915, Duell folder, PWC. The sleuthing metaphor was also used by one of Lowes's early reviewers, the Wordsworthian Leslie Broughton, who called *The Road to Xanadu* "a psychological detective story" (quoted in Thomas McFarland, "Foreword: John Livingston Lowes and Coleridge's Poems," in Lowes, *Road to Xanadu,* xi).

33. Lowes, *Road to Xanadu,* 38.

34. Lowes to Henry Holt, Oct. 15, 1915, Duell folder, PWC.

35. For *steel,* see Lowes to Morton Prince, n.d., 1915, Duell folder, PWC. Lowes's undated letter of 1915 to Prince reports a conversation with Curran from Apr. 2, 1915.

36. Lowes to Morton Prince, Oct. 26 and Nov. 1, 1915, Duell folder, PWC. At one point Lowes, seeking the name *Jasper,* asked PW if any family member was also the name of a stone. The board disappointed his trial of telepathy by guessing "J.A.E.D." (PWR 2:284–88).

37. Lowes to James Hyslop, Apr. 10, 1916, Duell folder, PWC; Lowes to Morton Prince, Nov. 19 and Nov. 23, 1915, Duell folder, PWC.

38. Lowes, *Road to Xanadu,* 59, 64–65; Norris, *Deconstructive Turn,* 138; Lowes, *Road to Xanadu,* 404–6.

39. Lowes, *Road to Xanadu,* ix.

40. T. H. McQueary to Walter Franklin Prince, Jan. 6, 1926, Duell folder, PWC.

41. Frank W. Putnam, *Diagnosis and Treatment of Multiple Personality Disorder,* 30. See also Michael G. Kenny, *The Passion of Ansel Bourne: Multiple Personality in American Culture,* 142–45. Kenny notes that Morton Prince named one alter "the Saint," another "the Devil," and the third "the Woman." For Lisa Appignanesi, Prince's description of Beauchamp's personality as "vividly misogynistic" is "a walking parody of the New Woman who thinks she is 'capable of running the world.'" See *Mad, Bad and Sad: Women and the Mind Doctors from 1800 to the Present,* 173.

42. Walter Prince, "The Doris Case of Multiple Personality," with a preface by James Hyslop.

43. A brief treatment of Walter Franklin Prince can be found in the serialized *Biographical Dictionary of Parapsychology,* ed. Helene Pleasants (259–61).

44. Arthur S. Berger, *Lives and Letters in American Parapsychology: A Biographical History, 1850–1987,* 82.

45. Walter Prince, *Psychic in the House,* 90–94, 264–66, 98; Berger, *Lives and Letters,* 344–45n201.

46. Prince, *Psychic in the House,* 277.

47. See Walter Prince, "A Review of the Margery Case," 212–13.

48. Prince, *Psychic in the House,* 29–30.

49. Walter Prince, "The Riddle of Patience Worth," 20–22. In addition to the blurry photo of eighteen-year-old Pearl with her father, the *Scientific American* article displays a more recent photo of what had been the Pollard home in Palmer, Missouri, and Curran's "present home," probably that of Dr. Henry Rogers on Lindell Boulevard just prior to their November 1926 marriage.

50. Walter Prince to Pearl Rogers, Apr. 25, 1927, and Rogers to Prince, titled "Undated message from P.W.," "Correspondence," Duell folder, PWC.

51. Rogers to Prince, titled "Undated message from P.W.," "Correspondence," Duell folder, PWC.

52. Rogers to Prince, Dec. 30, 1926, "Correspondence," Duell folder, PWC.

53. Ibid., Feb. 24, 1927.

54. Rogers to Prince, Dec. 30, 1926, and Jan. 6, 1927, and Prince to Rogers, Feb. 21, 1927, "Correspondence," Duell folder, PWC.

55. Walter Prince to McQueary, Apr. 19, 1927; McQueary to Prince, Apr. 22, 1927; Rogers to Prince, Apr. 22, 1927, Duell folder, PWC.

56. Pearl L. Wyman to Walter Prince, Feb. 25, 1934, "Correspondence," Duell folder, PWC.

57. T. J. Jackson Lears, *No Place of Grace: Antimodernism and the Transformation of American Culture, 1880–1920,* 48, 174. Lears cites Repplier's "Decay of Sentiment" (332n101). Litvag quotes liberally from "Dead Authors" (*SS,* 192–97).

58. See Melody Graulich and Elizabeth Klimasmith, eds., *Exploring Lost Borders: Critical Essays on Mary Austin,* and Barney Nelson, *The Wild and the Domestic: Animal Representation, Ecocriticism, and Western American Literature.*

59. Austin, "Automatism in Writing," 336–38. See also Augusta Fink, *I-Mary: A Biography of Mary Austin,* 21. For Austin's association of her creativity with mysticism, see Anna Carew-Miller, "Between Worlds, Crossing Borders: Mary Austin, Liminality, and the Dilemma

of Women's Creativity," in Graulich and Klimasmith, eds., *Exploring Lost Borders,* 105–25.

60. Quoted in Linda K. Karell, "Mary Austin, I-Mary, and Mary-by-Herself: Collaboration in *Earth Horizon,*" in Graulich and Klimasmith, eds., *Exploring Lost Borders,* 177.

61. Fink, *I-Mary,* 41.

62. Austin, "Automatism in Writing," 341, 346.

63. Ibid., 347.

Chapter 7 Pearl and Patience in the Twenties

1. Reedy to Anna George de Mille, May 10, 1920, William Marion Reedy Papers, MHM.

2. Quoted in Max Putzel, *The Man in the Mirror: William Marion Reedy and His Magazine,* 138.

3. On the Chopin-Reedy friendship see Emily Toth, *Kate Chopin: A Life of the Author of "The Awakening,"* 266–68.

4. Quoted by Kathleen Butterly Nigro in Corbett, *In Her Place,* 210–11.

5. See the biographical entries in Cuoco and Gass, eds., *Literary St. Louis,* on Reedy (78–87), Hurst (133–37), Akins (96–101), and Teasdale (122–27).

6. Quoted in Cuoco and Gass, eds., *Literary St. Louis,* 134.

7. Alice Hunt Sokoloff, *Hadley: The First Mrs. Hemingway,* 6. On Hadley's concluding "I didn't believe in Ouija boards and automatic writing," see Gioia Diliberto, *Hadley,* 34.

8. Charles E. Cory, "A Subconscious Phenomenon."

9. Ibid., 373–74, italics in original.

10. Quoted in Walter S. Jenkins, *The Remarkable Mrs. Beach, American Composer,* 81.

11. "Sennett, Goldwyn and Roach Films: 1917–1927," *Mabel Normand Home Page,* http://www.mn-hp.com/filmogp3.html. On Fannie Hurst, see Brooke Kroeger, *Fannie: The Talent for Success of Writer Fannie Hurst,* 361–64.

12. *What Happened to Rosa?* Grapevine Video; Betty Harper Fussell, *Mabel,* 117. See also Robert Klepper, *Silent Films, 1887–1996: A Critical Guide to 646 Movies,* 222–23.

13. Letter on *PWM* stationery to "Dears" (perhaps Mr. and Mrs. Charles Ives), Jan. 19, 1920, Box 6B.4.6, Patience Worth Collection, MHM.

14. *St. Louis Globe-Democrat,* June 2, 1922.

15. Holland, interview, n.d., 1957, Duell folder, PWC.

16. Kleymeyer to Duell, June 10, 1957, Duell folder, PWC.

17. Letters to the author, Apr. 11 and 23, 1999. Eileen and Ralph Kleymeyer, childless, divorced in the late 1950s, and Eileen, after marrying again, died in 1982. Ralph Kleymeyer remained certain only that the name of the alleged father had not been mentioned in any of the published material on Pearl Curran. He died in 2000 in Austin, Texas.

18. Holland, interview, n.d., 1957, Duell folder, PWC.

19. *Reedy's Mirror,* Dec. 18, 1918, 213. This was a special issue devoted to leading citizens of St. Louis and Kansas City.

20. Holland, interview, Feb. 12, 1957, Duell folder, PWC. This second interview, stipulating "2/12/57," adds to and expands on notes in the first, dated simply "1957."

21. Pearl Curran Rogers to Walter Prince, Jan. 21 and 27, 1927 (retyped by Duell), "Correspondence," Duell folder, PWC.

22. Cashman's obituary reported that he died at home "after an illness of several weeks" and that services would be conducted from the home to St. Rose's Catholic Church with interment in Calvary Cemetery (MHM, Vertical File).

23. Eileen Curran Kleymeyer, interview, New Orleans, 1957, Duell folder, PWC.

24. *St. Louis Post-Dispatch,* Nov. 7, 1926; Holland, interview, Feb. 12, 1957, Duell folder, PWC.

25. Henry Rogers to Walter Prince, Oct. 14, 1926, PWC.

26. Pearl Curran Rogers to Prince, Nov. 30, 1926, "Correspondence," Duell folder, PWC; *St. Louis Post-Dispatch,* Nov. 4, 1926.

27. Rogers to Prince, Sept. 23, 1928; Apr. 10, 1926; Mar. 25, 1927; Walter Prince to T. H. McQueary, Jan. 22, 1926, all in Duell folder, PWC.

28. See PWR 21:3488, 3495–97, 3503, 3560, 3565, 3569.

29. *St. Louis Times,* Oct. 29, 1928; Rogers to Prince, Nov. 12 and Jan. 5, 1928, Dec. 17, 1927, "Correspondence," Duell folder, PWC.

30. Rogers to Prince, Dec. 20, 1929, "Correspondence," Duell folder, PWC.

31. *St. Louis Post-Dispatch,* Oct. 27, 1929 (quoted in Litvag, *SS,* 254).

32. Pearl Curran to Mrs. Ives, July 17, 1919, Patience Worth Collection, MHM. Curran writes from 5714 Vernon Ave. on "John Howard Curran, Lands" stationery.

33. Rogers to Prince, Aug. 7, 1929, Nov. 12, 1928, "Correspondence," Duell folder, PWC.

34. Sadakichi Hartmann displayed several of their photographs in *The Valiant Knights of Daguerre: Selected Critical Essays on Photography and Profiles of Photographic Pioneers,* ed. Harold W. Lawton and George Knox (113, 123–24), in 1978. See also Beverly D. Bishop and Deborah W. Bolas, eds., *In Her Own Write: Women's History Resources in the Library and Archives of the Missouri Historical Society,* 60.

35. Bishop, "The Potter's Wheel," 87; Carpenter, *Sara Teasdale,* 72–73.

36. Sept. 22, 1924, *Poems from Patience Worth for Williamina Parrish, 1924–1928,* Patience Worth Collection, MHM.

37. Bishop, "The Potter's Wheel," 81–82.

38. See *CPW,* 311–21, and the Grace Parrish Scrapbook (Patience Worth Collection, MHM), assembled by Grace and Williamina Parrish (1898–1926). The twelve-page "Lamento Doloroso" appears in PWR 30, "Odds and Ends of Records and Short Stories by Patience Worth," a volume of writings and records gathered after Pearl's death. Pagination of the Record ends with vol. 29. References to "Lamento Doloroso" in the text cite the typescript's page numbering.

39. Susan Youens, "Excavating an Allegory: The Text of Pierrot Lunaire." Quoted in "Pierrot Lunaire in History," www.colleges.org/~music/modules/pierrot/history.html.

40. Zoë Akins, *Interpretations: A Book of First Poems.*

41. Mary Cass Canfield, foreword to *Mon Ami Pierrot: Songs and Fantasies,* ed. Kendall Banning, 11, 17.

42. Edna St. Vincent Millay, *Aria da Capo: A Play in One Act,* 45.

43. In addition to the MHM Grace Parrish Scrapbook, the St. Louis Public Library Special Collections hold several of these photo-portraits, the subject often unnamed or identified as Nino "Rouchi."

44. "Jean's Indication of the Last Incarnation of [attendees' names]," Grace Parrish Scrapbook, Patience Worth Collection, MHM.

45. Bishop, "The Potter's Wheel," 136.

46. Rogers to Prince, Jan. 30, 1927, "Correspondence," Duell folder, PWC.

47. Pearl Rogers to Grace Parrish, Apr. 9, 1927, Grace Parrish Scrapbook, Patience Worth Collection, MHM.

Chapter 8 The City of Angels

1. *Los Angeles Daily Times,* Mar. 24, 1928, sec. 1.

2. Ibid.

3. Campbell, "How Patience Worth's Ouija Board Baby Grew Up," *Every Week Magazine,* Mar. 7–8, 1931.

4. "Death Silences the 'Spirit Voice' of Patience Worth," *American Weekly, Inc.*, Feb. [n.d.] 1938, 89–92 (Box 6B.4.6, Patience Worth Collection, MHM).

5. "Spiritualism," *Los Angeles Times,* July 11, 1930, sec. 2.

6. Miss Chandler, PWR 26:4087; Miss Chandler, "Real `Ghost Writer,'" *Los Angeles Times,* July 21, 1930, Monday morning edition, sec. 2.

7. Alma Whitaker, "Sugar and Spice," *Los Angeles Times,* Aug. 27, 1930, Sunday morning edition, sec. 3.

8. Myra Nye, "Appeal Made for Friendship," *Los Angeles Times,* June 21, 1931, Sunday morning edition, sec. 3.

9. *Los Angeles Times,* Sept. 7, 1930, Sunday morning edition, sec. B.

10. "Ouija Board to Typewriter," *Los Angeles Times,* May 11, 1935, sec. 2, Women's Club Page.

11. Robert Windeler, *Sweetheart: The Story of Mary Pickford,* 168.

12. Windeler, *Sweetheart,* 163. See Gary Carey, *Doug & Mary: A Biography of Douglas Fairbanks and Mary Pickford,* 189–90, and Booton Herndon, *Mary Pickford and Douglas Fairbanks: The Most Popular Couple the World Has Ever Known,* 276.

13. Ralph Kleymeyer, letter to the author, Apr. 11, 1999.

14. Windeler, *Sweetheart,* 174, 179.

15. Campbell, "How Patience Worth's Ouija Board Baby Grew Up," *Every Week Magazine,* Mar. 7–8, 1931.

16. Kleymeyer to Duell, June 10, 1957, Duell folder, PWC. Rogers had "bought and restored a large three-story house on the beach," formerly owned by Edward Everett Horton, Kleymeyer believed.

17. Holland, interview, n.d., 1957, Duell folder, PWC.

18. Bailey Millard, "Will She Meet Her Astral Guide?" *Los Angeles Times Sunday Magazine,* Jan. 16, 1938, sec. H .

19. Ralph and Eileen Curran Kleymeyer told Duell essentially the same story, although Ralph Kleymeyer recalled Peters's name incorrectly and added that, after divorcing Peters, Patty took little interest in her child, Hope, leaving her with a nurse (Eileen Curran Kleymeyer, interview, 1957; Kleymeyer to Duell, June 10, 1957, Duell folder, PWC).

20. "Daughter of Late Psychic Found Dead," *Los Angeles Times,* Nov. 24, 1943, sec. 1.

21. Holland, interview, n.d., 1957, Duell folder, PWC; Kleymeyer to Duell, June 10, 1957, Duell folder, PWC.

22. Pearl Wyman to Walter Prince, from 917 Ocean Ave., Santa Monica, Feb. 25, 1934, Duell folder, PWC. All descriptions of Pearl's work with Gordon Ray Young in the following paragraphs are taken from this letter.

23. PWR 30: "Odds and Ends," n.p. See *SS,* where Litvag quotes "Naughty" and three more of what he calls "these indescribably banal and trivial poems" (258).

24. See PWR 26:4038, 4091, 4094; PWR 29:4363.

25. Eileen Curran Kleymeyer, interview, 1957; Kleymeyer to Duell, June 10, 1957, Duell folder, PWC.

26. *Los Angeles Times, Literature and Art: New Books, Book News,* Sept. 2, 1917, sec. 3, ProQuest Historical Newspapers.

27. *Los Angeles Times, The Times Literary Page,* June 23, 1918, sec. 3, ProQuest Historical Newspapers.

28. Eileen Curran Kleymeyer, interview, 1957, Duell folder, PWC.

29. A note on manuscripts: as Mrs. Robert Wyman, Pearl ends her 1934 letter to Prince with the note, "We have a complete record of all editing," but with the exception of the PWR, those records, including unpublished manuscripts, have not surfaced. (The original record-keeping procedures for the PW manuscripts were described in detail in *PWM,*

Sept. 1917, 15.) Their history is suggested only in letters and interviews following Curran's death.

In a letter to the Missouri Historical Society director, Mrs A. B. ("Dotsie") Smith claimed to have manuscripts of unpublished PW works, the novel "Samuel Wheaton," "The Shakespeare Play" (*sic*), and the unfinished story "The Madrigal" (letter to Charles van Ravenswaay, June 4, 1957, Patience Worth Papers 1916–1928, Box 1–2, Patience Worth Collection, MHM). While Smith shipped what is now known as the Patience Worth Record, she wrote van Ravenswaay again on July 28 to say that she would not be sending her personal correspondence with Curran and had not decided on "the disposition" of the manuscripts, which were apparently never sent to the MHM. In the same period, Ruth Duell wrote Director van Ravenswaay on July 15, describing visits to Smith at which she had urged her to send all manuscripts, clippings, and correspondence against the efforts of "the harpies here" who would have restricted access "in their peculiar cultish way." Though she believed Smith trusted her "discretion," Duell was evidently unsuccessful.

The last person in possession of "Elizabethan Mask," Eileen Curran Kleymeyer told Ruth Duell in her interview, was Roberta Wyman, who as Robert Wyman's adopted daughter had joined Patty and Eileen, "two wee uns and one sweetie" (PWR 28:4289), as audience for PW's urgently maternal poetry. After Pearl's death, all three young women were pressed by Smith and Max Behr for continued PW communications. Without enthusiasm and working only from memory, Eileen delivered PW imitations from the Ouija board, but Roberta's attempts "had no resemblance to the original," said Ralph Kleymeyer. Roberta's persistence gave her entrée to manuscripts in the possession of Max Behr, who married her, although according to Ralph, Max "detested Roberta." In 1957, Eileen described Roberta to Ruth Duell as "an unpleasant subject" and advised her not to attempt an interview. Both Eileen and Ralph identified Roberta as planning to write her own book on PW, Ralph objecting because, with no relevant skills, she intended to edit the Shakespeare manuscript and had only waited for Max to die in order to lay claim to it. According to Smith, Max left Roberta, who served in World War II as a WAC, his house at Pacific Palisades and his income of $17,500 per year when he died (Eileen Kleymeyer to Ruth Duell, Apr. 30, 1957; Ralph Kleymeyer to Duell, June 10, 1957; "Mrs. A. B. Smith" to "Madeleine," Jan. 12, 1957, PWC). Although the Pasadena Library received at some point a full run of *Patience Worth's Magazine* (now reported missing), no Los Angeles area library has a record of Pearl/PW manuscripts. At the time of the bequest in July 1957, Roberta Wyman lived at 28802 Gray Fox St., Malibu, CA.

30. PWR 29:4370. For obituaries see *Los Angeles Times,* Dec. 5, 1937, and *St. Louis Post-Dispatch,* Dec. 5, 1937. The *Los Angeles Times* gave 833 Ocean Blvd. as Curran's address at the time of her death, with no mention of Robert Wyman or the previous, Culver City address (PWR 28:4245) where they had lived after their marriage.

31. Elsie Martin, interview by Ruth Potter Duell, Apr. 7, 1956, Duell folder, PWC.

32. "Addendum: The Four Gospels," 22a, July 27, 1932, PWC.

33. Ibid., 22b.

Chapter 9 The Neural Pearl: Automaticity for All

1. *Collected Prose: James Merrill,* 87 (from an interview by Helen Vendler), 135 (from an interview by Fred Bornhauser). Timothy Materer points out that "a mixture of skepticism and naïveté" is characteristic of poets like Yeats and Merrill exploring metaphors of the occult. See his *Modernist Alchemy: Poetry and the Occult,* 1.

2. Merrill, *The Changing Light at Sandover,* 261–62.

3. Lowes to Morton Prince, n.d., 1915, describing a conversation with Pearl Curran of April 2, 1915, Duell folder, PWC.

4. M. D. Conroy, interview by Ruth Potter Duell, 1957, Duell folder, PWC. Conroy noted Curran's feeling a "pressure on top of the head" during PW sessions and, referring to her public appearances after John Curran's death, added, "Used to get $100."

5. Merrill, *Sandover,* 162, quoted in Polito, afterword to *A Reader's Guide to James Merrill's "The Changing Light at Sandover,"* 234.

6. London, *Writing Double,* 29.

7. Steven Johnson, *Mind Wide Open: Your Brain and the Neuroscience of Everyday Life,* 7–8.

8. Ibid., 173–78.

9. See Stephen E. Braude, "Dissociation and Latent Abilities: The Strange Case of Patience Worth." "Commentaries" by Jean Goodwin (49–53) and Jennifer Radden (55–59) follow Braude's article in the *Journal of Trauma and Dissociation* 1, no. 2 (2000).

10. Matthew Hugh Erdelyi, "Dissociation, Defense, and the Unconscious," 13.

11. Bernard Baars, "Psychology in a World of Sentient, Self-Knowing Beings: A Modest Utopian Fantasy," in Robert L. Solso, ed., *Mind and Brain Sciences in the 21st Century,* 3–4. The subject of interdisciplinary work in literature and the sciences was addressed in an influential special issue of *American Literature,* "Literature and Science: Cultural Forms, Conceptual Exchanges," ed. Wai Chee Dimock and Priscilla Wald. Among a new generation of interdisciplinary works see Brian Boyd, *On the Origins of Stories: Evolution, Cognition and Fiction;* the essays in *Introduction to Cognitive Cultural Studies,* ed. Lisa Zunshine; and *Toward a Cognitive Theory of Narrative Acts,* ed. Frederick Luis Aldama.

12. Edward O. Wilson, *Consilience: The Unity of Knowledge,* 214; Henry L. Roediger III, "The Future of Cognitive Psychology," in Robert L. Solso, ed., *Mind and Brain Sciences in the 21st Century,* 192–93.

13. Johnson, *Mind Wide Open,* 213.

14. Nancy Cartwright, *The Dappled World: A Study of the Boundaries of Science,* 1, quoted in Tim Thornton, "Reductionism/Antireductionism," in Radden, ed., *The Philosophy of Psychiatry,* 202; Carl Craver, "Beyond Reduction: Mechanisms, Multifield Integration and the Unity of Neuroscience," 388; Manuel DeLanda, "Virtual Environments and the Concept of Synergy," 357.

15. See Frank W. Putnam, *Diagnosis and Treatment of Multiple Personality Disorder,* 65–66.

16. Neuroimaging procedures have sought to identify the brain substrate of post-traumatic pathologies of dissociation, describing, e.g., differences in regional blood flow for DID patients who exhibit "at least two distinct mental states of self awareness, each with its own access to trauma-related memory." See Guochan E. Tsai et al., "Functional Magnetic Resonance Imagery of Personality Switches in a Woman with Dissociative Identity Disorder," and A. A. T. S. Reinders et al., "One Brain, Two Selves." For shifts in diagnostic views and terminology regarding dissociation, see John F. Kihlstrom, "One Hundred Years of Hysteria," in Steven Jay Lynn and Judith W. Rhue, eds., *Dissociation: Clinical and Theoretical Perspectives,* 365–94.

17. Jonathan Evans, *Thinking Twice: Two Minds in One Brain,* 6, 209.

18. Hilgard, *Divided Consciousness,* 204–9, 25–26,136.

19. Ibid., 249.

20. Ernest Hilgard, "Neodissociation Theory," in Lynn and Rhue, eds., *Dissociation: Clinical and Theoretical Perspectives,* 36.

21. Hilgard, *Divided Consciousness,* 195–98.

22. Marcel Kinsbourne, "What Qualifies a Representation for a Role in Consciousness?" in *Scientific Approaches to Consciousness,* ed. Jonathan D. Cohen and Jonathan W. Schooler,

349. Examples of ordinary dissociation are from Stanley Krippner, "Cross-Cultural Treatment Perspectives on Dissociative Disorders," in *Dissociation: Clinical and Theoretical Perspectives,* ed. Lynn and Ruhe, 357.

23. Erdelyi, "Dissociation, Defense, and the Unconscious," 4–8 (italics in original).

24. Daniel Dennett, "The Self as the Center of Narrative Gravity," 107.

25. Daniel Schacter, *Searching for Memory: The Brain, the Mind, and the Past,* 233–34.

26. Nancy Andreasen, *The Creating Brain: The Neuroscience of Genius,* 18, 37–43.

27. Erik Z. Woody and Kenneth S. Bowers, "A Frontal Assault on Dissociated Control," in Lynn and Rhue, eds., *Dissociation: Clinical and Theoretical Perspectives,* 57, 62. On "inappropriate . . . behavior," the authors are citing Tim Shallice, *From Neuropsychology to Mental Structure.*

28. Michiel B. de Ruiter et al., "Attention as a Characteristic of Nonclinical Dissociation: An Event Related Potential Study." Stephen Braude cites 1927 experiments by R. A. Messerschmidt ("Memory," 107). See Yves Rossetti and Antti Revonsuo's *Beyond Dissociation: Interaction between Dissociated Implicit and Explicit Processing,* 7.

29. See Jonah Lehrer, *Imagine: How Creativity Works,* 16–18. Lehrer cites authors Mark Jung-Beeman et al., "Neural Activity Observed in People Solving Verbal Problems with Insight," 500–510, and John Kounios et al., "The Prepared Mind: Neural Activity Prior to Problem Presentation Predicts Solution by Sudden Insight," 882–90.

30. Arthur S. Reber, *Implicit Learning and Tacit Knowledge,* 25, 23. See also Michael A. Stadler and Henry L. Roediger III, "The Question of Awareness in Research on Implicit Learning," 108.

31. Arthur S. Reber, "How to Differentiate Implicit and Explicit Modes of Acquisition," in *Scientific Approaches to Consciousness,* ed. Cohen and Schooler, 154. "The rule of thumb is that learning may occur when we do not intend it to happen, do not expect it or think that we do not study it" (Henry L. Roediger III, Yadin Dudai, and Susan M. Fitzpatrick, eds., *Science of Memory: Concepts,* 35).

32. Reber, *Implicit Learning,* 64; Daniel Schacter, "Implicit Memory: History and Current Status," 503.

33. John F. Kihlstrom, "Consciousness and Me-Ness," in *Scientific Approaches to Consciousness,* ed. Cohen and Schooler, 458.

34. William James, *Principles of Psychology,* 606.

35. Zusne and Jones, *Anomalistic Psychology,* 104–5; Howard Gardner, "Creative Lives and Creative Works: A Synthetic Scientific Report," 317.

36. Endel Tulving, "Cue Dependent Forgetting," 74, quoted by Henry L. Roediger III and Melissa J. Guynn, "Retrieval Processes," 198.

37. As Walter Prince's book neared completion, Curran succeeded in having him delete any suggestion that she had intended to amuse her father with the board, but Prince was unwilling to delete his reference to her staying away from the board for some time after Pollard's death. See Prince to Rogers, Feb. 21, 1927, "Correspondence," Duell folder, PWC.

38. Johnson, *Mind Wide Open,* 200; Schacter, *Searching for Memory,* 60–61.

39. Semon is Schacter's "stranger behind the engram" in his book with that title (*Stranger behind the Engram: Theories of Memory and the Psychology of Science* [Hillsdale, NJ: Erlbaum, 1982], 58–59, 87), in which he credits a 1905 review by Henry J. Watt with discerning the importance of Semon's ecphoric stimulus.

40. Daniel J. Levitin, *This Is Your Brain on Music: The Science of a Human Obsession,* 124–31.

41. Aniruddh D. Patel, *Music, Language, and the Brain,* 86, 324. Patel cites Judith Becker, "Anthropological Perspectives on Music and Emotion," in *Music and Emotion: Theory and Research,* ed. Patrik Juslin and John A. Sloboda.

42. John A. Sloboda, *The Musical Mind: The Cognitive Psychology of Music,* 19.

43. Andreasen, *Creating Brain,* 156.

44. See Fred Lerdahl, "The Sounds of Poetry Viewed as Music," 416, 427, and Mireille Besson and Daniele Schön, "Comparison between Language and Music," 273, both in Isabelle Peretz and Robert J. Zattore, eds., *The Cognitive Neuroscience of Music.*

45. Vera John-Steiner, *Notebooks of the Mind: Explorations of Thinking,* 8, 31, 54–55.

46. See Richard Powers, "How to Speak a Book," 31, and *Galatea 2.2,* 217–18.

47. See Randall Knoper, "American Literary Realism and Nervous 'Reflexion,'" 721–22.

48. Larry L. Jacoby, Jeffrey P. Toth, D. Stephen Lindsay, and James A. Debner, "Lectures for a Layperson: Methods for Revealing Unconscious Processes," 111. The concept of creative flow has been associated with the work of Mikhaly Csikszentmihalyi, who describes in *Flow: The Psychology of Optimal Experience* a creative process that cannot be commanded but is subject to modulation and regulation of attention. See also Larry L. Jacoby, Diane Ste-Marie, and Jeffrey P. Toth, "Redefining Automaticity: Unconscious Influences, Awareness, and Control."

49. John A. Bargh and Kimberley Barndollar, "Automaticity in Action: The Unconscious as Repository of Chronic Goals and Motives," 465.

50. Kinsbourne, "What Qualifies a Representation," in *Scientific Approaches to Consciousness,* ed. Cohen and Schooler, 342–43; Ran R. Hassin, "Nonconscious Control and Implicit Working Memory," in Ran R. Hassin, James S. Uleman, and John A. Bargh, eds., *The New Unconscious,* 211.

51. Bernard J. Baars, Michael R. Fehling, Mark LaPolla, and Katharine McGovern, "Consciousness *Creates Access:* Conscious Goal Images Recruit Unconscious Action Routines, but Goal Competition Serves to 'Liberate' Such Routines, Causing Predictable Slips," in *Scientific Approaches to Consciousness,* ed. Cohen and Schooler, 423.

52. Kinsbourne, "What Qualifies a Representation," in *Scientific Approaches to Consciousness,* ed. Cohen and Schooler,340–43, 348.

53. Herman H. Spitz, *Nonconscious Movements: From Mystical Messages to Facilitated Communication,* 122; Elizabeth F. Loftus and Mark R. Klinger, "Is the Unconscious Smart or Dumb?" 764.

54. Rhianon Allen and Arthur S. Reber, "Unconscious Intelligence," 314.

55. Uleman, introduction, 6, and Jack Glaser and John F. Kihlstrom, "Compensatory Automaticity: Unconscious Volition Is Not an Oxymoron," 190, both in Hassin, Uleman, and Bargh, eds., *New Unconscious.*

56. John A. Bargh and Tanya L. Chartrand, "The Unbearable Automaticity of Being," 476. Bargh (in *New Unconscious,* 53) cites Donald Merlin's use of the "demon" metaphor in *A Mind So Rare: The Evolution of Human Consciousness.* Merlin in turn distinguishes between the complex "demons of literacy" and the mechanized operations of artificial intelligence. Neither makes mention of the *daemon* of genius as humanistic precedent in Socrates and Goethe.

57. Reber, "How to Differentiate," in *Scientific Approaches to Consciousness,* ed. Cohen and Schooler, 137–38.

58. Daniel M. Wegner, *The Illusion of Conscious Will.* See especially chap. 7 (221–70). Page numbers from this work are given parenthetically in this and the next two paragraphs.

59. Eric R. Kandel, *In Search of Memory: The Emergence of a New Science of Mind,* 389–90.

60. B. F. Skinner's article "Has Gertrude Stein a Secret?" appeared in the *Atlantic Monthly,* Jan. 1934, 50–57.

61. Meyer, *Irresistible Dictation,* 221, 227.

62. Stein quoted ibid., 221; Solomons and Stein, "Normal Motor Automatism," 24; Stein, "Cultivated Motor Automatism: A Study of Character in Its Relation to Attention," 31. Meyer points out that Stein, though given as coauthor, did not contribute to Solomons's article, which originally appeared in the *Psychological Review* in 1896 and is reprinted in *Motor Automatism,* ed. Robert Wilson, along with Stein's report, which was originally published in 1898.

63. Stein, quoted in Solomons and Stein, "Normal Motor Automatism," 2.

64. Stein, quoted in Meyer, *Irresistible Dictation,* 221, 229; Gertrude Stein, *The Geographical History of America; or, The Relation of Human Nature to the Human Mind,* 92.

65. Meyer, *Irresistible Dictation,* 229; Solomons and Stein, "Normal Motor Automatism," 10; Ulla E. Dydo, *Gertrude Stein: The Language That Rises: 1923–1934,* 181. Meyer characterizes Stein's "xtra consciousness" as a laboratory-informed enactment of writing itself and goes on to move James's radical empiricism into, then beyond, the company of neuropsychological research, looking past reductionist namings to dynamic networks of neural process such as Gerald Edelman's neuronal group selection (in *Bright Air, Brilliant Fire: On the Matter of the Mind*) and its emphasis on successive neural mappings, and mappings of mappings, strengthened or weakened by continually reentrant experience. See Meyer, 121–28, and, on Edelman, 323–25.

66. Marco Iacoboni, *Mirroring People: The New Science of How We Connect with Others,* 132.

67. Allan Paivio, *Mind and Its Evolution: A Dual Coding Theoretical Approach,* 331.

68. Iacoboni, *Mirroring People,* 92–93, 133, 91, 96.

69. June E. Downey, *Creative Imagination: Studies in the Psychology of Literature.*

70. Spitz, *Nonconscious Movements,* 60–62, is quoting from Downey's study "Automatic Phenomena of Muscle Reading."

71. Downey, *Creative Imagination,* 15, 34–35. Following and occasionally differing with the 1896 Solomons study "Normal Motor Automatism," Downey used herself and Anderson as "reagents" in "Automatic Writing."

72. Antti Revonsuo, *Inner Presence: Consciousness as a Biological Phenomenon,* 109–10.

73. Ibid., 119.

74. Ibid., 285–92, 293, 298.

75. Marcus E. Raichle, "The Brain's Dark Energy."

Bibliography

Abbott, David. *Behind the Scenes with the Mediums.* Chicago: Open Court, 1907.

Akins, Zoë. *Interpretations: A Book of First Poems.* London: Grant Richards, 1912.

Aldama, Frederick Luis, ed. *Toward a Cognitive Theory of Narrative Acts.* Austin: University of Texas Press, 2010.

Allen, Rhianon, and Arthur S. Reber. "Unconscious Intelligence." In *A Companion to Cognitive Science,* ed.William Bechtel and George Graham, 314–23. Malden, MA: Blackwell, 1998.

Andreasen, Nancy. *The Creating Brain: The Neuroscience of Genius.* New York: Dana Press, 2005.

Appignanesi, Lisa. *Mad, Bad and Sad: Women and the Mind Doctors from 1800 to the Present.* New York: W. W. Norton, 2008.

Atherton, Gertrude Franklin Horn. *Patience Sparhawk and Her Times.* London: John Lane, 1897.

Auerbach, Nina. *Woman and the Demon: The Life of a Victorian Myth.* Cambridge: Harvard University Press, 1982.

Austin, Mary. "Automatism in Writing." *Unpartizan Review* 14, no. 28 (1920): 336–47.

Bargh, John A., and Kimberly Barndollar. "Automaticity in Action: The Unconscious as Repository of Chronic Goals and Motives." In *The Psychology of Action: Linking Cognition and Motivation to Behavior,* ed. Peter M. Gollwitzer and John A. Bargh, 457–71. New York: Guilford, 1996.

Bargh, John A., and Tanya L. Chartrand. "The Unbearable Automaticity of Being." *American Psychologist* 54, no. 7 (1999): 462–79.

Bargh, John A., and Melissa J. Ferguson. "Beyond Behaviorism: On the Automaticity of Higher Mental Processes." *Psychological Bulletin* 126, no. 6 (2000): 925–45.

Barker, Deborah. *Aesthetics and Gender in American Literature: Portraits of the Woman Artist.* Lewisburg, PA: Bucknell University Press, 2000.

Barresi, John. "Morton Prince and B.C.A.: A Historical Footnote on the Confrontation between Dissociation Theory and Freudian Psychology in a Case of Multiple Personality." In *Psychological Concepts and Dissociative Disorders,* ed. Raymond Klein and Benjamin Doane, 94–129. Hillsdale, NJ: Lawrence Erlbaum, 1994.

Barrett, Harrison D. *The Life and Work of Cora L. V. Richmond.* Chicago: Hack and Anderson, 1895.

Bauer, Mark. *This Composite Voice: The Role of W. B. Yeats in James Merrill's Poetry.* New York: Routledge, 2003.

Bean, Nellie Parsons. *My Life as a Dissociated Personality.* Boston: R. G. Badger, 1909.

Beecher, Charles. *Spiritual Manifestations.* Boston: Lee and Shepard, 1879.

Bentley, Toni. *Sisters of Salome.* New Haven, CT: Yale University Press, 2002.

Berger, Arthur S. *Lives and Letters in American Parapsychology: A Biographical History, 1850–1987.* Jefferson, NC: McFarland, 1988.

Bishop, Beverly D. "The Potter's Wheel: An Early Twentieth Century Support Network of Women Artists and Writers." Master's thesis, University of Missouri–St. Louis, 1984.

Bishop, Beverly D., and Deborah W. Bolas, eds. *In Her Own Write: Women's History Resources in the Library and Archives of the Missouri Historical Society.* St. Louis: Missouri Historical Society Press, 1983.

Bloom, Harold, ed. *Modern Critical Views: Merrill.* New York: Chelsea House, 1985.

Blum, Deborah. *Ghost Hunters: William James and the Search for Scientific Proof of Life after Death.* New York: Penguin, 2006.

Bourdieu, Pierre. *Language and Symbolic Power.* Ed. John B. Thompson. Cambridge, MA: Harvard University Press, 1991.

Boyd, Brian. *On the Origins of Stories: Evolution, Cognition and Fiction.* Cambridge, MA: Harvard University Press, 2010.

Brandon, Ruth. *The Spiritualists: The Passion for the Occult in the Nineteenth and Twentieth Centuries.* New York: Knopf, 1983.

Braude, Ann. *Radical Spirits: Spiritualism and Women's Rights in Nineteenth-Century America.* 2nd ed. Bloomington: Indiana University Press, 2001.

———. "Women's History *Is* American Religious History." In *Retelling United States Religious History,* ed. Thomas A. Tweed, 87–107. Berkeley: University of California Press, 1997.

Braude, Stephen E. "Dissociation and Latent Abilities: The Strange Case of Patience Worth." *Journal of Trauma and Dissociation* 1, no. 2 (2000): 13–48.

———. *Immortal Remains: The Evidence for Life after Death.* New York: Rowman and Littlefield, 2003.

Burgess, Charles A., comp. *Pictorial Spiritualism.* Chicago: Illinois State Spiritualist Association, 1922.

Burns Club of St. Louis. *Minutes, Notes and Speeches MCMXXXI–MCMXXXVIII.* For private distribution, Mound City Press, 1938.

———. *St. Louis Nights wi' Burns.* Burns Club of St. Louis, 1913, Washington University Special Collections.

Canfield, Mary Cass. Foreword to *Mon Ami Pierrot: Songs and Fantasies,* ed. Kendall Banning. Chicago: Brothers of the Book, 1917.

Carey, Gary. *Doug & Mary: A Biography of Douglas Fairbanks and Mary Pickford.* New York: E. P. Dutton, 1997.

Carpenter, Margaret Haley. *Sara Teasdale: A Biography.* New York: Schulte, 1960.

Cartwright, Nancy. *The Dappled World: A Study of the Boundaries of Science.* Cambridge: Cambridge University Press, 1999.

Cheney, Sheldon, ed. *The Art of the Dance: Isadora Duncan.* New York: Theatre Arts Books, 1969.

Chéroux, Clément, et al. *The Perfect Medium: Photography and the Occult.* New Haven, CT: Yale University Press, 2005.

Cohen, Jonathan D., and Jonathan W. Schooler, eds. *Scientific Approaches to Consciousness.* Mahwah, NJ: Erlbaum, 1997.

Connor, Steven. "Satan and Sybil: Talk, Possession, and Dissociation." In *Talk, Talk, Talk: The Cultural Life of Everyday Conversation,* ed. S. J. Salamansky. New York: Routledge, 2001.

Coon, Deborah. "Testing the Limits of Sense and Science: American Experimental Psychologists Combat Spiritualism, 1880–1920." *American Psychologist* 47, no. 2 (1992): 121–39.

Corbett, Katharine T. *In Her Place: A Guide to St. Louis Women's History.* St. Louis: Missouri Historical Society Press, 1999.

Cordingley, George V. *Impromptu Poems: By the Inspirational Poet.* N.p.: Beth Cooke Gray, [1901?].

Corelli, Marie. *Barabbas: A Dream of the World's Tragedy.* Philadelphia: Lippincott, 1894.

Cory, Charles E. "A Divided Self." *Journal of Abnormal Psychology* 14 (October 1919): 281–89.

———. "A Subconscious Phenomenon." *Journal of Abnormal Psychology* 14 (February 1920): 369–75.

Cottom, Daniel. *Abyss of Reason: Cultural Movements, Revelations, and Betrayals.* New York: Oxford University Press, 1991.

Cox, Robert. *Body and Soul: A Sympathetic History of American Spiritualism.* Charlottesville: University of Virginia Press, 2003.

Craver, Carl. "Beyond Reduction: Mechanisms, Multifield Integration and the Unity of Neuroscience." *Studies in the History and Philosophy of Biological and Biomedical Sciences* 36, no. 2 (2005): 373–95.

Crowley, John W. "From Psychologism to Psychic Romance." In *The Mask of Fiction: Essays on W. D. Howells,* ed. John W. Crowley, 133–55. Amherst: University of Massachusetts Press, 1989.

Csikszentmihalyi, Mihaly. *Flow: The Psychology of Optimal Experience.* New York: Harper Perennial, 1991.

Cullen, Richard Nelson, and Marcia Ewing Current. *Loie Fuller: Goddess of Light.* Boston: Northeastern University Press, 1997.

Cuoco, Lorin, and William H. Gass, eds. *Literary St. Louis: A Guide.* St. Louis: Missouri Historical Society Press, 2000.

Curran, Pearl Lenore. *Hope Trueblood,* by Patience Worth, communicated through Mrs. John H. Curran. Ed. Casper Yost. New York: Henry Holt, 1918.

———. *Light from Beyond: Poems of Patience Worth.* Selected and comp. Herman Behr. New York: Patience Worth Publishing Co., 1923.

———. "A Nut for Psychologists." *Unpartizan Review* 13, no. 26 (1920): 357–72; reprinted in Walter Franklin Prince, *The Case of Patience Worth, 392–403.*

———. Patience Worth Collection. American Society for Psychical Research, New York.

———. Patience Worth Collection. Missouri History Museum Archives, Missouri Historical Society, St. Louis.

———. Patience Worth Record, Missouri History Museum Archives, Missouri Historical Society, St. Louis.

———. "The Phantom and the Dreamer." In Yost, *Patience Worth: A Psychic Mystery.*

———. *The Pot Upon the Wheel,* by Patience Worth, dictated through Mrs. John H. Curran. Ed. Casper S. Yost. St. Louis: Dorset Press, 1921.

———. "*Redwing*—A Drama, by Patience Worth." *Patience Worth's Magazine* 1, no. 2 (September 1917)–2, no. 2 (February 1918).

———. "Rosa Alvaro, Entrante." *Saturday Evening Post,* November 22, 1919, 18ff.

———. *The Sorry Tale: A Story of the Time of Christ,* by Patience Worth, communicated through Mrs. John H. Curran. Ed. Casper S. Yost. New York: Henry Holt, 1917.

———. "The Stranger." In Yost, *Patience Worth: A Psychic Mystery.*

———. *Telka: An Idyll of Medieval England,* by Patience Worth. Ed. with a preface by Herman Behr. New York: Patience Worth Publishing Co., 1928.

Danielson, Susan. "The Woman Question, Free Love, and Nineteenth-Century American Fiction." In *The Canon in the Classroom: The Pedagogical Implications of Canon Revision in American Literature,* ed. John Alberti. New York: Garland, 1995.

Davis, Richard Harding. *Vera the Medium.* New York: Scribner, 1908.

DeLanda, Manuel. "Virtual Environments and the Concept of Synergy." *Leonardo* 28, no. 1 (1995): 357–60.

Deloria, Philip J. *Playing Indian.* New Haven, CT: Yale University Press, 1998.

Dennett, Daniel. "The Self as the Center of Narrative Gravity." In *Self and Consciousness: Multiple Perspectives,* ed. Frank S. Kessel, Pamela M. Cole, and Dale Johnson, 103–15. Hillsdale, NJ: Erlbaum, 1992.

Diliberto, Gioia. "Ghost Writer. " *Smithsonian,* September 2010, 84–100.

———. *Hadley.* New York: Ticknor and Fields, 1992.

Dimock, Wai Chee, and Priscilla Wald, eds. "Literature and Science: Cultural Forms, Conceptual Exchanges." *American Literature* 74, no. 4 (December 2002).

Ditmore, Michael G. "A Prophetess in Her Own Country: An Exegesis of Anne Hutchinson's 'Immediate Revelation.'" *William and Mary Quarterly* 57 (2000): 349–92.

Downey, June E. "Automatic Phenomena of Muscle Reading." *Journal of Philosophy, Psychology, and Scientific Methods* 5 (1908): 650–58.

———. "Automatic Writing." *American Journal of Psychology* 26, no. 2 (1915): 161–95.

———. *Creative Imagination: Studies in the Psychology of Literature.* New York: Harcourt Brace, 1929.

Dydo, Ulla E. *Gertrude Stein: The Language That Rises: 1923–1934.* With William Rice. Evanston, IL: Northwestern University Press, 2003.

Dyson, Erika. "Having Their Way with Science: Nineteenth-Century Natural Theology, the Spiritualist Movement, and the Mediumship of Cora L. V. Richmond." Undergraduate honors thesis, Mount Holyoke College, South Hadley, MA, 1999.

Edelman, Gerald. *Bright Air, Brilliant Fire: On the Matter of the Mind.* New York: Basic Books, 1992.

Eichenbaum, Howard, and Neal Cohen. *From Conditioning to Conscious Recollection: Memory Systems of the Brain.* New York: Oxford University Press, 2001.

Elwin, Jack. *The Parish Church of St. Peter, Portesham: A Tour through the Church.* Portesham, UK: n.p., n.d.

Erdelyi, Matthew Hugh. "Dissociation, Defense, and the Unconscious." In *Dissociation: Culture, Mind, and Body,* ed. David Spiegel, 3–20. Washington, DC: American Psychiatric Press, 1994.

Evans, Jonathan. *Thinking Twice: Two Minds in One Brain.* Oxford: Oxford University Press, 2010.

Federico, Annette R. *Idol of Suburbia: Marie Corelli and Late-Victorian Literary Culture.* Charlottesville: University of Virginia Press, 2000.

Field, Kate. *Kate Field: Selected Letters.* Ed. Carolyn J. Moss. Carbondale: Southern Illinois University Press, 1996.

———. *Planchette's Diary.* New York: J. S. Redfield, 1868.

Fink, Augusta. *I-Mary: A Biography of Mary Austin.* Tucson: University of Arizona Press, 1983.

Fishkin, Shelley Fisher. *Lighting Out for the Territory: Reflections on Mark Twain and American Culture.* New York: Oxford University Press, 1996.

FitzGerald, Edward, trans. *"Rubaiyat" of Omar Khayyam: A Critical Edition.* Ed. Christopher Decker. Charlottesville: University of Virginia Press, 1997.

Flower, B. O. "Garland in Ghostland." In *Critical Essays on Hamlin Garland,* ed. James Nagel. Boston: G. K. Hall, 1982.

Funk, Isaac K. *The Psychic Riddle.* New York: Funk and Wagnalls, 1907.

Fussell, Betty Harper. *Mabel.* New Haven, CT: Ticknor and Fields, 1982.

Gardner, Howard. "Creative Lives and Creative Works: A Synthetic Scientific Report." In *The Nature of Creativity: Contemporary Psychological Perspectives,* ed. Robert J. Sternberg, 298–321. New York: Cambridge University Press, 1988.

Garelick, Rhonda K. *Rising Star: Dandyism, Gender, and Performance in the Fin de Siècle.* Princeton, NJ: Princeton University Press, 1998.

Garland, Hamlin. *Forty Years of Psychic Research: A Plain Narrative of Fact.* New York: Macmillan, 1936.

———. *The Tyranny of the Dark.* New York: Harper, 1905.

Gauld, Alan. *A History of Hypnotism.* Cambridge: Cambridge University Press, 1992.

Goldenson, Robert. *Mysteries of the Mind: The Drama of Human Behavior.* New York: Doubleday, 1973.

Goldfarb, Russell M., and Clare R. Goldfarb. *Spiritualism and Nineteenth-Century Letters.* Rutherford, NJ: Fairleigh Dickinson University Press, 1977.

Graulich, Melody, and Elizabeth Klimasmith, eds. *Exploring Lost Borders: Critical Essays on Mary Austin.* Reno: University of Nevada Press, 1999.

Hadas, Pamela White. *Beside Herself: Pocahontas to Patty Hearst: Poems.* New York: Knopf, 1983.

Hall, David D., ed. *The Antinomian Controversy, 1636–1638: A Documentary History.* Middletown, CT: Wesleyan University Press, 1968.

Harris, Susan K. *19th-Century American Women's Novels: Interpretive Strategies.* Cambridge: Cambridge University Press, 1990.

Hart, Jim Allee. *A History of the "St. Louis Globe-Democrat."* Columbia: University of Missouri Press, 1961.

Hartmann, Sadakichi. *The Valiant Knights of Daguerre: Selected Critical Essays on Photography and Profiles of Photographic Pioneers.* Ed. Harold W. Lawton and George Knox. Berkeley: University of California Press, 1978.

Hassin, Ran R., James S. Uleman, and John A. Bargh, eds. *The New Unconscious.* Oxford Series in Social Cognition and Social Neuroscience. Oxford: Oxford University Press, 2005.

Hatch, Nathan O. *The Democratization of American Christianity.* New Haven, CT: Yale University Press, 1989.

Hawthorne, Nathaniel. *Twice-Told Tales: Centenary Edition of the Works of Nathaniel Hawthorne.* Ed. Fredson Bowers. Columbus: Ohio State University Press, 1974.

Herndon, Booton. *Mary Pickford and Douglas Fairbanks: The Most Popular Couple the World Has Ever Known.* New York: W. W. Norton, 1977.

Heywood, Rosalind. *Beyond the Reach of Sense: An Inquiry into Extra-Sensory Perception.* New York: E. P. Dutton, 1961.

Hilgard, Ernest. *Divided Consciousness: Multiple Controls in Human Thought and Action.* New York: John Wiley, 1986.

Hix, John. "Patience Worth—An Unsolved Phenomenon." *Scribner's Commentator,* January 1941, 83–88.

Holt, Henry. "That Patience Worth Baby." *Unpopular Review* 7 (January 1917): 193–98.

Howells, William Dean. *The Undiscovered Country.* Boston: Houghton Mifflin, 1880.

Hunt, Stoker. *Ouija: The Most Dangerous Game.* New York: Harper and Row, 1985.

Iacoboni, Marco. *Mirroring People: The New Science of How We Connect with Others.* New York: Farrar, Straus and Giroux, 2008.

Jacoby, Larry L., Diane Ste-Marie, and Jeffrey P. Toth. "Redefining Automaticity: Unconscious Influences, Awareness, and Control." In *Attention: Selection, Awareness, and Control,* ed. Alan Baddeley and Lawrence Weiskranz, 261–82. Oxford: Oxford University Press, 1993.

Jacoby, Larry L., Jeffrey P. Toth, D. Stephen Lindsay, and James A. Debner. "Lectures for a Layperson: Methods for Revealing Unconscious Processes." In *Perception without Awareness: Cognitive, Clinical and Social*

Perspectives, ed. Robert F. Bornstein and Thane S. Pittman. New York: Guilford, 1992.

James, William. *Principles of Psychology.* Cambridge, MA: Harvard University Press, 1981.

———. "Review of 'Planchette.'" In *William James on Psychical Research,* ed. Gardner Murphy and Robert O. Ballou, 19–23. New York: Viking, 1960.

Jastrow, Joseph. *Wish and Wisdom: Episodes in the Vagaries of Belief.* New York: Appleton-Century, 1935.

Jenkins, Walter S. *The Remarkable Mrs. Beach, American Composer.* Warren, MI: Harmonie Park Press, 1994.

Johnson, Anne [Mrs. Charles P.]. *Notable Women of St. Louis.* St. Louis: Woodward, 1914.

Johnson, Steven. *Mind Wide Open: Your Brain and the Neuroscience of Everyday Life.* New York: Scribner, 2004.

John-Steiner, Vera. *Notebooks of the Mind: Explorations of Thinking.* Rev. ed. Oxford: Oxford University Press, 1997.

Johnston, Mary. *To Have and to Hold.* Cambridge, MA: Houghton Mifflin, 1900.

Jung-Beeman, Mark, et al. "Neural Activity Observed in People Solving Verbal Problems with Insight." *Public Library of Science—Biology* 2 (April 2004): 500–510.

Juslin, Patrik, and John A. Sloboda, eds. *Music and Emotion: Theory and Research.* Oxford: Oxford University Press, 2001.

Kahane, Claire. *Passions of the Voice: Hysteria, Narrative, and the Figure of the Speaking Woman, 1850–1915.* Baltimore: Johns Hopkins University Press, 1995.

Kamensky, Jane. "Female Speech and Other Demons: Witchcraft and Wordcraft in Early New England." In *Spellbound: Women and Witchcraft in America,* ed. Elizabeth Reis, 25–52. Wilmington, DE: Scholarly Resources, 1998.

———. *Governing the Tongue: The Politics of Speech in Early New England.* New York: Oxford University Press, 1997.

Kandel, Eric R. *In Search of Memory: The Emergence of a New Science of Mind.* New York: W. W. Norton, 2006.

Kelly, Lori Duin. "Elizabeth Stuart Phelps, *Trixy,* and the Vivisection Question." *Legacy* 27, no. 1 (2010): 61–82.

Kenawell, William A. *The Quest at Glastonbury: A Biographical Study of Frederick Bligh Bond.* New York: Helix Press, 1965.

Kendall, Elizabeth. *Where She Danced.* New York: Knopf, 1979.

Kenny, Michael G. *The Passion of Ansel Bourne: Multiple Personality in American Culture.* Washington, DC: Smithsonian Institution Press, 1986.

Kerr, Howard. *Mediums and Spirit Rappers and Roaring Radicals: Spiritualism in American Literature, 1850–1900.* Urbana: University of Illinois Press, 1972.

Kerr, Howard, John W. Crowley, and Charles L. Crow, eds. *The Haunted Dusk: American Supernatural Fiction, 1820–1920.* Athens: University of Georgia Press, 1983.

Kessler, Carol Farley. *Elizabeth Stuart Phelps.* Boston: Twayne Publishers, 1982.

———, ed. *The Story of Avis.* New Brunswick, NJ: Rutgers University Press, 1985.

Kinnard, Roy, and Tim Davis. *Divine Images: A History of Jesus on the Screen.* New York: Carol, 1992.

Kittler, Friedrich. *Gramophone, Film, Typewriter.* Trans. Geoffrey Winthrop-Young and Michael Wutz. Stanford: Stanford University Press, 1999.

Klepper, Robert. *Silent Films, 1887–1996: A Critical Guide to 646 Movies.* Jefferson, NC: McFarland, 1999.

Kleymeyer, Ralph T. *Ancestors and Descendants of Some Early Settlers of the Evansville, Indiana, Tri-State Area.* Austin, TX: Nortex, 1993.

Knoper, Randall. "American Literary Realism and Nervous 'Reflexion.'" *American Literature* 74 (2002): 715–45.

Koppelman, Susan, ed. *The Stories of Fannie Hurst.* New York: Feminist Press at the City University of New York, 2004.

Kounios, John, et al. "The Prepared Mind: Neural Activity Prior to Problem Presentation Predicts Solution by Sudden Insight." *Psychological Science* 17 (October 2006): 882–90.

Kroeger, Brooke. *Fannie: The Talent for Success of Writer Fannie Hurst.* New York: Times Books, 1999.

Kucich, John. *Ghostly Communion: Cross-Cultural Spiritualism in Nineteenth-Century American Literature.* Hanover, NH: Dartmouth College Press, 2004.

Laughlin, James, Peter Glassgold, and Frederick R. Martin, eds. *New Directions in Prose and Poetry 40.* Norfolk, CT: New Directions, 1980.

Lears, T. J. Jackson. *No Place of Grace: Antimodernism and the Transformation of American Culture, 1880–1920.* New York: Pantheon Books, 1981.

Lee, Blewett. "Copyright of Automatic Writing." *Virginia Law Review* 13 (November 1926): 22–26.

Lehman, Amy. *Victorian Women and the Theatre of Trance: Mediums, Spiritualists and Mesmerists in Performance.* Jefferson, NC: McFarland, 2009.

Lehrer, Jonah. *Imagine: How Creativity Works.* Boston: Houghton Mifflin Harcourt, 2012.

Levander, Caroline Field. *Voices of the Nation: Women and Public Speech in Nineteenth-Century American Literature and Culture.* New York: Cambridge University Press, 1998.

Levine, Lawrence W. "William Shakespeare and the American People: A Study in Cultural Transformation." *American Historical Review* 89, no. 1 (1984): 34–66.

Levitin, Daniel J. *This Is Your Brain on Music: The Science of a Human Obsession.* New York: Penguin, 2007.

Litvag, Irving. *Singer in the Shadows: The Strange Story of Patience Worth.* New York: Macmillan, 1972.

Loftus, Elizabeth F., and Mark R. Klinger. "Is the Unconscious Smart or Dumb?" *American Psychologist* 47, no. 6 (1992): 761–65.

London, Bette Lynn. *Writing Double: Women's Literary Partnerships.* Ithaca, NY: Cornell University Press, 1999.

Lowes, John Livingston. *The Road to Xanadu: A Study of the Ways of the Imagination.* Boston: Houghton Mifflin, 1927.

Lupack, Alan, and Barbara Lupack, eds. *Arthurian Literature by Women.* New York: Garland Publishing, 1999.

Lurie, Alison. *Familiar Spirits: A Memoir of James Merrill and David Jackson.* New York: Viking, 2001.

Lynn, Steven Jay, and Judith W. Rhue, eds. *Dissociation: Clinical and Theoretical Perspectives.* New York: Guilford, 1994.

MacKaye, Percy. *Caliban by the Yellow Sands: Shakespeare Tercentenary Masque.* Garden City, NY: Doubleday, Page, 1916.

Maclaren, Ian. *The Potter's Wheel.* New York: Dodd, Mead, 1895.

Materer, Timothy. *Modernist Alchemy: Poetry and the Occult.* Ithaca, NY: Cornell University Press, 1995.

McGarry, Molly. *Ghosts of Futures Past: Spiritualism and the Cultural Politics of Nineteenth-Century America.* Berkeley: University of California Press, 2008.

McGuffey, William Holmes. *McGuffey's Fifth Eclectic Reader.* Rev. ed. New York, Cincinnati, Chicago: American Book Co., 1879.

McKee, Irving. *"Ben-Hur" Wallace: The Life of General Lew Wallace.* Berkeley: University of California Press, 1947.

Merlin, Donald. *A Mind So Rare: The Evolution of Human Consciousness.* New York: W. W. Norton, 2001.

Merrill, James Ingram. *The Changing Light at Sandover: A Poem.* New York: Knopf, 1993.

———. *Collected Prose: James Merrill.* Ed. J. D. McClatchy and Stephen Yenser. New York: Knopf, 2004.

Meyer, Steven. *Irresistible Dictation: Gertrude Stein and the Correlations of Writing and Science.* Stanford: Stanford University Press, 2001.

Millay, Edna St. Vincent. *Aria da Capo: A Play in One Act.* New York: Harper, 1920.

Miller, Clarence E. "William Marion Reedy: A Patchwork Portrait." *Bulletin of the Missouri Historical Society,* July 1961.

Moore, R. Laurence. *In Search of White Crows: Spiritualism, Parapsychology and American Culture.* New York: Oxford University Press, 1977.

Moresberger, Robert, and Katharine Moresberger. *Lew Wallace: Militant Romantic.* New York: McGraw-Hill, 1980.

Mott, Frank Luther. *A History of American Magazines, 1740–1930.* ACLS Humanities E-book. 5 vols. Cambridge, MA: Belknap Press of Harvard University Press, 1958–1968.

Mühl, Anita M. *Automatic Writing.* Dresden: Theodore Steinkopf, 1930.

Myers, Frederic W. H. "Automatic Writing; or, The Rationale of Planchette." *Contemporary Review* 47 (1885): 233–34.

Nelson, Barney. *The Wild and the Domestic: Animal Representation, Ecocriticism, and Western American Literature.* Reno: University of Nevada Press, 2000.

Norris, Christopher. *The Deconstructive Turn: Essays in the Rhetoric of Philosophy.* London: Methuen, 1984.

Owen, Alex. *The Darkened Room: Women, Power and Spiritualism in Late Victorian England.* Philadelphia: University of Pennsylvania Press, 1990.

Paivio, Allan. *Mind and Its Evolution: A Dual Coding Theoretical Approach.* Mahwah, NJ: Erlbaum, 2007.

Patel, Aniruddh D. *Music, Language, and the Brain.* Oxford: Oxford University Press, 2008.

Peretz, Isabelle, and Robert J. Zattore, eds. *The Cognitive Neuroscience of Music.* Oxford: Oxford University Press, 2003.

Phelps, Austin. *My Portfolio: A Collection of Essays.* New York: Scribner, 1882.

Phelps, Elizabeth Stuart. *Though Life Us Do Part.* New York: Houghton Mifflin, 1908.

———. *Three Spiritualist Novels by Elizabeth Stuart Phelps: "The Gates Ajar" (1868), "Beyond the Gates" (1883), "The Gates Between" (1887).* Ed. Nina Baym. Urbana: University of Illinois Press, 2000.

———. *Trixy.* Boston: Houghton Mifflin, 1904.

Phillpotts, Eden. *The White Camel.* Illus. Sheikh Ahmed. London: Country Life, 1936.

Pleasants, Helene, ed. *Biographical Dictionary of Parapsychology.* New York: Helix, 1964.

Podmore, Frank. *Modern Spiritualism: A History and a Criticism.* 2 vols. London: Methuen, 1902.

Polito, Robert, ed. *A Reader's Guide to James Merrill's "The Changing Light at Sandover."* Ann Arbor: University of Michigan Press, 1994.

Portesham Women's Institute. *Portesham: A Peep into the Past.* Broadoak, Bridport, UK: Portesham Women's Institute, 1984.

Powers, Richard. *Galatea 2.2.* New York: Harper Perennial, 1996.

———. "How to Speak a Book." *New York Times Book Review,* January 7, 2007, 31.

Powys, John Cowper. *Weymouth Sands.* New York: Harper and Row, 1984.

Prince, Morton. *Clinical and Experimental Studies in Personality.* Cambridge, MA: Sci-Art Publishers, 1929.

———. *The Dissociation of a Personality: A Biographical Study in Abnormal Personality.* New York: Meridian Books, 1957.

———. *The Unconscious: The Fundamentals of Human Personality Normal and Abnormal.* New York: Longmans, Green, 1906.

Prince, Walter Franklin. *The Case of Patience Worth.* 1927. Reprint, New Hyde Park, NY: University Books, 1964.

———. "The Doris Case of Multiple Personality," with a preface by James Hyslop. *Proceedings of the American Society for Psychical Research* 9, 10 (1915–1916).

———. *The Psychic in the House.* Boston: Boston Society for Psychic Research, 1926.

———."Psychometric Experiments with Señora María Reyes de Z[ierold]." *Proceedings of the American Society for Psychical Research* 15 (1921): 189–314.

———. "A Review of the Margery Case." In *The Case For and Against Psychical Belief,* ed. Carl Murchison. Worcester: Clark University, 1927.

———. "The Riddle of Patience Worth." *Scientific American* 135, no. 7 (1926): 20–22.

Putnam, Frank W. *Diagnosis and Treatment of Multiple Personality Disorder.* New York: Guilford, 1989.

Putzel, Max. *The Man in the Mirror: William Marion Reedy and His Magazine.* Cambridge, MA: Harvard University Press, 1963.

Pyle, Howard. *The Lady of Shalott: Decorated by Howard Pyle.* New York: Dodd, Mead, 1881.

Quen, Jacques M., ed. *Split Minds/Split Brains: Historical and Current Perspectives.* New York: New York University Press, 1986.

Radden, Jennifer, ed. *The Philosophy of Psychiatry: A Companion.* New York: Oxford University Press, 2004.

Raichle, Marcus E. "The Brain's Dark Energy." *Scientific American* 302 (March 2010): 44–49.

Reber, Arthur S. *Implicit Learning and Tacit Knowledge.* New York: Oxford University Press, 1993.

Reinders, A. A. T. S., et al. "One Brain, Two Selves." *NeuroImage* 20, no. 4 (2003): 2119–25.

Revonsuo, Antti. *Inner Presence: Consciousness as a Biological Phenomenon.* Cambridge, MA: MIT Press, 2006.

Reynolds, David S. *Beneath the American Renaissance: The Subversive Imagination in the Age of Emerson and Melville.* Cambridge, MA: Harvard University Press, 1989.

Richmond, Cora. *Ouina's Canoe and Christmas Offering: Filled with Flowers for the Darlings of Earth.* Ottumwa, IA: D.M. & N.P. Fox, 1882.

———. *The Soul: Its Nature, Relations, and Expressions in Human Embodiments.* Given through Mrs. Cora L. V. Richmond by Her Guides. 4th ed. Chicago: Spiritual Publishing Co., 1888.

Rieber, Robert W. *The Bifurcation of the Self: The History and Theory of Dissociation and Its Disorders.* Boston: Springer, 2006.

Roediger, Henry L., III, Yadin Dudai, and Susan M. Fitzpatrick, eds. *Science of Memory: Concepts.* New York: Oxford University Press, 2007.

Roediger, Henry L., III, and Melissa J. Guynn. "Retrieval Processes." In *Memory,* ed. Elizabeth Ligon Bjork and Robert A. Bjork, 197–236. San Diego: Academic Press, 1996.

Rossetti, Yves, and Antti Revonsuo. *Beyond Dissociation: Interaction between Dissociated Implicit and Explicit Processing.* Philadelphia: J. Benjamins, 2000.

Ruiter, Michiel B. de, et al. "Attention as a Characteristic of Nonclinical Dissociation: An Event Related Potential Study." *NeuroImage* 19, no. 2 (2003): 376–90.

Sargent, Epes. *Planchette; or, The Despair of Science.* Boston: Roberts, 1869.

Schacter, Daniel. "Implicit Memory: History and Current Status." *Journal of Experimental Psychology: Learning, Memory and Cognition* 123, no. 3 (1987): 501–18.

———. *Searching for Memory: The Brain, the Mind, and the Past.* New York: Basic Books, 1996.

Scharnhorst, Gary. *Kate Field: The Many Lives of a Nineteenth-Century American Journalist.* Syracuse, NY: Syracuse University Press, 2008.

Seltzer, Mark. *Bodies and Machines.* New York: Routledge, 1992.

Shakespeare, William. *The Old-Spelling Shakespeare: Being the Works of Shakespeare in the Best Quarto and Folio Texts.* Ed. F. J. Furnivall and W. G. Boswell Stone. 12 vols. New York: Duffield, 1908–1909.

Shallice, Tim. *From Neuropsychology to Mental Structure.* Cambridge: Cambridge University Press, 1988.

Shawn, Ted. *Every Little Movement: A Book about François Delsarte.* 2nd ed. Pittsfield, MA: Eagle Printing and Binding, 1963.

Showalter, Elaine, ed. *The New Feminist Criticism: Essays on Women, Literature, and Theory.* New York: Pantheon Books, 1985.

Sienkiewicz, Henryk. *Quo Vadis: A Narrative of the Time of Nero.* Trans. Jeremiah Curtin. Boston: Little Brown, 1896.

Skultans, Vieda. "Mediums, Controls and Eminent Men." In *Women's Religious Experience: Cross Cultural Perspectives,* ed. Pat Holden. Totowa, NJ: Barnes & Noble, 1983.

Sloboda, John A. *The Musical Mind: The Cognitive Psychology of Music.* Oxford Psychology Series, no. 5. Oxford: Clarendon Press, 1985.

Sokoloff, Alice Hunt. *Hadley: The First Mrs. Hemingway.* New York: Dodd, 1973.

Solomons, Leon M., and Gertrude Stein. "Normal Motor Automatism." In *Motor Automatism,* ed. Robert Wilson. Originally published in *Psychological Review* 3, no. 5 (1896): 492–512.

Solso, Robert L., ed. *Mind and Brain Sciences in the 21st Century.* Cambridge, MA: MIT Press, 1997.

Spitz, Herman H. *Nonconscious Movements: From Mystical Messages to Facilitated Communication.* Mahwah, NJ: Erlbaum, 1997.

Stadler, Michael A., and Henry L. Roediger III. "The Question of Awareness in Research on Implicit Learning." In *Handbook of Implicit Learning,* ed. Michael A. Stadler and Peter A. Frensch. Thousand Oaks, CA: Sage, 1998.

Stein, Gertrude. "Cultivated Motor Automatism: A Study of Character in Its Relation to Attention." In *Motor Automatism,* ed. Robert Wilson. Originally published in *Psychological Review* 5 (1898): 295–306.

———. *The Geographical History of America; or, The Relation of Human Nature to the Human Mind.* New York: Random House, 1973.

Stevens, Walter B., comp. *Burns Nights in St. Louis.* St. Louis: Buxton and Skinner, 1911.

Stevens, Walter B. *Centennial History of Missouri, 1820–1921.* St. Louis: S. J. Clarke, 1921.

Sword, Helen. *Ghostwriting Modernism.* Ithaca, NY: Cornell University Press, 2002.

Tan, Amy. *Saving Fish from Drowning: A Novel.* New York: Putnam, 2005.

Taylor, Eugene. *Shadow Culture: Psychology and Spirituality in America.* Washington, DC: Counterpoint, 1999.

———. *William James on Consciousness beyond the Margin.* Princeton, NJ: Princeton University Press, 1996.

Teasdale, Sara, comp. *The Answering Voice: One Hundred Love Lyrics by Women, Selected by Sara Teasdale.* Boston: Houghton Mifflin, 1917.

Thurschwell, Pamela. *Literature, Technology and Magical Thinking, 1880–1920.* New York: Cambridge University Press, 2001.

Toth, Emily. *Kate Chopin: A Life of the Author of "The Awakening."* New York: Morrow, 1990.

Tsai, Guochan E., et al. "Functional Magnetic Resonance Imagery of Personality Switches in a Woman with Dissociative Identity Disorder." *Harvard Review of Psychiatry* 7, no. 2 (1999): 119–22.

Tulving, Endel. "Cue Dependent Forgetting." *American Scientist* 62 (1974): 74–82.

Vendler, Helen. *Part of Nature, Part of Us.* Cambridge, MA: Harvard University Press, 1980.

Wall, Mia Grandolfi. *Rediscovering Pearl Curran: Solving the Mystery of Patience Worth.* PhD diss. New Orleans, LA: Tulane University Press, 2000.

Wallace, Lew. *Ben-Hur.* New York: Dodd, Mead, 1953.

Washington, Peter. *Madam Blavatsky's Baboon: A History of the Mystics, Mediums, and Misfits Who Brought Spiritualism to America.* New York: Schocken Books, 1993.

Watson, John. *Companions of the Sorrowful Way.* New York: Dodd, Mead, 1898.

Wegner, Daniel M. *The Illusion of Conscious Will.* Cambridge, MA: MIT Press, 2002.

———, Matthew E. Ansfield, and Daniel Pilloff. "The Putt and the Pendulum: Ironic Effects of the Mental Control of Movement." *Psychological Science* 9, no. 3 (1998): 196–99.

Weinstein, Sheri. "Technologies of Vision: Spiritualism and Science in Nineteenth-Century America." In *Spectral America: Phantoms and the National Imagination,* ed. Jeffrey Andrew Weinstock. Madison: University of Wisconsin Press, 2004.

Westerhoff, John H. *McGuffey and His Readers: Piety, Morality, and Education in Nineteenth-Century America.* Nashville, TN: Abingdon, 1978.

Whiting, Lilian. *After Her Death: The Story of a Summer.* Boston: Roberts, 1897.

Wilcox, Ella Wheeler. *The Worlds and I.* New York: George H. Doran, 1918.

Wilson, Edward O. *Consilience: The Unity of Knowledge.* New York: Alfred A. Knopf, 1998.

Wilson, Robert, ed. *Motor Automatism.* New York: Phoenix Book Shop, 1969.

Windeler, Robert. *Sweetheart: The Story of Mary Pickford.* New York: Praeger, 1974.

Worth, Patience. *See* Curran, Pearl Lenore.

Yenser, Stephen. *The Consuming Myth: The Work of James Merrill.* Cambridge, MA: Harvard University Press, 1987.

Yost, Casper S. *The Making of a Successful Husband: Letters of a Happily Married Man to His Son.* New York: G. W. Dillingham, 1907.

———. *Patience Worth: A Psychic Mystery.* New York: Henry Holt, 1916.

———. *The Quest of God: A Journalist's View of the Bases of Religious Faith.* New York: Fleming H. Revell, 1929.

Youens, Susan. "Excavating an Allegory: The Text of Pierrot Lunaire." *Journal of the Arnold Schoenberg Institute* 8 (1984): 94–115.

Zimmerman, David A. "Frank Norris, Market Panic, and the Mesmeric Sublime." *American Literature* 75, no. 1 (2003): 61–90.

Zunshine, Lisa, ed. *Introduction to Cognitive Cultural Studies.* Baltimore: The Johns Hopkins University Press, 2010.

Zusne, Leonard, and Warren H. Jones. *Anomalistic Psychology: A Study of Magical Thinking.* 2nd ed. Hillsdale, NJ: Erlbaum, 1989.

Index

"PW" stands for Patience Worth.

"Curran" is used throughout for Pearl Curran despite subsequent marriages and name changes.